Alternative Concepts of God

Alternative Concepts of God

Essays on the Metaphysics of the Divine

EDITED BY
Andrei A. Buckareff
and Yujin Nagasawa

OXFORD
UNIVERSITY PRESS

OXFORD
UNIVERSITY PRESS

Great Clarendon Street, Oxford, OX2 6DP,
United Kingdom

Oxford University Press is a department of the University of Oxford.
It furthers the University's objective of excellence in research, scholarship,
and education by publishing worldwide. Oxford is a registered trade mark of
Oxford University Press in the UK and in certain other countries

First Edition published in 2016

Impression: 1

Published in the United States of America by Oxford University Press
198 Madison Avenue, New York, NY 10016, United States of America

British Library Cataloguing in Publication Data

Data available

Library of Congress Control Number: 2015941533

ISBN 978-0-19-872225-0

Printed in Great Britain by
Clays Ltd, St Ives plc

Contents

Part IV. Causal versus Non-causal Accounts

Part V. Naturalism and Alternative Concepts

List of Contributors

MARILYN MCCORD ADAMS is Recurrent Visiting Professor of Philosophy at Rutgers University, USA.

JOHN BISHOP is Professor of Philosophy at the University of Auckland, New Zealand.

ANDREI A. BUCKAREFF is Associate Professor of Philosophy at Marist College, USA.

WILLEM B. DREES is Professor of Philosophy of the Humanities at Tilburg University, Netherlands.

PETER FORREST is Adjunct Professor of Philosophy at the University of New England, Australia.

BRIAN LEFTOW is Nolloth Professor of the Philosophy of the Christian Religion, Oriel College, Oxford, UK.

JOHN LESLIE is University Professor Emeritus of Philosophy at the University of Guelph, Canada.

HUGH J. MCCANN is Professor Emeritus of Philosophy at Texas A&M University, USA.

YUJIN NAGASAWA is Professor of Philosophy at the University of Birmingham, UK.

KEN PERSZYK is Associate Professor of Philosophy at Victoria University of Wellington, New Zealand.

KARL PFEIFER is Professor Emeritus of Philosophy at the University of Saskatchewan, Canada.

ROBIN LE POIDEVIN is Professor of Metaphysics at the University of Leeds, UK.

J. L. SCHELLENBERG is Professor of Philosophy at Mount Saint Vincent University, Canada.

ERIC STEINHART is Professor of Philosophy at William Paterson University, USA.

CHARLES TALIAFERRO is Professor of Philosophy at St. Olaf College, USA.

EMILY THOMAS is NWO Veni Research Fellow at the University of Groningen, Netherlands.

Acknowledgements

This volume originated in our project "Exploring Alternative Concepts of God," which was funded by the John Templeton Foundation. We wish to thank the Foundation for its generous financial and academic support. Neither the positions we present and defend in our respective contributions to this book nor the views of any of the authors who contributed to this collection reflect any of the commitments of the John Templeton Foundation. While the Foundation has generously supported this project, we have neither been constrained in our explorations nor directed to promote any particular perspective. We would particularly like to thank Michael Murray, John Churchill, Daniel Martin, and Alex Arnold from the John Templeton Foundation for their help in this project. Some of the contributors to this volume were interviewed for Robert Lawrence Kuhn's PBS TV documentary series *Closer To Truth*. The interviews and TV episodes based on them can be watched on the program website (<http://www.closertotruth.com>).

We would also like to thank Peter Momtchiloff and other staff of Oxford University Press and Sorin Sabou for their editorial support. Additionally, we are also grateful to anonymous reviewers for helpful comments and constructive suggestions. We also wish to thank the journal *Conceptus: Zeitschrift Fur Philosophie* for permission to use Karl Pfeifer's paper, "Pantheism as Panpsychism," originally published in volume 30 in 1997 of that journal and appearing here having been substantially revised and updated.

Finally, we are also grateful to our respective institutions, Marist College and the University of Birmingham, for their support of our work on this book and the larger project of which this was a piece. Andrei Buckareff, in particular, would like to thank the Vice President of Academic Affairs and Dean of Faculty at Marist College, Thomas Wermuth, and the Dean of the School of Liberal Arts at Marist, Martin Shaffer, for giving him regular course releases that afforded him extra time to work on this and other related projects.

Introduction

Alternative Conceptions of Divinity and Contemporary Analytic Philosophy of Religion

Andrei A. Buckareff and Yujin Nagasawa

1. Extending the Conversation in Philosophy of Religion Beyond Classical Theism

Variously labeled "classical theism," "omniGod theism," "traditional theism," and "mainstream theism," the prevailing orthodoxy in the Abrahamic religions—Judaism, Christianity, and Islam—has traditionally affirmed a conception of God as an omnipotent, omniscient, and morally perfect being who is the creator and sustainer of the universe. Importantly, God within this tradition is regarded as personal and ontologically distinct from the universe.[1] Additionally, the orthodoxy has included an endorsement of realism about theological language. Of course, there are points of disagreement among those who accept the dominant orthodoxy. For instance, some argue that God is a timelessly eternal being who exists entirely outside of time while others hold that God is sempiternal, existing at all times. There is also disagreement over how to understand the various omni-attributes. For instance, some hold that God's omniscience includes foreknowledge while others hold that it does not. There are, however, sufficiently many points of agreement to form a family resemblance between such views and to group them together in a class. It is the members of this class that collectively constitute something like the general standard or classical account of the divine in contemporary analytic philosophy of religion.

---

[1] That God is personal or a person according to what might be properly labeled as "classical theism" is controversial. If the progenitors of classical theism are taken to be the likes of Anselm, Ibn Rushd, Maimonides, and Thomas Aquinas, then it is not clear that they literally took God to be a person. They all recognized a point to anthropomorphic language while remaining hostile to taking any such representations of God literally. Thanks to John Bishop for bringing this to our attention.

The essays in this volume extend the dialectic over the metaphysics of divinity beyond classical theism and focus chiefly on alternative conceptions of God. While the chapters are for the most part sensitive to the dialectic over the concept of God in the context of Western philosophy and theology, many represent ways of thinking about the metaphysics of the divine that provide a bridge of sorts between the conceptions of divinity that we owe to the Abrahamic religions and conceptions of ultimate reality we find in non-Abrahamic religious and philosophical traditions. (We will say more about this last point in section 2.)

Some of the chapters in this volume include critiques of traditional theism (e.g., the chapters by Andrei Buckareff and Willem Drees). Others focus on critiquing alternatives (e.g., the chapters by Brian Leftow and Marilyn McCord Adams). While most of the essays present alternatives to traditional theism, some authors present conceptions of divinity that either (1) resist easy categorization (e.g., the views of Samuel Alexander examined by Emily Thomas in her essay), (2) defend views that are unconventional but are theistic (e.g., Charles Taliaferro's defense of theistic idealism), or (3) present alternatives to classical theism as well as to pantheism and panentheism (e.g., Eric Steinhart's religious naturalism and John Schellenberg's ultimism). But most of the authors who present positive alternative models of divinity that are alternatives to classical theism partially or fully defend some version of either pantheism (Peter Forrest, John Leslie, and Karl Pfeifer) or panentheism (John Bishop and Ken Perszyk and Yujin Nagasawa).

While the alternatives to traditional theism in the present collection are not limited to versions of pantheism and panentheism, most of the variants of alternative conceptions of God in the West have tended to be either pantheistic or panentheistic. In section 2 we will briefly sketch the general commitments of pantheistic and panentheistic conceptions of God, glossing over the fine-grained distinctions between the several variants of each. We will then discuss how examining such perspectives may help bridge the gap in the dialectic between conceptions of divinity that have emerged in the West with non-theistic conceptions that have been developed elsewhere. In the penultimate section we will consider why such conceptions of the divine have been marginalized in analytic philosophy of religion and how considering alternative conceptions of God could contribute to widening the scope of the field. We will summarize the contents of the chapters in this volume in the final section.

2. Alternative Conceptions of Divinity and Global Philosophy of Religion

According to traditional theism, God is ontologically distinct from the universe. There is no ontological overlap between God and the universe as the universe is God's creation. Pantheists and panentheists reject this idea because they believe that the universe is part of God. Very roughly, pantheists typically hold that the universe is *identical with*

God while panentheists typically hold that the universe constitutes God or is a *proper part* of God.

There are likely as many variants of pantheism as there are of classical theism. Pantheists differ with one another over their fundamental ontology and what features of reality provide the sort of unity and complexity necessary to ground our theological discourse. For instance, some pantheists are substance monists, taking space-time to be the one substance of which everything else is but a mode or collection of modes pinned to the one substance. Other pantheists reject substance monism, seeking the unity in some other feature of the universe. Still further, some pantheists regard pantheism as a non-theistic conception of divinity while others regard it as theistic and even think it is sufficient for grounding a conception of God as personal.

Similarly, panentheists differ over the nature of the relationship God bears to the universe. For instance, while some panentheists talk of emergent properties or emergent substances that are in some way ontologically dependent upon the universe, others eschew such a framework in favor of taking God to be constituted by the universe. On such a view, constitution is assumed to be a different relationship from identity. Hence, if Y constitutes X, X is not identical with Y. X and Y have different persistence conditions. The universe constitutes God when it displays a level of complexity and unity that is sufficient for God to exist. Still other panentheists analogize the relationship between God and the universe to the relationship between mind and body on non-reductive physicalism. Such panentheists hold that God supervenes on the universe and is ontologically dependent upon the universe. And like some pantheists, there are panentheists who take their ontology of the divine to be sufficient to ground a conception of God as personal while others are resolute in their denial of a personal God.

While we have taken a very broad view of the differences between pantheistic and panentheistic conceptions of divinity, our discussion should suffice to give the reader a reasonably robust sense of two of the most prominent alternative conceptions of God and the broad ontological commitments of such concepts of divinity. In the remainder of this section, we briefly consider the value of examining alternative concepts of God. In particular, we are interested in the value of such approaches for philosophers of religion who wish to take a more global perspective in their research, examining not just the traditional theistic picture of divinity that emerged in the West but also non-theistic conceptions of ultimate reality and considering how these alternative pictures of ultimate reality may relate to one another.

While this is no doubt a controversial claim, we are inclined to think that alternative conceptions of divinity such as pantheism and panentheism are better suited to engage with non-theistic conceptions of ultimate reality than versions of classical theism. We focus here on a recent statement of a panentheistic conception of God from an analytic philosopher: Mark Johnston's naturalistic panentheism that he develops in his recent book, *Saving God: Religion after Idolatry* (2009). We compare Johnston's conception of God with *tian* in Chinese philosophy. Our summaries of both will, no doubt, be rather superficial. But they should suffice to show that there are interesting similarities between the two that call for further examination.

Regarding the nature of the divine, Johnston asserts that we are "samplers of presence" who access the objective modes of presentation of other objects. The totality of objective modes of presentation that make up the realm of sense constitute Objective Mind (Johnston 2009, 154–5). To the extent that we grasp these modes of presentation we conform our minds to the Divine Mind, "which may be construed as the totality of fully adequate and complete modes of presentation of reality" (Johnston 2009, 155). While the Divine Mind is the "totality...of modes of presentation of reality," God is identified with reality, which is exemplified in the modes of Being that are disclosed to conscious agents who participate in Being by sampling modes of the presentation of reality constitutive of the Divine Mind and they are modes of the presentation of reality themselves. "The general form of reality is at least the outpouring of Being itself by way of its exemplification in ordinary beings and its self-disclosure to some of those beings" (Johnston 2009, 156). All existents, then, are expressions of Being, as is everything they encounter. God, as mentioned earlier, is the Highest One. And Johnston offers the following succinct characterization of the Highest One.

The Highest One=the outpouring of Being by way of its exemplification in ordinary existents for the sake of the self-disclosure of Being. (Johnston 2009, 158)

While Johnston does not present his view in terms of "truthmaking," we can construe the following account as a truthmaker claim for predicates applied truthfully to God:

Accordingly, the Love of the Highest One [can be] analogized as its outpouring in ordinary existents, its Will as self-disclosure, its Mind as the most revealing presentations found in the realm of sense, and its Power as the totality of the laws of nature. In these respects, the Highest One has by analogy the characteristics of a person, but a person far removed from ordinary personality. (Johnston 2009, 158)

Notice that this view may be sufficient for grounding a version of realism about theological discourse. But that fact, if it is a fact, is not what we are concerned with here. Rather, we are interested in the ways in which this sort of view can aid in the pursuit of a more global perspective in the philosophy of religion. If we go global, we quickly discover that there are conceptions of divine or ultimate reality developed in various cultures that differ in significant ways from the received view we get from orthodox theology in the Abrahamic religions.

For instance, in Chinese philosophy, *tian* (heaven) is central in Confucianism, Moism, and Taoism. There is no shortage of controversy over whether Confucianism is or is not properly religious (see Yang 2008). But there is at least one interpretation on which *tian* in early Confucianism is understood as an ultimate or transcendent reality. But insofar as *tian* could be understood as divine in some sense, our conception of it should be quite different from our conception of the God of classical theism. Regarding the views of Kongzi (Confucius) on *tian*, Liu Shu-hsien writes that "Heaven seems to be the ultimate creative power which works incessantly in the universe without exhibiting any personal characteristics, and [humankind] is to take Heaven as the model to follow" (1978, 413). Philip Ivanhoe goes further, noting that *tian* is "a concerned agent and a force for human good" (Ivanhoe 2007, 212).

Tian is complemented by *di* (earth). Commenting on the treatment of the relationship between *tian* and *di* in *Chung Yung*, Liu notes that *tian* and *di* are not the literal heaven and earth. Rather, these are forces. He writes:

Heaven creates and Earth sustains. These are the two main forces that keep the creative process in the universe going. In this process myriad things in the world receive their natures. (Liu 1972, 46)

Tian endows human agents with a character that is capable of ethical development (Ivanhoe 2007, 212). In living lives directed at the *dao* (the way), human agents must cultivate *cheng*. While *cheng* is rendered as "sincerity" in some places, it is not merely an ethical virtue. *Cheng* is ontological as well. Liu writes that "It means none other than Truth or Reality.... [C]h'eng is but another name for the all-encompassing metaphysical principle" (1972, 47). Roughly, the picture that emerges is one in which human agents are part of a larger reality that has a transcendent dimension and is directed at the development of the nature of human agents who, in turn, may participate in the creation and transformation of the universe.

The conception of what we may describe as the divine reality in Confucianism stands in contrast with classical theism. While *tian* is quite different from the God of classical theism as found in traditional Judaism, Christianity, and Islam, *tian*, like God, is regarded as the proper object of awe and reverence. Any devotion to *tian* is exercised in the life lived by an agent following the *dao* (Ivanhoe 2007, 215; see *Analects* 7.35 and 16.8). So there is a sense in which this conception of ultimate reality can be regarded as sufficient for a viable religious life, even if devotion is expressed differently from what one finds in the Abrahamic religions.

We expect that the similarities between Johnston's proposed conception of divinity and the concept of *tian* will not be lost on many readers. There are certainly similarities between conceptions of God found in some statements of classical theism and *tian*. But the similarities between the concept of God that we derive from Johnston's panentheism and the doctrine of *tian* are more evident.

For instance, on Johnston's alternative account of divinity, God is the "Highest One" and is identified with "the outpouring of Being by way of its exemplification in ordinary existents for the sake of the self-disclosure of Being" (Johnston 2009, 158). Compare this with the notion of *tian* as "the ultimate creative power which works incessantly in the universe without exhibiting any personal characteristics" (Liu 1978, 413). Apart from some apparent ontological similarities between these two conceptions of ultimate reality, on both Johnston's view and in Confucianism, devotion is exercised via cultivation of a moral character (see Johnston 2009, 183–6). Johnston uses a Christian framework, emphasizing turning one's loving self-concern towards others, but the idea is similar to that of living a life following the *dao*. They are not the same, but both focus on a devout life as a moral life and both provide an ontological framework that emphasizes the ground of being, if you will, as a form of being in virtue of which such a life is made possible.

The foregoing has all been rather quick and superficial. But we hope it suffices to illustrate our point that exploring alternative approaches to divinity could open up a new, global, horizon in the philosophy of religion. Before concluding this section, it is worth noting that we expect that at least some proponents of traditional theism may regard the foregoing frameworks as religiously inadequate and, hence, may be tempted to disregard them for that reason. But by examining such alternative conceptions of ultimate reality and bringing them in conversation with one another and, in turn, with classical theism we can open the door to providing a more thoughtful and careful adumbration of the desiderata of a religiously adequate conception of the divine or ultimate reality. We hope, moreover, that such a task can be done in a non-question-begging manner. This requires keeping in mind the range of appropriate ways in which one may express devotion and the acknowledgment that one's conception of ultimate reality may shape one's devotional practices.

3. Why Have Alternatives to Traditional Theism Been Marginalized?

While we see great value in taking a global perspective in work on philosophy of religion, asking that all philosophers of religion do global philosophy of religion may be asking for a bit too much. After all, in other philosophical sub-disciplines we do not expect specialists to know everything about every problem within the discipline, and historians of philosophy often focus only on a figure or era in the history of philosophy. If we move outside of philosophy and consider religious studies, someone who specializes in revival movements in nineteenthth-century American Christianity, for example, cannot be expected to know much if anything about Mahayana Buddhism, except, perhaps, if her research involves examining the relations between Buddhist and Christian communities in the United States during that period. Similarly, it may seem unreasonable to expect analytic philosophers of religion to engage with alternatives to traditional theism, particularly ones found in non-Western traditions.

It is indisputable that analytic philosophy of religion is largely an artefact of a Western culture (with roots in North America and Europe) that has engaged primarily with religious concepts in that particular cultural context. Within Western culture in the past two millennia traditional theism has dominated the literature and debates. Yet, some familiar alternatives to traditional theism have emerged. As our comparison of Johnston's conception of God with the conception of *tian* in Chinese philosophy illustrates, some of these examples resemble conceptions of the divine found outside of the Western Abrahamic religious traditions and perhaps open up avenues for taking a more global perspective. But these cases have been mostly ignored in debates over the metaphysics of the divine amongst analytic philosophers of religion over the past fifty years. Why has this been the case?

Some explain the lack of interest in sustained engagement with alternatives to traditional theism as a function of the dominance of traditional Christian theists in the philosophy of religion—thinkers who have largely set the agenda for everyone working in the field, determining which questions are worth thinking about. For instance, writing in 1995, Ninian Smart offered this explanation:

The philosophy of religion has greatly concerned itself with some old questions...but basically the agenda has been Western theism. This is what above all has exercised Wisdom, Flew, Hick, Hepburn, Philips and others. The tradition remains dominated, from the rear, by the idea of natural theology, or by something called theism, or more particularly Christian (sometimes Jewish) theism. (17)

Michael Levine (2000) presents an even more critical analysis:

Contemporary philosophy of religion now is...dominated by the religious agendas of Christian conservatives....That the religious find [contemporary philosophy of religion] largely irrelevant goes without saying—though there are various reasons for this. Instead of "faith seeking understanding," one is reminded of W. Somerset Maugham whose characterisation of philosophy pertains to most types, but particularly to the apologetics of contemporary Christian analytic philosophy of religion—including theodicy. "Philosophy is an affair of character rather than of logic: the philosopher believes not according to evidence, but according to his own temperament; and his thinking merely serves to make reasonable what his instinct regards as true." (89)

J. L. Schellenberg expresses a perspective that is similar to Levine's and Smart's. Schellenberg writes that, "in the [West]...philosophy of religion has been largely preoccupied with one religious idea, that of theism, and it looks to be moving into a narrower and deeper version of this preoccupation, one focused on specifically Christian ideas, rather than broadening out and coming to grips with its full task" (forthcoming, 3).

Are Smart, Levine, and Schellenberg correct? There is some reason to think they are, if not judging rightly, at least working in the vicinity of the truth. Recent surveys have suggested that the majority of philosophers are not theists. For instance, a recent survey conducted by the PhilPapers website suggests that most contemporary philosophers with faculty posts or PhDs without such an academic post are atheistic. Among 1,803 of such respondents 69.7% (1,257) said they accept or lean toward atheism, only 16.4% (295) said they accept or lean toward theism, while 13.9% (251) said they accept another alternative.[2] Thus, theists are a minority in philosophy. Yet theists, particularly traditional theists, are by far the majority within the philosophy of religion. In the same PhilPapers survey it was found that, among respondents who have PhDs who have an AOS in philosophy of religion, 70 of 101 (69.3%) indicated that they accept or lean

---

[2] See <http://philpapers.org/surveys/results.pl>. For more analysis of the survey results, see Bourget and Chalmers 2014.

toward theism; 20 of 101 (19.8%) accept or lean toward atheism; and only 11 of 101 (10.9%) accepted another alternative to either atheism or theism.[3] What we find among specialists in the philosophy of religion is the inverse of what we find among philosophers more generally. This may prove little for our purposes. After all, as Klaas Kray notes, the survey did not define "theism," "so it is possible—well, entirely expectable—that respondents interpreted this protean and multifarious term in different ways" (2013, 247).

In the interest of getting a clearer picture of the views of philosophers of religion, we ran a survey of our own on the Prosblogion, one of the most frequently accessed philosophy of religion blogs.[4] Not being social scientists by training, we expect that our survey most likely suffered from some methodological defects. Still, we think it was revealing.

While we did not offer a straightforward definition of "traditional theism" we decided to make distinctions between differing conceptions of the divine, distinguishing open theism, panentheism, pantheism, developmental theism, polytheism, and ultimism from traditional theism. The reason for this was, in part, due to the possibility that some who endorse non-traditional conceptions of divinity may refer to themselves by using the term "theist". Such persons may refer to "God" when they describe the object of their devotion or investigation but take the locution to denote something very different from what the traditional theist has in mind.

The survey drew 286 responses. The overwhelming majority (55.6%) described themselves as traditional theists. Coming in a distant second behind traditional theists were those who hold that no account of the divine is tenable (12.2%), while 11.5% of the respondents described themselves as open theists. The remaining respondents endorsed various alternative conceptions of the divine, including 10.5% who described their views as "other," followed by panentheists (5.2%) and ultimists (2.1%). Pantheism (1.4%), developmental theism (1%), and polytheism (0.3%) had the fewest advocates.

Of the 286 respondents only 250 answered all of the questions. Most of the 250 (46.4%) disagreed with the statement that "Alternative accounts of the divine, such as versions of pantheism and panentheism, or some other alternative to classical theism, can provide a metaphysically and religiously adequate framework for theological realists," while 36.8% of the respondents agreed with the statement and 16.8% had no opinion.

While most of the 250 respondents indicated that they believe that alternative accounts of the divine fail to provide a metaphysically and religiously adequate framework for theological realists, the overwhelming majority of the respondents (88.8%) indicated that they regard such accounts of the divine to be worthy of examination by analytic philosophers of religion and analytic theologians. Only 4.4% disagreed with

[3] See <http://philpapers.org/surveys/results.pl>.
[4] The complete summary of our findings can be found at *The Prosblogion*: <http://prosblogion.ektopos.com/2012/05/22/results_of_the/>.

the claim that such accounts of the divine are worthy of examination while 6.8% offered no opinion.

These data suggest that even among those who endorse traditional theism with research interests in the philosophy of religion, examining alternatives to traditional theism is regarded as a worthwhile endeavor. So what explains the relatively low level of engagement with alternatives to traditional theism in the philosophy of religion? One response can be found in a recent paper by Paul Draper and Ryan Nichols (2013). They argue that "the vast majority of philosophers of religion do not, when engaged in philosophical inquiry, *consciously pursue* any religious agenda." But there are a number of cognitive biases "operating at the nonconscious level" that combine with group influence and result in work with a particular character and focus that is not conducive to objective philosophical inquiry (2013, 423–4). While they focus on how this affects one's evaluation of the case for the God of traditional theism, this would have important consequences for thinking about the metaphysics of the divine and the comparative strengths and weaknesses of the various conceptions of God. Importantly for our purposes, Draper and Nichols echo Levine's contention that much philosophy of religion today amounts to smartly dressed apologetics. But, unlike Levine, they note that *both* defenders of traditional theism *and* atheists appear to be engaged in little more than apologetics. From our perspective, what is worth noting is that the dominant dialectic has mostly excluded alternative conceptions of divinity.

Why is this so? One answer is hinted at in Levine's quote above. That is, the limitations of the scope of the philosophy of religion may be owing to the many Christian philosophers who are motivated by "faith seeking understanding." This, however, suggests a motivation that is perhaps more subtle and not a matter of philosophers' intentionally ignoring alternatives. While it may be somewhat unfair to describe Christian philosophers who are interested in problems that emerge from their own faith tradition as engaged in apologetics, such individuals have an immediate motivation to focus their attention on problems that are of deep concern to them as religious persons. What has to be made clear to such philosophers is the value of engaging with alternatives that may allow them to take one step closer to a global perspective in their work in the philosophy of religion.

We would contend that studying alternatives to classical theism is useful for anyone interested in religion, including traditional theists, atheists, and agnostics. Traditional theists can compare their own concept of God with alternative concepts to clarify the strengths and shortcomings of theirs. Atheists and agnostics can consider alternative concepts and examine whether their atheism/agnosticism extends to alternative concepts.[5] In fact, such an activity is what philosophers are generally encouraged to pursue all the time. The point of doing philosophy is to study and discuss a variety of ideas so that one can better understand fundamental issues. It would be futile if philosophers

---

[5] The spirit of what we are suggesting, we believe, is in line with the proposal put forth by Klaas Kray in his essay, "Method and Madness in Contemporary Analytic Philosophy of Religion" (2013).

were to study only their own views. Studying alternative views is important and useful irrespective of the views one chooses to defend in the end.

It should be evident by now that the main purpose of the present volume is to encourage analytic philosophers of religion to examine alternative concepts of God, which many seem to think is a worthwhile project in its own right. A potential upshot of renewed work on such concepts of God will be, we hope, closer engagement with non-theistic traditions and a move towards a stronger global focus in the philosophy of religion.

4. The Essays

This volume is divided into five parts. The four chapters in Part I are devoted to the articulation and defense or critique of pantheism, which is perhaps the most well-known alternative to traditional theism.

In Chapter 1, Peter Forrest defends a version of pantheism he labels "personal pantheism," which is a variant of theism and not a rival, unlike most versions of pantheism. But while it is not a rival to theism, Forrest argues that his personal pantheism is superior to other theistic conceptions of divinity. On personal pantheism, God's relationship to the universe is analogous to what we find with non-reductive physicalism in the metaphysics of mind. Just as a human person may be identified with their body without the mental reducing to the physical, so God can be identified with the universe and understood as having various capacities that are correlated with things in the universe. On his account, the universe is a divine body. God is the universe qua personal. And God is aware of the states of the universe by proprioception. Moreover, God's action is identified with God's increasing the determinacy of the divine body (the universe) that begins in a state of maximal indeterminacy. Forrest assumes both the falsity of idealism *and* the falsity of naturalism. With respect to the latter, he asserts that some features of the universe resist scientific understanding. In particular, some attributes of humans and some other animals related to consciousness and agency. These attributes present us with *anthropic mysteries* that provide the basis for a "*Properly* Anthropomorphic Metaphysics" (PAM) that provides the grounds for a "*Defiantly* Anthropomorphic Theism" (DAT). He writes that, "Personal Pantheism is athropomorphic in the sense that the features of human beings not explained scientifically provide precedents for our conception of God" (p. 24). In contrast with an Anselmian methodology that admits divine attributes with no human precedent, DAT assumes an Ockhamist methodology that "attributes to God various human characteristics that cannot wholly be understood in a naturalistic fashion based largely on the theory of the brain" (p. 24). Forrest's case for his version of personal pantheism results from combining PAM with the Ockhamist methodology. He argues that the end product is not inimical to theism.

Karl Pfeifer focuses on how best to think about God's relationship to the universe and its parts on a pantheistic conception of the divine in Chapter 2. He suggests that

"God" be taken to be a *mass noun* and not a *count noun*. Count nouns (e.g. "plate," "cup," "bicycle") refer to numerically distinct objects (e.g., there are four plates on the table). Mass nouns (e.g. "beer," "gold," "cream") refer to stuff that is not countable per se and take on a new sense when they take a plural form. For instance, someone may say that beer has salubrious qualities and refer to the beers available at a local beer store. In the latter case, the plural is meant to express the varieties of beer versus beer as a general type of beverage. Also, unlike the referents of count nouns, the referents of mass nouns can typically be divided and fused and still be the proper referents of the same mass noun. If you divide some quantity of beer in half, you still have beer. Similarly, one can fuse two separate quantities of beer to compose a larger quantity of beer. He suggests that by regarding "God" as a mass noun, "we will...have an effective way of making certain pantheistic claims regarding identities across parts and wholes intelligible" (p. 43). Pfeifer's central claim is that wherever mentality is present, God is present; and mentality is pervasive. Pfeifer's panpsychism issues from an ontology of the dispositional properties of objects. The dispositional properties of objects exhibit intentionality, being directed at various sorts of manifestations with different manifestation partners (e.g., the solubility of salt is directed at dissolving when it is partnered with the power of water to dissolve salt). Assuming that intentionality is the mark of the mental, mentality is ubiquitous. Pfeifer takes higher-order intentional systems to be built up from lower-order intentional sub-systems of integrated dispositional properties. With this framework in place, we get a picture of the world as a mental system, God's brain, that can be divided into various mental sub-systems with various levels of information processing. This complex intentional system provides the truthmakers for theological discourse and may even make room for a conception of God as personal and in possession of some of the attributes traditionally ascribed to God, such as omniscience.

In Chapter 3, John Leslie defends a form of pantheism that affirms the existence of infinitely many separately existing infinite minds. Leslie starts his defense of this view with the question "why does the world exist?" While some philosophers dismiss this as an ill-formed question Leslie argues that it is a legitimate question which is answered by his version of pantheism. He rejects the common strategy of answering the question by specifying a truthmaker for the existence of the world in the realm of existing things. Instead he tries to answer it by evoking the Platonic thesis that there are some things whose existence is ethically required. He writes:

> The sheer possibility of there existing a good thing or things is itself enough to set up a need for such a thing or things to exist in fact, and in some cases such a need is itself able to act creatively—to account, that is to say, for coming into existence or for eternal existence. (p. 54)

This Platonic thesis entails, according to Leslie, that the world exists because it is an ethical requirement that it exist. Leslie develops his view further by incorporating the idea that no entity could be better than an infinite mind that eternally contemplated everything worth contemplating. He then says that such a mind, given its benevolence and power, would produce infinitely many more minds of the same type. Leslie there-fore deduces infinitely many infinite minds, each of which eternally contemplates everything that is worth contemplating such as the structures of infinitely many uni-verses, including our own universe. Leslie says that such a reality can be called "God."

In Chapter 4, Brian Leftow offers a critical assessment of naturalistic pantheism from a traditional theist's viewpoint. The core thesis of any version of pantheism seems to be the following: God and the universe are identical. There are several distinct inter-pretations of this identity claim but naturalistic pantheism holds that the universe at its basic level consists entirely of physical entities, and its only laws are those of physics. Naturalistic pantheism, according to Leftow, offers a highly non-standard candidate referent for "God." Since he focuses on naturalistic pantheism, which regards a natu-ralistic universe as at bottom physical, Leftow sets aside Eastern views that regard the universe as at least partly spiritual. Leftow is mainly interested in the tenability of natu-ralistic pantheism in relation to the standard Western religious usage of "God." In order to determine whether such an understanding of divinity is tenable, we first need to explain what it takes to be God. However, we cannot do this simply by listing the standard great-making properties, such as omniscience and omnipotence, because that would beg the question against naturalistic pantheism. Leftow therefore considers instead what it takes to play the God-role in human life. He contends that the essential religious element of the God-role is that God deserves worship. Leftow then argues that naturalistic pantheism fails to provide a tenable concept of God because the uni-verse, as it is understood by naturalistic pantheism, is not a conceptually appropriate object of worship.

Part II consists of essays that develop or critique versions of panentheism. While perhaps fewer people are aware of panentheistic conceptions of God and how they differ from versions of pantheism, panentheism may be more widely endorsed than pantheism.

In Chapter 5, Yujin Nagasawa considers a version of panentheism, which he calls "modal panentheism." Modal panentheism consists of two claims: (i) God is the total-ity of all possible worlds and (ii) all possible worlds exist to the same extent that the actual world does. Although this view initially appears very different from traditional theism, Nagasawa argues that it shares some unique features with traditional theism. For example, like traditional theism, it is based on the Anselmian definition of God as that than which no greater can be thought, although it employs an alternative interpre-tation of that definition. Also, according to Nagasawa, the modal panentheistic God shares many great-making properties with the traditional theistic God, such as omnis-cience, omnipotence, omnibenevolence, immutability, impassibility, eternity, neces-sary existence, omnipresence, independence, unsurpassability, and the property of being a cause of the universe. Nagasawa maintains, moreover, that modal panentheism provides answers to a number of difficult problems in the philosophy of religion, such as the problem of evil, the problem of no best possible world, the fine-tuning problem, the timing problem for the beginning of the universe, and the question why there is anything at all. However, according to Nagasawa, modal panentheism faces its own problem, which is a unique version of the problem of evil that is more powerful than the versions that traditional theism and pantheism face.

The problem of evil has often been treated as one of the motivations for rejecting classical theism. For instance, John Bishop (1998, 174–5) argues for rejecting classical theism and accepting an alternative conception of God owing in part to the threat posed by the argument from evil. In Chapter 6, John Bishop and Ken Perszyk consider the various problems of evil that attend different conceptions of God. They motivate an alternative conception of God by focusing on the difficulties for traditional omniGod theism posed by the problem of evil. And they note additional problems of evil faced by some other recent alternatives to omniGod theism. But while they argue that various conceptions of God face different challenges from different problems of evil, they admit that their "euteleological" pantheistic alternative faces its own unique challenges. On their account, God is identified both with love, which is the supreme good that is the Universe's *telos*, and with the reality that is directed towards realizing that end. This approach is consistent with ontological naturalism and avoids some of the problems of evil faced by omniGod theism. They concede, however, that euteleological theism might be judged religiously inadequate because it can offer only an austere notion of salvation: while they argue that there is a sort of salvific power of love, they admit that a universal victory of the power of love over evil would seem to require the supernatural power that they reject on their conception of God. They further acknowledge that an evidential problem of evil confronts their proposal. This is because the extent and nature of evil counts as evidence against the claim that the supreme good of loving relationship is the ultimate explanatory *telos* of the universe. They suggest that from a position of religious neutrality, this problem of evil may be insurmountable for euteleological theism. When wedded to certain Christian presuppositions, however, the scales may tip favorably for this conception of God.

In Chapter 7, Marilyn McCord Adams focuses primarily on critiquing the euteleological conception of God as the end or final cause at which the universe is directed. She discusses some different accounts of final causes from the history of philosophy, noting the difficulties with coming up with an adequate conception of a final cause. In doing so, she sheds light on Bishop and Perszyk's project and the problems their account faces. Adams questions whether euteleological theism can explain the universe as we know it. She also expresses skepticism about whether the sort of loving relationships required for the adequacy of euteleological theism can be had. Adams notes that, because "the vast majority of horror-participants never experience perfectly loving relationality" love will not conquer the evil of their participating in horrors (p. 138). Finding Bishop and Perszyk's proposal wanting, Adams discusses some other alternative conceptions of God she argues fare better than euteleological theism. But while, according to Adams, some other proposals fare better than Bishop and Perszyk's, in the light of difficulties the other alternatives face, she argues that theists would do better to remain committed to traditional theism.

The essays in Part III represent some further alternatives to traditional theism as standardly formulated. Theistic idealism, ultimism, and theological fictionalism are separately presented as alternatives and their implications are discussed.

In Chapter 8, Charles Taliaferro offers a defense of John Foster's theistic idealism. Naturalistic philosophers of mind today typically hold that we have a clearer idea of the physical than the non-physical and assume the primacy of the physical over the non-physical. They hence reject the idea that the non-physical, which is assumed to be ontologically distinct from the physical, can causally affect the physical. Taliaferro argues, however, that such a position is untenable. Unlike these naturalistic philosophers of mind—but like Foster—he accepts the ontological distinction between the physical and the non-physical and argues for the primacy of the *non-physical* over the physical. He tries to show this by providing reasons for thinking that our concepts of the mental and mental causation are more lucid and prior to our concepts of the physical and physical causation. These ideas entail the ineliminability of experience, which motivates Foster's idealism. Taliaferro argues that Foster needs theism to complete his idealism because it misses something that makes and sustains the cosmos as a place fit for experiencing beings like us humans. Foster did not intend to develop an alternative to Christian theism as he himself was a Christian. His theistic idealism is nevertheless construed as an alternative to traditional theism because it provides a more experientially based understanding of God's relationship to the cosmos than traditional theism.

In Chapter 9, J. L. Schellenberg claims that scholars choose between two extant approaches when exploring alternatives to traditional theism. The first approach is to develop detailed concepts of God that are distinct from the traditional concept of God. Such concepts include pantheistic and panentheistic concepts. The other approach is to develop an abstract concept according to which God is ineffable or transcategorial. Such concepts include John Hick's notion of the "Real." Schellenberg argues that we need a third approach because the first approach is too general and the second approach is too specific. The third approach that Schellenberg develops is based on the view he calls "ultimism." He says that ultimism is entailed by detailed religious claims but it does not entail them. This is because ultimism, although informative, has little content of its own. Schellenberg formulates ultimism in terms of three types of ultimacy: metaphysical ultimacy, axiological ultimacy, and soteriological ultimacy. He considers the historical development of human intelligence and claims that there may be many ways of adding detail to ultimism that we have not yet conceived. Yet, Schellenberg says, ultimism remains valuable even to more deeply enlightened descendants of ours because its contents are general enough and temporally stable. He concludes that the idea of God represented by ultimism should become central in the philosophy of religion.

In Chapter 10, Robin Le Poidevin considers the prospects for meaningful engagement between different varieties of theological realists and theological fictionalists in religious communities. Le Poidevin takes the realist to be someone who "takes God-talk…at face value, and as true by virtue of the way the world is independently of human belief" (p. 178). The fictionalist is characterized as a person who, "when engaging in religious language and practice, takes herself to be engaging in a (rather complex) game of make-believe" (p. 178). Importantly, the religious fictionalist does not take religious claims such as "God loves us" to be false. Rather, she takes them to be true "by virtue of the content of the relevant fiction" (p. 178). While the focus is on realists and fictionalists, Le Poidevin also considers anthropological reconstructionism, which treats theological discourse as about human ideals; non-cognitivism, the view that theological discourse lacks truth-value; and agnosticism. These three serve as a contrast class of views to the realist and fictionalist approaches that are his primary focus. Le Poidevin examines how the religious practices and commitments of these groups may differ. He does not deny that tension is likely between realists and fictionalists, or that some religious practices may be difficult to justify for the latter; but he strikes a cautiously optimistic tone in his chapter regarding the prospects for interaction between realists and fictionalists.

Classical theists assume that God is an agent whose activity makes a causal difference in the world. The essays in Part IV consider whether we must accept the notion of God as cause and, if we do, what the implications are for how we think of the metaphysics of the divine and the prospects for human agents to have a robust form of free will.

In Chapter 11, Willem Drees aims at offering a non-theistic way of thinking about the divine that takes ontological naturalism as both a resource and as a constraint on our theorizing about the divine. Focusing on both the cosmological and axiological dimensions of our conception of the divine, Drees considers two different ways of de-emphasizing or rejecting some traditional ways of thinking about the divine. First, he considers how we might think about the divine in non-causal terms as the ground of existence rather than in causal terms as the creator and first cause of the universe. This proposal is reminiscent of the proposal put forward by Paul Tillich in the first volume of his *Systematic Theology* (1951). But there are differences. For one, Drees eschews taking the ground of existence as being revelatory in the same way it is for Tillich. Drees then proposes an axiological framework that shifts from thinking in terms of a divine judge to thinking of the divine perspective as *sub specie aeternitatis*, a perspective that is not a particular perspective, and "thus not serving a particular self-interest" (p. 208). The divine perspective is impartial regarding the interests and concerns of agents. This perspective, in turn, is a model for our own perspective vis-à-vis others and provides a framework for the impartial evaluation of our own behavior and the behavior of others. Drees proposes a religious outlook that integrates both of the two perspectives on the divine he discusses into a single vision of divine reality that he claims is consistent with naturalism.

In Chapter 12, Andrei A. Buckareff considers some problems posed for those committed to theological realism by the thesis that God is an agent who acts in the universe and is an immaterial substance without spatiotemporal location. Buckareff asserts that theological realism involves the conjunction of two theses. The first is theological cognitivism, the thesis that at least some of our positive theological statements about God's attributes and divine agency express what we accept or believe and that the statements are truth-apt. The second commitment is the supposition that at least some positive theological statements are, in fact, true. Buckareff asserts that if we wish to avoid treating talk of divine action as merely metaphorical and avoid theological anti-realism, the question that naturally arises is "What must God *be like* if we are to truthfully employ action-predicates when we are making claims about divine action?" This question forces us to determine what the ontological commitments of our religious language are. Buckareff assumes a truthmaker criterion of ontological commitment on which the ontological commitments of some theoretical discourse are the things that must exist to make the sentences of that discourse true. Focusing on divine action sentences, Buckareff argues that if we wish to be theological realists about statements about divine action, then we must reject the traditional metaphysics of theism that takes God to be wholly immaterial and not spatiotemporally located. He argues that if God is an agent who performs discrete intentional actions, the effects of which can be indexed to locations in space-time, then God's actions have a spatiotemporal location. And if God's actions can be located in space-time, then God is located in space-time, being in some sense embodied by the universe. While he remains silent about how best to conceive of God's relationship to the universe, he explicitly defends the following two claims. First, traditional theism does not have the metaphysical resources necessary for us to be theological realists about divine agency. Second, because of this, theological realists about divine agency should endorse some version of either pantheism or panentheism.

While he is a proponent of classical theism, Hugh McCann defends a minority view in Chapter 13 that stands as an alternative to many standard versions of classical theism defended by analytic philosophers today. The free will debate provides the metaphysical backdrop for his contribution. He presents and defends a non-causal conception of libertarian free agency. The problem of how free actions can best be explained if we eschew a causal account of the explanation of our decisions by reasons is presented. Assuming that God is simple and timelessly eternal, McCann argues that for non-causalists the best approach to take is one where God's creative action as first cause provides for the existence of our decisions and other actions that are still related teleologically to our reasons. On McCann's preferred account, everything, including our actions, owe their origin and continued existence to God. He addresses some worries that may be raised by his interlocutors, including the worry that this approach is just a variant of theological determinism that would be incompatible with our having libertarian free will.

Many scholars pursue alternative concepts of God because of their dissatisfaction with the supernaturalistic implications of traditional theism. The two essays in the final part of the book, Part V, consider the tenability of alternative concepts within a naturalistic framework.

In Chapter 14, Emily Thomas sheds light on a unique view of God developed by the emergentist Samuel Alexander (1859–1938). Emergentist theologies commonly claim that the universe exhibits a hierarchy of emergence and that God has or will emerge from the universe most likely through evolution. Emergentist theologies that are defended by such contemporary scholars as Arthur Peacocke, Harold Morowitz, and Philip Clayton are construed as versions of panentheism, which places the universe within God. Thomas argues that Alexander's emergentist view is radically different ● from these others because it places God *within the universe*. According to Alexander's view, God will emerge as the final quality in a temporal and logical hierarchy of emergence. Thomas argues that Alexander's view is not only unique but also compelling. In order to show this, she contrasts it with Clayton's view. First, she defends Alexander's view against Clayton's criticisms. Clayton tries to undermine Alexander's view by showing that: (i) it is not fully naturalist, (ii) it "divinizes" human beings, and (iii) it "finitizes" God. Thomas claims that Alexander can successfully respond to these criticisms. She then raises two objections to Clayton's view. The first objection is that there is a tension in Clayton's view because, on the one hand, it relies heavily on naturalism in defense of emergence, but, on the other hand, it is based on a non-naturalist theology. The second objection is that Clayton's view seems to involve ontological redundancy because it posits an emergent God in addition to a creator God. Thomas concludes that Alexander's view, which does not face these objections, should be recognized as a serious contender among contemporary emergentist views.

In Chapter 15, Eric Steinhart focuses on religious naturalism. Religious naturalism is based on two main theses: (i) all religiously significant objects are natural, and (ii) some natural objects are religiously significant. There are many distinct versions of religious naturalism because there are many distinct ways of construing such concepts as *nature* and *religious significance*. Yet Steinhart argues that most versions of religious naturalism can be understood in terms of five contexts that they address: the *concrete* context, which is associated with nature in the largest and deepest sense; the *physical* context, which is associated with our universe; the *chemical* context, which is associated with our solar system; the *biological* context, which is associated with our earth; and the *personal* context, which is associated with human animals. Steinhart claims that religious naturalism does not have to be a solely theoretical enterprise. In fact, many religious naturalists perform naturalistic rituals in relation to each context. According to Steinhart, most religious naturalists affirm the existence of some natural creative power and regard it as divine or religiously significant. He contends that religious naturalism is remarkable because it shows that non-theistic religions are possible in the West.

Taken together, the essays in this volume represent a departure from some of the standard fare in analytic philosophy of religion. It is our hope that the essays in this volume will inspire further work on alternative conceptions of the divine. Whether that work is by proponents or critics, we expect that the benefits we will reap in the field will extend beyond considering a range of metaphysical options. It is our hope that it will contribute to a shift toward a more global perspective in the philosophy of religion.[6]

[6] We wish to thank Marilyn McCord Adams, John Bishop, Peter Forrest, Brian Leftow, Karl Pfeifer, John Schellenberg, and Eric Steinhart for their helpful feedback on an earlier draft of this introduction. Any mistakes that remain are our own.

References

Bishop, J. (1998). "Can there be Alternative Concepts of God?" *Noûs* 32: 174–88.

Bourget, D. and Chalmers, D. (2014). "What do Philosophers Believe?" *Philosophical Studies* 170: 465–500.

Draper, P. and Nichols, R. (2013). "Diagnosing Bias in Philosophy of Religion," *The Monist* 96: 420–46.

Ivanhoe, P. (2007). "Heaven as a Source for Ethical Warrant in Early Confucianism," *Dao* 6: 211–20.

Johnston, M. (2009). *Saving God: Religion after Idolatry.* Princeton: Princeton University Press.

Kray, K. (2013). "Method and Madness in Contemporary Analytic Philosophy of Religion," *Toronto Journal of Theology* 29: 245–63.

Levine, M. (2000). "Contemporary Christian Philosophy of Religion: Biblical Fundamentalism, Terrible Solutions to a Horrible Problem, and Hearing God," *International Journal for Philosophy of Religion* 48: 89–119.

Liu, Shu-hsien (1972). "The Confucian Approach to the Problem of Transcendence and Immanence," *Philosophy East and West* 22: 45–52.

Liu, Shu-hsien (1978). "Commentary: Theism from a Chinese Perspective," *Philosophy East and West* 28: 413–17.

Schellenberg, J. L. (forthcoming). "Divine Hiddenness and Human Philosophy," in A. Green and E. Stump (eds), *Hidden Divinity and Religious Belief.* New York: Cambridge University Press.

Smart, N. (1995). "The Philosophy of Worldviews, or the Philosophy of Religion Transformed," in T. Dean (ed.), *Religious Pluralism and Truth* (pp. 17–32). Albany, NY: SUNY Press.

Tillich, P. (1951). *Systematic Theology*, vol. 1. Chicago: University of Chicago Press.

Yang, Xiaomei (2008). "Some Issues in Chinese Philosophy," *Philosophy Compass* 3: 551–69.

PART I
Pantheism

1

The Personal Pantheist Conception of God

Peter Forrest

This chapter is a case for the pantheist conception considered as a species of theism, rather than a rival to it.[1] The starting point, the premise of the argument, is properly anthropomorphic metaphysics (PAM), which I propose as a rival to scientific natural-ism; I begin, then, by stating my version of pantheism, by expounding PAM, and by sketching my argument.

1. Personal Pantheism

My chapter is one of a collection on alternative *conceptions* of God, one of which I am expounding and arguing for. A conception is contrasted with a concept, a definition, and is a theoretical description of what satisfies that definition (Gallie 1956, Rawls 1971). This distinction often arises when the definition is either normative or intuitively extrinsic to the topic, and so when we think of the item in question we often rely upon a non-normative and intrinsic description. So I begin with the concept of *a god*. It is that of a worthy object of worship, where worship is an attitude often expressed by religious rituals, such as the paradigm of prostration before some representation of the object of worship. I claim no special expertise as a phenomenologist of worship, but I invite readers to agree that it involves both awe at the object and a consequent restraint of the worshipper's actions, expressed by saying, 'Not my will but thine be done', where, however the 'will' of the god being worshipped is often understood by analogy.

[1] Many thanks to Andrei Buckareff for his most useful comments both at the conference and subse-quently. The original title was 'A Case for Pantheism', but as he pointed out, most philosophers mean some-thing rather different by pantheism. I hope the qualification 'personal' conveys the difference between my proposal and other versions of pantheism. Many thanks too to a reader for Oxford University Press and to my colleagues Arcady Blinov and Adrian Walsh for their most helpful comments.

An atheist is someone who denies there is any worshipful being. If there is one object of worship that should be worshipped by us in a total or unconditional way, then it is *God*, which is by definition unique. Someone who holds there are gods but no God I consider a *polytheist* even if only one god is believed in. I restrict the term 'theist' for someone who holds there is a supremely worthy object of worship, God.

By a *conception* of God I mean a description of that which either is or would be supremely worthy of worship. Although God is by definition unique this does not exclude multiple conceptions of what would be the unique God if It existed. Theists and atheists tend to argue for and against God as described by their favourite conception. Presumably this is because they take it to be 'the one to beat', that which is considered more likely than rival conceptions. In this sense a conception of God is a hypothesis about the nature of God that is put forward as more likely than, or at least as likely as, rival hypotheses about the nature of God. Strictly speaking, therefore, an alternative conception of God might be proposed without much enthusiasm as the best of a bad bunch of hypotheses. For example John Mackie proposed John Leslie's Extreme Axiarchism as an alternative conception of God, in *The Miracle of Theism* (Mackie 1982). The case for an alternative conception of God may be said, therefore, to *undermine* theism if, as a corollary, that case significantly reduces the intellectual appeal of theism.

This paper argues that an alternative conception of God, Personal Pantheism, is superior to standard conceptions and argues that it does not undermine theism.[2] In fact I prefer Qualified Personal Pantheism, the 'Swiss Cheese' theory, in which human and similar minds are not parts of God but rather holes in God, who is identical to the rest of the Universe.[3] The considerations of this paper do not establish a case for qualified over unqualified pantheism. And I shall ignore the qualification, considering the Universe as it was before there were any non-divine minds. In that situation the physical universe is taken to be God's body but God is personal in the sense of being a conscious agent.

There are several standard conceptions, to which Personal Pantheism is an alternative. Some are neo-Platonist and Thomist conceptions of God as the One, the Beautiful, the Good, Pure Being, Pure Act, or in accordance with divine simplicity all of these identified. Rather different is the conception of God as an omnipotent omniscience person who, excepting Incarnation, has no body (Swinburne 2004). These standard conceptions all differ from pantheism by taking God to have created the Universe *ex nihilo* and to be a *spirit* in the stipulated sense of a substance (as opposed to a property

[2] Personal Pantheism is a Stoic thesis (Baltzly 2014, §3), but it is surprisingly hard to find other notable proponents. Grace Jantzen comes to mind as holding that the Universe is the divine body (Jantzen 1998, ch. 11). See also (Mander 2013, § 11).

[3] This qualification is also reminiscent of Stoicism, in which, as I understand it, God changes from being the whole world to only most of it, because we are the 'sparks from the divine fire'.

The Swiss might complain that their most famous cheese, Gruyère, has holes that are few, if any, and small. I am unrepentant.

or relation) that is not essentially embodied. By contrast, Personal Pantheism is materialist in the weak sense of denying that there are any spirits, divine or otherwise. The
standard conceptions often come with the qualification that what we say of God in a
positive fashion is by analogy, either in the Aristotelian *pros hen* sense or in the sense of
similitude. The conception that I am advocating is a literal one subject to two qualifica-
tions. The first is the 'Swiss Cheese' qualification mentioned above and here ignored.
The second is that my use of the term 'body' as the object of proprioception rather than
by definition something made of flesh and blood is a semi-technical stipulation.

Atheism is compatible with awe at the Universe, by which I mean the sum total of all
that is physical, and the natural order it exhibits. By pantheism I understand something more than awe, namely worship of the Universe.[4] This requires submission to the
'will' of the Universe. Most pantheists take the 'will' in question by analogy. And their
submission to it amounts to being reconciled to what is necessary. Maybe this was
Baruch Spinoza's attitude; maybe it was Margaret Fuller's attitude expressed by 'I accept
the universe'. Personal pantheists, however, take the 'will' literally. Personal Pantheism
is compatible both with polytheism and theism. I am advocating it as a version of theism, however, in that the God identified with the Universe is taken to be supremely
worthy of worship. On it we first conceive of the Universe to be the divine body and
then, just as so-called 'non-reductive physicalists' identify themselves with their bodies without reducing the mental to the physical, we identify God with the divine body.
So God has intellect, senses, and will, but these are correlated with the whole universe
the way that our intellect, senses, and will are correlated with our brain processes,
which act as ways of representing the world around us. Although anthropomorphic,
God differs from us not merely in the vastly greater extent of divine knowledge and
power, but also in that God is aware of the Universe whereas we are not (usually) aware
of the brain as such. Rather the way the brain appears from the inside is, by evolution
and divine purpose, a remarkably faithful representation of part of the Universe.

On this conception, God does not create the Universe *ex nihilo*. For that would be
self-creation, which is incoherent. Rather God starts as a maximally indeterminate
Universe, like the pre-Socratic *apeiron*, and the divine acts are ones of increasing
determinacy. (I shall return in section 9.2 to the theory of action as increase in
determinacy.)

2. Properly Anthropocentric Metaphysics

First I shall assume, for simplicity of exposition, that idealism is false. That is, I assume
that physical does not depend for its existence on the awareness of it. More important,
I assume, without here arguing, that Naturalism is false. That is, there are features of

---

[4] Michael Levine (1994), has defended a 'pantheistic' conception of God, without being himself a
pantheist. This 'pantheism' does not move beyond awe to worship.

the Universe that cannot be understood scientifically. These include rather general features of human beings (and some other animals) to do with consciousness and with reasons for action. These features are not mere mysteries but provide potential explanations of the scientific description. There is a tendency to condemn anthropocentricism, and, even more, to condemn theological anthropomorphism, which is why I call it *Properly* Anthropocentric Metaphysics (PAM), and why I call my theology DAT, *Defiantly* Anthropomorphic Theism. Personal Pantheism is anthropomorphic in the sense that the features of human beings not explained scientifically provide precedents for our conception of God. For Ockham's Razor weighs against those conceptions without precedent.

The version of Ockham's Razor being appealed to here is not that entities should not be multiplied but that *kinds* of entity should not be multiplied without good reason, and the more novel the kind, the better the required reasons. To be sure, God is a novel kind of being but Personal Pantheism keeps the novelty to a minimum thus reducing the Ockhamist objection to theism and hence supporting it as a conception of God. This Ockhamist methodology should be contrasted with that of Perfect Being Theology (Morris 1988), which following St Anselm, posits various divine attributes even if they have no human precedent, on the grounds that they would add to the divine value. The theological Ockhamist, by contrast, attributes to God various human characteristics that cannot wholly be understood in a naturalistic fashion based largely on the theory of the brain. These brain-transcending attributes are in the human case nonetheless structured in some fashion by the brain. But they are attributed to God without either the limitations or the structure due to the brain. (An obvious exception would be if evil is brain transcending. An evil being could not be a god, however powerful.) The contrast between the two theological methodologies may be illustrated by considering God's capacity to know the future. That seems a perfection but has no human precedent. The Ockhamist should not attribute it to God, the divine perfectionist should.

Perfect Being Theology would seem to be motivated in two ways. The first is that to posit a limitation is an intellectual complication and so to be avoided where possible on grounds of simplicity. The second is that the supremacy required for a being to be worthy of worship requires perfection. Agreed! But the first only warrants the non-limitation of those kinds of attribute we have independent reason to assign to God. The second only warrants those perfections required to be unconditionally trustworthy, notably moral perfection and infallibility (having no 'false knowledge').

3. The Argument in Outline

The comparison with standard conceptions of God depends on whether PAM supports Substance Dualism as a metaphysics for human beings (and *pace* Descartes, other animals). Substance Dualism asserts that the thing that is aware and acts is a spirit, that is, not essentially embodied. Substance Dualism may be contrasted with Property Dualism, the thesis that although Substance Dualism fails we humans have non-physical properties. PAM may well support Property Dualism, but that is not my present concern.

If PAM supports Substance Dualism then, without introducing totally novel kinds of entity, we may posit God as a spirit, with powers similar to that of a human soul, although vastly greater. On the other hand if PAM does not support Substance Dualism then Ockham's Razor renders the standard conceptions implausible. I argue that PAM does not support Substance Dualism. I also argue that the familiar qualia do not provide any precedent for the divine mind. My case for Personal Pantheism rests on the way that proprioception may, however, be extrapolated to the divine mind. I also provide an account of human agency as increasing the determinacy of a not wholly determinate spatiotemporal universe. Using this, and proprioception, as the precedents for the divine nature, I arrive at a version of Personal Pantheism in which:

1. The Universe is the divine body;
2. There is no divine soul;
3. God is aware of the Universe by proprioception; and
4. God acts by increasing the determinacy of the divine body, which starts in a state of maximal indeterminacy.

To show that Personal Pantheism does not undermine theism requires an argument for theism, which can be shown to be adaptable to Personal Pantheism. The role of such argument in supporting religious faith is contested, and mostly I leave it to readers to assess whether there is any undermining, although in section 12, I provide a specimen argument.

4. Awareness

Awareness and action are two of the topics where I reject the naturalistic account as inadequate. Because these topics provide the precedents for God, who is aware and who acts, a detailed theory of them should be a preliminary to Defiantly Anthropomorphic Theism. Such a detailed theory would have to take notice of debates in the philosophy of mind. My purpose in this chapter is less ambitious, however, and I need to consider awareness and action only so as to argue for Personal Pantheism over standard conceptions of God.

First, then, consider awareness. Perception, proprioception, and introspection are all species of awareness. It might well be the same as consciousness but it is a conceptual necessity that awareness takes an intentional object—you must be aware *of* something—whereas it makes sense to consider someone, a mystic or a foetus, being conscious without being conscious of anything. Whether in fact there ever is such objectless consciousness is disputed. To avoid these disputes I shall stick with the term 'awareness'. When certain complicated patterns of spiking frequencies in axons and firings of synapses occur—patterns that play a certain functional role—then there is awareness of something. For example, activity in the nerves that used to run down to an amputated limb result in the awareness of the limb that no longer exists. As this phantom limb example shows, awareness can come in modes; there is joyful awareness but also, as in this case, suffering awareness. As that example also shows, we have the baffling Intentionality Thesis: the things we are aware of don't have to exist. That which is aware must exist, however. It is the Self, but, apart from its unity, its nature is not revealed by introspection.[5] What is revealed by introspection, though, is that, either always or for the most part, the thing that is aware is attracted to what seems good and acts accordingly. As far as the phenomenology (the careful description of introspection) goes, a 'No Self' theory could be true, that is the Self might only exist in virtue of the contents of awareness. Likewise even if the 'No Self' theory is false the Self might depend for its existence on the brain.

5. A Misleading Precedent: The Qualia

Those who reject naturalism might suggest that not merely awareness and agency but the qualia and artistic-cum-intellectual creativity are also inexplicable by science and so precedents for our conception of God. I am not here concerned with the topic of artistic-cum-intellectual creativity, but I shall now argue against treating qualia as a precedent for a divine mind, distinct from the Universe, which, given DAT, would lead to a panentheist conception.

By the qualia I mean the peculiar phenomenological qualities of our sensations. This is illustrated by the thought experiment in which Frank Jackson considers Mary who knows all the relevant science but has not experienced colour (Jackson 1982, 1986). Regardless of how we interpret the Mary experiment we should acknowledge that she makes a discovery of some sort when first experiencing colour. What she discovers are putatively the qualia of colour sensations. And we may consider similar thought experiments for smell, hearing, taste, pain, hunger, thirst, and many other sensations. I now argue that these qualia are of no relevance to the argument from PAM to DAT. This is important as a way of focusing on what is relevant, namely proprioception.

Guided by functionalist theories in philosophy of mind we might well think that the qualia, how things seem, are (partially) explained by the functional roles of the associated brain processes.[6] This may be illustrated using two kinds of leech-like organisms whose life, prior to sexual maturity, is dominated by the twin goals of seeking the dark,

[5] There is confusion over the terms 'mind', 'soul', and 'self'. I stipulate that the Self is the mind abstracted from the details of the contents of awareness. The mind on the other hand includes these details. By a soul I mean either the Self or the mind if it is a spirit.

[6] Functionalism is the theory of mind that characterizes the various mental states by their role in a complicated network of causal interactions with other mental states with stimuli and with behaviour. It is then assumed, plausibly enough, that brain processes can play these roles.

to avoid predators, and seeking the warmth, to be near their next feed. The simpler organism operates by direct response to stimulus, moving away from light and towards warmth. Where these two goals conflict there is no motion. The other organism is more sophisticated. So if warmth is correlated with light it moves away from the light and warmth if it has just fed, but towards it otherwise. To do this it has a state playing the hunger role and it behaves by moving towards the warmth if hungry but away from the light if not hungry. As I understand it, on a functionalist theory the simpler organism has no mental states, whereas the more complicated has hunger states.

This functionalist theory of mental states notoriously omits the qualia, which PAM should not ignore. And it is an open question whether the more sophisticated leech-like organism really *feels* hunger, when in a hunger state. Maybe it feels nothing. But a functionalist may reasonably assert that if it feels anything it feels something like what we feel when are hungry. For the felt quale of hunger is such that it is not merely unpleasant but we know from that quale that we can end the hunger by eating. In this way its functional role is manifest in the state's quale. Now we might get rid of the hunger some other way, say by drinking coca leaf tea, but the functional role of hunger to prompt eating is manifest—unlike drinking coca leaf tea.

Functionalism does not fully explain the qualia but it is could provide a partial explanation based on the way that in simple cases the functional role is manifest in the quale. We then extrapolate, as best we can, to more complicated cases. For colour vision, for instance, the functional role of the hue-contrast is manifest—it is to divide up the visual field in salient ways—but the role of the intrinsic colour-quale is not manifest.

The alternative partial explanation is that it is not the functional role of the brain process that generates the qualia but rather something intrinsic to the brain process such as the pattern of spiking frequencies. We then rely on an evolutionary explanation to explain why, for instance, pain-aversive behaviour is not correlated with pleasant feelings.

The difference between the two partial explanations may be illustrated by considering extraterrestrials with brain-analogs in states playing the same functional roles as our mental states but in a quite different way (David Lewis's 'Martians', 1983). On the functional role explanation we may assume the extraterrestrials are aware in much the way we are, but on the other we must be agnostic about what it is like to be them.

Neither partial explanation is great news for DAT, because they both undermine the natural enough idea of extrapolating the qualia from our minds to the (initial) divine mind. Prior to God imposing the natural order, there were no functional roles. And such patterns as there might be in some initial Universe would be so unlike brain activity that if they should result in divine qualia we have no idea what these are like.

6. Divine Proprioception

The theological irrelevance of qualia focuses us on those sensations for which there is no corresponding Mary experiment. One of these is body-awareness, or proprioception.

We are aware of our own geometry. Likewise in kinaesthesia we have some sense of motion. I shall concentrate on proprioception in part because I anticipate that a unification of space and time will blur the proprioception/kinaesthesia distinction when considering God, and in part because the phenomenology is easier for proprioception than for kinaesthesia—the motion is distracting. That we know some geometry by proprioception without qualia is related to the primary/secondary quality distinction, with spatiotemporal structure being primary and the various qualia painted onto it as it were, resulting in secondary qualities. And it is independently plausible that our range of secondary qualities is too specific to human beings to be extrapolated to God. (Sure, I am an anthropocentric anthropomorphite but I extend 'anthropos' here to include any extra-terrestrials, as well as, in their degrees of approximation to our abilities, non-human animals.)

The neurophysiology of body-awareness is complicated but there is nothing mysterious about the brain's capacity to represent the body much as it is. As far as I know the distorted *cortical homunculi* concern touch, not proprioception, but the distortion might nonetheless suggest that the proprioception that provides a precedent for the divine mind is topological in character, based on adjacency.[7]

I conclude that the best human precedent for the nature of the divine mind is body-awareness. Assuming God is aware of the universe, this implies that God knows it like we know our bodies. Hence we may take the Universe to be the divine body and pantheism follows if there is no spiritual component to God.

7. Does the Unity of Consciousness Imply a Spiritual Self?

I now turn to why we might think that we human beings have spiritual part, a soul. This would be a precedent for God either being partly or entirely spiritual.

A normal person is not just aware of this and aware of that, but is aware of this and that together, as it might be the same words both read and heard. This is the phenomenon of the unity of consciousness, and I take the Self to be the common subject of the several items of awareness. That poses a Euthyphroid. Does the Self exist because consciousness is unified? Or is the unity of consciousness explained by the Self? Plausibly, the Self exists independently of the brain processes only if it is the cause of the unity, not an effect. In that case, the conceivability of disembodied existence establishes a presumption for the possibility of disembodied existence and hence for the spiritual nature of the self. PAM itself, unlike Naturalism, has no prior commitment concerning the correct account of the unity of consciousness. Therefore, PAM enthusiasts should accept the Self as a precedent for a spiritual God if and only if: (1) the unity of consciousness cannot be explained without appealing to a, perhaps short-lived, Self; and

---

[7] For an account of Space-time (or more accurately the Aether) based on adjacency see (Forrest 2012).

(2) there is no physical theory of the Self sufficiently plausible to outweigh the presumption based on the conceivability of disembodied existence. Concerning (1) it is worth noting that the popular idea that each human being has precisely one enduring spiritual part, the soul, offers only a spurious explanation of the Unity of Consciousness. For if this soul is the aware subject then in cases of divided consciousness, notably due to cutting the commissural fibres, there is one subject because there is one human being but there is a lack of unity.

A survey of theories of the Self is beyond the scope of this chapter (see Brook and Raymont 2014), so I shall sketch an account that coheres well with my emphasis on proprioception and does not seem open to objections. I recognize that some PAM enthusiasts will consider the idea of a spiritual Self a superior explanation, and hence have reason to reject Personal Pantheism. That said, my preferred account is to learn from Kant. By way of excuse I note that this is not as bad as my Hegel moments. I submit that the Self is constituted by the unity of the proprioceptive awareness, that is, by there being, in non-pathological cases, a single body image. I then consider the Self, thus constituted, to explain in turn the unity of consciousness for the other senses. For instance, the unity of the heard and seen words derives from the way that the apparent place of hearing, between the ears, and the apparent point of view, behind the eyes, can both be located within the body image, as well as the way that the muscles in the eyes themselves contribute to the body-image. Touch is especially well unified because the place of touch is located at a point on the body-image.

I put forward Personal Pantheism, then, as a conception of God for those who see no need to explain the Unity of Consciousness by appealing to a spiritual Self.

8. Self as Agent?

Many philosophical theists (e.g. Swinburne 2004) rightly emphasize the role of agency in our conception of God. Agency is the kind of causation in which part of the explanation of what happens is a reason or a motive. In the context of Aristotelian science reasons for acting may be treated as the final cause of the action, differing from other final causes precisely in the way the agent is aware of it, a precondition for choosing between final causes. We no longer need final causes in science, but PAM requires that there be something special about agency and is therefore attracted to the thesis that when a person acts the cause is either the person as a whole or some part, a soul maybe. In neither case is the cause just the combination of the beliefs and desires that partially explain the act. Whether the agent is taken to be the whole person or some spiritual part, there is something mysterious about agency.

The idea that agency is to be understood as the exercise of power by a spiritual substance may be diagnosed as due to the familiarity of Aristotelian brute teleology, especially in biology, but also in the prevalence of improper anthropomorphism applied both to nature ('It keeps trying to rain') and artefacts ('My old Mac really has it in for me'). By *brute* teleology I mean a system tending towards an end without being conscious of so doing, as in the use of teleological explanations in botany and much of zoology. Brute teleological explanations are superficial in the case of biology, and completely misguided elsewhere. It is plausible that we used to project agency onto the world around us and then, retreating from wholesale anthropomorphism, retain, with more or less seriousness, the language of final causes, which, although redundant elsewhere, make the idea of a powerful spiritual substance, the soul, seem less mysterious than it really is. The upshot is that although PAM owes us a theory of agency, it should not incline us towards belief in spirits in the attempt to explain agency.

I conclude that brute teleology has no valid precedents and that therefore by Ockham's Razor it should not be used in an attempt to explain agency. As a corollary I reject the quasi-teleological theories of John Leslie's Extreme Axiarchism and the explicitly teleological theory of John Bishop and Ken Perszyck, both featured in this volume. For on those theories it is either goodness itself or some good end that is said to explain, not our awareness of the good. Our experience of our own lives provides a precedent for agency, but brute teleology, in which the there need be no consciousness of the end, is without valid precedent. (Compare Aquinas' Fifth way based on the acceptance of teleology but the rejection of brute teleology.)

9. Speculation about Consciousness and Agency

I am not attempting to explain the fact that there is awareness and the fact that there is agency. Their existence may well be mysterious 'brute facts'. Rather I am speculating about how awareness and agency cohere with the world as described by the sciences.

9.1 Awareness

Compare awareness with chemistry. The laws of nature permit the existence of an enormous variety of complex molecules. As far as we know, they are, however, to be found only on some planets around some stars, associated with life or its precursors. Organisms that are aware are, presumably, even rarer. But there is a difference. That complex molecules are rare is not puzzling: they need the right circumstances to be formed. Awareness, however, poses a problem for PAM, that of explaining why it is associated with only some complicated systems, with the only uncontested examples being nervous systems.

We cannot solve the problem by positing spiritual Selves (souls) because we would have to explain why a given soul is aware of what a certain brain represents. One solution, but an unsatisfactory one, is to posit psycho-physical interaction laws. This is distasteful on grounds of ontological economy, because there would seem to be so many of them. But there is a more serious objection in the context of this chapter. For in two ways psycho-physical laws hinder the explanation of various features of our life and the world around us in terms of divine agency. The first is that the psycho-physical laws are flawed from a providential point of view, resulting in excessive and dysfunctional pain. Such flaws might be understood in a chillingly utilitarian fashion as balanced by the beauty of complexity resulting from simple basic laws, except that the psycho-physical laws are not simple. The second is that in treating the correlation between the mental and the physical as laws of nature we forgo any way of understanding God's power to create as ultimately the same as our capacity to act, unless we suppose God to be subject to the same psycho-physical laws as we are. But that is incompatible with explaining these laws as brought about by God. Therefore psycho-physical laws multiply mysteries. Hence, I reach the conclusion that theists should not invoke complicated psycho-physical correlation laws.

Another unsatisfactory solution is panpsychism, according to which there are many physical things all of which are aware.[8] This replaces the problem of just what things are conscious by the equally vexing problem of just what these things are conscious of. If an electron is aware, then perhaps it is aware of the electromagnetic field, but how far does this awareness extend? Does it just fade away at the inverse square of the distance?

The best solution to the problem I know of is Pervasive Awareness: there is awareness of all things. This then raises the question of just what Selves there are to be aware, which can be answered by appealing to those solutions to the problem of the Unity of Consciousness that do not rely on a spiritual Self.

9.2 Agency

Current physics and chemistry describe quantum states that are indeterminate between many classical states. For example, instead of thinking of a hydrogen atom as consisting of an electron in a definite orbit around the proton, the electron is assigned a 'probability' distribution for position and for momentum. These 'probabilities' are widely interpreted as measures of indeterminacy rather than either propensities or epistemic probabilities. One deservedly popular model for the indeterminacy, the Everett Interpretation, is that we inhabit not one but many worlds, and the indeterminate quantity (in this case the position or momentum of the electron) has determinate but different values in different worlds (Vaidnan 2014, Forrest 2007b).

When a quantity such as position is observed, it typically becomes more determinate, which we may model as the observer coming to occupy only some of the worlds previously occupied, namely those in which the quantity has the observed value, with the remainder being the ones in which the observed quantity takes some other value. In the standard example of the electron and the two slits, initially both the electron and the observer are in many worlds in 50% of which the electron goes through the first slit

---

[8] This definition excludes monistic panpsychism, which is indistinguishable from Personal Pantheism, and idealist theories such as that of Berkeley. Unlike Personal Pantheism, panpsychism is astoundingly popular. (See Seage and Allen-Hermanson 2013.)

and in 50% the second. If the electron is observed to go through the first slit then the observer is in only the 50% in which the electron goes through that slit.

We may assimilate action to observation by saying that when we act we make reality more determinate. In other words, we ensure we observe the outcome that we have chosen. Suppose you decide to raise your arm. Then you continue to exist only in those worlds in which you feel your arm rising.

The naturalistic version of the Many Worlds Interpretation implies that in the Twin Slit experiment both the electron and the observer splits in two, so that after the observation there is also an observer in the worlds in which the electron goes through the second slit. This rates a lewis or two on the scale of incredulous stares. If we apply it to actions, incredulous stares may be turned into refutation in two ways. First, in whatever way we have chosen, our counterparts have chosen otherwise. That undermines morality, or if this is more general, the gravity of our decisions (Adams 1979, 195). Hence, PAM implies there are no such counterparts. And second, there is the absurd consequence that it is rational for a happy loner to play quantum Russian roulette repeatedly. In quantum Russian roulette some quantum effect (say a Geiger counter and a radioactive source) results, we would ordinarily say, in a 1/6 chance of death. Even if you play it 100 times, with a chance of survival, we would ordinarily say, less than 1%, then you continue to survive—in less than 1% of worlds. The only penalty for addiction to Russian roulette would be the sadness of those you leave behind in the worlds in which you do not survive.

The worlds used to model quantum indeterminacy are spatiotemporal ones including all of time considered as a fourth quantitative dimension like those of space. There is, however, a temporal ordering of increasing determinacy modelled as a nested sequence of actual-at-a-time sets of worlds, with actual-at-a-time set X being a proper part of actual-at-a-time set Y just in case X is actual at a later time than Y. We are led then to distinguish the temporal ordering of earlier and later from the quantitative measure of temporal separation.

As the actual-at-a-time set of worlds in which we exist becomes successively smaller, the set of macroscopically determinate facts common to the worlds grows larger. The fuzzy boundary between past and future is thus the boundary between the macroscopically determinate and the macroscopically indeterminate.

This distinction between the ordering and the quantitative aspects of time has, I have argued elsewhere, the advantage of making sense of the rate of passage of time and of defending PAM against objections derived from Relativity (Forrest 2008). It has the theological consequence that God may be thought of as performing one or more acts without being restricted to a region of space-time, such as a supposedly absolute present. For God's initial act the only determinate facts are those that are necessary in the sense of being true at all the worlds. This moment of the temporal ordering is prior to all those in space-time associated with fuzzy boundaries between the macroscopically determinate past and the macroscopically indeterminate future.

THE PERSONAL PANTHEIST CONCEPTION OF GOD 33

10. The Case for the Personal Pantheistic Conception

Some PAM enthusiasts might judge Substance Dualism less harshly than I have, positing a spiritual Self as the unifier of consciousness and action. At very least, though, the
Personal Pantheist conception of God is of interest as not requiring Substance
Dualism. It is based on the judgement that believing in entities, such as a spiritual or
partly spiritual God without ontological precedent (in Science, supplemented, I say, by
PAM), offends against Ockham's Razor. Therefore, without entirely excluding such
standard conceptions of God, I commend the alternative Personal Pantheism as following from theological Ockhamism. I now reply to three objections and note an additional advantage.

10.1 The Objection from Synchronic Disunity

The account given of the unity of consciousness requires the spatiotemporal world of
which God is aware by proprioception to be unified. Yet the increase in determinacy
account of action implies that this world is a multiverse consisting of many rather different universes. How can it be unified?

I have argued elsewhere that we may consider the multiverse not as the sum of disconnected universes, as in Lewis's modal realism, but as a hyper-universe made up of
the many universes glued together (Forrest 2015). In the jargon of mathematicians the
hyper-universe is fibrated. An analogy might be the pages of a book. Provided the
characteristics of the universes vary continuously as we move from universe to universe, distant universes can be quite different without disrupting the unity.

10.2 The Threat of Diachronic Disunity

This threat presupposes that God has a temporally ordered sequence of states. The
classical conception of God, which is more specific than the standard conception,
states, however, that God is eternal, meaning not everlasting so much as timeless.
I shall now digress to give a case against strict divine eternity, and so explain why I take
the threat of divine diachronic disunity seriously. My case against strict divine eternity
is that it implies either: (1) that in the one state God both brings it about that our universe exists and knows how the creatures in that universe will act; or (2) God fails to
know at any time how creatures act. I reject (2) both as a more radical departure from
tradition than my own proposal and as positing a God not worth worshiping. For a
God that does not even minimally interact by knowing what we freely do could be the
object of awe but not trust and obedience. That leaves (1), itself a disjunction between:
(1a) God knows how creatures act because God creates them thus acting (the Thomist
position) or (1b) God knows how creatures would behave if created. I consider PAM
incompatible with the sort of determinism (1a) implies. In addition, any adequate
solution to the Problem of Evil commits theists, I say, to creaturely freedom in a libertarian sense, which is incompatible with predestination. So I reject (1a), leaving (1b),
itself the disjunction of: (1bi) God knows how creatures would act because their acts

would be determined by their circumstances, with (1bii) God has a special capacity, middle knowledge, to know what creatures would freely do. I reject (1bi) for the same reasons as I reject (1a). The last branch, (1bii), is Molinism, the subject of much discussion in recent years (see Perszyk 2011). Although conceding its coherence I reject it, on Ockhamist grounds, as without precedent in the human condition, and hence failing to cohere with the case from PAM to DAT. This is one of the topics where my rejection of Perfect Being Theology is relevant. Provided it *is* coherent, middle knowledge is plausibly taken as perfection.

Having rejected divine eternity I need to defend Personal Pantheism not merely from the threat of synchronic disunity, which I have done in the previous section, but from that of diachronic disunity. What makes the sequence of divine states the states of a single God rather than a sequence of gods, each giving rise to the next? This Phoenix conception of God as a sequence of gods (diachronic polytheism) is inadequate, because, on it, there is nothing worthy of worship. I am committed, then, to the diachronic unity of God.

As in the case of the synchronic unity I reject the appeal to a non-physical Self. In the human case we have the familiar combination of psychological continuity with the continuity characteristic of organisms, and much of the debate concerns what to say when the two fail to coincide. Neither, however, is adequate for the divine diachronic unity because they both presuppose there is already a structured universe with physical laws and fairly definite psychological tendencies. Yet the primal divine act predates this structure. There is then a problem finding a precedent in PAM for the divine diachronic unity required for God to be worthy of worship.

I shall now suggest three solutions to this problem. The most radical is to say that the all-powerful god that created only lasted for a single act, but one of the results of that act was a God who was constrained by the natural order enough to have psychological continuity, based on a certain kind of divine character. I rather like this speculation for Trinitarian reasons because the resulting worshipful God could be the sum of three gods, not independently worshipful (Forrest 1998).

The next solution I believe to be correct but it suffers from a certain lack of detail. It extends the proprioceptive theory of the Self to cover the specious present, maybe by incorporating kinaesthesia. In the human case there are many such overlapping short-lived Selves, and that might well constitute the most fundamental kind of diachronic unity. But in the divine case I argue that the specious present should cover all of time up to some moment. (The 'holes' in God that are creatures capable of acting are themselves ephemeral so our past is not part of our present consciousness. Therefore they should be part of the divine present consciousness.) Just as our successive Selves overlap, so do the divine Selves but with the difference that later divine Selves include earlier ones. So as the set of actual universes contracts, the history of the sequence of contractions endures and constitutes the growing divine memory.

In addition, or as a fall-back, I have a third solution. I warn readers that I am about to use the 'N' word: human beings can have a *narrative* identity, which confers, for good or ill, a kind of meaning on their lives. This narrative is constituted by a sequence of—more foul language!—*existential* choices, that is, choices that express the chooser's values and which constrain the circumstances of future choices. The way in which each choice influences the circumstances for the next choice provides a meaningful personal identity, although radical repentance might result in the replacing one such narrative person (Saul) by another (Paul). There may also be such things as collective narrative identities. Regardless of the importance of narrative identity for a meaningful, although not necessarily good, human life, narrative identity can be applied to Personal Pantheism, and we can, to a limited extent, come to know the divine narrative, which establishes the diachronic unity of the divine narrative self.

10.3 The Threat of Many Universes Polytheism

The theory of action based on many universes allows for an initial divine act that shatters the divine unity, replacing one God by many gods, each aware of and having power over a subset of the original plenitude of universes, say those with a given set of laws of nature. Do we have any reason to deny this version of polytheism? I have two replies. The first is that this not a version of polytheism as I have defined it. For each of the gods is God for the inhabitants, if any, of the universes that god controls. For the god of our universe is supremely worthy of our worship. So there is only one God.

My other reply is that the initial divine act is not arbitrary but based on God's being drawn to the good. From that I draw two conclusions. The first is that if there is anything genuinely objectionable about 'many universes polytheism' then God would not choose to bring it about. The second is that the shattering of the divine unity has occurred in two, lesser, ways. First in the generation of a Trinity of divine persons (Forrest 1998) and second, I say, in the divine withdrawal from parts of our universe, namely the 'holes', the parts that are creatures capable of independent action (Forrest 2007a).

10.4 The Advantage of Nature Worship

One of the advantages of Personal Pantheism is that we can incorporate the worship of nature into Abrahamic religions, which have been vehemently opposed to nature worship, because of its association with agriculture, sex, and procreation—great goods of course but not the stuff of worship. The romantic nature religion of poets (Wordsworth, or in a more Christian way Gerard Manley Hopkins) is quite compatible, however, with the Abrahamic tradition. The divine narrative identity can give such nature worship emotionally engaging detail. In this and other ways, we now know the natural world is grand and beautiful enough to be the divine body and worshipped as such.

11. Pantheism or Panentheism?

In his response to my chapter Andrei Buckareff notes that mine is not a typical pantheism and that many might prefer to call it panentheistic. The theory I have been expounding is that, excepting the holes, the universe is God's body. Does God also have a non-physical mind or soul? I judge such a soul to be redundant, and so consider my conception pantheistic.

There is, however, another technical sense in which, I hold, God is not the Universe. There are some properties that God has essentially that the Universe has accidentally. For God is essentially powerful. But I believe that God could abdicate all power by making the multiverse just consist of one universe. If God so acted then God would cease to exist, but the Universe would still exist. So even if there is no divine soul, and even if God and the Universe have the same non-modalized properties, they are non-identical. But I doubt whether such technical non-identity is what pantheists are denying. It is comparable to the non-identity of the statue and the lump of clay that constitutes it: the statue has an essential shape, say of a goddess—give or take an arm or two. But the lump of clay has that property accidentally.

Buckareff raises a further difficulty, based on Ross Cameron's recent work on ontological commitment (2008).[9] The problem is that Quine's criterion for ontological commitment turns out to be a criterion for the fundamental entities in the ontology. Thus if talk of minds can be 'paraphrased' in terms of talk of the mental contents minds are not to be included in the Quinean ontology. But, the objection goes, that does not show minds do not exist, just that they are not fundamental. This raises a problem with my conception of God. Might we not say that what is worthy of worship is the combination of divine body *and* mind, even if the divine mind depends for its existence on the divine body? So God is not just the Universe, God is also the divine mind, which depends on the Universe.

In response I grant that it would be idolatrous to worship the Universe in abstraction from the divine mind, but I do not mean by the Universe some such abstraction. Nonetheless if my usage is misleading then I guess it is better not to call my position pantheism *sensu stricto*. Maybe I should call it neo-Stoicism, but that would suggest detachment. I hope the qualification 'Personal' suffices.

12. The Case against Bayes-Proof Atheism and Agnosticism

Some atheists might agree that Personal Pantheism is a better conception of God than the standard ones, but go on to claim that this undermines the case for theism. I now argue that there is no such undermining, by considering the way in which PAM leads to DAT.

PAM supports DAT by undermining what I call Bayes-proof atheism and Bayes-proof agnosticism. The Bayesian Calculus of Probabilities describes how new information,

---

[9] Cameron's alternative criterion is stated in terms of states of affairs, but the relevant objection is not restricted to a theory of states of affairs.

either empirical or a priori but hitherto unnoticed, can increase or decrease the probability of a hypothesis, in this case theism.[10] Evidence that would significantly confirm a hypothesis with prior probability in the range 10% to 90%, say, will not rationally affect a prior probability of 0%. I say, therefore, that someone whose prior probability for theism is 0% is a Bayes-proof atheist. Of course, otherwise confirming evidence is not going to affect a prior probability of 100% either, but nor will evidence that would significantly disconfirm a hypothesis with prior probability in the range 10% to 90%. So I call that Bayes-proof theism. Finally, if we represent complete suspension of judgement as the whole interval of probabilities 0% to 100%, then that is Bayes-proof agnosticism. For such Bayes-proof attitudes, the Fitz Omar thesis typically holds (Fitzgerald 1859, quatrain 27):

> Myself when young did eagerly frequent
> Doctor and Saint, and heard great argument
> About it and about: but evermore
> Came out by the same door where in I went.

The situation is somewhat messy if we consider, say, the agnostic whose attitude is expressed by a range 1% to 99%. Evidence that would significantly confirm or disconfirm theism for the agnostic who initially has a range of probabilities 40% to 60% will have significantly less effect on one with range 1% to 99%. And likewise for the atheist whose initial range of probabilities is, say, 1% to 2%. I hope readers will indulge me if I ignore such atheists and agnostics and concentrate on the idealized totally Bayes-proof attitudes.

Bayes-proof attitudes are not immune to all rational argument but they are immune to *confirmation arguments*, as follows:

My hypothesis predicts something of which we have good evidence, but which yours does not. So my hypothesis is significantly more probable than it would otherwise be.

I endorse the following sort of argument that can be deployed against both Bayes-proof Atheism and Agnosticism and to rebut any naturalistic case against Bayes-proof theism:[11]

Theism is at least fairly plausible because we know in our own cases of facts concerning awareness and agency and so, without violating Ockham's Razor we may hypothesize an agent of unlimited awareness and unlimited power.

---

[10] We usually idealize the situation by assuming that rational belief systems are *completable* in Brian Ellis's sense (1979, 9). That is, we suppose that being shown the logical consequences of your beliefs will not require revision of them. Given this idealization, the hitherto unnoticed a priori must be restricted to the synthetic a priori. If, however, we are prepared to live with the required formal mess, we can make sense of discovering an analytic truth.

[11] The Cosmological Argument may also be deployed against Bayes-proof Atheism and Agnosticism. It supports pantheism over traditional theism if a totally indeterminate physical Universe is a more likely hypothesis for an initial necessary being than a non-physical simple God.

This argument depends on the principle that to posit a limited being reduces probability. That principle is neutral between conceptions of God, and has been defended, for instance, by Swinburne (2004, 97). I find it highly intuitive—but then I'm a metaphysician.

It does not follow from this argument that we should initially assign some definite probability, 50% say, to theism before looking at additional, empirical, evidence for God, say from purported revelation, religious experience, the moral order, and the suitability of our universe for life. My initial conclusion is precisely we should not adopt Bayes-proof atheism or agnosticism.

To show that the Personal Pantheism conception of God does not undermine theism I reply to two objections to the above case against Bayes-proof atheism or agnosticism, objections based on my reliance on the Personal Pantheist conception in place of the standard one.

12.1 HADD

Justin Barrett (2004) talks of HADD, the hyperactive agent detection device, pointing out the evolutionary advantage of attributing to agency events that have other causes. In arguing *against* Bayes-proof atheism and agnosticism, theists appeal to agency explanation. Because my position is anthropomorphic, treating the Universe as an agent, I am a more obvious target of this criticism than standard theists. My reply is that if I were to use the above argument *to support theism without further confirmation*, then that would be HADD at work, but as it is there is nothing hyperactive about my agency detection: all we are doing at this stage is not excluding agency, as would the Bayes-proof atheists and agnostics.

12.2 The Problem of Divine Imagination

To create is not enough for God to have the power to increase determinacy. In addition, God needs to be able to imagine the outcomes of divine acts. I used to think that Pervasive Awareness implied divine awareness of everything, including possibilia. But the case for Pervasive Awareness derives from the requirement not to posit unnecessary limits. Unlike Perfect Being Theology, it does not warrant assigning a novel power to God, merely not limiting a power to which PAM is already committed. Because in the human case our imagination is the awareness of what are actually the case (brain processes) representing some but not other possibilities, this does not extrapolate to a divine imagination. The standard conceptions of God do not justify the divine powers by extrapolation from the human case. So the problem of divine imagination threatens to undermine Personal Pantheism.

My reply concerning divine imagination is that initially all possible types of universe are actual components of the multiverse and that divine action concentrates on some rather than others. So at each stage what is still possible is real and consists of those of the universes between which the actual is still indeterminate.

13. Final Methodological Reflection

To advocate a certain conception of God is to plead for its inclusion as a hypothesis to be taken seriously, argued for and against. Seriousness is, however, relative to how much time we have at our disposal. Ideally we would consider many hypotheses that we dismiss as too fanciful to spend time on. Call this the Waste of Precious Time problem for alternative conceptions of God. Moreover, to argue for a certain conception of God is already to assume it is on the list of positions worth arguing about. Call this the Circularity problem. Both problems prevent not merely an adequate discussion of alternative conceptions of God but that of other ratbag ideas.

My defence of Personal Pantheism as an alternative conception of God contains a partial solution to these problems. The not here argued for assumption of PAM and of Ockhamism reflects the expectation that the intended audience already takes these seriously. The case from these assumptions to Personal Pantheism is, in outline, swift enough to merit attention from those who tend towards dismissal. If this case is initially fairly convincing then a more detailed but still pre-Bayesian examination is in order, resulting in a conception worth taking seriously.

References

Adams, Robert Merrihew (1979). 'Theories of Actuality', in Michael Loux (ed.), *The Possible and the Actual: Readings in the Metaphysics of Modality*. Ithaca, NY: Cornell University Press.

Baltzly, Dirk (2014). 'Stoicism', in Edward N. Zalta (ed.), *The Stanford Encyclopedia of Philosophy* (Spring 2014 edn), URL = <http://plato.stanford.edu/archives/spr2014/entries/stoicism/>.

Barret, Justin (2004). *Why Would Anyone Believe in God?* New York: AltaMira.

Brook, Andrew and Raymont, Paul (2014). 'The Unity of Consciousness', in Edward N. Zalta (ed.), *The Stanford Encyclopedia of Philosophy* (Winter 2014 edn), URL = <http://plato.stanford.edu/archives/win2014/entries/consciousness-unity/>.

Cameron, Ross (2008). 'Truthmakers and Ontological Commitment: Or How to Deal with Complex Objects and Mathematical Ontology without Getting into Trouble', *Philosophical Studies* 140: 1–18.

Ellis, Brian (1979). *Rational Belief Systems*. Washington, DC: Rowman and Littlefield.

FitzGerald, Edward (1859). *Rubaiyat of Omar Khayyam*. London: Bernard Quaritch.

Forrest, Peter (1998). 'Divine Fission: A New Way of Moderating Social Trinitarianism', *Religious Studies* 34: 281–97.

Forrest, Peter (2007a). *Developmental Theism: From Pure Will to Unbounded Love*. Oxford: Clarendon Press.

Forrest, Peter (2007b). 'The Tree of Life: Agency and Immortality in a Metaphysics Inspired by Quantum Theory', in Peter van Inwagen and Dean Zimmerman (eds), *Persons: Human and Divine* (pp. 301–18). Oxford: Oxford University Press.

Forrest, Peter (2008). 'Relativity, the Passage of Time and the Cosmic Clock', in *The Ontology of Spacetime II* (pp. 245–53). Amsterdam: Elsevier.

Forrest, Peter (2012). *The Necessary Structure of the All-pervading Aether: Discrete or Continuous? Simple or Symmetric?* Frankfurt: Ontos Verlag.

Forrest, Peter (2015). 'The Multiverse: Separate Worlds, Branching or Hyperspace? And What Implications are there for Theism?', in Klaas Kraay (ed.), *God and the Multiverse: Scientific, Philosophical, and Theological Perspectives* (pp. 61–91). London: Routledge.

Gallie, W. B. (1956). 'Essentially Contested Concepts', *Proceedings of the Aristotelian Society* 56: 167–98.

Jackson, Frank (1982). 'Epiphenomenal Qualia', *Philosophical Quarterly* 32: 127–36.

Jackson, Frank (1986). 'What Mary Didn't Know', *Journal of Philosophy* 83: 291–95.

Jantzen, Grace (1998). *Becoming Divine: Towards a Feminist Philosophy of Religion*. Manchester: Manchester University Press.

Levine, Michael (1994). *Pantheism; A Non-Theistic Concept of Deity*. London: Routledge.

Lewis, David (1983). 'Mad Pain and Martian Pain', in *Philosophical Papers*, vol. 1 (pp. 122–30). Oxford: Oxford University Press.

Mackie, John Leslie (1982). *The Miracle of Theism: Arguments For and Against the Existence of God*. Oxford: Oxford University Press.

Mander, William (2013). 'Pantheism', in Edward N. Zalta (ed.), *The Stanford Encyclopedia of Philosophy* (Summer 2013 edn), URL = <http://plato.stanford.edu/archives/sum2013/entries/pantheism/>.

Morris, Thomas V. (1988). *Anselmian Explorations: Essays in Philosophical Theology*. Notre Dame, Ind.: University of Notre Dame Press.

Perszyk, Ken (ed.) (2011). *Molinism: The Contemporary Debate*. Oxford: Oxford University Press.

Rawls, John (1971). *A Theory of Justice*. Cambridge, Mass.: Harvard University Press.

Seage, William and Allen-Hermanson, Sean (2013). 'Panpsychism', in Edward N. Zalta (ed.), *The Stanford Encyclopedia of Philosophy* (Fall 2013 edn), URL = <http://plato.stanford.edu/archives/fall2013/entries/panpsychism/>.

Swinburne, Richard (2004). *The Existence of God*. Oxford: Oxford University Press.

Vaidman, Lev (2014). 'Many-Worlds Interpretation of Quantum Mechanics', in Edward N. Zalta (ed.), *The Stanford Encyclopedia of Philosophy* (Winter 2014 edn), URL = <http://plato.stanford.edu/archives/win2014/entries/qm-manyworlds/>.

2

Pantheism as Panpsychism

Karl Pfeifer

1. Messy Stuff

Prima facie the term "pantheism" seems to apply to quite diverse theories. Some of these theories take as definitive what others take as optional, or even as positively excluded (e.g. whether pantheism is a type of theism, whether it allows for some manner of divine transcendence, and so on); some should perhaps even go by a different name altogether (e.g. "panentheism" rather than "pantheism"). I won't try to divine whether pantheism, in its various historical manifestations, can be adequately defined or is just another family-resemblance notion.[1] I will simply adopt as my starting point some rather minimal, and perhaps naive, but nonetheless typical reference-book characterizations of pantheism and speculate whether they can be interestingly fleshed out in the idiom of some contemporary philosophical concerns. Consider then these representative characterizations of pantheism:

(1) the view that "God somehow exists in everything or that everything is God." (*The Philosopher's Dictionary*)

(2) the view that "'God' is the name of the whole intelligible system of which finite beings are mere parts," or the view in which "the contrast between God and the world, a contrast which is at the heart of both Judaism and Christianity, is obliterated." ("Spinoza", *Encyclopedia of Philosophy*)

(3) "the belief that God is all there is, and that all things and persons are parts, aspects, or 'modes' of God." (*Collier's Encyclopedia*, 1960 edition)

(4) "The religious belief or philosophical theory that God and the universe are identical (implying a denial of the personality and transcendence of God); the doctrine that God is everything and everything is God." (*Compact Edition of the Oxford English Dictionary*)

---

[1] For good coverage of material relevant to this question, see Michael P. Levine, *Pantheism: A Non-theistic Concept of Deity* (London & New York: Routledge, 1994).

(5) "The doctrine that God is the transcendent reality of which the material universe and man are only manifestations." "Any religious belief that identifies God with the universe." (*Random House College Dictionary*)

(6) "a doctrine that equates God with the forces and laws of the universe." (*Webster's Ninth New Collegiate Dictionary*)

It is clear straightaway that without some equivocation these characterizations cannot constitute a consistent set. For example, transcendence would need to be understood differently in (4) and (5), if they are to be mutually compatible. As well, there is some tension among the claims that on the one hand identify God with the whole, as in (2), and on the other hand seem to locate Him "in" the parts, as in the first disjunct of (1), or identify Him with the parts, as on at least one reading of the second disjunct of (1). Such identification of God with the whole universe as well as (seemingly) severally with its parts formally recapitulates the traditional and seemingly intractable problem of the Holy Trinity—how can distinct things be identical to the same thing and yet not to each other?[2] Of course such tension might be ameliorated by selectively refraining from reading "is", "identify", "equate", and the like as meaning or implying strict numerical identity.

2. Massy Stuff

One such approach, allowing us to judiciously reinterpret the identity-terminology and yet retain strict numerical identity where it seems most wanted, is to view some pantheistic talk about God as having the logic of mass terms. There are two types of nouns, namely *count nouns* and *mass nouns*. "Cup", "chair", and "pencil", for example, are count nouns; we can enumerate what they refer to, saying for example that there are six cups in the cupboard, four chairs in the kitchen, and one pencil on the counter. Another way of expressing this point is that count nouns can readily be pluralized and the noun itself represents the unit that there is one or more of. "Gold", "butter", and "cream", on the other hand, are mass nouns; the "stuff" they refer to is not per se a countable unit, and does not take a plural form without some shift in sense. When, as sometimes happens, a mass noun is ostensibly pluralized, some other unit is implicitly understood to be the basis for enumeration. In a restaurant, for example, one might ask for two butters with one's toast, but in such contexts it is understood that one intends two of the standardized single-serving *pats* of butter that such commercial establishments often use.[3] Similarly, one might talk about the beers brewed in a certain country, but that would be understood as referring to different *varieties* of beer.

[2] For an analytic treatment of this topic, see Richard Cartwright, "On the Logical Problem of the Trinity", *Philosophical Essays* (Cambridge, Mass., and London: MIT Press, 1987).

[3] Some nouns have both a mass and a count sense: "creamer" can refer to the stuff one adds to one's coffee or to the single-serving containerfuls of the stuff used in restaurants; "lamb" can refer to the animal itself or to its edible stuff, its flesh.

Another feature that distinguishes the referents of count nouns from the referents of mass nouns is the possibility of composition and division. The various parts a chair may be divided into won't typically themselves be chairs, and if a number of cups are fused together, the composite won't typically itself be a cup. By contrast, if some gold is divided into parts, the parts will typically themselves be completely gold, and if gold is fused together with more gold the composite itself will still be entirely gold.[4]

I submit that if "God" is regarded as a mass term,[5] we will then have an effective way of making certain pantheistic claims regarding identities across parts and wholes intelligible, while still retaining strict numerical identity in a key role. Let us compare gold and God to make the point.

In our actual universe, gold may be found here and there, in mines and riverbeds, on fingers and (increasingly) pierced through bellybuttons and noses, in interstellar dust, and on farflung heavenly bodies. But wherever gold is found it is wholly gold, not just a part of gold. Suppose a possible universe containing gold throughout—no empty spaces, nothing consisting of earth, water, flesh, etc., just gold. In such a universe, gold as such would be present in every region. (As long as the regions aren't too small—real gold, after all, can't be subdivided indefinitely. There are parts of gold that aren't themselves gold and these will be encountered at the subatomic level.) Now imagine a similar possible universe consisting of a mysterious substance G throughout, such that G is present in every region, but unlike gold can be subdivided without limit. That is to say, there is no part of G whatsoever that is not itself G.

G in our imagined universe seems to coherently embody some of the prima facie problematic features attributed to God by our characterizations of pantheism: in the imagined universe, everything (the whole) is G and G somehow exists in everything (each of the parts). Moreover, insofar as it is one and the same substance G that is found here and there and everywhere, strict numerical identity obtains.[6]

Our actual universe is more complicated than our imagined universe, but I think the principles inherent in that conception can be carried over to our actual universe and made to cohere with some of the other notions presented in our characterizations of pantheism. G should not be thought of as a regular substance, limitlessly divisible,

---

[4] I use the qualification "typically" because there are limits. For example, the laws of nature may set the largest and smallest possible masses for particular kinds of stuff, beyond which division or composition results in something that is no longer of the same stuff. Human practices can also play a role. Two paper cups may be combined, one inserted inside the other, to create a cup for a liquid that would have been too hot to hold in either of the original cups; then the process can be reversed to yield parts of a cup that are themselves cups.

[5] This is not to say that "God" is to be regarded in only this way. My position here is that to make pantheistic God-talk intelligible we must regard it as equivocating between the count and mass sense of "God" (cf. n. 3) and determine which sense is appropriate to any particular claim of pantheism.

[6] Nevertheless, one and the same stuff can figure in different countables, which can be individuated and distinguished; e.g. countables such as parts and wholes (*this region* of the stuff vs. *that region* of the stuff) could still be distinguished despite sameness of stuff. Also different stuff (gold, silver, copper, etc.), different types of stuff, different instances of stuff, etc., will also be distinguishable and therefore countable. Masses and countables go hand in hand.

but otherwise on a par with common gold; that would overburden the analogy. Instead G should be thought of as belonging to a more fundamental descriptive category, something more like metaphysical substratum, a role which might be filled by something like the fields postulated in general field theories in physics, the point being that G must be of such a nature as to underlie and underwrite the diversity or lack of solid sameness manifest throughout our universe. If G is analogous to the infinite fields of field theory, where all subfields are also fields in a sense, and ordinary physical objects and phenomena are constituted by field distortions or perturbations, then we would also have a way of rendering intelligible how it could be that "all things and persons are parts, aspects, or 'modes' of G" or how it could be that "the material universe and man are only manifestations of G". So I submit that the conception of G that has been developed so far is a reasonably close fit to the pantheistic characterizations of God we proceeded from.

3. Brainy Stuff

Panpsychism is the view that mentality pervades everything, that even the basic physical constituents of the universe have mental states. I believe that given reasonable slack for the term "mental" a fairly presentable version of panpsychism can be given. What sort of slack is needed? For starters, I do not want to claim that rocks and trees might have souls or think or be conscious. (That would be animism. Admittedly some panpsychists of the past could be construed as animists, but panpsychism as such doesn't require it.) Nor do I even want to claim that rocks or trees or lesser configurations of matter have, if not full-fledged human mental states, then at least something like the lesser but still arguably mental states typical of lower organisms, say like the perceptual states of insects. The sense of the term "mental" in my variant of panpsychism will need to be charitably regarded as encompassing the proto or quasi. And what follows will need to be charitably regarded as a very preliminary and incomplete sketch of a conceptual space in which the full account might eventually be articulated. So I will be deferring some large questions. My intent here is not to establish panpsychism, but to argue, hypothetically, that given a certain conception of panpsychism, an interesting conception of pantheism can be built thereon.

Intentionality has traditionally been held to be the mark of the mental. But it has also been argued that the most typical characterizations of intentionality fail to distinguish mental states from physical dispositional states.[7] Consider the notion of "directedness". Desires, for example concern, are for, or are "directed at", certain objects or states of affairs. Similarly, inasmuch as dispositions are *eo ipso* dispositions to affect or be affected by certain objects or states of affairs, and, thus, to give rise to certain other

---

[7] C. B. Martin and Karl Pfeifer, "Intentionality and the Non-psychological", *Philosophy and Phenomenological Research* 46 (1986), 531–54. Although I speak mainly of dispositions, the point applies to physical causal dispositions, capacities, capabilities, powers, etc. in general.

states of affairs, a disposition can be said to be for, or directed at, a certain state of affairs. If the state of affairs remains merely possible, i.e. if the disposition is not manifested, the situation is comparable to that of (say) an unfulfilled desire, where many once took the recondite position that the object of the desire nevertheless has a mode of being termed "intentional inexistence". Thus the notions of "satisfaction" and "satisfaction conditions"[8] also carry over from intentional states to physical causal dispositions: a dispositional state is satisfied when the state of affairs that the disposition is for is brought about and otherwise not. Moreover, such similarities between intentional states and physical dispositional states will often be reflected in the language used to specify dispositional states. It will commonly be intensional (with an "s", i.e. nonextensional) in the same way that the language used to specify intentional (with a "t") states is commonly intensional (with an "s"). So to a significant degree, the behavior of physical dispositional states mimics that of mental intentional states.

   If the parallel between dispositional and intentional states is accepted and regarded as no mere coincident, then two metaphysical possibilities might be entertained. Intentional states may be regarded as a special type of dispositional state, or they may be regarded as basically tantamount to one another. Now the scholastic notion of intentionality was reintroduced into philosophy and psychology to provide a criterion for demarcation of the mental from the physical, where "mental" was understood primarily in terms of familiar everyday categories. If the notion of intentionality fails to provide a criterion that approximates the familiar everyday (intuitive, preanalytical) demarcation, then (A) one can choose to regard the introduced notion of intentionality as inchoate, go back to the drawing board, and try to redefine intentionality so that it will produce the desired demarcation, or else (B) one can just accept "the conclusion that intentionality is the mark, not, as Brentano thought, of the mental, but of the dispositional."[9] Since "intentionality" functions largely as a stipulative term of art, which option, (A) or (B), to take would seem to be largely a verbal issue.

   A further option (C) would be to bite the bullet and not only accept that intentionality, like dispositionality, is all-pervasive, but keep it as a mark of the mental as well. Whether to go down this route would not, I think, be a verbal issue of the same order. The term "mental" already has an everyday sense confined to the neighborhood of familiar states such as belief, desire, perception, judgment, and the like. Insofar as letting

   [8] John R. Searle, "What is an Intentional State?", *Mind* 87 (1979), 74–92.
   [9] U. T. Place, "Thirty Years On—Is Consciousness Still a Brain Process?", *Australasian Journal of Philosophy* 66 (1988), 208–19; quotation from p. 210. Also see his "Intentionality as the Mark of the Dispositional", *Dialectica* 50 (1996), 91–120. George Molnar, *Powers: A Study in Metaphysics* (Oxford: Oxford University Press, 2003), 61, likewise rejects the "Brentano Thesis", explaining, "I accept the intentionality of the mental, and go on to argue that something *very much like* intentionality is a pervasive and ineliminable feature of the physical world." His own italicized phrase suggests similarity rather than sameness, so what he subsequently calls "physical intentionality" could be construed as *quasi*-mental intentionality. On such a construal, Molnar's position may be regarded as a version of option (C), which I have adopted for present purposes.

the mental coincide with the dispositional results in extensions of this established usage, the term would need to be understood to be implicitly qualified as proto or quasi.

Anyway, taking the stipulated sense of "intentional" for the nonce to encompass those characteristics which unforeseeably turned out to earmark the dispositional and also regarding the dispositional per se as significantly proto- or quasi-mental—in other words, going with option (C) above—we have something that could with some justification be called "panpsychism" (again a term of art), although perhaps "panintentionalism" would be a better name.

All the options may be taken to presuppose certain relationships between dispositional levels. Clearly, the formal parallels between dispositional and intentional states notwithstanding, it is undeniable that dispositions in inanimate nature appear quite unlike the sophisticated dispositions involved in, say, the representations of the visual system, which "not only...fix direction upon quite specific perceptual objects (unlike the disposition of a bell, for instance, to ring when struck by any hard object whatever), but moreover they are dispositions that can be formed and altered in direct response to momentary changes in the sensory environment."[10] Or we could put the point in Fred Dretske's terms, where different "orders" of intentionality are distinguished,[11] and say that there is a world of difference between the low-grade first-order intentionality of simple physical phenomena and the higher-order intentionality of mental states like beliefs.

Yet, on Dretske's conception, higher-order intentional structures are constructed out of lower-order intentional states, with physical information-bearing structures as the basic building-blocks.[12] In a similar vein, I propose that the high-grade intentionality of ordinary mental states—let's call it "capital-I intentionality"—is a complex construction or "summation" of interlocking and nested dispositions of cruder sorts, prefiguring in cruder form some of the capital-I features.[13]

---

[10] Kenneth M. Sayre, 'Various Senses of "Intentional System"', *Behavioral and Brain Sciences* 10 (1987), 760–5; quotation from p. 763.

[11] Fred I. Dretske, *Knowledge and the Flow of Information* (Cambridge, Mass.: MIT Press/Bradford Books, 1981), esp. ch. 7.

[12] Dretske, *Knowledge and the Flow of Information*, 175; "information" is here to be understood in the technical, physical sense due to C. E. Shannon and W. Weaver, *The Mathematical Theory of Communication* (Champaign, IL: University of Illinois Press, 1949). This notion of "physical information" is not to be confused with information in the ordinary sense involving meaning or semantic content (Dretske, *Knowledge and the Flow of Information*, p. vii, pp. 41ff.), although it will of course figure in the explanation of how information in the ordinary sense comes about. Dretske employs the notion of physical information because he regards it as, *inter alia*, a useful terminological bridge between philosophy and disciplines like cognitive psychology and computer science (p. viii). However, this physical information is intentional in the same sense that dispositional properties are: "The ultimate source of the intentionality inherent in the transmission and receipt of information is, of course, the *nomic regularities* on which the transmission of information depends" (p. 76, Dretske's italics); hence this intentionality is causal-dispositional in the sense I have maintained.

[13] One of the large questions I am deferring here is how sensory awareness or consciousness enters the picture. (I'll plead that I'm in good company in this respect.)

John Searle has argued that (capital-I) intentional states only exist and function as they do in virtue of a "background"[14] consisting of the organism's abilities, capacities, habits, skills, and the like.[15] (While Searle himself regards the background states as nonintentional, that, as I have already indicated, is just a matter of taxonomical preference, and so they can be construed as intentional within the framework I have adopted here.[16]) The mental life of an organism such as ourselves will then essentially depend on a brain, or better, nervous system ("extended brain"), which embodies a system of simple dispositional (i.e. very crude intentional) states organized into systems of complex dispositional states, some of which are sophisticated enough to qualify as capital-I intentional, others of which constitute the background in which these are embedded. On this conception, intentional mental states at the personal level are a group effort, a product or summation of subsystems of intentional states which are really ultimately just constituted by subsystems of crude dispositional states. Switching back to a Dretskean idiom, we can say (roughly) that the brain gathers together and integrates information from the nervous system as a whole, and certain centralized gatherings will enter into informational structures that constitute the capital-I personal-level intentional states of the organism.

Where exactly do these capital-I intentional or high-level integrated informational states occur? Clearly they must be in the brain, but it seems we often cannot do much better than that; they seem to be rather smeared about. Since the capital-I intentional states we are talking about are states attributed at the personal level, we can regard the capital-I states, if not their cruder constituent states, as smeared over the whole brain and leave it at that.

Alternatively, we might recall Daniel Dennett's delightful story, "Where Am I?",[17] wherein a brain is left behind in a vat, continuing to maintain input/output relations and execute its normal control functions via radio links to the (rest of) the body, which is off somewhere else engaged in various tasks too dangerous to risk exposing the brain to. The burden of the story is that although the essential information processing is presumably happening in the brain, the person has difficulty thinking of himself as not being where his body is, namely at the interface of the sensory organs with the environment.

[14] John R. Searle, *The Rediscovery of the Mind* (Cambridge, Mass., and London: MIT Press/Bradford Books, 1992), ch. 8.

[15] These can be lumped together with dispositions, as far as the mimicry of intentional characteristics is concerned.

[16] Searle, in fact, holds that strictly speaking only conscious states can be intentional, and unconscious "mental states" are given the courtesy of transferred mentalistic epithets only if they are such that it is possible for them to be conscious (presumably this requires that unconscious mental states involve dispositions for their conscious manifestation). That is not my current position. However, if someone were to come up with a compelling story of quasi-, proto-, or fully fledged phenomenal properties at the most fundamental physical level, that could definitely help my account (cf. n. 13).

[17] Daniel C. Dennett, *Brainstorms: Philosophical Essays on Mind and Psychology* (Montgomery, VA: Bradford Books, 1978), ch. 17.

So the content of high-level intentional (in this case perceptual) states can seem just as relevant to personal location as where the states having that content actually are.

Let's now turn back to God. In a nutshell, I want to promote pantheism as tantamount to construing the universe as God's *brain*. The universe is a panpsychic system of information-bearing dispositional-intentional states, multileveled and organized in multitudinous ways, with information smeared all about. Here and there where persons exist, very high-level integrations of information exist that coalesce into capital-I intentional states. Within those persons there are sometimes competing coalescences of capital-I states (multiple-personality cases) that may nevertheless also be integrated at various levels of organization (cf. the sometime mutual awareness of such personalities for one another, their "internal conversations"). Multiple-personality cases aside, the normal human case will also involve somewhat hierarchically organized lesser coalescences of decreasing intentional complexity that can be regarded as homuncular in nature.

Suppose the universe to be, then, a system of dispositional cum intentional cum informational states (which include the local coalescences constituting the central brainstates of organisms such as ourselves); further suppose there to be some sort of overarching integrative summation of these informational states, such that the summation incorporates them all in a capital-I intentional manner. Then, like Dennett's fictional character (but minus the ambivalence introduced by disjoint body and brain), we may regard the owner of those centralizing capital-I intentional states as being located at the informational sources giving rise to those centralizing states, namely *everywhere*, and such interfacing with *every* informational source might be regarded as tantamount to omniscience. The distinct persons and other thinking organisms found here and there could be regarded as God's subpersonal homunculi or as embedded personalities that contribute to what goes on at God's personal level. Moreover, capital-I intentional states at God's personal level can be regarded as smeared over His "brain", the universe.

Let me be clear that none of this is intended to imply that such a God must involve a new level of being emerging from the physical stuff. Rather, there is just one ontological level, the physical stuff, which provides the truthmakers for various nonontological levels of description and explanation, some of which may be psychological or theistic.[18]

Traditional pantheism is generally nontheistic, where theism generally takes God to be a "person".[19] However, in the picture I have sketched, pantheism might be more, or less, theistic, depending upon the particular nature of the overarching integration of

---

[18] Cf. John Heil, *From an Ontological Point of View* (Oxford: Clarendon Press, 2003), 10: "We can accept levels of organization, levels of complexity, levels of description, and levels of explanation, without commitment to levels of reality in the sense embraced by many self-proclaimed anti-reductionist philosophers today. The upshot is a conception of the world and our representations of it that is ontologically, but not analytically, reductive."

[19] Levine, *Pantheism*, 2.

states—on the state of God's brain, as it were. If the dispositional-intentional states of the universe are indeed organized relevantly similar to those of a human brain, then there is room for variations of centralized organization, variations which might be constitutive of self-consciousness, of unselfconscious consciousness (presumably the condition typical of most nonhuman animals), of coma (yet even comatose humans may still harbor enough dormant high-level intentional states to regain functional personhood), or even of schizoid consciousness (allowing perhaps for some sort of Manichean pantheism).

In this chapter I argued that a problematic aspect of pantheism could be made intelligible by treating "God" as a mass term, and then went on to sketch a conception of panpsychism, cashed out in terms of a "panintentionalism" that admits of various organizational possibilities for causal dispositional states, comparable to the organization of intentional states in human brains. So *if* the universe is like a brain—well, why not let it be God's brain?[20] Panpsychism can be tantamount to pantheism. This panpsychist picture also dovetails with the "massy" notion of God, in that it provides a way of construing the idea that God is everywhere in "spirit" as well as substance, and in that "brain" can be a mass term too.

---

[20] One might worry that, omniscience apart, none of the traditional mainstream-Abrahamic great-making "omni" properties have been suggested for this conception of God. I regard that as a virtue, inasmuch as there have been many other religious traditions whose gods lack some or all of those properties. Moreover, as John Bishop has argued in "Can There Be Alternative Concepts of God?", *Noûs* 32/2 (1998), 174–88, even a concept of God adequate to the tradition of Christian theism may not require a suite of "omni" properties, just as some heretics within that tradition have insisted. Admittedly, however, it's still an open question whether those properties can in principle be accommodated by my pantheistic conception of God.

3

A Way of Picturing God

John Leslie

1. The Mystery of Existence

Descriptions of the world's character are often strongly influenced by ideas about why there is any world, instead of just abstract facts about mere possibilities. Suppose you believed that something worth calling "God" explained why the world exists. It would be strange if this did nothing towards, for instance, making you believe you had a chance of surviving the death of your body. Whereas if you instead thought the world was simply there, for no reason whatever, then this would probably make you think it a world in which bodily death could not possibly be survived. Things which, against the background of one way of answering why there is a world, can seem altogether plausible, become absurd against another background. "*Why does the world exist?*" could therefore be philosophy's most fundamental question.

It indeed seems to me that the world's existence is a problem, and that it could have its solution in a reality worth calling "God". In contrast, the reality of mere logical possibilities seems to me no problem whatever. An infinite realm of logical possibilities has to exist, eternally and unconditionally. Imagine something which, though it might not be fully possible (and I myself think it isn't), does at least strike me as something logically possible, something involving no actual contradiction: namely, that an Annihilation Machine wiped out every actually existing thing, itself included. There would remain infinitely many realities. It would be real, it would genuinely be the case, that a world had once been there. It would be real that if two sets of two lions were ever to come into existence, there would then exist four lions. The sudden coming into existence of up to infinitely many lions really would be a logical possibility, and similarly with the sudden arrival of any number of universes: huge spatiotemporal systems, largely or entirely separate from one another. And it would be real, presumably, that some of the things which might come into existence would be intrinsically good.

That lions were logically possible, and that two sets of two of them would make four of them: could such facts ever generate lions or anything else? The answer is No. Suppose a lion sprang into existence from utter emptiness. There would be no logical contradiction here; it would be unlike the sudden arrival of a round square; yet how could this explain the lion? All that would be true is things like the following: that IF the lion had twice times two heads THEN it would have more than three. If round then not square, and if four-headed then more than three-headed: all the facts of logic and of mathematics are IFfy-THENny like these, so they cannot create anything. They present only requirements which things would have to satisfy for their existence not to be self-contradictory—*ruled out*—instead of requirements that might explain why there actually is a realm of existing entities: objects that are "concrete", not "abstract" like the possibility of there being a lion.

How about ethical truths, though? Might not Plato be right when he suggests in Book Six of his *Republic* that The Good, something itself "beyond existence", is "what gives existence to things"? Because, in an absence of all existing things, wouldn't it still be true that the coming to exist of good things really would be something fortunate, the fulfilment of what was *ethically required*? So might not an ethical requirement or set of compatible requirements account for the existence of a complex world, or perhaps of a world-creating deity? I see nothing absurd in this Platonic suggestion. It strikes me as quite probably right. Still, many philosophers think it a crazy suggestion, and before making it this article of mine may have tried to block various paths leading towards better ways of explaining why there is a world.

2. "Mustn't all truthmakers be existing things?"

Here is a first place where I could have gone wrong. I asked you to imagine the annihilation of the world in its entirety. But mayn't this conflict with the picture of Time accepted by many physicists, the picture which, as Einstein expresses it, presents physical reality "as a four-dimensional existence instead of, as hitherto, the evolution of a three-dimensional existence"? If Time is just an aspect of a four-dimensionally existing block, then how could this block *change* from existing to not existing? *At what point in time* could the entire block suddenly vanish?

I answer that, as a logical possibility at least, anything whatever could suddenly vanish. The disappearance of the four-dimensional block would occur in a variety of Time that is forever flowing completely unconditionally, necessarily, as can be seen when you reflect that even an entire four-dimensional cosmos, a sum total of everything in existence with clocks that measured distances along its time dimension, would have repeated logical opportunities of vanishing, its constantly prolonged survival being a matter of ever increased good fortune if it were a good cosmos, or of bad fortune, were it a bad one. If the whole thing vanished then there would be no trace of its once having existed; but so what? I accept Einstein's block universe; physics certainly suggests that it is real, and its reality would mean that after my death I would still exist "back there along the fourth dimension", which I find comforting; yet although some strong philosophers have tried to prove the block's reality by arguing that there otherwise would be nothing in existence to *make it true* that dinosaurs had once existed, I would not dream of using such reasoning. It strikes me as almost as weak as A. J. Ayer's suggestion in the first edition of his *Language, Truth, and Logic* that truths about the past are simply truths about what we call records and traces, an idea liked by the villain of George Orwell's *Nineteen Eighty-Four*. Plato did get at least one thing right. Truths *do not* always need "truthmakers" among actually existing things. If you and I exist as parts of a four-dimensional block, and if the entire block suddenly vanished, and if any other existing things all vanished as well, then it would of course still be true that you and I had once existed. Nothing whatever could suddenly make it true that you and I had never existed. The sole truthmaker needed for a thing's once having existed is *that thing's once having existed*, period. Omnipotence might perhaps be able to destroy a four-dimensional block, but it could not then proceed to destroy the truth that the block and all its contents had once been there.

Similar remarks apply to the Modal Realism of David Lewis. Lewis writes that all logically possible things are in existence somewhere. So long as they can be described without contradiction, all the Greek gods do *really exist,* although of course not locally. They exist not in our world, but in other worlds equally real. Now, almost all philosophers reject this, rightly. In a wonderful article in *Midwest Studies in Philosophy: Volume Nine*, Peter Unger points out that the realm of real existence would be in a way much simpler if it contained all logical possibilities; it would be describable in very few words ("Contains Everything Logically Possible", for instance). Simplicity is often rightly wanted by scientists and therefore, Unger reasons, Lewis's world-picture is probably correct. But this is nothing like reasoning that "logically possible" and "existing somewhere" must be like "bachelor" and "unmarried man", or that the things in Modal Realism's gigantic cosmos would be essential as "truthmakers" for truths about logical possibility.

How about mathematical truths? Had something wiped out all mathematicians, or all countable objects, would it genuinely remain true that two and two made four? The answer must presumably be Yes. It looks excessively odd to fancy that two and two would suddenly cease to make four when the last mathematician was annihilated, or the fourth last existing thing. While far from being idiots, some philosophers would call me mistaken here; but what does this show? Simply that in philosophy decisive arguments are in short supply. Clever people, agreeing that two and two must always make four, can conclude that there must always be at least four concrete things; the existence of Something and not Nothing is thereby explained! Yet it can make more sense to conclude instead that mathematical truths never depend on the concrete existence of anything.

Here is another point of much the same kind. Many intelligent humans would protest that God, an infinite being, would be secure against any Annihilation Machine. Through logical necessity, they proclaim, God exists eternally. And they then at times declare that God's infinite understanding is the truthmaker of all logical possibilities, all mathematics, all facts about what things, if they existed, would have an existence intrinsically good. Admittedly it is seldom claimed that God's logical necessity can be proved by us. What is nonetheless maintained is that God could not be perfect without it. Likewise, it may not be claimed that we can grasp just how God grounds all truths of logic, mathematics, and ethics. Instead it may simply be said that a being who failed to ground those truths would not be supreme enough to be God. Himself necessarily existent, God must, it is held, be the ultimate source of absolutely everything else, controlling all things except where he has voluntarily limited his power, as when he gives us freedom of the will. Even the laws of logic rely for their validity on the fact that God eternally contemplates them. Otherwise God would not be genuinely perfect.

Although believing in a reality I call "God" I accept no particular religion. How does that claim about genuine perfection strike religion-less people like me? If hoping to convert us to any religion, better avoid any such claim. Because God could not contemplate anything unless God's existence *were itself* logically possible, and how could *that* in turn depend on God's act of contemplating it? For anything to exist, it must first be a logical possibility, most of us unbelievers would say. Not "first" in a temporal sense, but first as a matter of one fact's being the prerequisite of another. And if anyone is to know that two and two make four, it must first be true that two and two do make four. The attempt to view God's infinite intellect as the ground of all logical, mathematical, and ethical truths, for instance of whether the existence of dragons or of a deity is logically possible, can look a curiously unfortunate consequence of placing all truthmakers in the realm of existing things. Some who make the attempt are highly skilled philosophers. They proceed with much heart-searching, conscious of the folly of saying that God could have made it true that two and two made five or that torturing babies for fun was good. But they do strike me as making a strange mistake.

Yet, you may ask, if logical possibilities do not need God as their truthmaker, God to ground them, what then makes them genuine, not fictitious, in the way that logical possibilities are genuine instead of fictitious? The answer is that the logical possibility of a dragon, for example, would be simply that a dragon could exist without contradiction—that *IF any dragon existed* then this wouldn't be like *there existing a bachelor with seven wives*. No person or thing would cause this to be the case; it just would be the case, unmysteriously, regardless of whether there actually had existed, did now exist, or would in future exist any dragons, any minds thinking about dragons, or anything else whatsoever. Now, likewise with God. The logical possibility of God's existence, the fact that the divine properties weren't self-contradictory, would not itself be *derived from* anything: for instance, from God's actually existing to think about the logical possibility of God's existence.

3. "Yet what could create a thing, without itself being one?"

While, however, truths may not always have truthmakers among actually existing things, must not creative power be found only in such things? Well, not if Plato is right!

The Platonic suggestion, remember, is that the answer to why there's a world is to be found here: that the existence of some thing or things is ethically required. The sheer possibility of there existing a good thing or things is itself enough to set up a need for such a thing or things to exist in fact, and in some cases such a need is itself able to act creatively—to account, that is to say, for coming into existence or for eternal existence.

Just why would this Platonic idea be crazy? Isn't *required existence* what we would be looking for when asking why a divine being or the entire cosmos exists? And cannot ethical requirements be unconditional instead of depending (like *moral* requirements, requirements of duty) on whether there already exist any agents? Had something wiped out the entire realm of existing things, wouldn't this be a highly unfortunate truth although there would now exist no "truthmaker" to contemplate and regret it? And does not "unfortunate" here function as an ethical word, a word expressing the idea that an ethical requirement would no longer be fulfilled, now that the cosmos had been annihilated? The protest that of course the requirement "would only be ethical and not creative" can sound an oddly question-begging dismissal of Plato's theory. It is a theory, after all, which has attracted numerous philosophers. Neoplatonists, for instance, such as Dionysius, Plotinus, Paul Tillich, Hans Küng, who make "God" the name simply of a good creative force—a force of *creatively effective* ethical require-ment. Or people like Aristotle, A. C. Ewing, Peter Forrest, John Polkinghorne, Keith Ward, who speculate that the reason why a divine person exists lies in that person's goodness—a goodness which is a reason for such a person to exist, because goodness is not just another property like being pleasurable or having a mass of twenty tons. The ethically required existence of good things is their being intrinsically marked out for existence: marked out for existence by their own natures, rather than in the trivial way in which blue objects are marked out for existence in the eyes of someone wanting to paint the world blue, or through anyone's chancing to prescribe actions that favor them. Today many philosophers view such requiredness as merely "invented", and cer-tainly it could be very wrong to see its presence as *provable* in any strong sense (for what examination of things seems able to prove is just that they do have such and such natures, rather than that the existence of things with those natures is required in any absolute fashion); but belief in it is central both in philosophical tradition and in ordi-nary talk about goodness. If there is any such reality as goodness as traditionally and ordinarily conceived, then having non-trivial requiredness, being marked out for existence in a non-trivial way, is what such goodness *is*. But if you want, call the requiredness "axiological" instead of "ethical". It might help you to remember that the kind of requiredness that is ordinarily believed in involves much more than just moral duties to produce good things, or to keep them in existence.

True enough, ethically required existence might be "only ethical" in the sense that it never in fact could explain anything's existence, for Plato's theory is speculative instead of guaranteed correct through the sheer meaning of the words "ethically required" or "an axiological reason for such and such to exist". But its speculative nature does not make nonsense of it, and how else could we explain why there actually exists Something and not Nothing? Ordinary causal requirements for things to exist—for there to exist roses, say, or well-baked cakes—depend on the prior existence of other things such as water, earth, and competent cooks. And logical requirements can, I think, get no grip on the difference between existence and nonexistence for the following reason. The necessities of logic and mathematics are always "structural" in a wide sense, this being what allows us to mirror them with the structures of logical and mathematical proofs. Structural relationships can mean that a thing or group of things, when it has certain properties, *necessarily* has others as well: a square, for instance, must have diagonals which cross at right angles. And to get an idea of the way in which one structural necessity can *mirror* another, think of asking whether a particular table necessarily cannot be maneuvered through a particular kitchen door: you could test the matter with the table and kitchen door of a suitably chosen doll's-house. Well, Kant's way of dismissing any Ontological Proof of God's Existence—he claims that existence "is not a predicate"—has this much to be said for it. Although existence plainly is in some sense "a predicate", there being a clear distinction between possibilities which are actualized and others which are not actualized, there is *no structural difference* between merely possible things (possible dollar coins, for instance, or possible deities) and the corresponding actually existing things, and hence nothing for an Ontological Proof to seize on here.

Note, though, that a necessity, even when not logically provable, can still be unconditional, absolute, holding in all possible worlds—so that any explanation which pointed to it would be more than the kind of "subsumption under a universal correlation" seen in "This cat purrs because the fact is that all cats do." Plausibly, a pleasurable experience of playing chess will have some intrinsic goodness and will be intrinsically better than an experience of being burned alive. Well, this cannot be proved logically. "Intrinsically good" is not just another way of saying "pleasurable" or anything at all like "pleasurable". Still, it is clear that either some particular pleasurable experience of playing chess is intrinsically good to some degree—that, considered in itself and without regard to any causal consequences it may have, it is better than nothing, necessarily—*or else* it has neither intrinsic goodness nor intrinsic badness because good and bad are mere illusions, *this instead being where the necessity lies.* For the language of good and bad does at least make one thing evident: that it could not be the case that in one possible world a pleasurable experience was intrinsically good while in another possible world a precisely similar experience was intrinsically bad or with an intrinsic value that was illusory. We are stuck here with necessity, one way or the other. Either exactly such an experience would in itself have some degree of ethically required existence, necessarily, or else it would fail to have it, once again necessarily. And similarly with the Platonic suggestion that the ethical requirement for the existence of something, of an eternally existing divine mind perhaps, would itself be creatively effective. Either that is right or it is wrong, in each case necessarily, for it would be absurd for it to be a matter of mere chance.—"What could *make* the requirement creatively powerful?" The question would miss the point of the Platonic suggestion. The requirement would be powerful by itself, not made so by anything outside it. You might almost as well ask what "made" phenomenal yellow, the color as experienced, lie nearer to phenomenal orange than to phenomenal red. The reason why it lies there isn't the logical reason that orange *is defined as* yellowish red, for even savages without language would have seen that lemons looked more color-similar to oranges than to strawberries. And neither is it that a deity's command has forced phenomenal yellow, orange, and red to lie where they do. Instead they simply lie there necessarily, thereby forcing "yellowish red" to mean what "orange" means.

If, however, something is the case in all possible worlds, mustn't it then be "logically necessary" in a commonly accepted sense? Indeed it must, for nowadays many philosophers define being logically necessary as being the case in all possible worlds. Still, their strategy looks unfortunate. Apart from raising problems of how to understand possible worlds other than by saying "They are worlds whose absence isn't logically necessary" (which would mean that logical necessity was being defined in terms of itself) it erodes the crucial distinction between those absolute necessities that are logically provable and other absolute necessities which are not. If the existence of a divine mind were due directly to the ethical need for it, as a matter not of chance but of necessity, then this would be a case of necessity "based on the natures of things", holding in all possible worlds, unconditional, absolute, *but not* "a case of logical necessity" in the sense that I urge you to give to those words.

Could we not say, though, that an ethical need for a thing to exist could never *as such* be responsible for that thing's existence, not even in the case of an eternal divine mind whose existence was supremely good? Indeed we could, for in a sense that is so. The sense in question is the sense in which a cow *as such* is female but not brown. This does not mean that brown cows cannot exist. The difficulty here is that an ethical requirement which was creatively effective would be a reality with two sides to it: an ethical side and a creative side. Now, you could always separate the two sides mentally, then saying that the ethical requirement would not "as such" be creative. However, this wouldn't ruin a Platonic approach to explaining divine existence.

4.   "But don't evils show that Plato is wrong?"

It is often held that Platonic talk of creative ethical requirements is absurd when the world is so defective a place. Visibly, ethical requirements regularly remain unfulfilled unless intelligent agents strive to fulfill them.

"Visibly"? Why should we hurry to accept this? Although it may not be obvious that ethical requirements can create things, we see much possible evidence of their creative power. There is a universe instead of a blank, utter emptiness. While the world might have been entirely chaotic, causal laws have an elegance that scientists admire. Such laws seem "fine-tuned" in ways encouraging the evolution of intelligent life. Yet which philosophers protest most vehemently that ethical requirements "are never themselves seen creating anything"? They are the very folk who treat the world's existence, its causal orderliness, the apparent fine-tuning, as *visible signs* of a benevolent Creator! Confronted by destructive earthquakes, disasters befalling good men, the absence of meals appearing out of thin air to feed the hungry, such folk hasten to explain that ethical requirements often conflict with one another, it being impossible for them all to be satisfied simultaneously. It is good, they say, that we inhabit a world generally obedient to causal laws rather than one of constant miracles. It is good that we can sometimes decide what to do instead of being puppets; from this it follows that various ethical requirements would be satisfied only if we freely gave them our support. When we failed to give it, the ethical requirement for us to give our support would be *overruled* by the ethical requirement for us not to be puppets. Well, why cannot admirers of Plato make these same points? Why cannot the absence of a blank, the presence of causal orderliness, the fine-tuning, be due to ethical requirements which themselves act creatively, instead of to a benevolent Creator who gives effect to them? And why cannot evils then be due to how one ethical requirement sometimes overrules another?

Still, those who view Goodness as somehow behind the world's creation can often seem to picture a surprisingly second-rate world—a world far inferior to what could have been expected had ethical requirements been influential because a Creator recognized them or because they themselves exerted creative power. For what, after all, is the best imaginable kind of entity? The right reply would seem the one which theists so often give: namely, that no entity could be better than an infinite mind which eternally contemplated everything worth contemplating. But why, then, would there exist anything other than a mind or minds of that sort? Why in particular would any such mind, if benevolent and able (as theists so often insist) to create absolutely anything that was logically possible, produce anything except more minds, infinitely many minds, of the same type?

Some philosophers would answer by appeal to Identity of Indiscernibles. There cannot, they declare, be two things exactly alike, let alone infinitely many such things. Yet this invites the reply that Identity of Indiscernibles wouldn't forbid the simultaneous existence of infinitely many infinite minds, one of which contemplated *absolutely everything* worth contemplating while the rest each failed to contemplate some utter triviality that was contemplated by all the others.

A second answer could be that Uniqueness is supremely desirable. But, I ask, why? Why would an infinite mind be any less intrinsically good through existing side by side with others? Why should it resent the fact that other minds had experiences just as much worth having as its own experiences? The intrinsic goodness of any particular thing is the goodness that it has *in itself*, the goodness that it would have if everything else were annihilated, as distinct from any "instrumental value" that it may have through bringing benefits to other things. Such goodness is by definition such that it cannot be lowered through the existence of other things. What could lower it, though, would be such ingredients as envy, or resentment at having equals.

A third possible answer is that a single infinite mind would contain all the goodness that could be required: infinite goodness, so that nothing could be better. But again, why? If there existed twenty infinite minds, each contemplating everything or almost everything that was worth contemplating, would it be quite all right to annihilate all but one of them "because the nineteen others would supply mere repetition of the same infinite value"? Or suppose instead that the twenty minds each had infinite *negative* value through experiencing infinitely many inescapable torments. Could this truly be *no worse*—"mere repetition"—than if there were just a single such mind, so that there'd be no ethical advantage in annihilating nineteen to put them out of their agony? Do not be dazzled by the word "infinite"! Imagine an infinite number of islands each inhabited by people with lives only just worth living, lives with a value only marginally above zero. In total, there would be an infinity of value here, yet it would be far better if the lives were greatly worth living.

A fourth answer could be that of Spinoza. There cannot exist two infinite things, he tells us. Anything outside a thing would limit it, thereby making it less than infinite. Yet once again, why? If there existed a world outside a divine being, how would that "limit" this being's infinitude? In the following respect only: that the being would then not be infinite *in the sense of including everything*. But why would including everything be automatically better than existing side by side with other things?

A fifth answer might be that any two infinite minds could gain in value through being fused into one. But I reply that if the minds had precisely identical properties then the result of such fusion would be no different from the situation where one of the minds had been annihilated—for Identity of Indiscernibles surely applies in the case of any single thing; nothing could possess all its own properties *twice* so that, for instance, it was green all over *and in addition* green all over. And if instead the minds differed very, very slightly, with the first of them contemplating absolutely everything that was worth contemplating while the second contemplated all of this with the exception of a single triviality, then after they had fused the situation would be exactly as if the second, less perfect mind had been annihilated.

5. A Pantheism of Infinitely Many Infinite Minds

It is hard to avoid the following conclusion. If a Platonic creation story is right, or even if there instead just happened to be an infinitely good, infinitely powerful Creator, then there must exist an infinite number of infinite minds, and nothing else. Each of the minds eternally contemplates everything (or if Identity of Indiscernibles is correct, then at least almost everything) that is worth contemplating—this including, presumably, not only such things as infinitely many beautiful mathematical facts but also the structures of infinitely many universes, perhaps obeying infinitely many slightly different physical laws.

Well, I think we have no shred of evidence that Reality differs from that. Reality could be much as seems pictured by Spinoza in much of what he writes, if we leave aside his insistence on just a single infinite thing. My pantheism is of infinitely many separately existing infinite minds. The universe in which we find ourselves is nothing but a structure contemplated by one such mind; its contemplation of this structure is what this universe *is*; hence the universe is entirely contained in it, as a pattern carried by its thought. Probably the mind in question contains infinitely many other universes as well. It would in that case be wholly unlikely that ours was the very best universe. Yet it would at any rate be good enough to deserve its place inside that mind—which, please note, is very different from its being a dark area needed for a painting to be beautiful.

Here the point to be grasped firmly is that the infinite mind inside which we existed would carry the patterns of innumerable things, and that the reality of those things would simply be this infinite mind's contemplation of those patterns. A Spinozistic pantheism does not picture, on the one hand, a divine mind, and on the other a gigantic collection of infinitely inferior entities existing outside it for it to contemplate. Now, if an infinite mind contemplated the entire structure of our universe then one thing it would contemplate would be just how it felt to be living your life, for instance. And as Spinoza and other pantheists have appreciated, it would not *in that part of its thought* be aware of anything other than what you were aware of. In that part of its thought it would not know every single beautiful mathematical fact, or exactly what every other human or every elephant was thinking, or that our universe was only one among many. Compare the case of John Barrow's speculation that our universe is nothing but a pattern of activity inside an artificial mind, a gigantic computer. What shred of evidence could you have against this? With a chair of mathematical sciences, Barrow is not picturing what every child knows to be wrong. True, we don't feel that it's inside a computer that we exist. But neither do we feel that earth is whizzing around the sun.

We need not here suppose, any more than Spinoza does, that an infinite mind and its thought would be very much like a human mind and human thought. All the same, when such a mind contemplated, pictured, represented to itself, the structure of some logically possible universe that was immensely complex, then this mind would itself have to be of immense complexity. True enough, it could be "just a single existent" in the following sense: that all the infinitely many elements of that complexity would stand to it much as a stone's length and its roughness stand to the stone (the length couldn't suddenly wander off on its own). Nevertheless it would be complexly structured, just as is any human mind, and just as is our universe. Only then could this universe be a structure inside it.

What, though, of our experience of Time? If an infinite mind contemplated everything worth contemplating, why would it ever change to contemplating anything different? Wouldn't it eternally contemplate the same things, which is what many theists have believed? The answer, I suggest, should be on Einsteinian lines. We have absolutely no evidence against the theory ("the B-theory of Time") that our universe exists four-dimensionally instead of three-dimensionally and evolvingly. All experiences that could be present in the one case could be equally present in the other. Appeals to how it feels to run to catch a train, or to our ignorance of the future, cannot settle anything here. Einstein's world is a block that is eternally unaltered, a four-dimensional whole in which all change is merely relative, the difference between successive three-dimensional cross-sections, yet Einstein accepted that people run to catch trains, not always knowing whether they will succeed. And running could be needed even if trains were patterns in an eternal mind that never altered.

Note, though, that an eternal mind inside which you and I existed, a mind whose thought-patterns included all our thought-patterns, would lack the omniscience so often attributed to God. Among logically possible worlds, infinitely many would be scenes of utter chaos, and such a mind would no doubt know this. It would, however, fail to contemplate those worlds in all their immensely messy and uninteresting details. The point is that one has to avoid a situation like the one pictured by David Lewis. Real existence, says his Modal Realism, extends to all logical possibilities and hence to all logically possible worlds which, although with histories identical with that of our world right up to the present instant, develop thereafter in utterly chaotic ways. Now, for argument's sake let us grant that those suddenly chaotic worlds would be, as Lewis suggests, no greater in number than the worlds which continued onwards non-chaotically, because there would be infinitely many in each category and because the infinities would be "equal in number" on Cantor's understanding of that phrase. Even if we grant all this, the crucial point is that *the range* of the suddenly chaotic worlds would be vastly greater, there being so huge a variety of logically possible ways in which chaos could appear: cabbages and kings vanishing, for instance, or exploding or turning into ice cubes. This would mean that in Lewis's scheme of things we should expect to die at the very next moment because of turning into ice cubes or whatever. And immediate death ought likewise to be expected if we viewed ourselves as elements in the thoughts of an infinite mind which contemplated in full detail all logically possible universe-patterns, instead of just a comparatively tiny range of universe-patterns that were non-chaotic and therefore worth contemplating.

Difference in range—or, as it is often called, difference in measure—is a difficult technical notion, but comparing the ranges of various infinities can be essential in cosmology. Our universe may well be infinitely large. If it is, then infinitely many stones are presumably hopping around in huge circles through quantum fluctuations. But let not infinity dazzle you! Expect all stones that you ever will see to behave more conventionally, whether or not our universe is infinite.

6. Where Would God Fit into All This?

If infinite minds, and infinitely many of them, do manage to be logically possible then they would be found inside the immense Modal Realist cosmos of all worlds that can be described without contradiction. Anyone who believes in the existence of those minds and of nothing else is being extremely narrow-minded by comparison with David Lewis. Yet if Modal Realism is rejected then an infinite collection of infinite minds could well be deemed highly implausible, supposing that things existed for no reason whatever. In contrast, such a collection seems virtually forced on us if we accept the Platonic suggestion that The Good—what's ethically (or "axiologically") required—accounts for all existence.

How could God fit into this world-picture? All would depend on what one chose to mean by the word "God". Now, this in turn implies that one's choice of its meaning could be very unimportant. It might have no effect whatever on what one actually believed. My picture is markedly Spinozistic. Many have called Spinoza an atheist. His world differs greatly from what is preached from a great many pulpits, so maybe "atheist", "philosopher who rejects God", would portray him least misleadingly for typical users of Ordinary Language. Yet what is important is that his words often seem to describe an infinite mind that includes all reality, a mind which (as is easier to appreciate if you read his straightforward *Short Treatise* before struggling with his *Ethics*) exists for the Platonic reason that its existence is ethically required. While its "perfection" places it far beyond what Spinoza calls mere goodness, this doesn't at all mean that he thinks it is not good. But say if you like that he does not believe in God, and then say the same about me.

How, though, do I prefer to use the word "God"? Nowadays I marginally prefer applying it to the whole shebang: the collection of infinitely many infinite minds in which I believe. Not being a Christian, I have no trouble with the idea of infinitely many infinite minds, or with calling each of them "divine". If I became a Christian, what then? Well, the Bible was not written as a metaphysics text, and there might be nothing too strange in a Christian who used the word "God" for an infinite ocean of being, its waters consisting of endlessly many separately existing minds, each of them infinite in its complexity. Or else, perhaps, for an infinite mind of which you and I are parts, other infinite minds then becoming "other deities"—with "the deity" then operating like "the island", which for me means Vancouver Island where I live.

Alternatively, do what I have sometimes done instead. Apply the word "God" not to an infinite reality which is pictured as existing through its own creative ethical requiredness, but instead to that requiredness itself. This is the way of many Platonists, particularly the ones often called "Neoplatonists". It can lead to the accusation that they downgrade any divine mind by treating something outside it as responsible for its existence. But first, why would it be "downgrading" anything if you attributed its existence to a supremely strong ethical requirement? And secondly, why should a creative ethical requiredness grounded on something's very own nature, a requiredness that would rightly be counted as one of its very own properties, be classified as "outside" it? When Platonists are described as making ethical requirements into Top Dogs, things that actually created God, this may be only the hostile critic's way of talking. So far as concerns what is actually believed, there is no difference at all between (a) declaring that ethical requirements are creatively responsible for infinite, eternal minds, and (b) saying instead that these minds exist eternally because of their own ethical requiredness.

Finally, note that Spinoza's infinite divine mind, although it includes the strictly limited, very ignorant lives of you and me, also has an "overviewing" component, an area filled with knowledge as if in a single glance of everything in that mind's other areas. Spinoza attributes to this area what we might call loving divine personhood. Well, the infinite minds in which I believe could each contain such an area. It might even be particularly worth naming "God". It could include not only knowledge of everything worth knowing, but also a wish to share more and more of the knowledge with people like you and me, enjoying our joy as we came to enjoy it in one another's company. Unlike Spinoza, I find it hard to accept a divine mind which is going to contemplate our mental lives only retrospectively after the deaths of our bodies. Suppose you constructed an intelligent, truly conscious, happy computer. You would have no right to smash it. Similarly if an immensely clever extraterrestrial created such a computer in its own head, through thinking about its workings in full detail; the extraterrestrial ought not to destroy that computer by stopping thinking about it. Now, suppose your and my thought-patterns truly were patterns inside a divine mind. Why shouldn't they continue onwards after our bodies had died, so that we could start exploring the wonders of divine knowledge? It would require no miracles inside the physical world which we had until then inhabited, with brains to generate our thoughts and hearts to pump blood to the brains, for our personal identities could survive without all of that. And if it were good, then a Platonic creation story could make it plausible.

Further Reading

For further development of these ideas, please see other writings of mine such as "Efforts to Explain All Existence", *Mind* (April 1978), 181–94; *Value and Existence* (Oxford: Blackwell, 1979); "How to Draw Conclusions from a Fine-Tuned Universe", pp. 297–311 of R. J. Russell, W. R. Stoeger, and G. V. Coyne (eds), *Physics, Philosophy and Theology* (Vatican City State: Vatican Observatory, 1988); *Universes* (London: Routledge, 1989); "A Spinozistic Vision of God", *Religious Studies* (September 1993), 277–86; "Cosmology", "Cosmos", "Finite/Infinite", "World", "Why There Is Something", in J. Kim and E. Sosa (eds), *A Companion to Metaphysics* (Oxford: Blackwell, 1995); pp. 155–70 of *The End of the World: The Science and Ethics of Human Extinction* (London: Routledge, 1996); "The Anthropic Principle Today", pp. 163–87 of R. Hassing (ed), *Final Causality in Nature* (Washington: Catholic University of America Press, 1997), reprinted as pp. 289–310 of my edited *Modern Cosmology and Philosophy* (Amherst, Mass.: Prometheus Books, 1998); "Our Place in the Cosmos", *Philosophy* (January 2000), 5–24; "The Divine Mind", pp. 73–89 of A. O'Hear (ed.), *Philosophy, the Good, the True and the Beautiful* (Cambridge: Cambridge University Press, 2000); *Infinite Minds* (Oxford: Oxford University Press, 2001); "The Meaning of 'Design'", pp. 123–38 of J. B. Miller (ed.), *Cosmic Questions* (New York: The New York Academy of Sciences, 2001), reprinted as pp. 55–65 of N. Manson (ed.), *God and Design* (London: Routledge, 2003); "Cosmology and Theology", in the *Stanford Encyclopedia of Philosophy* at <http://plato.stanford.edu/archives/sum2003/entries/cosmology-theology>; *Immortality Defended* (Oxford: Blackwell, 2007);

"How Many Divine Minds?", pp. 123–34 of P. Basile and L. B. McHenry (eds), *Consciousness, Reality and Value: Essays in Honour of T. L. S. Sprigge* (Frankfurt: Ontos Verlag, 2007); "A Cosmos Existing through Ethical Necessity", *Philo* Special Issue on Theism and Naturalism (Fall/Winter 2009), 172–87, reprinted as pp. 126–41 of J. Leslie and R. L. Kuhn (eds), *The Mystery of Existence: Why Is There Anything At All?* (Malden, Mass.: Wiley-Blackwell, 2013); "A Proof of God's Reality", pp. 411–27 of A. Hutter, F. Hermanni, T. Buchheim, and C. Schwöbel (eds), *Gottesbeweise als Herausforderung für die moderne Vernunft* (Tübingen: Mohr Siebeck, 2012), reprinted as pp. 128–43 of T. Goldschmidt (ed.), *The Puzzle of Existence: Why Is There Something Rather Than Nothing?* (London: Routledge, 2013); and "God and Many Universes", pp. 192–210 of K. J. Kraay (ed.), *God and the Multiverse* (New York: Routledge, 2014).

Similar ideas have been developed recently by others. For a defense of the "monist" theory that a single whole, mental throughout, carries all the vastly complex patterns of our universe, see Timothy Sprigge, *The Vindication of Absolute Idealism* (Edinburgh: Edinburgh University Press, 1983). For the view that God's existence is due to the ethical need for God to exist, see A. C. Ewing, *Value and Reality* (London: George Allen and Unwin, 1973), John Polkinghorne, *The Faith of a Physicist* (Princeton: Princeton University Press, 1994), Keith Ward, *Religion and Creation* (Oxford: Oxford University Press, 1996), and Peter Forrest, *God without the Supernatural* (Ithaca, NY: Cornell University Press, 1996). For the idea that God might instead be viewed as the Platonic Principle that ethical grounds for the cosmos to exist are responsible for its existence without the aid of a divine person, consult once again that book by Peter Forrest, and see Mark Wynn, *God and Goodness* (London: Routledge, 1999) plus another book with just the same title by Hugh Rice (Oxford: Oxford University Press, 2000); also books by Nicholas Rescher including *Nature and Understanding* (Oxford: Oxford University Press, 2000) and *Axiogenesis* (Lanham, MD: Lexington Books, 2010), although Rescher prefers to call the grounds "axiological" instead of "ethical". By "ethical" he always means "moral", "concerning duties".

For there being at least no contradiction in the idea that ethical needs, as ordinarily and traditionally conceived, could themselves be creatively powerful, see chapter 13 of J. L. Mackie's *The Miracle of Theism* (Oxford: Oxford University Press, 1982), building on the account in his *Ethics: Inventing Right and Wrong* (Harmondsworth: Penguin Books, 1977) of ordinary thought and philosophical tradition. Also appendix D—"Why Anything? Why This?"—to vol. 2 of Derek Parfit, *On What Matters* (Oxford: Oxford University Press, 2011).

4

Naturalistic Pantheism

Brian Leftow

Traditional Western theism thinks of God as wholly distinct from the universe. Pantheism asserts that there is a God, but denies the distinctness. I now distinguish some versions of pantheism. Having done so, I argue that one of them does not provide a tenable concept of God.

1. Pantheism

"Pantheism" can name both a general tendency of thought and a particular sort of position. The general tendency is to merge God and the universe. I will take the characteristic claim of pantheism proper to be that

P.   God and the universe are identical.

This is to some extent stipulative. Some writers insist on (P), yet call themselves panentheists rather than pantheists. Others deny (P) and yet call themselves pantheists—e.g. John Leslie, who calls the universe a structure carried by the thought of an infinite mind, or William Mander, who identifies the universe with part of God's knowledge.[1] Terminology in this area is regrettably loose. Still, I want a reasonably precise thesis to discuss, and at least a great many who think of themselves as pantheists (or who are thought so by others) would accept (P).

Mander suggests that there have been four interpretations of (P).[2] On one, associated with Spinoza, God and the universe are the same substance. This is a straightforward strict identity. There are also teleological interpretations, as in Schelling or Samuel Alexander: the universe is moving toward being God, and so "God as actually possessing deity does not exist but is an ideal, is always becoming; but God as the whole

---

[1] John Leslie, *Infinite Minds* (Oxford: Oxford University Press, 2007); William Mander, "Omniscience and Pantheism," *Heythrop Journal* 41 (2000), 199–208.
[2] http://plato.stanford.edu/entries/pantheism/.

universe tending towards deity does exist."[3] This is strict identity, but with the "theism" in pantheism yet to come. On a third reading, Mander writes, (P) asserts that

BI.   God is "being itself" manifest in all beings.

This is (putting it mildly) hard to fathom. One might take (BI) in Platonist terms, as that all things somehow "participate" in God just qua existing. But then it gets no clearer unless we parse participation in terms of efficient causation of a resemblance, as Aquinas did— and in that case we have simply a way to describe traditional theism, which would deny (P). We might instead parse (BI) along the lines of God constituting the universe or being something like a property all things possess (at least, we might if unhobbled by Kantian scruples about existence being a predicate), but these too deny (P). Finally, Mander writes, we might "express the identity of God and nature... by reference to the thought that all things come from God, rendering them both identical with each other and with the one source from which they came."[4] Whatever "identical" is doing in that claim, it is not expressing identity. He gives as an example Eriugena's thesis that "God is... the nothing from which all things are made" and Spinoza's distinction between *natura naturans* and *natura naturata*. Spinoza takes us back to ordinary strict identity. Eriugena takes us deep into fog.

There are, then, a variety of positions broadly of pantheist tendency, but not a variety of ways to interpret the pantheist identity claim. Still, there are different ways to interpret the nature of what an identity claim implies to exist.

2. The Pantheist Identity

An identity statement tells you that where you might have thought there were two things, there is just one.[5] But given the identity, we can still ask what that one thing is like. If Clark Kent = Superman, one person has all the properties Superman ever really has and all the properties Clark ever has. But he may have all, some, or no properties we had *thought* Clark or Superman had. Perhaps he has traits we'd associated with each: if Superman = Clark Kent, he's really a reporter but not really a weakling. If he has some traits of each, he might have Superman traits and Kent traits in any proportion. An identity statement only begins rather than ends the process of characterizing the "things" identified.

At the extreme, sometimes an identity eliminates: it might tell us that what's really there has almost no attributes we'd associated with one of the terms identified. When we identify temperature with mean molecular kinetic energy, we mean that only mmke, as we'd understood it, is really there. One extreme way God/universe identity can go is to "eliminate" the universe: thus in advaita Vedanta, Brahman = the universe, and the consequence is taken to be that there is really just one simple, immutable,

---

[3] Ibid.   [4] Ibid.
[5] Take "thing" here very broadly. Aquinas held that God is not in the category of substance (*ST* Ia 3, 5 *ad* 1), and neither universal nor particular (*ST* Ia 13, 9 *ad* 2). All the same, he asserted identity claims about God (e.g. in articulating the Trinity). Whatever God turns out to be, if there is just one God, then (some would say) Yahweh = Allah, and (others would say) the Father is the same God the Son is.

atemporal, spiritual thing. The extreme opposite to Vedanta eliminates all distinctive attributes of the theistic God: takes it that all there really is, is the physical universe. Pantheism which eliminates everything distinctively theistic is naturalist. For naturalistic pantheism—henceforth NP—the universe at its basic level consists entirely of the basic entities of physics, and its laws are only those of physics.

Another sort of view starts with a naturalist universe, then adds to it a level of law or explanation not finally reducible to physical law: examples might be a law of karma or the existence of some objective universal natural teleology, as in Alexander's view above. A universe running in part by moral law—tending to the good in some way—has inherited via (P) one distinctive aspect of the theist God. It has not quite eliminated Him. As it features non-physical laws, we can call this non-naturalist pantheism. Add anything at all of the relevant sort to a purely naturalist universe, and you have a non-naturalist universe, even if its ontology is purely natural. Non-naturalist pantheism is a genuine faith-position. It is not obvious that the universe is (say) teleological. One could provide a natural theology for personalist pantheism by arguing the existence of objective teleology.

Finally, there is pantheism which includes so much of the theist concept of God that it treats the universe as a single conscious entity. Toward the high end of this, one would claim that the standard theist God exists, but happens to be identical with the universe, every part of which He has created to embody Him; universe-eliminating pantheism, as in Vedanta, is the limiting case of this. The boundary between "non-naturalist" and other forms of non-naturalist pantheism is that between having and not having a unified universal consciousness.

With its versions differing so greatly, it would be surprising if any one argument against pantheism scored equally against all versions. So in a single paper, one must choose a narrower target. I now argue against NP.

3. The God-Role

NP offers a highly non-standard candidate referent for "God." It is non-standard relative to Eastern as well as Western religions. For a universe that is "really" Brahman is not naturalistic. A naturalistic universe is at bottom physical, not spiritual. This is one reason Eastern religions are not in my crosshairs: my target here is only *naturalistic* pantheism. A second reason is that I mean to treat pantheism insofar as it is addressed to those whose context is standard Western theism. I am about to make the relation of NP's non-standard God-candidate to standard Western religious usage of "God' an issue for NP. This is not a constraint for those raised Hindu. They have no reason to conform their use of "God" to Western canons, if they use the word among themselves.[6]

---

[6] If they use the word in expressing their own theologies to Western theists, they will at the least court confusion.

But when pantheism is offered to those whose religious background is Western theism, relation to standard Western uses of the term does become relevant.

The non-standardness of its God-candidate requires NP to walk a tightrope. It transfers "God" away from its standard Western religious uses, yet it must also show that its use of the term is not purely equivocal with respect to ordinary Western usage. For if NP uses "God" equivocally, NP does not after all offer a concept of God, taking "God" to have anything like its ordinary Western use. If "God" names something, NP claims that Western theists are wrong about what it names. But then if the meaning of a name is just its referent and the term is used purely equivocally, NP will wind up saying that "God" in its use and "God" in Western religion are like "Brian" said of me and "Brian" said of Brian Dennehy—terms with only a set of letters in common. That would leave it unclear, for instance, that what pantheism is offering really has anything to do with religion at all. So NP has to show that there is something significant common to its use and standard Western uses. If "God" has no sense, NP must show that the reference-fixers NP gives it have something in common with those it has in Western theism. If "God" has a sense, NP must claim that its genuine sense has significant commonalities with what Western theism has taken its sense to be or with its Western theist reference-fixers, and yet makes a naturalist universe the best or only candidate to satisfy it.

To evaluate NP's claims, we need some account of what it takes to be God. In order not to beg the question against NP, we cannot make this consist in having any of the standard divine attributes. NP eliminates these, yet claims to have a concept of God. So we need a way to talk about being God which is dialectically neutral—one NP and Western theism can accept equally. I seek such an account in what it is to play the God-role in human life. I will not offer a full account of this here. I base what I do say on actual religious practice and talk. Even if we do not create God and our notions of the God-role are shaped in response to input from its occupant, we create the God-role: it is the way we live that determines what the role of God is in our lives, and the way we speak and think (and are disposed to) that determines what *our* concept of God is. We determine the God-role, even if we do not determine what fills it.

To be God, something must be the sole item to play this role. The bare syntax of "God" makes this clear. Either "God" is a proper name, or "God" is a title (like "Pope") only one thing at a time can correctly bear.[7] If I said that Yahweh is God, Allah is God, and Yahweh ≠ Allah, I would be mis-using "God."[8]

---

[7] For the latter see Nelson Pike, *God and Timelessness* (New York: Schocken Books, 1970).

[8] Suppose there are many causally and spatiotemporally isolated universes. If NP is true, are there then many Gods? John Leslie suggests that given many universes, each might have its own divine mind, and "the divine mind" might have an indexical element: like "the galaxy," it would pick out *ours* (*Infinite Minds* (Oxford: Oxford University Press, 2001), 148). "God" might work the same way. It would then still be true that only one thing at a time can be God, since the other universes' times do not overlap our own. If we don't say this, my own intuition is that even on NP, one should say that there are many gods and no God. For if we don't say this, we then treat each "God" as in effect the deity of a limited portion of the (scattered) whole of spacetime reality—and surely that is a role for Baal and Chemosh, not God.

I submit that it is also part of the God-role to be an "ultimate reality." Just what "ultimate" means varies with religion. In the West, it makes a claim about causation; God creates and sustains everything that is not God, and nothing happens but what He permits. This is a theological claim, but it has parallels or roots in ways ordinary believers act, think, and speak: they *treat* and talk about everything as rooted, sustained, and permitted by God. In some versions of some Eastern religions, the ultimate reality— Brahman—is causally ultimate, but in others, it's a bit more as if Brahman is the ultimate stuff of reality, the one thing of which all else is a modification or manifestation.[9] Even polytheist religions distinguish God from the gods along ultimacy lines. Proclus, a Neoplatonic polytheist, writes that

> God and the One are the same because there is nothing greater than God and nothing greater than the One…(Plato's) Demiurge is a god, not God. The god that is the One is not a god, but God simply.[10]

Proclus' One is ultimate causally—the origin of all else—and also in value ("greatness"). If God's full manifestation or existence is the goal toward which reality moves, as in the pantheists noted earlier, God is teleologically ultimate. Other pantheists treat God as ultimate in the sense of all-inclusive. Thus the role of being ultimate reality is rather plastic—but it would have to be, to be a role common to very diverse religions and philosophical systems.

If it is part of the role to be an ultimate, and it is part of the role to be the sole item playing the role, it is part of the God-role to be the *sole* ultimate reality. *De facto*, religions that make a God/gods distinction have always held that there's just one God. On my account, this must be so: anything that shares "ultimate reality" duties isn't *really* ultimate, and so doesn't count as God. In Zoroastrianism, there are co-equal good and evil deities, Ormuzd and Ahriman. They together explain where the universe comes from and why it is as it is. So what is the universe's ultimate source? All we can say is: Ormuzd and Ahriman. Ormuzd alone is not the ultimate source. Nor is Ahriman. And so it seems best to say they are gods, but neither is God. If either were God, both would be God, and so there would be two Gods—which violates the syntax of "God."

4. The Religious Element

I take it, then, that to qualify for the title "God," something must be at least the sole ultimate reality. I have allowed that "ultimate" can be specified in various ways, and that pantheists can offer their own gloss on this. The least one can say in defense of their glosses is that it would be hard to insist on a more typically theist gloss without begging the question against them. So far, then, pantheism of some sort is not ruled out as a concept of God. But there is more to the God-role than this. It is part of the God-role as we

---

[9] I *suspect* that this has roots in ordinary Eastern belief and practice, but my knowledge here is very limited.
[10] Proclus, *Commentary on Plato's Parmenides*, trans. Glenn Morrow and John Dillon (Princeton: Princeton University Press, 1983), 32–3.

have crafted it to play a distinctive role in religious life. One could argue that this is the most important part of it, for the term "God" is primarily religious, not philosophical.

De facto in the world religions, God offers salvation (however one construes that). Thus Mark Johnston suggests that *de facto*, the religious element of the role includes doing so.[11] Bishop and Perszyk seem to make a stronger claim: "it is essential to the God-role that God is the one who brings…salvation."[12] But Johnston also notes that it is "thinkable," not a contradiction, that God exist but not offer salvation.[13] If as we conceive God it is contingent that God saves us, it is not necessary to playing the God-role in human life that God offer salvation. This seems correct. For one thing, as we think of God, it is possible that God create humans and they not need to be saved: for Christians, it is contingent that there was a Fall (however that be construed), for others it is contingent that we ever sin. In such cases, God would continue to be God and to play the God-role in human life, but salvation would never be offered. Making it essential to the role to save would also ignore cases. The Deists believed in someone who was the Jewish God and the Christian Father intrinsically, but had a wholly non-interventionist providential policy. If God the Father was God, so was the Deist God. It is quite imaginable that God create us, set us in an at least moderately hospitable environment, inform us of the right and best way to live, and then take no further interest in us: a loving but very distant *paterfamilias*, who has distributed His estate and then retires. Why not? That wouldn't be God as Western religions depict Him, but their depiction is based on a set of contingent actions they believe He has taken, not merely on the requisites of being God. Nor were Deists necessarily irreligious. Their God deserved worship for His intrinsic excellence and His creative activity, and a Deist could consistently give it.[14] Of course, this argument

---

[11] Mark Johnston, *Saving God* (Princeton: Princeton University Press, 2009), 11–12.

[12] John Bishop and Kenneth Perszyk, "Concepts of God and Problems of Evil," in Yujin Nagasawa and Andrei Buckareff (eds), *Alternate Conceptions of God* (Oxford: Oxford University Press, 2016).

[13] Johnston, *Saving God*, 12.

[14] One can turn this sort of argument against me (my thanks here to William Mander). Plotinus' system features two supreme items, the One and Nous. Augustine's God is in very large measure Nous, granted (inconsistently, I'd say) the simplicity of the One. Augustine's concept of God became the backbone of medieval Christian theology till Duns Scotus. So if medieval Christian theologians had a concept of God, so did Plotinus. But it makes no sense to worship Plotinus' Nous or One: though each is in its own way aware, neither is aware of us here below. So something can be God even though it is not a conceptually proper object of worship. My quick response: Augustine's changes in his Plotinian inheritance included making God aware of and responsive to us. These were precisely the changes needed to make a fit object of worship out of entities which otherwise were not. The Deists did not change the Judeo-Christian God-concept in ways that made it senseless to worship a Deist God. So the parody fails, because the parallel is not sufficiently close. My answer, though, comes at a cost. It implies that though Plotinus considered the One the content of mystical experience, strictly speaking there was nothing in His system that fitted the God-role as we now have it. This is not an unheard-of combination, though—atheist Zen Buddhists pursue mystical experience of some sort. And look more closely at Plotinus' One and Nous. The One is not personal, not omniscient, omnipotent, or morally good, not directly our creator, not our sustainer: on closer inspection, why would any Western theist even be tempted to call it God? Merely being causally ultimate does not seem enough (cf. the text's later Bang singularity case). All those things are also true of Nous, though it is at least conscious and knows all necessary truths. So again, I do not see why a Westerner should find the claim that it is God appealing. It is not even causally ultimate: it is the One's creature.

might not move Bishop and Perszyk, who think the God of Western theism isn't really a fit claimant for the title "God." If He is not, sufficient resemblance to Him is not sufficient for being God. But any who want to redeploy "God" and not simply drift into equivocity must begin their case from intuitions within the "going" religious traditions about what is to count as God. If these traditions provide an argument that something non-salvific can do so, it is not clear on what basis they could ignore this.

I think that the essential religious element of the role is deserving worship; to be God, something must deserve worship.[15] God has a role in human life: as cars are things to drive, God is something to worship. Deserving worship has two notes. One is being a conceptually appropriate object, a thing whose nature makes worship a fit, sensible, not nonsensical response. It is conceptually appropriate to worship the theist God, but not to worship a toaster. At a minimum, to be conceptually appropriate for worship, an item must be able to be aware of us addressing it and to understand enough of our address for there to be a point to it, and be sufficiently superior to us in some way to deserve a worship-attitude. Persons might meet these criteria, but Godzilla might too. The other is being a worthy object of worship. Satan deserves worship in the first but not the second sense. His devotees do something morally but not conceptually problematic. I note in support of the worship requirement that I know of no organized religion with gods or a God which did not worship these/this. If we gather our grasp of the God-role from the concept of God's role in human life, then if we do not make worship-worthiness part of the role, we put in question our basis for including anything else in it, since very little is a more common feature than worship in religious thought and practice, or taken to be more central to these by the religious. We also claim, implausibly, that it is just some sort of large-scale coincidence that all deities get worshiped, rather than there being something intrinsic to the concept of deity that ties it to worship.

Further, if there is anything in current cognitive-scientific speculation about the origins of religion, the connection to worship is no accident. On the most popular theories, god-concepts originate as those of invisible enforcers of the social code, or else as products of a hyperactive agency detection device. Either way, god-concepts originate as concepts of powerful personal agents interested in us. They are concepts of things we can address which are potentially harmful or beneficial features of our environment. So it makes sense to deal with them. As we cannot see them, hear them, etc., we can only interact with them if we communicate with them; as we conceive them, it makes sense to try to do so, and to try to find *effective* ways to speak to them. If this sort of story is broadly on target, worship might well originate in the quest for an effective way to address these—a way which gets their attention and communicates to them what we wish to say.

Every religion distinguishes between things which do and things which do not deserve worship. (God or gods deserve it; non-divine things do not.) So every religion operates with the concept of worship-worthiness, and it is hard to believe that any

---

[15] For other writers who endorse at least this strong a connection between the concept of God and desert of worship, see Pike, *God and Timelessness*, 149–50 and 150 nn. 9, 10.

religion has ever claimed that God (however conceived) does not deserve worship. I take it, then, that it is part of the God-role to be a worthy object of worship.

I make only two claims about what worship is, both obvious given actual religious practice. One is that worship is a form of address: when we worship, we *say things to* what we worship. We sing hymns *to* God; we pray *to* God; we declare *to* God our belief in Him. We do not intend this as some sort of psychological self-help, or for moral improvement. The point of the practice is for these words to be heard and understood. The other is that worship always involves praising, at some point. Practice makes this clear, but it's even part of the word's etymology: it is from the Anglo-Saxon worth-ship, the proclaiming of worth. So if something is to deserve worship, it must deserve praise, at least in some respect.[16]

The first point leads directly to my argument against NP. Nothing can deserve worship if trying to worship it cannot accomplish the point of worship. It cannot accomplish the point of worship to address something which cannot be aware of or understand what we say. Thus things which cannot be aware or understand are not conceptually appropriate objects of worship.[17] Only something able to be aware of and understand us can count as God.[18] NP's universe is not conscious. So if I am right about the worship requirement, a naturalist universe cannot play the role of God in human life. If so, NP does not provide a tenable concept of God.

5. Pantheist Replies

NP might reply that (a) it does make sense to worship NP's universe, with worship construed as in the Western monotheisms, (b) the way I construe worship is too indebted to Western monotheism—other things legitimately called worship are more pantheist-friendly, (c) the worship requirement itself is illegitimate, e.g. because it is too indebted to Western theism and so begs the question against the pantheist's claim to have a concept of God, or (d) the worship requirement is not wholly illegitimate, but is too strict: we should include in the God-role only being a proper object of some or other recognizably religious attitudes or activities.

6. Worshiping the Universe?

Taking up (a), we must distinguish two ways to understand worship: call them subjective and objective. In the subjective sense, I worship just if I mean to: I cannot try to

---

[16] Other practices in worship may have changed radically since the Stone Age, but anyone who wanted to claim that worship in the caves of Lascaux did not involve *these* things would face two obstacles. One, *de facto*, is the utter lack of evidence to support the claim. The other, *de jure*, would be justifying the claim that this radically different something deserves to be called worship—that *our* term "worship" applies to it, however analogously.

[17] As is also noted (though not in these precise terms) in Graham Oppy, "Pantheism, Quantification and Mereology," *Monist* 80 (1997), 332, and Michael Levine, *Pantheism* (London: Routledge, 1994), 315.

[18] Pike, *God and Timelessness*, argues in very much the same direction, but without drawing the conclusion: see 149–54.

worship and fail. Thus in the subjective sense, if I try to worship my toaster, I worship it, even though it is not an appropriate object of the attitude; if I try to worship God by murdering my wife, I do worship Him by doing that, even though the action is not in fact an appropriate way to worship God; if I try to worship Zeus, I succeed, even if there is no Zeus. In another sense, I can try and fail to worship. If there is no Zeus, I cannot succeed in worshiping him, though I can try to; if God has commanded me not to murder, I cannot succeed in worshiping Him by murder, even if I mean to; if a toaster is not a conceptually appropriate object of worship, I cannot succeed in worshiping one. In the subjective sense, there is no issue about whether one can worship NP's universe. Clearly one can, just because one says so. The pantheist who wants to meet the worship requirement does not want to leave pantheist practice (if such there be) no better off than toaster-worship or worship by murder. The pantheist who pushes (a) wants to claim that one can in the *other* sense worship the universe by standard Western sorts of practice: that it is conceptually appropriate to do so and that there could be appropriate ways to do it.

I see only one way to make this out. The theistic concept of God, for NP, could be a "personification" of the universe. The pantheist could say that while there really is no such person as the theist God, we can picture the universe to ourselves as the theist God. The pantheist could in support of this argue that the universe actually has some attributes ascribed to the theist God. It exists at all times, either because times are just a function of relations between events or because spacetime is a substance it includes. It exists in all places for related reasons. If time is eternalist, the universe is in a sense indestructible: even if it is spatiotemporally finite, it is just "there," given—it is not the sort of thing that can disappear. If one expanded it to the Lewis multiverse, it would exist necessarily (having a part in every world, and existing "there" by having a part there, as a year exists now by having a part now). Its forces have great power, and power over us. They inspire awe. The universe makes us and unmakes us; in it we live and move and have our being. And still more could be said, though perhaps not as plausibly. So NP might claim that it makes sense to worship the universe in the guise of a personification.

I think what to say about this depends on just what we think the object of such worship would be. Suppose that the worship is directed just to the personification: in worshiping God, I do not intend to worship the universe, and perhaps this entails that I do not really worship the universe. In that case, worshiping God is like writing a letter to Santa: I direct my act to an object I conceive in a way appropriate to that act, but the object is not there. Whatever precisely one makes of this, it does not help the pantheist. The pantheist who makes the present move wants to say that it makes sense to worship the universe, because it makes sense to worship a personification and, by so doing, one worships the universe. If one worships *only* the personification, one does not worship the universe.

Suppose on the other hand that the worship is also or only of the universe; I do not mean to worship the universe, but in fact, because the theist God is just the universe misconceived, that is what I am doing. If this is so, it seems to me, we are just back to our original argument. I may *think* that the object of my worship is conceptually appropriate to it. But it is not, in fact. Suppose my parents have taught me arithmetic as a series of stories about Mr Number, who listens to us when we calculate. In fact Mr Number is just a personification of the positive integers. It does not make sense to talk to numbers. If by talking to Mr Number I talk to numbers, it does not genuinely make sense to talk to Mr Number, though I may think it does. Things would not differ if I could not but think of arithmetic under the guise of Mr Number, or could not but think of the universe personally when I am feeling religious. This would simply mean that I am constrained by my makeup to misrepresent the facts in a way that inclines me to conceptually inappropriate activities and thoughts. So too, a nominalist might say, we naturally form numerical concepts, which we express with numerals, which in turn incline us to the false belief that there are abstract numbers and to speak as if we could make singular reference to such things. So I do not think the personification move helps NP, and I do not see another way for it to make a go of (a).

A pantheist might reply that theists, too, personify God, because God is not a person in any ordinary sense. They do so because otherwise it is very difficult to talk about Him. But then (pantheists might say) aren't I hoist with my own petard?[19] I think not. If God is a person of an extraordinary sort, He is still a person. If He is not a person, still He is personal. Even the most anti-anthropomorphic theists, so long as they do not simply subside into negative-theological silence, admit that God knows, God wills, and God is good, in some legitimate sense of these terms: Even Aquinas' theory of analogy tells us that these are really, literally true of God, though the way these properties are realized in God—the sense in which they are true of Him or what it is in God that satisfies these terms' senses—is ultimately beyond us.[20] So for Western theists, beyond whatever personification and even anthropomorphizing we do in our religious lives stands something to which worship is straightforwardly appropriate. This is precisely what we do not have with NP.

7. Pantheist-Friendly Worship?

I turn now to (b), to construals of worship that claim, in effect, that one can worship without addressing what one worships. Istvan Aranyosi argues that we think an impersonal pantheist deity fails as an object of worship because it does not elicit appropriate emotions.[21] But as he sees it—Sufism being his main example—worship is of two sorts: exoteric, which is merely the following of certain rules, and "esoteric," the worship of

---

[19] So Yujin Nagasawa, in correspondence.   [20] *ST* Ia 13.

[21] Istvan Aranyosi, *God, Mind and Logical Space* (Basingstoke: Palgrave MacMillan, 2013), 168. Aranyosi's brand of NP identifies God with logical space rather than the physical universes, but this difference does not matter for present purposes.

"experts" in worship, which is the pursuit of mystical experience.[22] This, he says, is "about a psychological-spiritual state of the subject who worships...not about any cognitive-theoretical construct...the main focus is a state to be reached by the worshipper."[23] The state's content is beyond description; so no description of a deity could be worse or better at articulating its content; and so a pantheist "object" for it is as good as any other.[24] Aranyosi might say, then, that construing worship as talking-to is too bound to exoteric practice; "true worship" is beyond speech.

Well, mystics themselves would be surprised to hear that they aim only at a psychological state. They would say that they aim at union with God, and that a description of God is integral to the pursuit. This is true even of the Sufi prayer Aranyosi instances, which consists largely in recitation of names (canonical descriptions) of God. His other example, Christian Palamism, involves a verbal formula invoking Christ and His mercy.[25] Prayer, whether the Sufi *dhikr* or the Palamist Jesus prayer, is talking to. So the mystic pursuit Aranyosi sees as "esoteric" worship is no exception to the talking-to account. Again, in the Christian mystical tradition more generally, meditation on the nature of God and the life of Christ plays a central role in leading up to the union experience.

Again, the esoteric/exoteric distinction is foreign to the Western monotheisms apart from Sufism; to the rest of us, what we are doing is grade-A standard worship, which has nothing to do with following rules (save insofar as these preserve good order at worship services) and everything to do with speaking to God. More to the point, while mystics say repeatedly that their experience is beyond description, they also say a good deal about its content: their point is that it is beyond *fully adequate* description. The most basic thing they say, repeatedly, is that they are sure they experience the God of Western theism, not of something else.[26] They themselves, then, would emphatically deny that a naturalist universe is as good as any other as the object of their quest. Finally, the having of mystical experience is precisely *not* a form of worship. It is often described in the language of bridal embrace. We do not worship our spouses at such moments. Mystics frequently say that at the apex of their experience, they lose all sense of distinction between themselves and God. Worship supposes a sense of this distinction: if you are worshiping, you do not mean to be talking to yourself, and especially not praising yourself.

William Mander suggests that worshiping consists in feeling awe toward, loving, feeling dependent on, and valuing to the highest degree.[27] If this is correct, worship is just having certain attitudes and emotions, not a matter of address. (Perhaps address's typical role is just to evoke these attitudes.) And Mander would claim that the universe is a sensible object of these attitudes. I suggest that his analysis of worship is incorrect. Many contemporary mathematicians (particularly the Platonists among them) have felt awe toward mathematics and loved it. The most dedicated among them may well have valued

---

[22] Ibid. 169.   [23] Ibid. 169–70.   [24] Ibid. 168–9.   [25] Ibid. 169–70.

[26] For a careful discussion, see Nelson Pike, *Mystical Union* (Ithaca, NY: Cornell University Press, 1992).

[27] Personal correspondence.

it to the highest degree. Anyone who sees its role in the physical world cannot fail to feel dependent on it in some sense. Yet no contemporary mathematician has meant to worship mathematics.[28] I doubt that one can worship anything unintentionally, and doubt even more that mathematicians would accept that they have worshiped mathematics in spite of not meaning to. (To support the claim about unintentional worship: suppose an atheist drops into a church on a hot day, just to cool off in the shade. He looks down at his shoes to check some dirt, and so doing, bows his head. Just then he recalls a beautiful recording of "Amazing Grace" and listens to it in his mind, just to savor the music, to enjoy an aesthetic experience. Has he worshiped? Surely not. But what was missing?) Some aesthetes have probably been awed by certain artworks' beauty, valued them to the highest degree, loved them (if we can love mathematics or the universe, we can love statuary—in each case, in *some* sense of the word) and felt dependent on them for the meaning of their lives. Again, none would accept that he or she has worshiped them *malgré lui*, and I think few others would find that claim plausible either. So the complex of attitudes and emotions Mander offers is not sufficient for worship. Pantheists will of course note that the reasons one might value the universe to the highest degree differ from reasons mathematicians and aesthetes might have for mathematics and artworks: the universe, they might say, deserves this attitude because it subsumes everything (including mathematics and artworks) and we causally depend on it.[29] But Mander's suggestion includes only emotions and attitudes, not reasons. Pantheists might reply then that what matter here are not just attitudes and emotions, but having the right reasons for them, namely those just mentioned. But while the suggestion about reasons seems plausible, the specific reasons suggested look like special pleading. Christians would be guilty of the same if they insisted that something is worship only if it is done because its object deserves love for salvific actions done on our behalf. Mander's complex of emotions and attitudes is not necessary for worship either. I often take part in Christian worship without feeling anything, but with full sincerity and an intention to offer worship to God. Surely I manage to worship in these cases, if there is such a God: but if I am not feeling anything, the feelings in the Mander complex are not necessary conditions of worshiping, nor then the Mander complex as a whole. And I could worship without acknowledging dependence on God too: I might simply praise Him for His natural power, goodness, etc.

Harold Wood offers the most elaborate account of what a pantheist might treat as worship.[30] As Wood sees it, pantheism is a sort of nature mysticism, whose religious goal is oneness with God (i.e. the universe). Thus pantheist worship would be "devotion to the universe, a celebration of life," whose purpose is to make us more conscious agents of natural forces and affirm our place in nature. Its practice might include "artistic

---

[28] The Pythagoreans are said to have worshiped numbers. Whatever they did, though, is not relevant to my present point, which is simply that what Mander offers does not suffice for worship.

[29] So Yujin Nagasawa, in correspondence.

[30] Harold Wood, "Modern Pantheism as an Approach to Environmental Ethics," *Environmental Ethics* 7 (1985), 151–63. I summarize the piece as available at <http://pantheist-net.planetpatriot.net/society/modern_pantheism_approach.html>.

expression, nature observation, or…outdoor activities" meant to promote wonder, reverence, and awe at nature, celebrating the life-cycle or natural cycles.[31]

There are puzzles here. I literally don't understand how anything a mountain or a tree just as such could inspire could count as reverence. One can celebrate life and its cycles in any way a pantheist would without intending to offer worship; birthday and New Year's parties are not inadvertent acts of worship, there being no such thing. One can also have the feelings mentioned without intending to worship, and again, I do not think one can worship inadvertently. (It would be hard to convince Jews, Christians, or Muslims that, in feeling wonder and awe at nature, they have unintentionally committed what they should consider an act of idolatry.) So the crux of Wood's account has to be the notion of (expressing) devotion to the universe. But I do not know what it could mean to be devoted to a naturalistic universe. It has no interests one could promote or defend. There is obviously nothing one can do to obey its will, as it has none. There is nothing one can do, think, or feel to align oneself with the good of a naturalistic universe. It has no good. Nothing is good for it. It is just there, and it will be there whatever form it takes, by our agency or without it. If it had an intrinsic teleology of some sort, then even if it is wholly impersonal, aligning oneself with that teleology (or what one takes that teleology to be) might be a way to be devoted to it. But NP's universe has nothing of the sort. It is ruled only by the laws of physics.

It is tendentious to think that one would act for good of a naturalistic universe or in its interest by (say) defending nature against human depredations. Anything we make is as much a part of the natural order as a mountain, since *we* and all are doings are so: cities are natural for the same reason beehives are. I might be devoted to a particular forest, and want to keep it from development, but in so doing I express the opposite of devotion to the developers and the people who might live in the houses they put up: and their interests are as natural as the forest's "interest." As we are a part of nature, so are any interests we have. A pantheist can do just about anything and be subjectively worshiping the universe. But there does not seem to be some sort of act a naturalistic universe itself makes more appropriate than others as a way to worship it. Thus it seems that there is no success condition by reference to which one could in the other sense worship a naturalistic universe, some way to succeed in expressing devotion to it the way keeping kosher expresses devotion to God.

NP might jump on this: perhaps it follows that whatever one does, meaning thereby to express devotion to the universe, one succeeds in worshiping a naturalistic universe. How wonderful to have a religion where every act can be an act of worship, if one thinks of it that way! Isn't this something Christians claim for Christianity? Well, not quite. Christians do not think one can vomit to the glory of God. Naturalistic pantheists should. Nothing makes Druid chanting at Stonehenge more appropriate as NP worship than collective vomiting, save perhaps our tendency to find chants more

---

[31] Wood, "Modern Pantheism as an Approach to Environmental Ethics."

uplifting. But that is a matter of practices' effect on us, not of their appropriateness to the object of worship. Now vomiting could perhaps be a way to worship *something*.[32] It might please Bacchus or Pan, if it had suitable causes. But it would be appropriate to them because their particular tastes made it more suitable (at certain points in the orgy) than other things. But my point is not that vomiting is just intrinsically unable to count as worship. It is that Christianity does establish substantive success conditions for worship, picking out activities which would be uniquely appropriate to and would succeed in worshiping the Christian God if He exists (vomiting not among them), and NP does not. To NP, vomiting is as good or bad as anything else. NP might reply: as we are part of the universe, that vomiting does not uplift us is enough to make it inappropriate as worship, since we are part of the object of worship, and a particularly central part in such ceremonies. But we might as easily see in our digestive difficulties our harmony with and subjection to natural forces, our conscious acceptance of ourselves as physical, natural beings, etc. And it is the role of religion to educate us as to the attitudes we should take—which might include getting over disgust at anything natural. Nothing in NP favors the one point of view over the other. So again, there is no way to define an objective success condition for NP "worship."

Here is another try: perhaps any who increase the net good in the universe, improving it in some way, thereby act for the good of the universe and align themselves with that. They improve it, and in making it better act for its good, in a sense. And perhaps any who do so intending thereby to present an offering to and thereby worship the universe, succeed in doing so. But one cannot present an offering to something that cannot receive it. If I intone, "here, O toaster, is some bread, in tribute to your toast-making powers," I do not turn the bread into an offering to the toaster: I may subjectively worship the toaster, but I do not worship it in the other sense. If adding good to the universe is not a way to present an offering to it, it is not clear under what other category of worship it could figure. It is not praise, prayer, etc. It might count as an act of devotion, broadly construed. But acts of devotion, while religious, need not count as acts of worship. If I promise God to mop the floor and then do so, I do it out of devotion, but I may think while doing it of nothing but mopping. My mopping is not then an act of worship. If I think about honoring my promise as I mop, I still do not thereby worship. If I present my mopping to God as an offering, as honoring Him by keeping my promise, I make it an act of worship—but that is something beyond its being an act of devotion, done by fitting it into a recognized category of worshipful acts. By moving to acts of devotion, we have really changed the subject, from whether one can worship a naturalist universe to whether one can make it the focus of some sort of life that might count as religious. We've stretched the meaning of "worship" beyond its being a

[32] Here I'm partly indebted to William Mander.

category of recognizable acts or attitudes, as does naturalist pantheist George Chryssides:

To worship would be to submit one's own life to the principle of order...inherent in the world...to recognize what is possible and desirable to change within the natural flow of things, and what is not...submitting his or her will to this natural order, and...ensuring that one's emotions and actions are in harmony with [it].[33]

Further, there is in any case the question of whether I can make anything *count* as an act of devotion to the universe. I can perform acts of devotion to a particular part of it, e.g. my wife. But what counts as devotion to the whole as such? And I doubt I can really perform acts of devotion to "the more natural" things like forests. In the same sense in which I can't make an offering to my toaster, I can't do an act of devotion to my toaster. Why would forests or naturalistic universes differ?

Here is one more try: perhaps a naturalistic universe promotes a set of values not in tending teleologically toward realizing them—naturalist universes don't do that—but simply in that it is the ground of the exemplification of objective normative properties. If it does, those who act in accord with these norms act as the universe dictates, aligning their wills with values the universe promotes. Perhaps this counts as expressing devotion to it, at least if done with an intention of devotion to the universe. But "promotes" and "dictates" are wildly metaphorical. A naturalistic universe does not promote any value. It simply exists, and the values just happen to be there, if they are.[34] The most that is really true is that there are the normative facts, and we should be guided by them. If being guided by normative facts is what it is to express devotion to the universe, then any moral person does so without intending to. Yet one *can't* express devotion to something if one does not mean to do it. Might the pantheist therefore express devotion to a naturalist universe by acting morally and meaning thereby to do so? This runs into the vomit problem: in the same sense that the universe promotes moral action by grounding normative properties, it promotes nausea by containing the gross and disgusting. So why think that acting morally expresses devotion to the universe in some way inducing vomiting does not? Again, there is no objective basis for a success condition for devotion here. But more basically, again, devotion is one thing, worship another. This really pushes us beyond consideration of worship into the final strategy, a focus on broader sorts of religious attitude. So if NP moves to acts of devotion, I submit, it really ceases to try to meet the worship requirement. Mystical experiences, attitudes, feelings, and acts of devotion may well exhaust the possibilities for wordless worship. So I do not see much hope for NP in (b).

[33] George Chyrssides, "Subject and Object in Worship," *Religious Studies* 23 (1987), 371.
[34] I cannot here go into whether there could *be* objective normative properties in a naturalist universe. The issue is just too large. But permit me to just express skepticism about that.

8. Denying the Worship Requirement

Let's now consider (c), the move of simply denying the worship requirement. NP might just assert flat out that God is not the sort of thing to which worship is appropriate, and so it is not really part of the God-role to be worship-worthy. But for reasons I now lay out, the claim that God is in fact not a proper object of worship is a tough sell.

Our concept of God does not just have its origin in religion in general. It originated in the Western monotheisms.[35] NP in effect proposes to wrest the word "God" from its original context and claim that in its new employ it has enough in common with its original use, sense, or reference-fixers to make its new use not simply an equivocation. But suppose you tell a Western theist, "there is a God, and this is what God really is: God is a naturalist universe. God is not something you can sensibly worship." The theist will be irremediably puzzled. The reply will be: if just about everything I associated with "God" isn't true of its genuine referent, even down to its not deserving worship, what makes that referent deserve the title "God"?

NP might reply with a lecture on the philosophy of language. "Theist," it might say, "'God' is a proper name. It was conferred in an initial baptism. Now either that baptism was of nothing, really, or it was of some part of the universe, or it was of the universe: and whatever was baptized is what you've really been referring to all along, if anything, since the causal theory of reference is gospel truth. So get used to the idea. Nothing has ever satisfied most descriptions you associate with 'God.' The universe satisfies at least some of them. It might well be what you've really been talking about all along, and at any rate, it's the best candidate available. The best available God-candidate doesn't deserve worship. Be a pantheist."

Let's ask how a theist would react to this lecture. To do so, let's suppose the lecturer had instead been a naturalist but not a pantheist, and had said "I do know what 'God' names. It names the sole ultimate reality. It names the causal source of all, just as it should. It names the Big Bang singularity. There is no such being as the God of theism, but the singularity plays as much of His role as is played. So it's God. And for the same reasons it's not apt to worship the universe, it's not apt to worship the singularity." Suppose that the theist has a Damascus Road moment and accepts that the theist God does not exist. The ex-theist now considers his options. Would it be more sensible for him to become an atheist, or to decide that the singularity is God? Atheists would think atheism the sensible thing. For they do believe that there is no theist God, but the singularity plays His causally ultimate reality role, and are nonetheless atheists, not pantheists. Surely any Western theist would also think atheism the more sensible reaction. Theists will think it just too big a change in what's associated with "God" to sensibly

---

[35] This is not to say that the concept of God, as vs a god, had no currency in writers coming out of (say) Greco-Roman paganism. But their usage has not had an independent influence on the current concept of God; to the extent that their ideas affected this, it was through their absorption by Christian, Jewish, and Muslim theology.

continue to use the term. That is as good a sign as we can get that taking the word "God" over to apply to a thing not of the right sort to be worshiped simply changes its meaning, use, or reference-fixers too far. I do not see how expanding the referent to the whole universe, not just the singularity, would change this. Even if the universe is in some sense eternal, omnipresent, etc.: there would be nothing left of the theist's *religion*, and without a religion, what use for "God"?

The Psalmist wrote against the idols of his day,

> The idols of the nations ... have mouths, but cannot speak, eyes, but cannot see.
> They have ears, but cannot hear, nor is there breath in their mouths.
> Those who make them will be like them.[36]

Jeremiah similarly declaimed,

Everyone is senseless and without knowledge; every goldsmith is shamed by his idols. The images he makes are a fraud; they have no breath in them.[37]

Isaiah mocked,

Some pour out gold from their bags and weigh out silver on the scales; they hire a goldsmith to make it into a god, and they bow down and worship it. They lift it to their shoulders and carry it; they set it up in its place, and there it stands. From that spot it cannot move. Even though someone cries out to it, it cannot answer; it cannot save them from their troubles.[38]

The Psalmists and prophets are the original sources of Western religion. If they got it wrong, nothing that grew from them got it right. NP in effect says to them, "well, you had a point insofar as the non-living things worshiped in your day weren't big enough. But pick out the *biggest* non-living thing, and, well, that's it. That's what really is God. Something without breath (life). Something that cannot speak, see, hear, or act to save. The idolaters were more right than wrong." Again, Western theists will find this irremediably puzzling. If the prophets and Psalmists were so thoroughly wrong about what God is—if the tradition has been wrong from the very outset—why think that anything else is God? Why should we think that a term that got associated from the start with a radically incorrect stereotype should remain in use? Why not just conclude that the Old Testament authors were wrong that anything is God?

NP continues to use a term Western theism invented, but in effect commits to offering an error-theory of Western theism. Now if it is to serve NP's purposes, an error-theory has to be of a specific sort. It has to explain away theism and the most central of its religious activities—worship, prayer, etc.—without being an error-theory of *religion* as a whole, or of Western religion, or of taking *any* religious attitude to anything, or even of belief that something plays the God-role. Further, the justification it permits for believing that something is God cannot be simply pragmatic—that there are benefits to health, society, etc. in doing so. The pantheist wants to maintain that some existent *deserves* to be called God.

---

[36] Ps. 135: 15–18; cf. Ps. 115.   [37] 51: 17–18.   [38] 46: 6–8.

There are many error-theories of religion as a whole—Marx, Freud, Dennett, take your pick. By pantheist lights, they throw out the baby with the bathwater. The simplest error-theory that keeps the baby might run like this: the universe evokes certain feelings. Mechanisms cognitive science is uncovering provided us with concepts of disembodied non-natural agents. Feelings the universe in fact evoked were somehow transferred to these agents, away from their true and proper source. So religion as such is no error—the feelings are an apt response to something real—but everything distinctively theistic about religion is. One would need a story about the transfer here. But the deeper worry is that this theory does what's required only if what's left when theist elements are abstracted away—what a naturalist universe itself can evoke—are genuinely religious feelings, reactions, and attitudes. As we have seen and see further below, that may well not be so.

Mark Johnston offers an error-theory NP can use. He does not think his positive views are a version of NP, but what he thinks defeats (P) is "the general form of reality... the outpouring of Being itself by way of its exemplification in ordinary beings."[39] If all there is according to Johnston is a naturalist universe with this "form," one can be pardoned for wondering whether we do not after all have NP, but with the universe conceived in a peculiar way. In any case, Johnston's argument is basically this: we know independent of religious tradition some truths about what God would have to be like.[40] These are enough to show that the God the Bible depicts cannot be the true God.[41] If He is not, He is an idol. We know where idols come from. From one perspective, they personify natural forces. From a deeper perspective, we try by making idols to domesticate Deity: to conceive the divine in such a way that if we behave suitably toward it, it will satisfy our unreformed desires rather than transforming us.[42] If the biblical God is an idol, monotheism has been just an evolution from polytheism's many small idols to having one large one.[43] So the "error" in Western monotheism stems from the corruption of our natures. Worship as usually conceived is not what true worship would be, since it is not something a genuine deity would ask of us.[44] It is part of the error in religion; it is inherently idolatrous. So any true God would not be a proper object of it. The Western conception of God as a non-natural person to be addressed is idolatrous. God properly conceived is impersonal.[45]

Dealing with Johnston's biblical criticism would take a paper of its own. So I confine myself to noting that Johnston's account of idolatry does not well fit the biblical religions. If idols are personified natural forces and monotheism's deity is just "the last remaining god of a polytheistic pantheon... invested with... virtues of the expelled gods,"[46] the biblical God is the personification of many natural forces. But He is not. The Bible pictures Him as having a control which extends beyond the physical, as no mere "face" or master of natural forces could. And it invests Him with moral qualities,

---

[39] Johnston, *Saving God*, 156.   [40] Ibid. 35–6.
[41] Ibid. 57ff. Johnston means his critique to extend to all the Western monotheisms, but like such other "courageous" critics of theism as Dawkins, he manages not to discuss the Koran.
[42] Ibid. 16, 20, 23.   [43] Ibid. 39, 123.   [44] Ibid. 24–5.   [45] Ibid. 95–6.   [46] Ibid. 123.

powers, and knowledge not part of any such role. Nor is it the role of natural forces to create *ex nihilo*. Moreover, any who think the biblical religions do not aim at complete personal transformation has an odd, jaundiced view of their contents. The Law aimed to regulate all the main areas of life, in a way and direction quite different from the lives the Hebrews saw around them. If you "love the Lord your God with all your heart and with all your mind and with all your strength" (Deut. 6: 5), if you "talk about . . . these commandments . . . when you are sitting at home and when you go on a journey, when you lie down and when you rise up" (Deut. 6: 7) and "love your neighbor as yourself" (Lev. 19: 18), you will be transformed out of all recognition. And the ethic of the New Testament pushes against every impulse of unredeemed nature: that is what Nietzsche had against it. If the biblical approach to God is not a manifestation of what Johnston identifies as idolatrous impulses, he has no case that the biblical forms of worship are idolatrous, nor then that a true God could not be their proper object.

Johnston's case that the proper conception of God is of something impersonal runs this way: only the most perfect being can be God. But

If there is . . . a separate creation . . . Consider . . . the joint reality made up by (God) and the separate creation . . . this joint reality might be a more appropriate object of worship than the sub-part of reality that is (God. But) only (God) deserves worship. So there is no separate creation. What is called creation is some part or aspect or . . . mode of (God) . . . The existence of other beings can . . . not augment the goodness of (God). Otherwise the . . . sum . . . of other beings and the supposed (God) would be still . . . more worthy of worship . . . It would be a better competitor for the name of (God and) there can be no such competitor.[47]

So God must include Creation. But God is not a soul whose body is Creation, because "the concept of a non-natural mental realm is bankrupt."[48] So God is just an impersonal naturalistic universe.

To be fair, Johnston calls this reasoning "too compressed"[49] and denies that his book is "a work of philosophy."[50] But still. I'll confine myself to saying two things about it. One is that the options for views on which God includes Creation are not just NP and "dualist" panentheism. If the mental realm is natural, fine: the universe could still have its own mental properties, as natural as ours, and be a fit subject of address, just as we are. This was the Stoic picture, I think, and arguably was Spinoza's. The other is that the argument assumes without support something few Western theists would accept, that the perfection of God apart from Creation is finite. If it is infinite, then the sum of a finite Creation and God does not have more value than God does. Nothing surpasses God's perfection. At worst, God and the sum are tied. But of God and the sum, only God can be addressed: and even in the event of a tie, that is enough to qualify only God as the proper object of worship. Further, the theist in the street probably has no views about mereological sums at all, but if the theist in the street accepts, at least implicitly, that God is the most perfect being, he or she surely means by this that God is the most

---

[47] Ibid. 95–6.   [48] Ibid. 127.   [49] Ibid. 96.   [50] Ibid., preface.

perfect being in the ordinary ontology—which does not include arbitrary sums of ordinary objects. You could drive a truck through the holes in Johnson's argument.

Indian philosophy may have produced error-theories NP could use, and arguments for them, but I do not know that terrain. Again, there were views near NP's error-claim in nineteenth- and early twentieth-century Idealism, but the arguments for them are so thoroughly entangled in their authors' overarching systems that I doubt anything worth considering can be torn free of these contexts. At best, anyone not antecedently convinced of the relevant sort of idealism will have to be persuaded into that before the arguments can have much bite—which would be a very large task. Further, it's also at least a question whether NP could really appropriate arguments developed in support of what was in fact non-naturalist pantheism or pantheism of the more theistic sort. I take it, then, that we do not yet have a promising candidate for the sort of error-theory NP needs.

9. Religious Attitudes without Worship

Suppose that nothing discussed above really does amount to worship, separately or conjoined, and that dispensing with the worship requirement is unpromising. Still, there is strategy (d): perhaps it is enough to meet the religious requirement of the God-role that it make sense to have other religious attitudes to the universe. One has to make this move with care. Catholics, for instance, insist that one can venerate saints and angels but not worship them. Worship, they say, is appropriate only to God. Veneration is a religious attitude short of worship implemented in a variety of acts. If there are religious attitudes other than worship whose proper objects are other than God, not just any non-worship religious attitude can serve (d)'s purpose. One needs an attitude clearly appropriate only to God. Let's consider some candidates.

Theists are grateful to God. But when I am grateful to my wife, there is nothing religious about it. Gratitude is not always religious; to make it so, something must be added, or it must be embedded in some larger complex of attitudes and activities, or it must have a distinctively religious object. If it's the last, then NP can't appeal to gratitude to settle the question of whether its universe is a religious object: for then to assert that we can have distinctively religious gratitude to the universe would beg the question at issue. Mander suggests that one can be grateful to the universe as one can to an institution.[51] If so, perhaps gratitude embedded in other attitudes or directed to (say) something deemed supremely valuable might do the trick for NP. But I doubt that gratitude to an institution will do the trick here. Such gratitude is possible because it is really gratitude to the people past and present who have made it what it is and currently

---

[51] William Mander, "Pantheism," <http://plato.stanford.edu/entries/pantheism/#NatCos>.

constitute it. It analyzes without remainder into this. One can't treat gratitude to a naturalist universe similarly.

Theists trust God. Gregory Vlastos suggests that, impressed by its natural order, one might trust the universe to continue to uphold one in being.[52] Paul Faulker calls this predictive trust:

I trust my apple tree to bear apples, not oranges. I trust its boughs to bear my weight, if they look strong and healthy. I trust my reliable old alarm clock to wake me tomorrow, as it did yesterday.[53]

We speak of trust, Faulkner suggests, when we not only expect, but depend on things turning out as we expect.[54] Now the primary context for talk of trust is interpersonal. We learn what trust is, and how to talk about trust, by trusting people. The talk gets extended from there. Extended far enough, it becomes just metaphor. I think Faulkner's examples are metaphorical, and that Vlastos is taking a metaphor too far. If I trust you to do A, I do not just expect and perhaps depend on your doing A. I have faith in you in this respect. (Faith in God, as distinct from (say) faith that He exists, seems to consist in nothing other than trusting Him. If that's right, perhaps "trusts" and "has faith in" are synonyms in interpersonal contexts.) I know that you might choose to let me down, but my assessment of your character leads me to treat this possibility as remote. Talk of having faith in my alarm clock or in a tree sounds like a joke, at least to me, and that is one sign of metaphor. It is obviously metaphorical to speak of either letting me down. If I'm right about this, trust, like worship, is properly and literally directed only to agents. In any case, like gratitude and unlike worship, trust is not an intrinsically religious attitude.

Mander, again, writes that

Religion gives meaning to human lives by assigning them a...place within a grander scheme or narrative. It gives its adherents a sense of their part in a coherent universe. It tells us that the universe is...a whole in which we have our proper location. The pantheist may regard the cosmos as divine for very similar reasons. To think of oneself as part of a vast interconnected scheme may give one a sense of being "at home in the universe."[55]

This does not distinguish religion from metaphysics. Any metaphysic may also assign us a place in a grand narrative, make coherent sense of the universe, and so make us feel at home in it. But these things don't suffice for a metaphysic to have religious significance or include anything to which religious attitudes are appropriate. They would be true, for instance, of a naturalist metaphysic which explicitly denied pantheism.

---

[52] So Gregory Vlastos, quoted at Levine, *Pantheism*, 51.
[53] Paul Faulkner, "On Telling and Trusting," *Mind* 116 (2007), 880.
[54] Ibid.   [55] Mander, "Pantheism."

Still, see what we have. The universe can evoke something like mystical experience (of "oneness with all things"). It can provoke awe, for its spatial and temporal size, for the power of its forces, for these forces' making and potentially unmaking us. One can feel humble before what awes one. One can admire the universe's beauty. One can love it the way one loves a painting or a home. One can feel dependent on parts of it, and perhaps that transmits to a feeling of dependence on the whole. One can feel the universe awesome and fearful, and if one also feels it mysterious, marvelous, a wonder, then it is at least a candidate for evoking Otto's famed numinous experience: Otto sees these as its constituent notes.[56] One can value it to the highest degree. If my arguments above are correct, there is nothing distinctively religious one can do about these experiences and attitudes—there is no way to put them into practice. But still, they are there. So we can ask whether a life in which they are prominent is religious, and if it is, whether the universe's role in these attitudes and feelings then makes it conceptually appropriate to call it God. To muddy the waters further, if not religious (whatever that means, precisely), we can ask whether it is a "spiritual" life (whatever *that* means) and whether *that* is enough to make "God" conceptually apt.

I reply that someone could have these attitudes and experiences and still be living only what Kierkegaard called an aesthetic life.[57] One could simply enjoy the experiences, visit nature the way one would visit a museum, and value the universe simply because one values the experiences. (One might value paintings the same way.) One could treat Christianity the same way, visiting churches for the music and perhaps the pleasure of briefly simulating a religious frame of mind (like acting a part in a play). But an "aesthetic" life is precisely *not* religious. It is one of passive enjoyment. So what is listed above is not sufficient for having a religious life. Nor then are the feelings and attitudes mentioned a sufficient basis for saying that a naturalist universe satisfies what *should* be the religious clause within the God-role. It is possible to have these attitudes and experiences without having a God, even a pantheist God. I suggest that something similar is true about the spirituality question (I am hesitant, though, as I don't really know what "spirituality" apart from organized religion is supposed to be). The aesthete just described could spend much time enjoying "spiritual" experiences and emotions—but someone who only dabbles in this way is precisely not "spiritual." Whatever precisely "spirituality" is supposed to be, my impression is that it is not meant to be a sort of entertainment. So I do not think this is enough to qualify the universe for the title "God" under the "spirituality" heading either.

---

[56] Rudolph Otto, *The Idea of the Holy* (Oxford: Oxford University Press, 1950), 12–13, 193–4. I owe the point to Levine, *Pantheism*, 48.

[57] See Søren Kierkegaard, *Either/Or* (London: Penguin, 1992).

I submit, then, that NP's universe cannot meet the religious requirement on "God." Now there might seem to be a simple way around this: perhaps NP could just substitute for "God" a term "God*,"[58] which NP might explain in at least these ways:

1. God* =df. God not properly worshiped,
2. God* =df. God according to NP,
3. God* =df. God according to pantheism,
4. God* =df. God not according to Western theism, or
5. God* =df. the ultimate reality and most valuable being.

NP will then say that

G*.   the universe is God*

and forswear talk of God.

Recourse to "God*" would have a point only if NP granted my argument about "God." If NP does not grant this, it need not substitute "God*" for "God." But if NP grants my argument, the move won't work. (1)–(4) include "God." Now God fills the God-role, analytically. The God-role includes being a proper object of worship. So if I am correct about the God-role, if the universe is God* and (per (1)) is God not properly worshiped, then something fills the God-role which does not fill the God-role. This is clear if "God" is a title-term whose sense expresses requisites of bearing the title, for then its sense includes being properly worshiped. But it is also true if "God" is a proper name, for we mean to assign the name to something that actually satisfies the name's reference-fixers, and these prominently include the God-role.

(G*) fares little better on (2), if my argument is correct. For on (2), God* is something that plays the God-role according to NP. But if I am correct, NP's supposed deity could not play the God-role.

Now pantheism is either naturalist or non-naturalist. So on (3), (G*) implies:

6. the universe is NP's God or non-naturalist pantheism's God.

If my argument is correct, (6) is true only if the universe is non-naturalist pantheism's God, for NP does not have a God, a player of the God-role—NP has only a God*. So (6) is true only if NP is false. So on (3), (G*) is true only if NP is false: checkmate for NP. The same sort of disjunctive move applies on (4): though there will be many more disjuncts, the disjuncts will all be NP or things incompatible with NP.

(5) dispenses with "God" and so avoids the problems just noted. I jib at it even so, just because "God*" includes the string "God": that brings with it unearned and potentially misleading overtones, connotations, and suggestions. Our evaluation of NP would be fairer if NP dispensed with that string altogether, and simply said that it holds that the universe is the ultimate (all-inclusive) and most valuable reality. But if I am

---

[58] So Yujin Nagasawa, in correspondence.

correct about the God-role, one might simply reply "fine. But what's that got to do with God? I believe that the universe is all there is, and includes all the value there is. I understand that claim fully. Still I do not see that it provides me with any reason to engage in religious, quasi-religious, or spiritual behavior." So NP must either contest my account of the God-role or admit that its God-candidate fails to play the role. I do not see hope in just granting my case and trying to side-step it. As I think the case succeeds, I draw a simple moral: pantheism and naturalism don't mix. If you want to be a pantheist, don't be a naturalist.[59] Whether there can be a viable form of non-naturalist pantheism is however a tale for another day.

[59] My thanks to William Mander and Yujin Nagasawa for comments.

PART II

Panentheism

5

Modal Panentheism

Yujin Nagasawa

What could be more stupid than to deny that supreme excellence to that universal nature which embraces all things?—Cicero

1. Introduction

Modal panentheism consists primarily of the following two theses:

(1) God is the totality of all possible worlds.
(2) All possible worlds exist to the same extent that the actual world does.

As I explain in detail in this chapter, the first thesis can be construed as a version of pantheism or panentheism depending on how we understand the ontological status of possible worlds. The second thesis corresponds to what metaphysicians call modal realism.[1] It says that the actual world is not the only possible world that exists; all possible worlds exist and they are as real as the actual world. So modal panentheism says that all possible worlds exist and God is the totality of those worlds.

The aim of this chapter is to consider modal panentheism as an alternative to traditional theism. In section 2, I argue that we can derive modal panentheism—perhaps counterintuitively—from the Anselmian definition of God, which is widely accepted among traditional theists. In section 3, I argue that the modal panentheistic God shares many specific great-making properties that are commonly ascribed to God by traditional theists. Such properties include omniscience, omnipotence, omnibenevolence, immutability, impassibility, eternity, necessary existence, omnipresence, independence, unsurpassability, and the property of being a cause of the universe.[2] In section 4, I argue that modal panentheism provides compelling answers to many difficult problems in the philosophy of religion, such as the problem of evil, the problem of no best

---

[1] Modal realism is most notably defended by David Lewis (1986).
[2] The ascriptions of these attributes to God are matters of dispute. For example, it is disputed whether or not God is eternal. Some claim that God's relationship with time should rather be understood as timelessness or omnitemporality. I set these disputes aside in this chapter.

possible world, the fine-tuning problem, the timing problem for the beginning of the universe, and the question why there is anything rather than nothing. However, I argue in section 5 that there is a variation of the problem of evil for modal panentheism which is difficult to resolve. Section 6 concludes.

2. The Anselmian Definition of God

Traditional theism so called is shared across the Judaeo-Christian-Islamic tradition. It is widely agreed that traditional theism is based on the definition of God (or a close variant thereof) introduced or anticipated by Anselm in the eleventh century:

(3) God is that than which no greater can be thought.

Anselm famously uses this definition to construct the ontological argument for the existence of God (Anselm, originally 1077–8, 1979).

How does traditional theism interpret the above definition? More specifically, how does it interpret the notion of greatness in the definition? Harwood presents the most common interpretation as follows: God (or the Maximally Great Being, as Harwood calls it) 'is one that has all possible positive qualities to the highest possible extent and is totally devoid of negative qualities' (Harwood 1999, 478). So, for example, if knowledge, power, and benevolence are positive qualities (or great-making properties) while ignorance, vulnerability, and malevolence are negative qualities (or worse-making properties), then God has knowledge, power, and benevolence to the highest possible extent while totally lacking ignorance, vulnerability, and malevolence.[3] Based on this interpretation traditional theism typically holds that God is an omniscient, omnipotent, omnibenevolent, immutable, impassible, eternal, necessarily existent, omnipresent, independent, unsurpassable, personal cause of the universe.[4]

Modal panentheism appears to differ radically from traditional theism, where the nature of God is at stake. Surprisingly enough, however, we can also derive modal panentheism from the Anselmian definition of God, albeit based on an alternative interpretation of that definition according to which greatness in the definition of God should be understood not in terms of the extent of positivity or great-making there is but in terms of the scope of that which it encompasses. So, on this interpretation, the more encompassing a being is the higher the greatness of that being is. It is easily overlooked but pantheists and panentheists often understand God's greatness in this way. God's complete comprehensiveness, its capacity to encompass all of reality, represents God's ultimate significance. God is the greatest being, according to

---

[3] I use the term 'it' rather than 'he' or 'she' to refer to God throughout this chapter because our main focus is on modal panentheism, which does not regard God as a person or personal being.

[4] There is a debate about whether or not God, or any being, can simultaneously have multiple great-making properties to the highest possible extent. Some people claim, for example, that it is impossible for God (or any other being) to be omniscient and omnipotent simultaneously. I set this debate aside in this chapter. See Nagasawa (2008).

this understanding, because God encompasses absolutely everything and there is nothing beyond it. Balbus, Cicero's character in *The Nature of Gods* who defends Stoic pantheism, says, for example, 'What could be more stupid than to deny that supreme excellence to that universal nature which embraces all things?' (Cicero, originally 45 BC, 1972, 137).[5] According to this understanding, God, as that than which no greater can be thought, is the maximally encompassing being. And modal panentheism holds that such a being is the totality of all possible worlds as it encompasses everything.

Suppose now that modal actualism is true, that is, only the actual world exists. In this case, insofar as existing things are concerned, the 'totality of all possible worlds including the actual world' is equivalent to the actual world alone because, according to modal actualism, everything that exists is actual and no merely possible worlds exist. This means that modal actualism and the thesis that God is the totality of all possible worlds jointly entail pantheism, according to which God is identical with the actual world.

Modal panentheism says, on the other hand, that modal realism (i.e., thesis 2 above) is true; that is, all possible worlds exist to the same extent that the actual world does. According to modal realism, actuality is merely indexical. There is no ontological difference between the actual world and other possible worlds. The actual world is special for us merely because it is *our* world, just as some other possible world is special for the inhabitants of that world. All possible worlds are ontologically on a par although they are causally isolated from one another.[6] Given modal realism, the totality of all possible worlds including the actual world is more encompassing than the actual world alone is. Modal panentheism is a version of panentheism rather than pantheism because it entails existence beyond the actual world which we inhabit, namely, other possible worlds. That is, the actual world is only a proper part of God. (Having said that, I hasten to add that modal panentheism can be construed as a version of pantheism if we define

---

[5] An anonymous referee doubts that this quote from Cicero supports the construal of greatness in terms of encompassment. The referee contends that Balbus says only that there is something which encompasses all things and it would be foolish not to call that thing great. According to the referee, that is not the same as saying that it is great *because* it encompasses all things.

However, if encompassment has nothing to do with greatness, it is puzzling why Balbus uses the phrase 'that universal nature which embraces all things' rather than simply 'that universal nature'. The quote in question follows this passage, which I think supports my construal: 'The various creatures of the universe may meet with many external obstacles to their perfect development. But no obstacle can frustrate the development of the universe itself. The universe moulds and *embraces all things*. Therefore, we must admit the existence of that forth and final stage of being, which no power can assail. This is the stage of being on which the whole of nature depends. It is thus above all things and nothing has any power against it, and is the universal dwelling-place of reason and of wisdom' (Cicero, originally 45 BC, 1972, 137, emphasis added).

In any case, whether or not my interpretation of Cicero is correct, it is quite common for pantheists and panentheists to construe God's greatness in terms of encompassment.

[6] Modal possibilism says that some existent things are in the actual world and some other existent things are not in the actual world. Modal realism is an extreme form of modal possibilism.

pantheism as the view that God is identical with reality or the sum of all there is, rather than only the actual world which we inhabit. Ultimately, therefore, it is a matter of definition whether modal panentheism is a version of pantheism or panentheism.)

Pantheism is known to face the problem of unity: How can we consider the world a single unified entity given that it consists of uncountably many individual objects? Modal panentheism faces a parallel problem: How can we consider the totality of all possible worlds a single unified entity given that it consists of uncountably many individual objects? Pantheists typically appeal to causal links or the laws of nature to explain the unity, but modal panentheists may be able to maintain a stronger unity by appealing to a unity that is based on modality. If our world is a four-dimensional object consisting of space and time, then perhaps the totality of all possible worlds is equivalent to logical space or a five-dimensional object consisting of space, time, and modality. God, according to this view, is the most encompassing being because it extends maximally in space, time, and modality. Nothing can extend further than such a being.

Defending modal realism itself is outside the scope of this chapter. However, one strategy that could motivate modal realism in this context would be to construct an argument similar to the ontological argument: That than which no greater can be thought is, according to modal panentheism, the totality of all possible worlds. Suppose, for the sake of argument, that some of the worlds in the totality of all possible worlds do not exist. It then follows that another totality can be thought that is greater than the totality of all possible worlds. Such a totality is thought to encompass all possible worlds and all of these worlds are thought to exist. However, it is contradictory to say that a being can be thought that is greater than the totality of all possible worlds because the totality of all possible worlds is, by definition, that than which no greater can be thought. Hence, it is impossible that some of the worlds in the totality of all possible worlds do not exist. Therefore, all possible worlds in the totality of all possible worlds exist. Therefore, modal realism is true.[7]

I am aware that many, especially those who are critical of the ontological argument, would not find the above argument compelling. However, in this chapter I will not discuss the soundness of the above argument or any other argument for modal realism. Instead, I try to motivate modal realism indirectly by showing how modal panentheism, which is based on modal realism, can solve a number of central problems in the philosophy of religion.

---

[7] The fact that we can construct a version of the ontological argument for modal realism/modal panentheism supports the point that the modal panentheistic concept of God is structurally parallel to the traditional theistic concept of God despite the fact that these concepts are based on distinct interpretations of God's greatness. If, however, one is antecedently skeptical of the ontological argument, then the observation that we can construct a version of theargument for modal realism/modal panentheism might make such a skeptic question these views even further. Thanks to an anonymous referee for this point.

3. Great-Making Properties

We have seen that despite its uniqueness modal panentheism is, just like traditional theism, derived from the Anselmian definition of God as that than which no greater can be thought. Nevertheless, it still appears that modal panentheism differs radically from traditional theism. As we have seen, while traditional theism regards God as the being that has all possible positive qualities to the greatest possible extent, modal panentheism regards God as the totality of all possible worlds. I maintain, however, that the modal panentheistic God at least in some sense shares several properties with the traditional theistic God.[8] Such properties include omniscience, omnipotence, omnibenevolence, immutability, impassibility, eternity, necessary existence, omnipresence, independence, unsurpassability, and the property of being a cause of the universe.

According to modal panentheism, God is the totality of all possible worlds, a being that encompasses all possible states of affairs and, moreover, all such possible worlds are real. This means that all possible instances of knowledge, power, and benevolence are real and encompassed by God. This implies that, at least in one sense, the modal panentheistic God is omniscient, omnipotent, and omnibenevolent.[9] (One might claim that the modal panentheistic God cannot be omniscient, omnipotent, and omnibenevolent because although it encompasses all possible forms of knowledge, power, and benevolence it also encompasses all possible forms of ignorance, weakness, and malevolence. Here is a possible response to such a claim: Consider, as a parallel example, a group of three people A, B, and C. A knows x and y, B knows z, and C is totally ignorant. In this scenario, we are inclined to say that the group as a whole knows x, y, and z and that the ignorance of C does not cancel out what A and B know. Similarly, the ignorance/weakness of an individual does not seem to undermine the knowledge/power of the totality to which the individual belongs. Omnibenevolence is more difficult to address but perhaps the same reasoning applies if Aquinas is right in saying that to sin is merely to fall short of a perfect action.[10])

Also, since the totality of all possible worlds is equivalent to logical space the modal panentheistic God is immutable, impassible, eternal, and necessarily existent. The modal

---

[8] Oppy (1997) and Steinhart (2004) make similar points.

[9] Notice that, if pantheism is true, God encompasses only all pieces of knowledge that *exist in the actual world*, all powers that *exist in the actual world*, and all forms of benevolence that *exist in the actual world*. This hardly entails that God is omniscient, omnipotent, and omnibenevolent.

[10] There is a further question about the possession of knowledge, power, and benevolence by the modal panentheistic God. It is assumed here that the modal panentheistic God is omniscient, omnipotent, and omnibenevolent because it subsumes all possible forms of knowledge, power, and benevolence possessed by individuals. One might say, however, that this is an instance of the fallacy of composition because it is assumed erroneously here that if an individual has certain properties, the whole, which encompasses them, has these properties as well (thanks to Klaas Kraay for this perspective on this point). I do not have space to discuss this criticism in detail here but I believe that modal panentheists can respond to it. For example, they can appeal to the fact that we commonly attribute collective knowledge, collective power, and collective morality (if not benevolence) to a group of people, such as a company.

panentheistic God is also omnipresent and eternal in the sense that it encompasses all spatiotemporal locations in all possible worlds.[11] The modal panentheistic God is also independent because, as the totality of all possible worlds, its existence does not rely ontologically on any other existents. In fact, there is nothing external to God as there is nothing outside the totality of all possible worlds. The modal panentheistic God is also unsurpassable since there cannot be anything greater than the totality of all possible worlds; the totality of all possible worlds is the most encompassing being possible. Furthermore, the totality of all possible worlds can even be seen as a cause of the universe. A necessary being is commonly understood as a self-caused being that does not require any external cause of its existence. Since God, as the totality of all possible worlds, is a necessary being it is also a self-caused being. Now the totality here is assumed to encompass everything, including the universe. This means that, in one sense, the modal panentheistic God is a cause of the universe as well.

Perhaps the only prominent properties of the traditional theistic God that the modal panentheistic God lacks are the property of being a person and the property of having free will. Traditional theism normally says that God is a person (or a personal being) with free will. Modal panentheism does not ascribe such a property to God even though it entails that God encompasses all possible persons and all beings with free will. In this sense, perhaps God is a partially personal being or a partially free being even though it is not a free person in itself. In order to ascribe freedom and personhood to a thing there has to be an appropriate bearer of these properties. However, the totality of all possible worlds does not seem to qualify as a bearer of such properties.

Nonetheless, as we have seen, the modal panentheistic God at least in some sense shares many properties with the traditional theistic God. It seems reasonable, therefore, to view modal panentheism as a form of theism, although ultimately, of course, it is a matter of definition whether or not any given view can be seen as a form of theism.

4. Modal Panentheism and Problems in the Philosophy of Religion

One of the main reasons to prefer modal panentheism to traditional theism is that it offers answers to many difficult problems in the philosophy of religion, answers that are not available to traditional theism. Such problems include the problem of evil, the problem of no best possible world, the fine-tuning problem, the timing problem for the beginning of the universe, and the question why there is anything at all.

---

[11] This of course does not mean that the modal panentheistic God is omnipresent and eternal in exactly the same sense in which the traditional theistic God is. In particular, modal panentheism does not entail that God is wholly present everywhere, undivided in His being.

Consider the problem of evil first:

The Problem of Evil: If an omnipotent and omnibenevolent God exists, the actual world has to be free from evil. However, there certainly is evil in the actual world. Therefore, God does not exist.[12]

Modal panentheism can quickly dismiss this problem. A hidden assumption in the above-stated version of the problem is that God is, if it exists at all, a being that would, given its omnipotence, omnibenevolence, and free will, eliminate evil. Modal panentheism simply rejects this assumption by saying that it is a mistake to think that God is a being that performs morally significant actions using free will. God is, according to modal panentheism, the totality of all possible worlds and not a being with free will. This response is, however, not very interesting because it does not explain why there has to be evil in the first place.

Modal panentheism explains the existence of evil as follows: Again, given modal realism all possible worlds exist. This means that every single possible state of affairs is instantiated. Many states of affairs that include evil—states of affairs which include instances of moral evil such as murders, rapes, terrorism, and slavery, and instances of natural evil such as disasters and catastrophes caused by earthquakes, tornadoes, floods, and droughts—are metaphysically possible. If so, it is unavoidable that evil is instantiated. In sum, once we accept modal realism, it is necessarily the case that there is evil.

But why does there have to be evil in the actual world instead of some other possible world? Why do *we* in the actual world have to suffer? Modal panentheism responds to these questions by saying that there is no reason that the actual world, instead of some other possible world, has to be free from evil. Modal realism does not privilege the actual world over other possible worlds. As we saw earlier, according to modal realism, actuality, which distinguishes the actual world from other possible worlds, is nothing but indexicality. That is, the actual world appears ontologically special to us merely because *we* happen to exist in the actual world. However, counterparts to us exist in other possible worlds similar to the actual world. If we do not suffer from evil, then our counterparts, who are as real as we are, must suffer from evil in their worlds. Given that we and our counterparts are morally equivalent, there is no reason for them to suffer instead of us, and vice versa. As Michael Almeida says, this is comparable to a situation in which a rescuer can save each of two persons but not both of them (Almeida 2011, 9). In such a situation, it is not legitimate to ask why person x rather than person y had to be rescued. Similarly, it is not legitimate to ask why the actual world rather than some other possible world has to contain evil.

We can apply the same reasoning to many other problems in the philosophy of religion. Consider, for example, the following:

The Problem of No Best Possible World: If there is an omnipotent and omnibenevolent God, then the actual world has to be the best possible world. However, the

---

[12] See Adams and Adams (1990), Peterson (1992), Plantinga (1974), and Rowe (2001).

actual world certainly is not the best possible world. Therefore, God does not exist.[13]

Notice how this problem differs from the problem of evil. The problem of no best possible world is not necessarily concerned with the existence of evil in the actual world. In fact, the problem would remain even if the actual world had been completely free from evil, as long as the actual world is not the best possible world. Leibniz famously bites the bullet and responds to the problem by saying that the actual world *is* the best possible world. However, most people disagree with him; it is easy to conceive of a possible world that is better than the actual world. For example, we can conceive of a world identical to the actual world except that a certain minor mishap in the actual world does not take place in that world. Modal panentheism responds to the problem of no best possible world in the same manner in which it responds to the problem of evil: (i) It is wrong to assume that God is a being with free will that would, given its omnipotence and omnibenevolence, create the best possible world; (ii) there exist worlds like the actual world that are not the greatest possible because all possible worlds exist; (iii) there is no reason to think that the actual world, instead of some other possible world, has to be the best possible world as all possible worlds are ontologically on a par.

The problem of evil and the problem of no best possible world raise primarily moral concerns. They ask how an omnipotent and omnibenevolent God could be morally justified in creating the actual world given certain observed conditions of that world. Yet modal panentheism can also respond to problems that raise purely metaphysical concerns regarding the nature of the actual world:

> *The Fine-Tuning Problem*: Some philosophers and scientists claim that the existence of life is grounded on an extremely delicate balance of initial conditions that obtained at the beginning of the universe in the actual world. For example, Stephen Hawking estimates that if the rate of the universe's expansion one second after the big bang had been smaller by even one part in a hundred thousand million million, life could not have existed in the universe. (Craig and Sinnott-Armstrong 2004, 9)

However, life does exist in the universe in the actual world, which appears miraculous.[14]

> *The Timing Problem for the Beginning of the Universe*: According to scientists, the universe in the actual world is approximately 15 billion years old. Why did the universe have to begin to exist 15 billion years ago? Whether the universe is created by God or through a natural process the age of the universe seems to be completely arbitrary.[15]

---

[13] See Adams (1972), Kraay (2008), Langtry (2008), and Rowe (2004).

[14] See also Barrow and Tipler (1988), Carr (2007), and Leslie (1996).

[15] See Leftow (1991). G. W. Leibniz also addresses the question 'Why didn't God create everything a year sooner than he did?' in his exchange with Samuel Clark in 1716.

The Problem of Why There is Anything at All: As J. J. C. Smart says, 'That anything exists at all does seem...a matter for the deepest awe' (Smart 1955, 194). Biology might explain why there are animals and plants, and cosmology might explain why there are planets and galaxies. However, why there is anything at all rather than nothing in the actual world is the deepest metaphysical mystery that no one seems able to answer.[16]

The fine-tuning problem might not arise if, as the multiverse hypothesis says, there are infinitely many universes in the actual world. However, even if there can be only one universe in each possible world, this problem does not arise for modal panentheism. This is because modal panentheism can still allow infinitely many universes by letting each possible world in the totality of all possible worlds (i.e., infinitely many possible worlds) contain one universe. Modal panentheism says that it is not surprising that there is a fine-tuned universe because there are infinitely many universes subject to infinitely many conditions across possible worlds. Why the actual world contains a fine-tuned universe is not a question for modal panentheism because, again, modal realism does not discriminate among possible worlds.

In response to the timing problem modal panentheism says that there are, in the totality of all possible worlds, infinitely many universes of an infinite variety of ages, and our 15-billion-year-old universe is only one of them. It is not surprising that there is a universe that is 15 billion years old because, given modal realism, some world has to contain such a universe. Why the actual world has to contain such a universe is not a legitimate question because, again, the actual world and other possible worlds are ontologically on a par.

The question why there is anything at all might not arise if there cannot be an empty world.[17] However, even if there can be an empty world, this problem does not arise for modal panentheism. It just happens to be the case that the actual world is not an empty world. There is no reason to think that the actual world, instead of some other possible world, has to be empty.

Notice that each of the problems that we have seen focuses on a 'mystery' concerning a specific condition of the actual world that appears incompatible with the existence of an omnipotent and omnibenevolent God or that, by itself, appears totally arbitrary or probabilistically/metaphysically unlikely to obtain. The problem of evil asks why there is evil in the actual world given the existence of an omnipotent and omnibenevolent God. The problem of no best possible world asks why the actual world is not the best possible world given the existence of an omnipotent and omnibenevolent God. The fine-tuning problem asks why the actual world has to contain a universe that is fine-tuned when it is probabilistically very unlikely. The timing problem asks why the actual world has to contain a universe that is 15 billion years old, which seems

---

[16] See Goldschmidt (2013), Kuhn (2007), Leslie and Kuhn (2013), and Rundle (2004).

[17] See Baldwin (1996), Efird and Stoneham (2005), and van Inwagen (1996).

arbitrary. The question why there is anything at all asks why there is something rather than nothing in the actual world, which seems metaphysically unlikely.

Modal panentheism can respond to any problem within the same logical structure. It says that all possible worlds exist and are equally real, so there is no special reason that the actual world—that is, one of infinitely many possible worlds—has a specific condition. If we consider the converse of this point we can derive an interesting conclusion: *all of these 'mysteries' arise because we assume erroneously that the actual world is the only possible world that exists*. Once we give up such an assumption these mysteries disappear.

5. The Problem of Evil for Modal Panentheism

In section 4, I argued that the problem of evil is among problems in the philosophy of religion that modal panentheism can resolve. Accordingly I have shown that the following three questions do not raise serious concerns for modal panentheism:

Q1:   Why is there evil given the existence of God as an omniscient, omnipotent, and omnibenevolent free being?

Q2:   Why is there evil at all?

Q3:   Why is there evil in the actual world, i.e., *our* world?

First, Q1 cannot be directed against modal panentheism. This is because Q1 is based on an assumption that modal panentheism rejects, namely, the assumption that God is a being that can freely choose to eliminate evil. Second, modal panentheism successfully responds to Q2 by saying that every single possible state of affairs is instantiated in the totality of all possible worlds, which is, according to modal panentheism, identical with God. Given that it is possible for evil states of affairs to be instantiated, it is not a surprise that they are instantiated in the totality. Third, Q3 is not a legitimate question for modal panentheism because, according to modal panentheism, all possible worlds are ontologically on a par. Since the actual world is by no means privileged it is not a question why *our* world, rather than some other possible world, includes evil.

It is a great strength of modal panentheism in contrast to traditional theism that it can offer straightforward answers to the above questions concerning evil. However, ironically, modal panentheism faces a different form of the problem of evil because of its own unique feature. In what follows, I argue that this problem raises a serious challenge for modal panentheism.

The problem that modal panentheism faces is a variation of the following problem that *pantheism* faces:

The Problem of Evil for Pantheism: Pantheism says that God is identical with the actual world. However, there certainly is evil in the actual world and God is not an evil being. Therefore, pantheism is false.

The actual world includes many awful instances of moral and natural evil. Pantheism has to say that these instances are part of God and yet it is difficult to regard anything that includes instances of evil to be God. This problem is based on the following question:

Q4:   Why is there evil in the world if God is identical with the world?

This question is distinct from Q1, Q2, and Q3 as it is directed specifically to pantheism. The problem of evil for pantheism is powerful because pantheists cannot undercut it by making typical moves that traditional theists make in response to the problem of evil. For example, pantheists cannot appeal to the free will theodicy by saying that God is not responsible for evil because evil is caused by free humans. This is because even if evil is caused by free humans pantheists still have to hold that free humans themselves are part of God. Whatever free humans do is, according to pantheism, part of God. Neither can they appeal to the soul-making theodicy by saying that evil is necessary for the spiritual growth of humans beyond their physical existence. This is because pantheism holds that there is no reality beyond the physical world that humans inhabit. Neither can they appeal to skeptical theism by saying that, while our epistemic limitations do not allow us to fully comprehend God's reason, evil is necessary in God's grand scheme beyond the physical world. This is because pantheism is not compatible with the existence of a God that has a grand scheme beyond the physical reality.

The bad news for modal panentheism is that the problem of evil for pantheism intensifies when it is applied to modal panentheism.

The Problem of Evil for Modal Panentheism: Modal panentheism says that God is identical with the totality of all possible worlds. However, the totality of all possible worlds includes all possible instances of evil, including the very worst possible instances of evil, and God is not an evil being. Therefore, modal panentheism is false.

This problem is based on the following question:

Q5:   Why are there the worst possible instances of evil in the totality of all possible worlds if God is identical with it?

This question is distinct from Q1–Q4 as it is directed specifically to modal panentheism. We have seen that pantheists cannot undercut Q4 by making moves that traditional theists typically make in response to the problem of evil, and neither can modal panentheists undercut Q5 by making such moves.

The problem of evil for modal panentheism is more intractable than the problem of evil for pantheism. While pantheism entails only the thesis that all *actual* instances of evil (i.e., all instances of evil in the actual world) are part of God, modal panentheism entails the much stronger thesis that all *possible* instances of evil (i.e., all instances of evil in all possible worlds), including the very worst possible instances of evil, are part of God. This means that modal panentheism entails that there is, as part of God, a state of affairs in which, for example, millions of innocent children are tortured for an extended period, possibly eternally, for no reason.[18]

Again, modal panentheism adopts the interpretation of God's greatness that is not based on the degree of positivity or great-making but on the scope of that which it encompasses. Hence, according to modal panentheism, the more encompassing a being is the higher the greatness of that being is. The amount of evil that God subsumes therefore actually enhances, rather than diminishes, the greatness of God.

Conversely, if God fails to encompass some evil state of affairs (or any state of affairs at all) it fails to qualify as the greatest possible being on this interpretation. However, it is highly counterintuitive to think that utterly awful states of affairs are part of God if God is worthy of religious veneration. What this observation seems to teach us is that it is not correct to interpret God's greatness in terms of encompassment. While modal realism might not be an incoherent metaphysical view and it depends on one's definition of God whether the totality of all possible worlds is identified with God according to modal realism, such a definition entails disturbing moral implications which are difficult to accept.

One might think that we can solve this problem by appealing to Lewis's defence of modal realism. Modal realism faces a moral problem that is related to the problem of evil for modal panentheism. The moral problem for modal realism is this: Given the claim of modal realism that all possible worlds exist, the total amount of good and evil does not change whether or not we act morally in the actual world. Whether or not we act morally to prevent and eliminate evil in the actual world, the same evil is instantiated in some other possible world anyway. Therefore, modal realism appears to discourage us from acting morally.

Lewis's response to this problem is that evil events in other possible worlds should not be our moral concern. He writes:

> For those of us who think of morality in terms of virtue and honour, desert and respect and esteem, loyalties and affections and solidarity, the other-worldly evils should not seem even momentarily relevant to morality. Of course our moral aims are egocentric. And likewise all the more for those who think of morality in terms of rules, rights, and duties; or as obedience to the will of God. (Lewis 1986, 127)[19]

One might try to apply similar reasoning to the problem of evil for modal panentheism and maintain that we should not be bothered that there are utterly awful evil states of

---

[18] An anonymous referee says that it is not clear how the problem of evil intensifies for modal panentheism because the amount of evil that occurs is irrelevant to the difficulty or seriousness of the problem. I agree with the referee that a single instance of evil is sufficient to formulate the problem of evil, but the problem *is* strengthened significantly if all possible instances of evil, including the very worst possible instances of evil, are obtained. That would constitute the quantitatively and qualitatively most significant form of what Marilyn McCord Adams calls the problem of horrendous evil (Adams 1999).

[19] For the moral implications of modal realism see Adams (1979) and Heller (2003).

affairs in worlds other than the actual world. When we talk about what is good and what is evil, one might say, our main concern is what is good and what is evil in *our* world and our moral concerns should not extend to other possible worlds that are causally and spatiotemporally isolated from the actual world. And, given the laws of nature and other contingent facts, evil that can be instantiated in the actual world is only finite in quality and quantity. However, such a response does not succeed in saving modal panentheism. Lewis might be right in saying that we should not be bothered by evil in other possible worlds when considering the moral significance of actions in our own world. That is, even though the total axiological value and the total amount of good and evil in the sum of all possible worlds do not change whatever action we perform, we should not be discouraged from acting morally in the actual world. Yet this does not entail that we should not be bothered by evil in other possible worlds in relation to the thesis that the totality of all possible worlds is identical with God. The adoption of an egocentric point of view allows us to set aside other possible worlds *in considering our moral actions* but it does not allow us to set aside other possible worlds *in considering the totality of all possible worlds identified as God.* It is still puzzling how the totality of all possible worlds could be worthy of religious veneration if it includes so much evil.

The problem of evil for modal panentheism is intractable. It seems more intractable than any other forms of the problem of evil, as it involves, quantitatively and qualitatively, the most significant instances of evil, which exist, according to modal panentheism, as part of God.

6. Conclusion

Modal panentheism offers a unique alternative to the traditional concept of God. It coheres with the Anselmian definition of God as that than which no greater can be thought (at least on a certain interpretation) and preserves some of the great-making properties that are commonly ascribed to God (again, at least on a certain interpretation). It also offers answers to many fundamental problems in the philosophy of religion and shows that apparent mysteries on which these problems are based are not actually mysteries. However, it faces its own problem. The problem of evil is widely recognized as one of the most difficult challenges to traditional theism but a variation of the problem that modal panentheism faces seems to be even more difficult.[20]

[20] I would like to thank Andrei Buckareff, Klaas Kraay, Robert Lawrence Kuhn, Eric Steinhart, and two anonymous referees for their comments on an earlier version of this chapter. I discuss 'multiverse pantheism', which is closely related to modal panentheism, in my earlier paper (Nagasawa 2015). I presented that paper at a workshop at Ryerson University in February 2013. I would like to thank the workshop organizers and participants, as the current chapter also benefited from discussions that took place at that event. This chapter was written as part of my Templeton project with Buckareff, 'Exploring Alternative Concepts of God'. I am very grateful to the John Templeton Foundation for their generous support.

References

Adams, Marilyn McCord (1999). *Horrendous Evils and the Goodness of God*. Ithaca, NY: Cornell University Press.

Adams, Marilyn McCord and Adams, Robert Merrihew (eds) (1990). *The Problem of Evil*. Oxford: Oxford University Press.

Adams, Robert Merrihew (1972). 'Must God Create the Best?', *Philosophical Review* 81: 317–32.

Adams, Robert Merrihew (1979). 'Theories of Actuality', in Michael Loux (ed.), *The Possible and the Actual*. Ithaca, NY: Cornell University Press.

Almeida, Michael (2011). 'Theistic Modal Realism?', *Oxford Studies in Philosophy of Religion* 3: 1–14.

Anselm (originally 1077–8, 1979). *Anselm's Proslogion*. Trans. M. J. Charlesworth. Notre Dame, Ind.: University of Notre Dame Press.

Baldwin, Thomas (1996). 'There Might be Nothing', *Analysis* 56: 231–8.

Barrow, John D. and Tipler, Frank J. (1988). *The Anthropic Cosmological Principle*. Oxford: Oxford University Press.

Carr, Bernard (ed.) (2007). *Universe or Multiverse?* Cambridge: Cambridge University Press.

Cicero (originally 45 BC, 1972). *The Nature of Gods*. Trans. C. P. McGregor. London: Penguin Books.

Craig, William Lane and Sinnott-Armstrong, W. (2004). *God? A Debate between a Christian and an Atheist*. Oxford: Oxford University Press.

Efird, David and Stoneham, Tom (2005). 'The Subtraction Argument for Metaphysical Nihilism', *Journal of Philosophy* 102: 303–25.

Goldschmidt, Tyron (ed.) (2013). *The Puzzle of Existence: Why is There Something Rather Than Nothing?* London: Routledge.

Harwood, Robin (1999). 'Polytheism, Pantheism, and the Ontological Argument', *Religious Studies* 35: 477–91.

Heller, Mark (2003). 'The Immorality of Modal Realism, or: How I Learned to Stop Worrying and Let the Children Drown', *Philosophical Studies* 14: 1–22.

Kraay, Klaas J. (2008). 'Creation, World-Actualization, and God's Choice Among Possible Worlds', *Philosophy Compass* 3: 854–72.

Kuhn, Robert Lawrence (2007). 'Why this Universe? Toward a Taxonomy of Possible Explanations', *The Skeptic* 13: 28–39.

Langtry, Bruce (2008). *God, the Best, and Evil*. Oxford: Oxford University Press.

Leftow, Brian (1991). 'Why Didn't God Create the World Sooner', *Religious Studies* 27: 157–72.

Leslie, John (1996). *Universes*, new edn. London: Routledge.

Leslie, John and Kuhn, Robert Lawrence (eds) (2013). *The Mystery of Existence: Why is There Anything at All?* Oxford: Wiley-Blackwell.

Lewis, David (1986). *On the Plurality of Worlds*. Oxford: Blackwell.

Nagasawa, Yujin (2008). 'A New Defence of Anselmian Theism', *Philosophical Quarterly* 58: 577–96.

Nagasawa, Yujin (2015). 'Multiverse Pantheism', in Klaas J. Kraay (ed.), *God and the Multiverse: Scientific, Philosophical, and Theological Perspectives*. London: Routledge.

Oppy, Graham (1997). 'Pantheism, Quantification and Mereology', *The Monist* 80: 320–36.

Peterson, Michael L. (ed.) (1992). *The Problem of Evil: Selected Readings*. Notre Dame, Ind.: University of Notre Dame Press.

Plantinga, Alvin (1974). *God, Freedom and Evil*. London: George Allen and Unwin.

Rowe, W. L. (ed.) (2001). *God and the Problem of Evil*. Oxford: Blackwell.

Rowe, W. L. (2004). *Can God Be Free?* Oxford: Oxford University Press.

Rundle, Bede (2004). *Why is There Something Rather than Nothing?* Oxford: Oxford University Press.

Smart, J. J. C. (1955). 'The Existence of God', *Church Quarterly Review* 156: 194.

Steinhart, Eric (2004). 'Pantheism and Current Ontology', *Religious Studies* 40: 63–80.

van Inwagen, Peter (1996). 'Why is There Anything at All?', *Aristotelian Society Supplementary Volume* 70: 95–110.

6

Concepts of God and Problems of Evil

John Bishop and Ken Perszyk

Our wider interest in this chapter is in the following questions: How does 'the problem of evil' arise in different ways relative to different conceptions of God? May some conceptions of God be judged more adequate than others on the basis of how they give rise to a problem of evil, and how serious that problem is?

We have a specific interest in the question of how a particular conception of God stands in relation to the problem of evil—a 'euteleological' conception based on what we think is an important though relatively philosophically neglected aspect of theistic religious belief, namely that God is the supremely good end (*telos*) of the Universe and that this is what ultimately explains the existence of all that is.

The phrase 'the problem of evil' may be used to refer to importantly different problems. In particular, a distinction is sometimes made between the 'intellectual' or 'theoretical' and the 'existential' or 'pastoral' problems of evil.[1] The problem of evil from which our present discussion begins does have an essential intellectual component, though at its root it is an existential problem—a problem for lived human existence. But, at the outset, we will leave the labels aside, and be content to specify 'the problem of evil' with which we are concerned as expressed in this question: how is it possible to (continue to) believe in God with intellectual integrity in the face of full, clear-sighted, acknowledgment of actual evil?[2]

---

[1] See, for example, Plantinga 1985, 36–7.

[2] 'Actual evil' means all that is, was, and looks set to continue to be significantly defective in the actual world. What all the 'defects' are, and how 'significant' in each case, is up for discussion. But the defects certainly include the serious suffering of humans and non-human animals, both as the result of the actions of personal agents and from purely 'natural' causes. These defects are objectively real: they are not merely 'constructed' by either individual or social consciousness (though, had they been so, their construction would arguably itself have been a significant defect).

1. The Argument from Evil as Directed against the Existence of a Personal OmniGod

The standard way of explaining how evil challenges the intellectual integrity of theistic faith is to refer to an 'Argument from Evil' (AFE) with the following basic form: If God exists, evil does not exist; evil does exist; hence God does not exist. An AFE, if it succeeds, shows that it is unreasonable to believe in God and accept that evil is actual—although AFEs differ in the kind of unreasonableness they attribute to theists. Some AFEs, if successful, show that theistic belief (that accepts the actuality of evil) is unreasonable because it is internally inconsistent. The success of other AFEs, however, would allow the consistency of theistic belief, but show it to be unreasonable because it is held contrary to the weight of the total available evidence.

An AFE will succeed in showing theism to be unreasonable only if its proponents employ the conception of God to which the theist is in fact committed. This was clearly recognized at the time discussion of the AFE was revived in the analytical tradition by J. L. Mackie (1955) and H. J. McCloskey (1960). Mackie's so-called 'logical' argument from evil (an AFE of the type that alleges logical inconsistency) takes God to be an omnipotent, omniscient, and perfectly good agent. It also makes assumptions about what these attributes entail—for example, that an omnipotent agent is able to achieve any logically possible state of affairs, and that a perfectly good agent seeks to eliminate evil so far as it can. Accordingly, in responding to an AFE, defenders of theist intellectual integrity have a choice: either they may accept its (explicit and implicit) characterization of the divine and attempt objections to the argumentation, or they may accept the argumentation but challenge the assumed conception of God. This second option is to be understood broadly: challenges to a conception of the divine include challenges to presuppositions about what aspects of that conception imply.[3]

The history of theist responses to Mackie and McCloskey—and to the 'evidential' argument of William Rowe (1979) that later took centre stage—does not contain much dispute about *the basic* conception of God assumed by these AFEs. (Process theology seems to be the exception here, since it rejects, or at least significantly restricts, divine omnipotence.[4]) Most theist philosophers in the analytical tradition take as fundamental the 'personal omniGod' conception of the divine, according to which God is 'an all-powerful, all-knowing, wholly good person (a person without a body) who has

---

[3] Both options may be employed at once, of course: it may be apt for the theist to reply to the proponent of a given AFE: 'the God you think you've shown it unreasonable to believe in is not, in fact, the God of religious tradition—but your argument doesn't succeed anyway'.

[4] William Hasker's summary is useful: 'Process theists generally do not describe God's power as "omnipotence". They resist vigorously the suggestion that God as they conceive of him is weak or ineffectual. God, they say, does not have all the power that there is, but he has the most power that any being could possibly have, and to see this power as weakness is gravely to underestimate the ability of persuasive love to gain its ends, given sufficient time and patience' (2004, 137). For a defence of the process view of God's persuasive power, see, for example, Cobb and Griffin 1976, 52–4, and Hartshorne 1984, 20–6.

created us and our world' (Plantinga 2000, 3). Nevertheless, amongst personal omni-God theists there has been a good deal of discussion about what the divine attributes that belong to this basic conception actually entail, and how this relates to the existence of evil and its place in God's providence.[5]

A 'Logical' Argument from Evil, Normatively Relativized to Relationship Ethics

We have recently argued, however, that there is a version of AFE which leaves many theists with no option but to reject this personal omniGod conception, and, accordingly, to be committed to some alternative.[6]

Our argument is a *normatively relativized* version of the 'logical' AFE. It arises from recognizing the importance of *the normative assumptions* implicit in attempts to explain how evil may be consistent with the existence of a personal omniGod. Our argument emerges from the dialectic generated by Mackie's AFE, which initially asserted that the existence of any evil at all was inconsistent with the existence of a God who is both perfectly good and all-powerful. That argument fails, if it may be assumed that it is logically possible for God to have a morally adequate reason for permitting some evil. Now, the truth of that assumption needs defence, since morally adequate reasons for permitting preventable evil seem prima facie to arise only from limitations in power. An account of omnipotence as subject to logical limitation does, however, secure the possibility that God may be unable to avoid evils that are *logically* implicated in outweighing goods—and that keeps alive the possibility of a divine 'excuse' for permitting, or indeed, causing evil. That there could really be such an excuse is then established by speculative theodicies that show evils as logically necessary means for, or logically unavoidable side-effects of, important and plausibly outweighing 'higher' goods (such as the 'Vale of Soul Making' theodicy and the Free Will theodicy).[7]

There are many serious sufferings, however, that seem gratuitous—not implicated logically or otherwise in any imaginable outweighing 'higher' good. Proponents of AFE may thus focus specifically on these apparently gratuitous forms of evil, such as the drawn-out suffering of Rowe's (1979) dying fawn badly burnt in a forest fire.[8]

---

[5] There have, for example, been disputes about whether divine omniscience includes foreknowledge of free actions, about how to define omnipotence, and about whether perfect goodness entails impeccability.

[6] See Bishop and Perszyk 2011.

[7] For the Vale of Soul Making theodicy, see John Hick (1978), and for Free Will theodicy, Alvin Plantinga (1974a and 1974b). We agree with Plantinga that 'the aim is not to say what God's reason [for permitting evil] *is*, but at most what God's reason *might possibly be*' (1974a, 28), but we do not follow him in insisting that only a consistency 'defence' (rather than a 'theodicy') is required. We agree with David Lewis (1993, see 151–2) that it will not be enough merely to show that God's existence is logically consistent with the existence of evil: what is needed is a morally adequate reason that could (logically) constrain omnipotence, and 'speculative theodicy' seems the apt name for an account of such a reason.

[8] This specific attention to apparently gratuitous evils was perhaps more fundamental to Rowe's famous refocusing of AFE than the corresponding 'evidential' shift to the conclusion that theistic belief is unreasonable, not because it is outrightly inconsistent with accepting the existence of these evils, but because it is contrary to the weight of the evidence they present.

Notoriously, however, this argument from seemingly pointless evils is open to the 'sceptical theist' reply that, for all we limited creatures know, sufferings that seem pointless *to us* are *in fact* logically implicated in outweighing goods, themselves, perhaps, of a type beyond our knowledge.[9]

Note, however, that speculative theodicies assume that it is consistent with God's moral perfection that he causes or permits evils logically implicated in outweighing 'higher' goods; and sceptical theists make the same assumption, applying it to evils whose logical connection with higher goods is beyond our ken. But this normative assumption is decidedly questionable. The outweighing value of a supremely good end does not necessarily justify using evil means to achieve it, nor putting up with evil side-effects. As Marilyn Adams (1999) puts it, a perfectly good personal God needs to 'defeat' evil: God will ensure he is good *to* each participant in 'horrendous evils', not merely that he 'balances off' these evils against ultimately achieved outweighing goods.[10] Adams has herself offered sophisticated, theologically rich, theodicies that seek to meet these further requirements: the theme of Adams's type of speculative theodicy is that God ultimately defeats horrendous evil by bringing its participants (perpetrators as well as victims) into the fulfilment of eternal relationship with him.[11]

Adams's approach does indeed improve on standard theodicies that merely claim that the goods that implicate evils are good enough to outweigh them.[12] But we doubt whether her improvements are enough. God's perfection as a personal agent has to count as such according to our best theory of that kind of perfection. That best theory, we think, will hold that a perfectly good personal agent maintains, so far as it can, perfectly loving personal relationships with all other persons. Now, the personal omni-God is the creator in the sense that he is the unproduced producer and sustainer of all else that exists.[13] God is thus ultimately, if indirectly, causally responsible for all horrendous evils. So if God does finally bring participants in those evils into the joy of eternal relationship with him, he will be coping with the effects of evils *that he himself ultimately produced*. And we think it is reasonable to hold that the way God would then be related overall to participants in horrors would necessarily not be consistent with

---

[9] This 'sceptical theist' approach was initiated in recent discussion by Stephen Wykstra (1984).

[10] For Adams's explanation of what she means by 'horrendous' evils, see Adams 1999, 26, and for her discussion of the distinction between 'defeating' and 'balancing off' evils, 20–1.

[11] Adams here builds on Hick's theodicy: see Adams 1999, 49–55 and ch. 8.

[12] Adams's approach does have some limitations, however. By placing emphasis on what God can do to defeat *horrendous* evils (evils that prima facie prevent the lives of those who participate in them from being overall worth living), Adams tends to leave in the background (though still unanswered?) the issue of why God permits *ordinary* human—and perhaps more problematically—*non-human animal* suffering. Adams's strategy for an account of God's defeat of horrors—namely, by identifying 'ways that created participation in horrors can be integrated into the participants' relation to God, where God is understood to be the incommensurate Good' (1999, 157)—would seem to require considerable theological innovation if it is to be applicable to Rowe's fawn, for example.

[13] Some of what God produces and sustains is, of course, *directly* produced by producers other than himself, producers that he ultimately produces and sustains as producers.

God's playing a perfectly good part in loving personal relationship.[14] *Relative to* a relationship ethic that sustains this judgement, then, an omnipotent personal God logically could not be perfectly good—and it would thus follow that, if there were such a God who *was* perfectly good he would have to turn away, sadly, from the project of creating finite creatures for eternal relationship with him if that project did indeed entail causing some of them to participate in horrendous evils.

Our argument is thus a *normatively relativized* 'logical' argument from evil (NRLAFE): it maintains that evils allegedly defeated in God's ultimate consummation would still be inconsistent with God's perfect goodness as a personal agent, *relative to* certain reasonable normative commitments about what would constitute such perfect goodness. Our NRLAFE, then, does not claim merely that evil's existence is inconsistent with that of the personal omniGod, but that evil's existence *and its being dealt with in a best attempt to defeat it by the omnipotent personal creator* is inconsistent with that agent's being perfect qua personal agent.

The normative account of perfection as a personal agent to which our NRLAFE appeals deals in the notion of (perfectly) right relationship, rather than just in the notions of right action and good character. We think that theists will generally applaud the idea that the supreme good is, or involves, supremely good relationship amongst persons. Christians, in particular, with their understanding of the Godhead as a Trinity of Persons united in eternal love, will surely be committed to a normative ethics that has at its core an ethics of right relationship. We think it reasonable to conclude, then, that a significant number of theists will agree that serious reasons for doubting whether God can be the personal omniGod are expressed by our NRLAFE.

It may be urged that there is a more accessible NRLAFE, as suggested by the argument Dostoevsky puts into the mouth of Ivan Karamazov. That argument takes the straightforward normative stance that no personal agent who has, but does not exercise, the power to prevent some given evil (for example, the torturing to death of a child) could be morally perfect. Such an NRLAFE is existentially compelling for many—including some theists, who will accordingly have a vital interest in exploring alternatives to the personal omniGod conception of the divine. Other theists, however, will think that this 'Ivan Karamazov' version is theoretically naive, failing to give sufficient weight to God's role as creator—as the unique personal agent who has to decide whether or not to go ahead with the project of realizing the supreme good given that so doing logically implicates terrible evils. We believe that our 'right relationship' NRLAFE may give pause to at least some of these more sophisticated reflective theists, thus deepening the justification for a theist search for alternatives to the personal omniGod.

---

[14] Perhaps, too, the 'horizontal' interpersonal relationships amongst the finite participants in horrors who are ultimately all brought into eternal relationship with God would also be defective (for example, the relationships between Hitler and those whose destruction he devised), though the defect may not be quite the same as the one that affects the 'vertical' relationship between God and participants in horrors. Interesting questions about whether there are limitations on forgiveness and its effectiveness evidently arise here.

Motivating this Argument's Key Normative Judgement

But may not theists reasonably reject the normative judgement on which our 'right relationship' NRLAFE rests—namely, that God's way of relating personally to created persons will be flawed if he first sustains and then seeks to defeat the evil of horrendous suffering?

People who play first a causal then a restoring role in the suffering of others need not, simply on that account, have flawed personal relationships with those sufferers. Compensating for suffering to which one contributed either unintentionally or with good intentions may be consistent with, or even promote, truly loving relationship with the sufferer. What *would* be morally flawed would be to cause suffering, or let it happen, *in order to* then relieve it—with the motive, perhaps, of being hailed as a saving hero. And we think it telling that it's natural to express *what's bad* about such manipulative behaviour by describing it as 'playing God'.

Surely, though, there can be nothing wrong with *God's* playing God? And, in any case, it will be urged, God does not cause horrors *with the intention of* finally defeating them. God allows them for other reasons, well explored in theodicy—for example, he intends there to be significant moral freedom in the creation and must therefore put up with logically implicated evils, yet he willingly accepts ultimate responsibility by achieving a final consummation in which evil is defeated. God's original responsibility for creation implies, however, that, if God does create a world with freedom, horrific evil, and a consummation that supposedly defeats this evil, then *the existence of that whole set up is something God directly intends.* Arguably, it then follows that God *does* cause horrors with the intention of defeating them, since he certainly sustains them with the intention of implementing an overall plan that is completed in their supposed defeat.

To reinforce this last point, consider the case of a doctor who causes a patient intense suffering for the sake of saving him from an otherwise fatal condition and then arranges for a thorough recuperation so effective as to defeat the evil of the suffering. Nothing morally flawed so far—but now add that it is actually the doctor who intended *the whole set up*, including the disease which necessitated the painful intervention. Would the doctor then be secure in claiming that he had not caused the suffering for the sake of relieving it?[15]

It might still be objected, however, that, though God causally sustains horrors, he does not directly—but only obliquely—intend them, since they result from the exercise of creaturely free will that God permits. Since our aim is not to establish as rationally obligatory the judgement that a personal God who first sustains and then redeems evils introduces imperfection into his relationship with creatures, but only to show that this judgement is *a* reasonable one, we are content not to attempt to resolve here the complex issues raised by this objection, but simply to observe that one may reasonably doubt whether the distinction between what is directly and what is obliquely intended can apply to an all-powerful agent whose agency is required to sustain every aspect of the natural universe.

---

[15] See Plantinga's (2004) discussion of 'cosmic Munchausen syndrome by proxy', and our criticisms (Bishop and Perszyk 2011, 123).

It seems, then, that there *are*, after all, grounds for anxiety about God's 'playing God', as the personal omniGod must. If God is both a person and the all-powerful producer and sustainer of all else that exists, he may not be able to relate to created persons in ways consistent with the highest perfection of personal relationship, because he cannot escape playing too dominant a role in those relationships.[16] The Being who is ultimately causally implicated in sustaining each created person's every thought, feeling, and action arguably cannot Itself be a person who could establish with those creatures the best kind of interpersonal loving relationship.

One might try to meet this problem of a personal omniGod being too dominant by a shift in a 'deistic' direction according to which God's creative role is purely original and there is no need for God to sustain creation once it is 'in place'. There are various degrees of this strategy—for example, God's *general* role in sustaining creation might be granted, but an exception made for autonomously free (libertarian) created agents. We are inclined to think that such attempts to place God at a suitable distance from created persons will fail, because we suspect that it is incoherent to take God to be productive creator *ex nihilo* while denying that certain aspects of the creation (in particular, the free actions of autonomous agents) require God's creative activity to sustain them in existence. But, if we are wrong about this, the problem raised by our 'right relationship' NRLAFE remains in any case, even for a 'deistic' personal omniGod who must retain at least original causal responsibility for setting up a Universe in which evil is a known or likely component.

Perhaps it is a mistake, however, to evaluate God's way of relating to created persons from a specifically *moral* perspective? Marilyn Adams appeals to the medieval consensus that it makes no sense to attribute to God any moral *obligations* to his creatures.[17] Yet if divine metaphysics has it that God is literally a person who enters into personal

---

[16] Some personal omniGod theists are sensitive to concern about God's potential dominance in personal relationship with creatures. For example, Eleonore Stump (1979) suggests that petitionary prayer serves as a kind of buffer, safeguarding us from being overwhelmed by God and promoting a close relationship with him. We will not pause, however, to consider this or other potential lines of reply, since our intention is to mention rather than press the wider point that perfectly loving relationship between an omnipotent personal agent and created persons may be altogether impossible. On the subject of prayer, however, we think it pertinent that Christ taught his disciples to address God as 'our *Father*'. Since fathers and mothers are not the producers but the begetters and nurturers of their children, the implication is that we are to relate to God as beloved children and heirs, not as products to their producer.

[17] See Adams 1999, 82–3, for her account of God's 'incommensurate' 'metaphysical' goodness. See also p. 64 for her situating her own 'remodelling' of divine agency as following the classical tradition that 'understands God to be of the wrong metaphysical category to have obligations to creatures'. But that tradition treats cautiously talk of God as a person: Adams emphasizes, however, her 'distinct metaphysical bias' in favour of God's being a person (80–1).

It is also pertinent to note that Adams is uneasy about classifying her account of the compossibility of God's existence with the existence of horrendous evils as a theodicy because she thinks that theodicies operate on the assumption that God's goodness is fundamentally moral goodness. But she is keen, nevertheless, to tell a story whereby God can be good to each created person by guaranteeing a life that is a great good to him or her on the whole, and by defeating horrors within the context of the individual lives of those who participate in them. If we use the term 'theodicy' for any theistic answer as to how theism could be true given actual evils, she is (by her admission elsewhere—Adams and Adams 1990, 3) not only offering a theodicy but an 'explanatory theodicy'.

relationships with created persons, it is hard to see how God's participation in those relationships can escape evaluation in accordance with the relevant moral norms. Locke observed that our modern conception of a person is a forensic one—to be a person is to be capable of bearing moral responsibility for outcomes that occur through one's own agency.[18] To the extent that it is suggested, then, that moral evaluation does not apply to God qua personal agent, so too our grip is loosened on just what is meant by holding that God is a person.[19]

But even if Adams is right to suggest that we here need 'evaluative lenses' other than the moral (1999, 202), we think the force of our 'right relationship' argument will still appear through those different evaluative lenses. Those different evaluative lenses might, for example, be aesthetic. Adams remarks that 'the history of a personal relationship is a story with its own formal aesthetic properties; which ones they are greatly affects the value the relationship contributes to the lives of the persons involved' (1999, 144). But could those 'formal aesthetic properties' be of the finest and best if the overall personal relationship includes one person's sustaining the destruction of the very personhood of the other—for that is what participation in horrors can involve? Would such a defect be capable of being healed? 'Given the horrendous evils God permits,' Adams says, 'God must have extraordinary aesthetic imagination to overcome them' (147). And he *does* overcome them, she thinks, by bringing participants in horrors into the eternal 'contemplation of Divine Beauty', which, she says, 'not only balances off but engulfs participation in horrendous evils' (147). We are prepared to concede that *the evils themselves* may be 'engulfed' in eternal contemplation of divine beauty: our doubt concerns the overcoming of the defect *at the level of the overall relationship* with created persons that we think a personal God would still introduce as the one who sustained the horrors in the first place.

2. The Existential Problem of Evil, Salvation, and 'the God-Role'

So much for the motivation for seeking an alternative to the conception of God as the personal omniGod. What alternatives are there, and how do they fare in the face of the problem of evil? To begin to answer this question we must first consider what governs

---

[18] See John Locke, *An Essay Concerning Human Understanding*, book ii, ch. 27, s. 26.

[19] We think that Adams may have slipped from her apt and compassionate observation that *human* moral wrongdoing cannot account for horrendous evils and her inference (again, apt) that 'moral categories are inadequate to grasp what is so bad about horrendous evil' (1999, 60) to holding that a personal God's relation to horrors must *therefore* transcend questions of moral responsibility. If the Creator God is a person, then surely he *is* inescapably morally responsible for horrors in a way in which no human could possibly be? Elsewhere, Adams seems to admit this: 'Whether one believes in Adam's fall or credits evolution, God is the One Who sets us up in an environment in which we are radically vulnerable to participation in horrors. Primary responsibility for this occurrence must rest with God!' (Adams 2001, 196). We concede that there may be grounds for unease about taking God's responsibility to be moral responsibility—but we think that those grounds will point towards the inadequacy of a personal conception of God.

the acceptability of potential alternatives: from where do we obtain criteria for acceptable conceptions of the divine?

The theist concept of God is the concept of that which plays a certain role in the beliefs and practices of theist 'forms of life'.[20] We may call this 'the God-role'. The adequacy of a particular conception of God is then a matter of whether God on that conception is *fit* to play the God-role. Thus, to the extent that there can be different views about what constitutes the God-role, so there will be different views about what is fit to play that role. Core elements of the God-role seem relatively uncontested, however. God has to be worthy of being 'believed in', where believing in God amounts to a special kind of overall practical commitment, well described by Paul Tillich in terms of 'ultimate concern'. Believers ultimately trust in, and submit wholly to God—they take God as their object of worship—in the faith that so doing promises 'ultimate fulfilment', 'salvation' in more traditional terms.[21]

Mark Johnston has recently suggested a usefully 'religiously neutral' account of salvation and what it is we need to be saved from. Salvation, Johnston proposes, is properly coming to terms with the 'large scale structural defects in human life that no amount of psychological adjustment or practical success can free us from', including 'arbitrary suffering, aging (once it has reached the corrosive stage), our profound ignorance of our condition, the isolation of ordinary self-involvement, the vulnerability of everything we cherish to time and chance, and, finally, to untimely death' (2009, 15).[22] These 'large scale structural defects' count as evils. But there may be a way of living such that we 'overcome', or are 'saved' from, these evils, and it is essential to the God-role that God is the one who brings this salvation. At root, then, there is *an existential* problem of evil—namely, the problem of living in such a way that the evil of these defects is overcome.[23]

If it is essential to the God-role that God enables our resolving this existential problem of evil, it will then not be a *purely* theoretical difficulty if it turns out to be hard to

[20] For further discussion, see Bishop 1998.
[21] See Tillich 2001, 1 and 21.
[22] Johnston focuses on defects at the individual level. We think it important to add the 'large-scale structural defects' of our communal, national, and global *collective* existence: for example, the way in which institutions can cause serious harm despite the generally good intentions of the individuals involved in them; the phenomenon of herd behaviour; our slowness to adapt collectively to dramatically changing contexts—e.g. vastly increased human population, the far-reaching effects of human existence on the environment, etc. Coming to terms with the structural defects of our existence *in its widest context* arguably also requires a proper orientation to the defects in the lives of animals under the 'regime' of evolutionary development, with its millennia of predation, parasitism, and species extinctions.
[23] Johnston points out, in effect, that you do not have to be a theist to recognize this existential problem of evil. Maybe, too, you do not have to be a theist in order to make progress in resolving it. But if you are a theist, your believing in God will be key to your approach to resolving this existential problem, and your concept of God will be of one who brings salvation from being corrupted, overcome, or destroyed by evil. Note that seeking to resolve the existential problem of evil will be an open-ended challenge, continuing throughout life and, on some accounts, beyond it: 'yes' will be a presumptuous answer to the question 'are you saved?', 'I trust that I am being so', closer to the mark (an observation recalled [by Bishop] from a sermon by Kallistos Ware at Vespers at Pusey House, Oxford, 24 January 2009).

understand how this existential problem could have arisen if the God who saves is real. The intellectual difficulty in understanding how evil can arise in God's creation will then be an obstacle to resolving the existential problem through absolute trust in God, and so the intellectual difficulty will have existential importance.[24]

A satisfactory conception of God, then, will have to be such that, under that conception, (1) a significant existential problem of evil arises in the world that God creates; (2) believing in God is believing in that which enables our properly dealing with this problem (in other words, enables our salvation); and (3) believing in God is justifiable given our acceptance of the reality of the evil that gives rise to the problem. It will therefore not be surprising if any serious contender for an adequate conception of God faces some version of the intellectual problem of evil.[25]

3. Varying Conceptions of God, Varying Problems of Evil

It seems plain, then, that an intellectual barrier to resolving the existential problem of evil through trusting in God is likely to arise for any conception of God worth its salt. Those who—like ourselves—find that barrier insurmountable under the personal omniGod conception had better be on guard lest their preferred alternative should generate a problem of evil as bad or worse. Before we outline our 'euteleological' conception of God, we will consider more generally (but with no attempt at comprehensiveness) how alternatives to the personal omniGod may arise, noting the contours of the problems of evil they generate. This will provide useful background for understanding the advantages and disadvantages of our own preferred conception.

Separating Creator from Saviour?

The particular difficulty with the personal omniGod to which we have drawn attention will be removed by any conception of God that separates out the roles of creator and saviour. If God were not the ultimate producer of all that exists, we could celebrate his redeeming work without the unsettling thought that the evil from which he saves us has its ultimate origin in him. But that suggestion seems hopeless, since it is absolutely essential to the God-role that God be creator.

Peter Forrest's (2007) developmental theism, however, *does* tease these two roles apart by positing that God *develops* from a primordial omnipotent producer who creates a Universe that can achieve the supreme good though at great (if ultimately outweighed)

---

[24] Plantinga (1985) thus makes too sharp a distinction between the intellectual problem of evil and the existential/pastoral problem of evil.

[25] This account of how the intellectual problem of evil arises depends on taking it as essential to the God-role that God brings salvation in the face of evil. That assumption is uncontested so far as the Christian tradition is concerned. But there is significant disagreement over what salvation would involve, and how widely it may be achieved—for example, as between Christians whose sympathies are with Calvinism and those who favour universalism.

cost, to a morally perfect being seeking to be good to each creature but—through the kenosis of creation—no longer all-powerful. A related suggestion distinguishes God in the role of designer of universes from God in the role of producer. Evils the designer might properly countenance might yet be evils the producer could not sustain, given the differences between perfect goodness qua designer and qua sustainer. Forrest's speculation offers a way through this dilemma, which might otherwise suggest that a personal omniGod ought to leave the business of creating Universes well alone.

The God of developmental theism may not, perhaps, fall foul of our version of the Argument from Evil. The *developed* God may be morally beyond reproach in his ways of relating to creatures—though perhaps an aesthetic perspective might yet register the shadow of the primordial God. The developmental theist may still confront a problem of evil, however, focused more on God's power than his goodness. Is a God who *now* lacks absolute overall control enough of a power for good to fill the role of trustworthy saviour? We may note, then, an important respect in which the intellectual problem of evil may vary: whether it resides in understanding how God could be good enough to care about saving us given his presiding over the existence of evils in the first place, or whether, granted God's goodness, the problem is to understand how God's power could suffice to deliver us from those evils.[26]

Naturalism about the Divine

The personal omniGod is supernatural. What prospects are there, then, for *naturalism* about the divine? What we mean here by 'naturalism' should not be confused with what might best be called 'natural scientism', which holds that what is real is exhausted by what natural science (at its ideal limit) recognizes as existing. Natural scientism either eliminates the divine altogether or else reduces it to something identifiable within some appropriate natural science—psychology, most likely. Anti-realist or 'constructionist' understandings of God are reductionist in this way, taking God to be a psycho-socially constructed entity in a fiction that functions in advantageous ways—in particular, by encouraging solidarity in commitment to a community's central values.

Naturalism about the divine, by contrast, is wholeheartedly realist. It is 'naturalist' just in the sense that it is 'anti-supernaturalist': it is a religious perspective for which the divine reality is not a *separate*, supernatural, reality, but belongs to one, unified, order

---

[26] Attempts to respond to the Argument from Evil against personal omniGod theism vary according to the extent to which they entertain limits on divine power—and the knowledge on which that power partly depends. For example, open theists take God to lack the middle knowledge attributed by Molinists, and can thereby depict the exercise of God's omnipotence as more constrained in a way which they hope will generate less of a problem in reconciling evils with God's perfect goodness (see, e.g., Hasker 2004, 101–2). Nevertheless, the intellectual difficulty to which they are responding is of the former type: the problem for personal omniGod theists is in understanding how the Supreme Person with all things under his control (however the details of the logical limitations on that control may pan out) could have the goodness to be trusted to save us from evils which could not have existed other than (ultimately) under his control.

of reality.[27] The obvious example of a naturalist concept of the divine is pantheism. If God does not belong to a distinct supernatural order, God must either be constituted by the Universe as a whole, or else by some part or aspect of it. But the supreme onto-logical greatness that God must have (another generally uncontested element in the God-role) excludes the latter alternative, so a theistic naturalism appears committed to identifying as divine the whole of what exists.

But pantheism is not the mere introduction of the term 'God' as a synonym for the Universe. Rather, as Michael Levine (1994) explains, it is commitment to the claim that the Universe has *a certain kind of unity* that is divine. Its constituting such a unity will be beyond the scope of natural scientific theorizing, although it may be true that all that concretely exists is open to description in physical terms (so pantheism may be consistent with a certain kind of 'emergentist' materialism or physicalism). A notional complete physical description of the Whole will, however, fail to capture the all-encompassing divine unity that is realized by what it describes.

Rejecting the Personhood of the Divine

The omniGod is a person, uniquely supreme. Can there be viable conceptions of the divine that reject divine personhood?

If the divine can be understood without taking God to be 'a' person, then the problem of evil focused on God's goodness as a responsible moral agent will be avoided. But the-ists may well be inclined to reject non-personal conceptions out of hand, on the grounds that relating to God as a person is essential to theist religious life and spirituality.

But this may be to confuse what is essential to religious *psychology* with what is essential to religious *understanding*: relating to God as person to person may be psy-chologically essential even though God is not to be understood as a person. Non-personal conceptions of the divine, then, should not *ipso facto* be excluded—though one may expect, in defence of any given non-personal conception, some explanation of the psycho-spiritual sanity of relating in profoundly personal ways to what is not in fact a person.

Pantheist Conceptions as Falling Short of Theism

We think that the most interesting alternative or alternatives to the personal omniGod conception will depart both from its supernaturalism and from its 'personalism'—they will amount, that is, to naturalist and non-personal conceptions of the divine.

We will therefore reflect a little further on pantheism, since it is a non-personal nat-uralism about the divine, although one that fairly obviously falls short of anything that could fit the theist God-role—for at least two reasons.

---

[27] Forrest uses the term 'anti-supernaturalist' in a weaker sense to mean the rejection of divine interven-tion in the natural historical causal order (see Forrest 1996). Forrest's anti-supernaturalism does not, there-fore, make him a theistic naturalist in the sense we are here describing: even if God does not—or even cannot—intervene in the natural historical order, God's reality may still belong firmly to a separate, and higher, ontological order.

Under pantheism God's role as creator reduces to the Universe's status as a creation understood somewhat vaguely as its having 'a certain kind of' unity, 'an interconnect-edness' that somehow 'makes all things one'. But theism, of course, does not reductively identify God with that overall unity, but rather with its source, principle, and ultimate purpose or end.

And the pantheist God seems hardly to fill the saviour role at all—although Michael Levine observes that practical commitment to pantheism may function to 'save' believ-ers from what obstructs their living well. But this, for a theist, is too severely reduced a notion of 'salvation'—as consisting in an ecologically expanded neo-Aristotelian flourishing according to which to function well humanity must relate itself properly to the whole environment of which it is a part.[28]

Pantheist Problems of Evil

What problem of evil—if any—emerges for pantheism? Is there an intellectual prob-lem about how the world could be as pantheism says it is, given the evils whose existen-tial challenge is (putatively) met or assuaged by believing in the pantheist divinity? There will be such a problem if those evils are evidence for the non-existence of the pantheistic unity. But they clearly will not be, since a *pan*theist unity must be one that *encompasses* evil, somehow integrating it into the divine whole.[29]

The idea that a practical orientation towards the pantheist unity might be 'salvific' is not threatened, then, by the existence of evil. What is problematic, though, is the ade-quacy of a pantheist solution to the existential problem of evil. How strong a 'saviour' is the pantheist God, and how worthwhile the 'salvation' such a God may bring? Arguably, pantheists may live more harmoniously with the wider environment—but this 'salvation' is achieved, to the extent that it is, by 'raised consciousness' on the part of humans. Specifically divine saving *action* is not in the picture. Furthermore, given that the pantheist unity encompasses evil, a pantheist orientation may encourage qui-escence in the face of evils that ought rather to be actively opposed—so if that amounts to salvation there is an ethical issue as to whether it is worth having.[30, 31]

---

[28] See Levine 1994, ch. 4.4.

[29] For Levine's own discussion of the problem of evil for pantheism, see his 1994, ch. 4.2. Note that the claim that evil is integrated into the divine pantheist unity need not entail that the divine *itself* is evil even in part, since what counts as divine is *what integrates* all the elements, including evil, into the whole: it may follow, however, that the divine is partly *constituted by* evils.

[30] William James passionately rejected his father's Swedenborgianism on these grounds. James instead adopted a religious worldview for which the universe is 'melioristic', able to be improved by those who will but believe that it is able to be improved (see James 1911, 229).

[31] We make the general observation that conceptions of God as saviour will essentially be correlated with conceptions of what salvation is, and how securely and extensively God's saving action achieves it. These soteriological conceptions will themselves be open to evaluative criticism. (Such criticism was, of course, implicit in our 'right relationship' NRLAFE against personal omniGod theism: the postmortem salvation that a personal omniGod could achieve, even if it involves universal bliss, would not be truly worthwhile—even if, no doubt, one would settle for it if one found oneself in the relevant kind of possible world!)

Johnston's Theology of 'Outpouring' Being

Pantheist 'salvation', furthermore, offers nothing beyond calm acceptance in the face of Johnston's 'large scale structural defects in human life'. Theist religious traditions announce a more robust form of salvation, widely assumed to require both supernatural agency and personal immortality. Johnston, however, rejects supernaturalism and the associated belief in personal immortality as the subtlest of religiously entrenched idolatries, and proposes a naturalist and non-personal conception of God *as adequate for theism*.

According to Johnston, 'The Highest One = the outpouring of Existence Itself by way of its exemplification in ordinary existents for the sake of the self-disclosure of Existence Itself' (2009, 116). Johnston describes his view as 'a process panentheism'. It is pan*en*theistic because it takes God to be 'wholly constituted by the natural realm [, but]...numerically distinct...by virtue of having this different form' (127), that is, as specified on the right hand side of the above identity. And it is a *process* panentheism because the divine is not 'Being itself' (as Johnston maintains—controversially—that it is for Aquinas) but the concrete *activity* of Being's 'outpouring', activity that, he says, 'could be analogically described as Loving, for it is *the self-giving* outpouring of Existence Itself...' (our emphasis, 113).

It is doubtful, however, whether God under this conception can deliver salvation of a suitably robust kind. How does the self-disclosing outpouring of Existence Itself enable our properly dealing with the existential problem of evil—beyond a calm acceptance that a non-theistic pantheism could supply? Indeed, how can it do so, given that some of this 'outpouring', 'analogically describable as Loving', involves serious suffering and the persistence of the large scale defects themselves?[32] Nevertheless, the conceptual space that Johnston opens up seems to us of the first importance, namely the possibility of a conception of God that is non-supernaturalist and non-personal but nevertheless fit to count as genuinely theistic, and, indeed, Christian.

4. A 'Euteleological' Conception of Divinity

We now outline our proposal for an occupant for this conceptual space.[33] Christian belief understands God not only as creator, but also as the ultimate purpose, or end, of all that is. The core of the euteleological conception is that God's being the ultimate supremely good *telos* (end, purpose) of the Universe *is the very same thing* as God's being its ultimate cause. The Universe may then count as a cosmic unity even though it has *no* supernatural

---

[32] For a fuller discussion of Johnston's rejection of supernaturalism and critique of his positive alternative conception of the divine, see Bishop 2012.

[33] This is the same proposal we have made in Bishop and Perszyk 2014, where we placed particular emphasis on considering how a euteleological understanding can accommodate divine action, both in creation and in history. We have since sought to explore the contours of this proposal in more metaphysical detail than we have space for here in Bishop and Perszyk, forthcoming.

producer, and is a creation *ex nihilo* in a quite literal sense. To count as a creation, the Universe must indeed have an overall explanation of its existence *ex nihilo*—an explanation in terms of a creator. But, on the euteleological conception, that explanation does not appeal to the productive action of an agent who is somehow prior to the Universe. That explanation is rather *irreducibly* in terms of the Universe's having an overall end or purpose—a purpose that is actually realized and supremely good. (Hence the 'eu' in 'euteleological': it is not just that the Universe is inherently directed upon the supreme good as its end, but the good news is that this end is actually fulfilled.)

Standardly, teleological explanations reduce to causal explanations. Explaining the Universe's existence as for the sake of the supreme good therefore looks as if it must be reducible to an intentional explanation of the Universe as produced by an agent with that intention—the personal omniGod (or something near enough to it). The euteleological explanation of the Universe's existence, however, is *not* thus reducible. That may make it unique amongst teleological explanations. But explanatory uniqueness is unsurprising, when what is explained is a unique explanandum, the existence of the Universe as a whole.[34]

The euteleological explanation of the Universe's existence has affinities with John Leslie's axiarchic explanation, since both may be broadly described as explaining the Universe in terms of the good. On Leslie's proposal, the Universe exists because it is good that it should do so.[35] On the euteleological proposal, the Universe exists because *it realizes* the supreme good which is its *telos*. Provided one uses the notion of efficient causation in a suitably wide sense, so that an effect's efficient cause is just whatever explains why that effect is actual, our proposal *preserves* the claim that the Universe has an ultimate efficient cause (while denying that this ultimate efficient cause is an Unproduced Producer of all else).[36] Leslie's proposal may also preserve an overall efficient cause, but only if the good can be such a cause, which will require the standard Platonic stance of taking the good to be a transcendently real ideal. On the euteleological account, however, appeal need be made only to immanent realizations of the good.

But what exactly is God, on the euteleological proposal? Is it that God is to be identified with the realized supreme 'telic' good in the Universe? Suppose we accept,

---

[34] In Bishop and Perszyk 2014, we note that the standard account of God as supernatural producer of the Universe also has unique explanatory features insofar as it posits productive action by an immaterial (and, on some views, atemporal) being. We follow Hartshorne in responding to the riposte that divine action is analogous to human agency (on a libertarian, agent-causationist account) by maintaining that 'for the creation-out-of-nothing idea there was no *noncontroversial* analogous phenomenon whatsoever' (Hartshorne 1984, 58). Of course, a viable explanation of the Universe's existence must bear *some* analogy with familiar forms of explanation—but we think an irreducible euteleological explanation meets that requirement in relation to intentional explanation even though reference to a productive causal agent is dropped. With a genuinely irreducible teleological explanation, however, there will be no possibility of explaining, so to say, the mechanism by which it works.

[35] See Leslie 1979, ch. 1 and 1989, ch. 8.

[36] We are much indebted to Thomas Harvey for the observation that the Aristotelian and Thomist conception of efficient causation is broader than our modern understanding which either accepts the Humean reduction of efficient causation to regularity subsumed under natural law or else takes it to be the relation of agent to action, producer to product.

following Christian tradition, the revelation of the nature of the supreme good as love—as perfectly loving personal relationship.[37] Would God then be the sum total of the perfectly loving relationships actually achieved throughout history? But wouldn't such a God be 'too small'—too immanent and too dependent for its existence on a myriad of contingent prior existents?

It may be replied that particular loving relationships would be only *instantiations* of the divine qua supreme telic good—though, *pace* Platonism, these instantiations need not be imperfect with respect to the ideal they instantiate. (The Christian incarnational principle implies that the divine is *fully* manifested within history, paradigmatically, but not exclusively, in Christ: 'God is love, and whoever remains in love remains in God, and God in him.'[38]) These instantiations of the divine do, of course, depend on other contingent beings in the order of productive causality, but the whole point of the euteleological proposal is to suggest that ontological priority need not be priority in the order of productive causality—the divine may thus be ontologically prior to, and the creator of, all else even though it is not the ultimate productive cause of all else.

On the euteleological conception, the divine may be identified, not just with Love, as the supreme good which is the ultimate *telos* of all that exists, but, at the same time, with reality at its most profound or ultimate—that is to say, with reality as inherently directed upon the supreme good, and actually existing only because that end is fulfilled. It is thus essential to the ontological priority of the divine on the euteleological conception that *particular* instantiations or incarnations of it *do not exhaust the divine*—though *that there are* such incarnations is necessary, since the actuality of the Universe could not *be explained* as existing to realize its *telos* if its *telos* were not actually realized.[39] But the divine transcends its particular manifestations through its status as all-encompassing reality existing for the sake of, and only because of, the realization of love, the supreme good. (A further dimension to the transcendence of the divine over its particular manifestations, this time within the natural Universe, will emerge below.[40])

---

[37] This Christian account of the supreme good may avoid the risk of anthropocentricity if perfectly loving personal relationship is understood as one species of the supreme good of a wider relational genus (in which non-personal beings may in principle participate). It is a task for Christian ethics to give a substantive account of the nature of love and loving relationship, drawing on scriptural understandings of *agape* and theological ideas such as the *perichoretic* dynamic of intra-Trinitarian relationships.

[38] I John 4: 16 (New Jerusalem Bible). Consistently 'remaining in love', and so incarnating the divine, may indeed be unique to Christ ('The Incarnation')—yet *wherever* there is authentic love, nothing is then lacking of the essential character of the divine. Keeping the 'new commandment' to love one another as Christ has loved us is not (under divine grace) an impossibility, and when that commandment is kept there is no 'mere approximation' to the ideal.

[39] The fact that incarnation is essential to divinity is expressed in Christianity, of course, by the Incarnate Word's status as Second Person of the Trinity. We note also that the idea that a particular incarnation—indeed Christ, The Incarnation—may depend on other beings in the order of productive causality seems entrenched in Christian tradition: witness the acceptance of Mary as *theotokos* ('God-bearer') at the Council of Ephesus in 431.

[40] This euteleological conception may fairly be described as a *panentheist* conception of the divine. The *Oxford Dictionary of the Christian Church* defines 'panentheism' as 'the belief that the Being of God includes and penetrates the whole universe, so that every part of it exists in Him, but (as against pantheism) that His Being is more than, and

Problems of Evil for a Euteleological Conception

Since, on the euteleological account, God is not a person, the problem of God's moral responsibility for evil does not arise. On the euteleological conception, God is not the ultimate productive cause of evil—though 'he' remains the ultimate explainer of its existence. The evils and defects of existence may be explained as inherent in the evolutionary development under natural law of sufficient levels of physical complexity for the realization of the supreme good to be a real possibility. However, on the euteleological conception, no supreme agent is personally responsible for the decision to actualize such an evolutionary development. (Of course, finite evolved persons *are* partly causally responsible for some evils, and, under certain conditions, bear a degree of moral responsibility for them as well.)

The other kind of intellectual difficulty in trusting God in resolving the existential problem of evil does, however, arise for the euteleological conception. Is the God who is Love, the ultimate *telos* of the Universe whose realization explains its very existence, *powerful enough* to be rightly trusted for *worthwhile* salvation from evil? Without supernatural personal agency, how could the divine love be *effective* for salvation? And how widely could salvation be achieved?

In response, euteleological theists may add to their basic claim that realized love ultimately (but *not* productively) explains why the Universe exists, a further claim which *is* about productive causal power—namely a claim about the productive power of realized love *within* the Universe. This further claim is precisely that love *is* able to bring salvation—a worthwhile resolving of the existential problem of evil. This salvific power of love, though not supernatural, may nevertheless count as *transcendent*, in the sense that it is an emergent power (the power of something *relational*) whose operations could not be the object of any *scientific* understanding.[41] There is widespread witness to the salvific power of love in the Christian scriptural/ecclesial tradition.[42] Yet, in the experience of that tradition, the divine power to save is not an all-controlling power—in that mode it appears weak—but rather it is gently persuasive, relentlessly inventive, and ultimately victorious.[43]

---

is not exhausted by the universe' (Cross and Livingstone 2005,1221). (For a historical overview of panentheism, see Cooper 2006, chs 2–13.) While the above is widely accepted as a generic definition of 'panentheism', its usefulness may be questioned: for example, to say that 'the Being of God includes and penetrates the whole universe' does little more than repeat the literal meaning of 'pan-en-theism' (all-in-God) without explaining what 'in God' is supposed to mean. Different types of panentheism may result in part from different attempts to explicate this notion. For further discussion, see, for example, Clayton and Peacocke 2004.

[41] Nevertheless, an understanding of the power of love, as the power of something relational, may need to rest (through analogy at least) on a scientific understanding of how powers emerge out of complex interrelation of entities.

[42] Much more needs saying, of course, about how the power of love can be salvific, enabling our properly coming to terms with Johnston's 'large scale structural defects'. A Christian moral psychology will have at its core an account of the transformative power of divine love to overcome self-centredness and replace it with what Hick (1989) calls 'Reality-centredness'. Christian moral psychology may be contested, of course (by Nietzscheans, for instance): our point here is just that it may fairly be presupposed by a Christian euteleological conception of the divine.

[43] Here the euteleological theist takes a leaf from the process theist's book. See n. 4.

How secure and complete a victory could the power of love achieve, though? Not the universalist victory as Adams understands it, in which all participants in horrendous evils ultimately come to share in everlasting relationship with God. Supernatural power seems clearly required for such an outcome. But it seems to be required, too, on other conceptions of a final and just consummation, such as Kant's, in which all and only those who deserve happiness are ultimately made happy, or Stump's (2010), where all created persons obtain their heart's desire, with the saved enabled by transformative grace to desire eternal union with God.[44]

If there is no overarching supernatural control, and 'all' we have to rely on for salvation by divine agency is the power of love within creation, that power may seem too weak to deserve our ultimate trust. Participating fully in perfectly loving relationship may indeed constitute worthwhile salvation (perfect love casts out fear, enabling us properly to come to terms with evil, sin, and death).[45] What may seem doubtful, however, is whether love's productive power for good is powerful enough to ground hope that this salvation is achievable.

But is there not a worse problem for the euteleological proposal—a threatened return to an argument from evil? We agree that a significant problem of evil *does* remain for euteleological theism even though it avoids the specific version focused on the implications of evil for God's moral perfection as a personal agent. The problem is that actual evils and defects count against the world's being as euteleological theism says it is. Arguably, the nature and extent of actual evils and defects are *evidence* that the supreme good of loving relationship is *not* the ultimately explanatory *telos* of the Universe, and any 'salvation' achieved by participation in perfect love is purely a happy accident.

We argued earlier, however,[46] that commitment to the reality of the divine under any viable conception will be *bound* to face a problem of evil. There is a general problem of evil counting against the existence of a God who brings salvation and enables our

---

[44] On the question of the extent of salvation, we think that a personal omniGod would do his best to save all, and universal salvation would then be secured unless a finite will could eternally resist divine salvific power. Yet a God who is *not* a person with supernatural control might still count as saviour even though only 'an elect' are saved. (The Calvinist stance that seems ethically excluded for personal omniGod theism might thus lose its offensiveness on a non-personal conception of the divine—though 'election' would then need to be understood analogically, and not as involving anyone's making a decision as to who is in and who is out.) That God saves even though salvation may not be universal is, anyway, the view that euteleological theists will need to take. Since Christians have been notably divided over how bearable it would be for not all to be saved, the fact that salvation may not be universal on the euteleological conception is not by itself enough to dismiss it.

[45] Euteleological Christian theism may thus share with Marilyn Adams the view that salvation consists in being brought into full relationship with God. It may also follow Adams in agreeing that being in full relationship with God is an incommensurable good. Of course, since, on the euteleological view, God is not 'a' person, it will have to be explained how relating personally to what is not a person is both a sane psychological possibility, and, plausibly, an essential component of participation in the supreme good. While we believe that such an explanation can be given, the required discussion in the psychology and phenomenology of theistic religious commitment is beyond our present scope.

[46] See section 2.

coming properly to terms with evil. Evil from which we desire to be 'delivered' is—or, at least, is experienced as—inherently *dysteleological*. That is to say, the very existence of such evil is naturally taken as indicating the *absence* of any ultimate or overall 'well ordering' that overcomes or 'properly deals with' it. This general dysteleological problem of evil applies—in different ways—to different conceptions of the God who saves from evil.[47]

This wider problem of evil as it affects the euteleological proposal does not yield a 'logical' Argument from Evil, however, since there seems no *inconsistency* in accepting the existence of actual evils while also holding that the realized supreme good both explains the Universe's existence and exercises saving power within it. But an 'evidential' or 'inductive' Argument from Evil *does* confront euteleological theism, since the evidence of actual evil is arguably evidence against the truth of the euteleological scenario.

That the nature and extent of evil in the Universe makes the falsity of euteleological theism more likely than not may indeed be the reasonable view—*from a position of initial neutrality*. For euteleological Christians, however, their overall view of the world (based as it is on a claim to revelation) may also be *a* reasonable one, making sense of the existence of actual evils coherently with the reality of a God who saves. A crucial— here, just the right word—factor in this coherence is the revealed Good News (i) that living steadfastly in truly loving relationship ('carrying out the divine will') is a genuinely achievable ideal for human beings, even in contexts of injustice, persecution, and violence, and (ii) that when this ideal is achieved it carries a power for good whose greatness transcends any conceivable measure.

This revealed Good News is enacted in the death and resurrection of Christ. On a non-supernaturalist view (such as the euteleological theist's), Christ's love in his passion so resonates with the purpose of existence, decisively demonstrating its ultimacy, that there is resurrection—not a restoration of the *status quo ante*, but a transformation into new life boundlessly fertile in its self-giving that others may undergo the same rebirth. Christological resources are thus needed in response to the dysteleological problem of evil faced by the euteleological conception of the divine (though it need not follow that such a conception could fit only a Christian theism, since it may be that other kinds of revelatory grounded resources fill the same functional role as Christology for other theist religious traditions).

The fact that such an appeal must be made to specific—Christological—resources drawn from revelation is, we think, dialectically quite in order. Christian belief in the God who saves from evil is undermined only if evil's existence, in its actual character and extent, provides decisive intellectual grounds *from the Christian's own perspective*

---

[47] Hick uses the term 'dysteleological evils' to mean evils which apparently do not promote soul-making—and he boldly argues that the mystery this creates is conducive to soul-making. (See Hick 1978, 330–1, discussed by Adams 1999, 52.) We are here using the term differently, following Thomas Harvey (unpublished essay), who draws attention to our need for a term for the wider problem of evil counting against the existence of any God who can supposedly save us from it.

for holding that there can be no such God. We have argued that evil may well provide such grounds when the Christian's perspective affirms that God is the personal omni-God—at least when that perspective also includes an ethical stance under which whatever the personal God does to try to cope with evil he cannot avoid introducing a flaw into the overall personal relationships he has with created persons. For Christians who adopt the euteleological conception of God, however, there is no similar obstacle—and the obstacle posed by the dysteleological evidential force of evil may be countered by appeal to the (claimed) revealed truth of traditional Christological doctrines.[48]

To provide a full defence of the reasonableness of a Christian euteleological theism, then, it would be necessary to show that a viable Christology can be maintained under the euteleological conception of divinity, even though God is not a supernatural person under this conception. It will also be necessary, furthermore, to defend the reasonableness of accepting truth-claims as divinely revealed, both in general, and specifically for the case of the Christological doctrines. We can take up neither of these major challenges here. For the present we will be satisfied if we have managed to recommend, as worthy of further consideration, a theistic perspective from which there is no supernatural personal omniGod, yet a worthwhile Christian resolution of the existential problem of evil may still be had based on a non-supernaturalist, non-personal, euteleological conception of the God who saves as the Love which is the Omega and thereby also the Alpha.[49]

References

Adams, M. (1999). *Horrendous Evils and the Goodness of God*. Ithaca, NY: Cornell University Press.
Adams, M. (2001). Afterward, in S. Davis (ed.), *Encountering Evil: Live Options in Theodicy* (pp. 191–203). Louisville, KY: Westminster John Knox.
Adams, M. (2006). *Christ and Horrors: The Coherence of Christology*. Cambridge: Cambridge University Press.
Adams, M. and Adams, R. (eds) (1990). *The Problem of Evil*. Oxford: Oxford University Press.

[48] Our response to the problem of evil thus agrees with Marilyn Adams in accepting the importance of theological content that goes beyond the bounds of 'restricted' theism. Adams has made a notable contribution to Christology in her response to the problem of evil (see Adams 2006). A euteleological Christology would no doubt look significantly different from hers.

[49] We are grateful for helpful comments and criticisms from audiences at a workshop organized by Nick Trakakis at the Australian Catholic University in Melbourne (21 June 2012), at a workshop at the University of Birmingham on 'Alternative Concepts of God' organized by Yujin Nagasawa and Andrei Buckareff (19–20 July 2012), and at the Philosophy Research Seminar at the University of Glasgow (4 December 2012). In particular, we wish to thank Thomas Harvey for valuable comments and suggestions, and each of the following individuals, who kindly acted as commentators at the workshops mentioned: Marilyn McCord Adams, Andrew Gleeson, Bruce Langtry, and Graham Oppy (at the Melbourne workshop), and Sarah Coakley, and Hugh McCann (at the Birmingham workshop). These commentators have set us a challenging and wide-ranging agenda for further development and defence of a euteleological conception of the divine: though their comments have prompted significant changes to earlier versions of this chapter, we have made no attempt to deal here with all the issues raised.

Bishop, J. (1998). 'Can There be Alternative Concepts of God?', *Noûs* 32: 174–88.

Bishop, J. (2012). 'In Quest of Authentic Divinity: Critical Notice of Mark Johnston's *Saving God: Religion after Idolatry*', *European Journal for Philosophy of Religion* 4/4: 175–91.

Bishop, J. and Perszyk, K. (2011). 'The Normatively Relativised Logical Argument from Evil', *International Journal for Philosophy of Religion* 70: 109–26.

Bishop, J. and Perszyk, K. (2014). 'Divine Action beyond the Personal OmniGod', in J. Kvanvig (ed.), *Oxford Studies in Philosophy of Religion*, vol. 5 (pp. 1–21). Oxford: Oxford University Press.

Bishop, J. and Perszyk, K. (forthcoming). 'A Euteleological Conception of Divinity and Divine Agency', in Thomas Schärtl, Christian Tapp, and Veronika Wegener (eds), *Rethinking the Concept of a Personal God*. Münster: Aschendorff.

Clayton, P. and Peacocke, A. (eds) (2004). *In Whom We Live and Move and Have Our Being: Panentheistic Reflections on God's Presence in a Scientific World*. Grand Rapids, Mich.: William Eerdmans Publishing Company.

Cobb, J. and Griffin, D. R. (1976). *Process Theology: An Introduction*. Philadelphia: Westminster.

Cooper, J. (2006). *Panentheism: The Other God of the Philosophers—From Plato to the Present*. Grand Rapids, MI: Baker.

Cross, F. L. and Livingstone, E. A. (eds) (2005). *The Oxford Dictionary of the Christian Church*, 3rd edn revised. Oxford: Oxford University Press.

Forrest, P. (1996). *God without the Supernatural: A Defense of Scientific Theism*. Ithaca, NY: Cornell University Press.

Forrest, P. (2007). *Developmental Theism: From Pure Will to Unbounded Love*. Oxford: Clarendon Press.

Hartshorne, C. (1984). *Omnipotence and Other Theological Mistakes*. Albany, NY: State University of New York Press.

Hasker, W. (2004). *Providence, Evil and the Openness of God*. London and New York: Routledge.

Hick, J. (1978 [1966]). *Evil and the God of Love*. New York: Harper and Row.

Hick, J. (1989). *An Interpretation of Religion*. New Haven: Yale University Press.

James, W. (1911). *Some Problems of Philosophy: A Beginning of an Introduction to Philosophy*. New York: Longmans, Green.

Johnston, M. (2009). *Saving God: Religion after Idolatry*. Princeton: Princeton University Press.

Leslie, J. (1979). *Value and Existence*. Oxford: Basil Blackwell.

Leslie, J. (1989). *Universes*. London: Routledge.

Levine, M. (1994). *Pantheism: A Non-Theistic Concept of Deity*. London: Routledge.

Lewis, D. (1993). 'Evil for Freedom's Sake?', *Philosophical Papers* 22: 149–72.

McCloskey, H. J. (1960). 'God and Evil', *Philosophical Quarterly* 10: 97–114.

Mackie, J. L. (1955). 'Evil and Omnipotence', *Mind* 64: 200–12.

Plantinga, A. (1974a). *God, Freedom, and Evil*. Grand Rapids, MI: Eerdmans.

Plantinga, A. (1974b). *The Nature of Necessity*. Oxford: Clarendon Press.

Plantinga, A. (1985). 'Self-Profile', in J. Tomberlin and P. van Inwagen (eds), *Alvin Plantinga* (pp. 3–97). Dordrecht: D. Reidel.

Plantinga, A. (2000). *Warranted Christian Belief*. Oxford: Oxford University Press.

Plantinga, A. (2004). 'Supralapsarianism or "*O felix culpa*"', in P. van Inwagen (ed.), *Christian Faith and the Problem of Evil* (pp. 1–25). Grand Rapids, MI: Eerdmans.

Rowe, W. (1979). 'The Problem of Evil and Some Varieties of Atheism', *American Philosophical Quarterly* 16: 335–41.

Stump, E. (1979). 'Petitionary Prayer', *American Philosophical Quarterly* 16: 81–91.

Stump, E. (2010). *Wandering in Darkness: Narrative and the Problem of Evil*. Oxford: Clarendon Press.

Tillich, P. (2001 [1957]). *Dynamics of Faith*. New York: Harper & Row/Harper-Collins Publishers.

Wykstra, S. (1984). 'The Humean Obstacle to Evidential Arguments from Suffering: On Avoiding the Evils of "Appearance"', *International Journal for Philosophy of Religion* 16: 73–94.

7

Horrors

To What End?

Marilyn McCord Adams

1. Personal Omni-God versus Alternative-God

In a series of solo and joint papers,[1] John Bishop and Ken Perszyk take the problem of horrendous evils seriously.[2] Horrors are not small, medium, or large-scale evils, but evils of a prima facie life-ruinous kind. For Bishop and Perszyk, the existence of horrors drives them to theological reconstruction. Beginning with the Christian conception of (what they style) "personal omni-God" (that is, God conceived of as omniscient, omnipotent, and perfectly good), they mount a Norm-Relative Logical Argument from Evil (NRLAFE, for short) that no such God exists. Their NRLAFE constitutes their negative case. Then they forward their own positive proposal, the (what I shall call) "alternative-God" of euteleology.

Bishop and Perszyk reckon that not just anything could qualify as God. Replacements for personal omni-God would have to be credible fillers of two theoretical roles: Creator, the ultimate explainer of the world's existence; and Savior, the one who rescues created persons from evils.[3] Moreover, Bishop and Perszyk take it as fixed that whatever counts as God must be perfectly good. They recognize that norms are philosophically contentious; unanimity about them among rational philosophers is not to be had. They style their argument from horrors against the existence of personal omni-God "norm-relative" because it rests on their distinctive construal of "perfect

---

[1] John Bishop, "How a Modest Fideism may Constrain Theistic Commitments: Exploring an Alternative to Classical Theism," *Philosophia* 35 (2007), 387–402; "Towards a Religiously Adequate Alternative to OmniGod Theism," *Sophia* 48 (2009), 419–33; John Bishop and Ken Perszyk, "The Normatively Relativised Logical Argument from Evil," *International Journal of the Philosophy of Religion* 70 (2011), 109–26; "Concepts of God and Problems of Evil," Chapter 6 in the present volume, 106–27.

[2] See Bishop, "How a Modest Fideism may Constrain Theistic Commitments," 393–4; "Towards a Religiously Adequate Alternative to OmniGod Theism," 426–8; Bishop and Perszyk, "Concepts of God and Problems of Evil," s. 1, 108–10.

[3] Bishop, "Towards a Religiously Adequate Alternative to OmniGod Theism," 420–1; Bishop and Perszyk, "Concepts of God and Problems of Evil," ss 2–3, 113–19.

goodness" in terms of perfectly loving relationality (as opposed, say, to retributive justice). They insist that their ethics of right relationship can find Christian inspiration (say, in traditional doctrines of the Trinity or in the love commandments), while stressing that their LAFE (Logical Problem of Evil) is NRLAFE because it will be sure to convince only those who understand "perfect goodness" their way.[4]

In fact, Bishop and Perszyk seem to offer several distinct arguments for their negative conclusion, and these rest on two further assumptions about how personal omni-God would fill the Creator-role:

omni-God would fill the Creator-role by being the efficient productive and sustaining cause of all else,

and

[Q] in creating and sustaining, personal omni-God would exercise meticulous providence over all that happens in creation.

[P] combines with the existence of horrors to imply that personal omni-God would produce and sustain the horrors from which It then saved people.

[Argument 1] Bishop and Perszyk are convinced that

[R] if a person X produces and sustains the horrors from which X rescues another person Y, then X cannot be in right relationship with Y.

Both solo and joint articles express the sense that—in view of horrors—there would be something morally deficient in personal omni-God's *combining* the Creator and Savior roles.[5] [Argument 2] Bishop also suggests that personal omni-God who created a world with horrors *would not be able* to occupy the Savior-role at the same time. For to save created horror-participants would mean establishing a perfectly loving relationship between God and creatures. But not even God can alter the past. Once God has produced the horrors from which creatures suffer, God will never be able to erase that blot on their relationship history and so will never be able to set things right.[6] [Argument 3] This last suggests that the real and sufficient difficulty is with personal omni-God's producing and sustaining horrors in the first place.[7] [Argument 4] Bishop offers yet another argument that has nothing to do with horrors. Rather he suggests

[4] Bishop, "Towards a Religiously Adequate Alternative to OmniGod Theism," 425; Bishop and Perszyk, "The Normatively Relativized Logical Argument from Evil," 114–15; "Concepts of God and Problems of Evil," s. 1, 108–13.
[5] Bishop, "How a Modest Fideism may Constrain Theistic Commitments: Exploring an Alternative to Classical Theism," 397; Bishop and Perszyk, "The Normatively Relativised Logical Argument from Evil," 121–2; "Concepts of God and Problems of Evil," s. 1, 111–13.
[6] Bishop, "Towards a Religiously Adequate Alternative to OmniGod Theism," 427–8.
[7] Bishop, "Towards a Religiously Adequate Alternative to OmniGod Theism," 428; Bishop and Perszyk, "The Normatively Relativised Logical Argument from Evil," 121–2.

that personal omni-God's relations with created persons would fall short of perfect love, because—by [Q]—God would be utterly manipulative in relation to them.[8]

Turning to their positive case, Bishop and Perszyk recommend replacing personal omni-God with alternative-God. Like personal omni-God, alternative-God is the supreme good, which Bishop and Perszyk construe in terms of their norm of perfectly loving relationality.[9] Alternative-God fills the Creator-role, not by being the efficient productive and sustaining cause of all else, but by being the "ultimate end," "the purpose," "the overall point," that for the sake of which the universe ultimately exists. Alternative-God fills the Savior-role, because the "transcendent power" of love conquers evil.

For my part, I am unpersuaded by Bishop's and Perszyk's NRLAFE, and so remain as devoted to personal omni-God as ever.[10] In this chapter, however, I want to bracket worries about their negative case to focus instead on their positive position and on the alternative-God they offer us. Bishop and Perszyk are not the first to hold that God is the end or final cause, but not the efficient or productive cause of the universe.[11] Aristotle assigned the unmoved mover that job. But teleology is and was a murky subject. What does it mean to identify alternative-God as ultimate end? In what follows, I will review some ancient and medieval understandings and difficulties, in an effort to shed light on the theologically reconstructive moves that Bishop and Perszyk are making. If I have got them wrong, my array of alternatives may at least help to make explicit what they do not mean to say.

2. Ends and Explanations

2.1 Aristotelian Roots

In *Physics* II.3, Aristotle sets out a theory of explanation that is multi-dimensional. If we ask "why does X exist?" or "what accounts for the existence of X?" four different kinds of causes or explanatory factors are relevant. One may respond by mentioning [i] the matter out of which X comes to be and which persists as a constituent of X [= the material cause of X], or [ii] the form or definition or parts of the definition of the essence of X [= the formal cause of X], or [iii] what brings about X's coming to

[8] Bishop, "How a Modest Fideism may Constrain Theistic Commitments," 395; "The Normatively Relativised Logical Argument from Evil," 123–4.

[9] Bishop, "How a Modest Fideism may Constrain Theistic Commitments," 397–9; "Towards a Religiously Adequate Alternative to OmniGod Theism," 431–2; Bishop and Perszyk, "Concepts of God and Problems of Evil," s. 1, 107–13 and s. 4, 120–1.

[10] I lay out my reply to their positive case in "Ignorance, Instrumentality, Compensation, and the Problem of Evil," *Sophia*, 52.1 (2013), 7–26.

[11] Bishop, "How a Modest Fideism may Constrain Theistic Commitments," 400–1; "Towards a Religiously Adequate Alternative to OmniGod Theism," 429–32; Bishop and Perszyk, "Concepts of God and Problems of Evil," s. 1, 107 and s. 4, 119–21.

be [= the efficient cause of X], or [iv] the end or "that for the sake of which" X comes to be [= the final cause of X].[12]

Aristotle's first example of a final cause is health, for the sake of which the agent might take a walk, take a purge, swallow drugs, or submit to surgery. Health is the goal that explains why the agent would do or suffer these latter things.[13] Thus, for Aristotle, *the paradigm of acting for the sake of an end is the action of an intelligent voluntary agent*. Aristotle also suggests that the end for the sake of which other things are done or suffered is not merely *last*, but also *a good or at least an apparent good*.[14]

What about non-rational natural agents? All parties to the dispute agree that there are regular determinate sequences in nature, sequences that have characteristic end-points. They also concur that for many, even all natural kinds, there are regular determinate sequences whose end-points are the last perfecting form or function for things of that kind. But this would not be enough to make those end-points *final causes*, because causes are supposed to have *explanatory value* in relation to the agent's actions and effects. *How does being merely last and best explain what went before?*

When Aristotle contends that nature is like art, he relies on analogies to persuade us to find something like the rational agent's cognition (intention) and appetite in non-rational natural agents as well. He asks us to consider, what if the shipbuilder's art were in the wood instead of the shipbuilder's mind? The ship would be produced by the same process then as now. But now the shipbuilder intends to produce a ship, and his art dictates that to fulfill this goal he should produce X for the sake of Y and Y for the sake of Z and Z for the sake of the ship. If the art were in the wood, it would direct wood-development towards the same end (= the ship) and take it through the same set of ordered changes. To persuade us that such natural wood-development was teleological and not merely naturally necessary, Aristotle would need to get the intentionality of the artist (that purposes the end and the sequences for the sake of the end) into the wood.[15]

Aristotle concludes that in nature there are to be found natural necessities (always-or-for-the-most-part regularities) that are for the sake of an end. He thinks this is most obvious in the case of non-human animals (e.g., by nature and for the sake of an end, the swallow builds a nest and the spider spins its web). But he finds it also true where plants are concerned (e.g., plants grow leaves for the sake of fruit and send down roots for the sake of nourishment).[16]

2.2 "Platonizing" Sources

In *Physics* II, Aristotle is concerned with *agents acting* for the sake of an end. By contrast, in the *Monologion* and *De Veritate*, Anselm is more focused on the ends of *natures*. Anselm does not use the word "end" (*finis*) but speaks of that-for-which-a-thing-was-made-or-came-to-be (*ad quod factum est*) and that-for-which-the-powers-were-given.

---

[12] Aristotle, *Physics* II.3.194a24–35.   [13] Aristotle, *Physics* II.3.194a24–35.
[14] Aristotle, *Physics* II.3.195a23–25.   [15] Aristotle, *Physics* II.8.199b28–31.
[16] Aristotle, *Physics* II.8.199a20–30.

Anselm's picture is that the end (the perfection that is the goal) explains why the nature includes certain powers and not others.[17] Anselm holds (as do Aquinas and Henry of Ghent) that creatable natures are at bottom ways of imperfectly imitating the Divine essence.[18] The powers are given to enable beings of that nature to strive towards Divine being a certain way. This gives the natures an ec-static reach that makes God the ultimate end of every creatable nature. Each nature also has a proximate end: to use Aristotle's language, the perfecting form or functional state that is normative for that nature. Because bovinity is aimed at grass-munching and cud-chewing activities, digestive, reproductive, and locomotive powers (powers to do "the cow-thing") are given. Because humanity is aimed at ranking goods and loving them in proportion to their worth, reason is given for discerning and evaluating, while will-power is given for loving accordingly.[19]

On this understanding, *creatable* natures have a double teleological structure, but the Supreme Nature (= Supreme Goodness = the Divine essence) does not.[20] Its power is not bent on striving to be something else. It *is* maximal being, goodness, and excellence.[21] Rather the Divine essence functions as the ultimate end of creatable natures insofar as It is an exemplar, form, or rule.[22] Creatable natures strive with all of their powers to be Supreme Goodness, but their powers are insufficient to be It and instead they reach only their proximate end or the last perfecting form or functional state of the creatable natural kind.

Where creatable natures are concerned, however, all of them have ends, whether animate or inanimate, rational or non-rational. Therefore, this notion—that creatable *natures* have ends to which their constitutive powers incline them, ends which have explanatory value insofar as they are *prior to* and *explain why* the nature is constituted by these rather than those powers—seemed to reinforce the conclusion drawn from Aristotle's analogy between art and nature. Likewise, it seemed to fit with Aristotelian talk of natures having appetites or natural inclinations for their last perfecting forms or functional states.

Putting these ideas together, Aquinas uses his doctrine of Divine ideas to make good on Aristotle's reasoning about the shipbuilder and the wood: God is the cosmic artist.[23] God's art is the Divine ideas of creatable natures, which are in turn God's cognition of the Divine essence as imperfectly imitable this way, that way, and the other way (e.g., bovinely, oakishly, fire-wise).[24] When God creates, it is that very intelligible content in

[17] Anselm, *Monologion* 68–9; Schmitt I: 78–9; *De Veritate* 3; Schmitt I:180–2; *De Veritate* 5; Schmitt I: 191.27–192.14.

[18] Anselm, *Monologion* 31; Schmitt I: 48.13–50.13.

[19] Anselm, *Monologion* 68–9; Schmitt I: 79.1–9, 13–18.

[20] Anselm, *Monologion* 17; Schmitt I: 31.15–18; *De Veritate* 10; Schmitt I: 190.1–4.

[21] Anselm, *Monologion* 15–16; Schmitt I: 128.1–131.8.

[22] Anselm, *Monologion* 9; Schmitt I: 24.10–14.

[23] Aquinas, *Summa Theologica* I, q. 2, a. 3, where his premise is that things without cognition must be directed to an end by something that has cognition.

[24] Aquinas, *Summa Theologica* I, q. 14, a. 5 c; q. 15, a. 1 c. See also *Summa Theologica* I, q. 58, aa. 6–7.

God's mind that comes to exist in the particular thing as its essence. In God's intention, the determinate causal sequences built into the nature is God's Divine-art-dictated means to getting a perfect specimen of—say—bovinity and to getting this sort of Godlikeness represented in the real world. It is the fact that the Divine art *is in nature* that allows us to say that these naturally necessary actions are for the sake of an end. Because the Divine intentionality is what makes the naturally necessary sequence teleological, one can say—as Aquinas does—that natural agents are *externally ordered* to the end. But on Aquinas' scheme, they do not fail to be *somehow self-ordered* insofar as the Divine art is *their* nature. This self-ordering gets "cashed" in terms of the natural agent's having built-in natural inclinations.[25]

2.3 Ends and Values

Likewise, this Platonizing rationale for discovering ends in creatable natures links ends with normativity. The Divine essence is the exemplar that all creatable natures imperfectly approximate. The proximate end for the sake of which the powers are given defines the norm for what the species actually can reach. Ranking goods, reason dictates that Supreme Goodness (a being a greater than which cannot be conceived) should be loved the most, above all and for its own sake, whereas lesser goods are to be loved for Its sake. Likewise, nature-constituting powers drive a nature towards its last perfecting form or nature, acquiring which enables things that have that nature to be perfect specimens.

This conclusion seemed to resonate with ideas in Aristotelian action theory: that the ultimate end is loved for its own sake and others insofar as they are ordered (as means) to that end. Thus, if Z is the end, the goodness of Z plus X's and Y's ordering to Z as means, together furnish an agent with reason for willing X or Y. Moreover, because it is irrational (contrary to right reason) to will the greater for the sake of the lesser good, right reason dictates that ends should be better than means, and the ultimate end noblest of all. Thus, we find Scotus arguing that the most eminent being must be the first final cause, because it would be altogether inappropriate to order the most eminent being as a means to some lesser good as an end.[26]

2.4 Re-Psychologizing Final Causality

Nevertheless, Scotus and Ockham find the notion of explanatory ends in nature problematic. Against Anselm, Aquinas, and Henry of Ghent, Scotus contends (and Ockham agrees) that creatable natures are not constituted at metaphysical bottom by imitability relations. To be sure, creatable natures *are* imperfectly similar to the Divine essence. But relata are metaphysically prior to their relations. Creatable natures are constituted

---

[25] Aquinas, *Expositio in Libros Physicorum Aristotelis*, Book II, Lectio 14, n. 8 [71799].

[26] Scotus, *De Primo Principio*, c. 2, n.11; Wadding III.219–20. See also Allan B. Wolter and Marilyn McCord Adams, "Duns Scotus's Parisian Proof for the Existence of God," *Franciscan Studies* 42 (1982), 248–321; esp. 250–1.

as definable by this genus and that differentia, prior in the order of explanation to their being imperfectly similar to Godhead. It follows that creatable natures do not in themselves, by their very metaphysical constitution, have a transcendent teleological reach. Scotus and Ockham agree, it pertains to creatable natures to be constituted as they are (e.g., that species S is defined by genus G and differentia D) of themselves. So to be constituted pertains to them of metaphysical necessity and does not require any further explanation.[27]

Accordingly, Scotus returns his attention to Aristotle's original position: what needs to be explained is the existence of things and the actions of agents. Distinguishing between end-points and final causes, Scotus reasons that ends *explain* only by somehow accounting for the action of the efficient cause in producing the effect. In non-rational natures, Scotus finds, the explanatory priorities go the other way around. The nature-constituting powers are *efficient* causal explanations of the end-points and perfecting forms regularly found in nature. Those ends do nothing to explain the action of those nature-constituting powers, but are *merely the resultants* of such action.[28] Scotus contends that the only case in which the end explains efficient causal action is intelligent voluntary agency, where an agent A cognizes and loves an end F, and A produces something else E for the sake of F. On this "psychologized" analysis of final causality, F *explains* the existence of E, not by acting as an efficient cause of E, but by being an object of the agent A's love, a love-object for the sake of which A efficient causally produces E.[29] Scotus remarks that the end F *moves* A to produce E *metaphorically*.[30] Ockham follows Scotus in psychologizing the notion of final cause and in routing its explanatory power through the efficient cause's loves. Ockham remarks that the end F does not have to be real to exercise the function of conferring lovability on E via an order (real or apparent to A) between E and F.[31]

Ockham draws an important further consequence: if the analysis of final cause is psychologized, and if one holds (as Scotus and Ockham do) to the liberty of indifference, then one should not take it to be axiomatic that the end is nobler than what is for

---

[27] Scotus, *Lectura* I, d. 35, q.u, nn. 20 and 22; Vaticana XVII.451–3; *Ordinatio* I, d. 35, q. 7, nn. 30 and 32; Vaticana VI.258–9.

[28] Scotus, *De Primo Principio*, c. 2, n. 3; Wadding III.215; c. 4, n. 5; Wadding III.238; *Ordinatio* I, d. 2, p. 1, qq. 1–2, nn. 76–7; Vaticana II.175–6.

[29] Scotus, *Ordinatio* I, d. 2, p. 1, qq. 1–2, n. 89; Vaticana II.180–2; I, d. 8, p. 2, q.u, n. 240; Vaticana IV.289; *Op.Ox.* IV, d. 49, q. 4, n. 4; Wadding X.381.

[30] Scotus, *De Primo Principio*, c. 2, n. 4; Wadding III.216. See also Ockham, *Quaestiones Variae* q. 4; OTh VIII.108–9, 113. For a fuller discussion of Scotus' treatment of final causality, see my "Final Causality and Explanation in Scotus' *De Primo Principio*," in Chumaru Koyama (ed.), *Nature in Medieval European Thought: Some Approaches East and West* (Leiden: Brill, 2000), 153–83.

[31] Ockham, *De Fine, Quaestiones Variae*, q. 4; OTh VIII.98–154; esp. 103–4, 107. Ockham discusses final causality in many texts and not always to the same effect, where causes in nature are concerned. For an analysis of this complicated textual picture, see my "Ockham on Final Causality: Muddying the Waters," *Franciscan Studies* 56 (1998) (Festschrift for Girard Etzkorn), 1–46.

the sake of an end.[32] Ockham makes this point scandalously explicit, when he insists that the liberty of indifference can not only will evil *considered as evil*,[33] *but also evil for the sake of evil*.[34] Such action would be perverse because contrary to right reason. But incompatibilist free agents are at liberty to be irrational and so to make evil their aim!

3. Make Love Your Aim!

Bishop and Perszyk have proposed alternative-God (= Supreme Goodness = perfectly loving relationality) as the ultimate end of the universe.[35] Will our review of ancient and medieval disputes and models help us get a better grip on what they have in mind? Maybe a little.

[1] First of all, it is clear that Bishop and Perszyk mean to forward alternative-God as an *explanatory* end.[36] Otherwise, alternative-God would be disqualified from filling the Creator-role. Moreover, like Anselm's Supreme Goodness, alternative-God is supposed to be, not only prior in the order of explanation, but *ontologically* prior to what gets explained.[37]

[2] Nevertheless, Bishop and Perszyk explicitly insist—against John Leslie's axiarchic theory—that alternative-God is *not*—like Anselm's Supreme Goodness—*a transcendent ideal*. What rankles most in this Platonizing notion is its apparent implication that instantantiations of perfect love here below would have—like Anselm's creatable natures—somehow to fall short of the ideal. By contrast, it strikes Bishop and Perszyk important to claim that perfectly loving relationality *is* fully manifested *within* history, paradigmatically but not exclusively in Christ.[38]

From these comments, one might think that Bishop and Perszyk were opting for an Aristotelian ontology of immanent universals, according to which there is no transcendent Platonic form (e.g., of bovinity), but only individual instantiations (e.g., particular cows), most of which fully exemplify bovine nature. In Aristotle himself, the ontology of immanent universals is combined with his commitment to the eternity of the species to yield the conclusion that, for each time, every universal has some individual instantiations or other. For Aristotle, the immanent universal would not simply

---

[32] Ockham, *Scriptum in I Sent.*, Prol., q. 11; OTh I.308; *Quodlibeta* IV, q. 1; OTh IX.298; *Expositio in Libros Physicorum Aristotelis* II, c. 12; OPh IV.393; *Summulae Philosophiae Naturalis* II.4; OPh VI.224.

[33] *Quaest. in IV Sent.*, q. 16; OTh VII.351, 357–8; *Quaestiones Variae*, q. 6, a. 10; OTh VIII.285; *Quaestio de Connexione Virtutum*, q. 7, a. 3; OTh VIII.367.

[34] *Scriptum in I Sent.*, Prol., q. 11; OTh I.306; d. 1, q. 1; OTh I.375; *Quaestiones Variae*, q. 4; OTh VIII.103–7, 120–43. For a fuller discussion of Ockham's views about the scope of the will, see my "Ockham on Will, Nature, and Morality," in Paul Vincent Spade (ed.), *Cambridge Companion to Ockham* (Cambridge: Cambridge University Press, 1999), ch. 11, 245–72.

[35] Bishop and Perszyk, "Concepts of God and Problems of Evil," s. 4, 119–21.

[36] Bishop and Perszyk, "Concepts of God and Problems of Evil," s. 1, 107. s. 4, 122.

[37] Bishop and Perszyk, "Concepts of God and Problems of Evil," s. 4, 120–21.

[38] Bishop and Perszyk, "Concepts of God and Problems of Evil," s. 4, 119–20.

be identified with the sum total of its instances, because it may be contingent that a universal is instantiated by these instances rather than those (e.g., bovinity by Beulah and Elsie rather than Samantha and Jill). But there wouldn't be anything actual over and above its actual instances with which the immanent universal would be identified.

Bishop and Perszyk do want to deny both that alternative-God is a transcendent ideal and that alternative-God is "'just' the sum total of the truly good loving relationships actually achieved throughout history."[39] Nevertheless, they do not seem to take over Aristotle's idea that the species must be eternal, because they imagine that it took the universe some time to evolve beings complex enough to be capable of perfectly loving relationality (namely, human beings).[40] Moreover, while at pains to insist that some loving relationships are perfect specimens, they do not commit themselves to the implausible idea that most are. Belief that universals must be immanent is perhaps logically independent of the claim that they are always instantiated. Perhaps Bishop and Perszyk assume with David Armstrong that an immanent universal exists omnitemporally if and only if it is instantiated somewhere or other, at some time or other in four-dimensional space-time. That way perfect loving relationality would exist, provided there is, was, or will be some instance of it somewhere, some time, somehow. But their papers do not make clear whether or not that is what Bishop and Perszyk meant to say about alternative-God, and so I remain unsure whether or not their alternative-God is best understood as the immanent universal perfectly loving relationality.[41]

[3] It is possible to quibble whether *perfectly* loving relationality is really possible between humans the way Bishop and Perszyk claim. Suppose we grant this point for the sake of argument. It follows that the universe has causal powers sufficient to evolve partners who exercise their agencies to form right relationships. Less controversial, I hope, is the observation that the universe has causal powers sufficient to evolve individuals who participate in horrors. Both love and horrors are causal *resultants* of the universe as we have it. Aristotle's question re-arises: *how do we get from the claim that something is a resultant, to the conclusion that it is an end that explains?*

[4] Shall we imagine that the universe as a whole is a giant Anselmian creatable nature, and identify Love (= perfectly loving relationality) as that for the sake of which humans come to be, and that for the sake of which the universe's human-evolving powers are given? Does Love explain why the universe has these powers, the way that per-

---

[39] Bishop and Perszyk, "Concepts of God and Problems of Evil," s. 4, 120–21.

[40] Bishop and Perszyk, "Concepts of God and Problems of Evil," s. 4, 122.

[41] In conversation, they were inclined to deny that alternative-God has temporally interrupted existence. But, again, it was not clear to me whether that was because they thought non-existence would keep alternative-God from exercising the role of ultimate end. Certainly, Scotus and Ockham both admit that the final cause "moves" only metaphorically and can exercise its final causality even if it does not really exist (see section 2 above). This conclusion fits nicely with their "psychologized" analysis of final cause, which Bishop and Perszyk seem to reject.

fect-specimen bovinity was supposed by Aristotle to explain the powers and causal sequences involved in bovine embryonic development? How do we eliminate the parallel hypothesis that horrors explain why the universe has human-evolving powers, that horrors are that for the sake of which human-evolving powers are given? What justifies us in saying that Love is the point of evolving humans while horrors are not? For Aristotle, explanatory ends in nature had to be the always-or-for-the-most-part resultants of natural causal sequences. The fact remains, where human evolution is concerned, horror-participation is a much more common resultant than perfectly loving relationality. Only a lucky few escape being individual human horror-participants. Fewer still enjoy perfectly loving relationality. If the universe as a whole were a giant Anselmian creatable nature, nothing so rare could qualify as its *natural* explanatory end.

[5] Should we instead agree with Scotus and Ockham that last and best do not automatically explain? Should we hold with them that for F to be an explanatory end with respect to E, there must be an intelligent voluntary agent who loves F, and for the sake of F wills E? Love rather than horrors might turn out to be the point of the universe if personal omni-God loved perfectly loving relationality and for the sake of it endowed the universe with human-evolving powers. Horrors rather than Love would be the point of the universe if a personal omnipotent and omniscient being loved horrors and willed the universe to have human-evolving powers for the sake of horror-participation. Ockham is explicit: personal omni-God possesses the liberty of indifference and owes nothing to anyone. Ockham thinks that where personal omni-God is concerned, it is *logically possible* for Horrors rather than Love to turn out to be the Divine aim. Happily, Ockham is convinced that in fact personal omni-God is maximally amiable, a God who freely and contingently makes Love the Divine aim. For Scotus and Ockham, it would be the intentions and decisions of a transcendent intelligent voluntary agent that made either resultant the universe's aim.

This interpretation of how the universe as a whole comes to have an explanatory end is the one Bishop and Perszyk are most concerned to resist![42] Even if what Ockham's personal omni-God most wanted out of the universe was perfectly loving relationality, that God would be responsible for producing a universe with powers that result in rampant human horror-participation. The thrust of Bishop's and Perszyk's negative case is that filling the Creator-role as productive cause of the horror-evolving frame would not be compatible with perfectly loving relationality between personal omni-God and human horror-participants.

If intelligent voluntary agents are the way to select among causal resultants and to turn some rather than others into explanatory ends, the obvious candidates for the role—on Bishop's and Perszyk's euteleological scheme—would seem to be human beings. Love explains by being that at which individual human beings aim and for the

---

[42] Bishop and Perszyk, "Concepts of God and the Problem of Evil," s. 1, p. 1, p. 111–13, s. 3, 117, and s. 4, 119–20.

sake of which they will other things. In the course of their discussion, Bishop and Perszyk shift from the language of "ends" to speak of "the point." Love is the point of much that many humans do and suffer, because love or perfectly loving relationality is, or is imagined to be, a principal source of positive meaning in human lives.

[6] Does Bishop's and Perszyk's claim—that God is the ultimate explanatory end of the universe—come down to the claims [i] that perfect loving relationality is the best resultant our universe has to offer and [ii] that it looms large in human meaning-making as that for the sake of which humans would do and suffer much and so [iii] as an important contributor to what positive meaning there is in human lives? Are they saying merely that the universe is so structured that Love is possible, and that humans are so structured that making Love their aim would confer positive meaning in their lives? If so, I do not see how alternative-God will do very well at filling either the Creator- or the Savior-role. The most that alternative-God will explain, will be why certain human beings act as they do. Alternative-God will not explain the rest of the universe (e.g., its horror-producing powers), unless you drop the assumption that ends explain by somehow accounting for the action of the efficient cause and insist that alternative-God explains simply by virtue of being the best (where bestness is a/the rational target of a voluntary agent's aim).

Nor is it plausible to suppose that alternative-God will save humans from horrors. To their credit, Bishop and Perszyk admit that their euteleology will not be able to under-write universal salvation.[43] Sadly for alternative-God, this proves an understatement. The vast majority of horror-participants never experience perfectly loving relationality. Love will not conquer horror-participation for them. Many personal omni-God devotees—I among them—have claimed that loving relationality between God and horror-participants could not only "swamp," but even defeat horrors. But for Bishop and Perszyk, only human lovers are available. Loving relationality between humans usually does not survive horror-participation. Even when it does, I have maintained, there is not enough to us or to it to balance off, much less defeat horrors.[44] Where we are talking about merely human partners, love does not and cannot conquer all. It remains a blessing for the lucky few, whose aim and labor for it is not frustrated by horrors.

Overall, Bishop and Perszyk still leave me wondering, what is the alternative-God of euteleology, and how does alternative-God explain?

4. Neglected Options

A Trio of Issues? Bishop and Perszyk admit up front: personal omni-God and the alternative-God of euteleology are not the only options. They themselves review a

[43] Bishop and Perszyk, "Concepts of God and Problems of Evil," s. 4, 122–3.
[44] See my *Christ and Horrors: The Coherence of Christology* (Cambridge: Cambridge University Press, 2006), ch. 2, 29–48.

variety of others: e.g., Peter Forrest's developmental theism, pantheism, Mark Johnston's panentheism.[45] In closing, I want to come at the issue of theoretical alternatives from a different angle. It strikes me that Bishop and Perszyk have been insufficiently attentive to distinctions among the following three propositions:

[1] Supreme Goodness is a transcendent ideal;
[2] Supreme Goodness is personal;
[3] Supreme Goodness is personal omni-God.

Anselm and other personal omni-God devotees accept each and all of [1]–[3]. Bishop and Perszyk respond by rejecting all of them, evidently denying [1] and [2] as if in a package-deal that goes with denying [3]. Other responses have been defended, however. Plato himself held to [1] but rejected [2] and [3]. Aristotle in effect gets behind [1] and [2] but not [3], insofar as his unmoved mover is a transcendent thinker, but not an omnipotent free producer of the rest of what there is. If Bishop and Perszyk must—as they think they must—give up on [3] personal omni-God, might it not be theoretically advantageous to go for an alternative-God that was more than an immanent universal whose actual instantiation depends on human lovers escaping horror-participation? Are there other ways to reject [3] while retaining [1] and [2]?

Whiteheadian Process Theology? Charles Hartshorne and David Griffin, themselves Whiteheadian process theologians, insist on [2], while rejecting [3], declaring classical omnipotence to be a "theological mistake."[46] Where [1] is concerned, their panentheism drives them to distinguish. God is not transcendent in the classical sense, because it is not metaphysically possible for God to exist all by Godself in the world. Hartshorne affirms, God is related to the rest of what there is as soul to body, and a bodiless God would be metaphysically impossible.[47] On the other hand, modal arguments prove God to be necessarily existent, necessarily omniscient, and perfectly good.[48] Everything else is contingent. Take each and all of the actual individuals. God could have existed without *them*. The rest of what there is, is included in God's body but is not identical with God's body, because if other contingent things had existed, they would have constituted God's body instead.[49]

Hartshorne and Griffin reject classical omnipotence because they hold that all creatures are "mini-minds" with something analogous to incompatibilist freedom. They conclude that it will be metaphysically impossible for any creature to be "forced" by another agent to act this way rather than that.[50] Divine power with respect to creatures

---

[45] Bishop and Perszyk, "Concepts of God and Problems of Evil," s. 3, 115–19.
[46] Charles Hartshorne, *The Divine Relativity* (New Haven: Yale University Press, 1948), ch. III, 116; *Omnipotence and Other Theological Mistakes* (Albany, NY: State University of New York Press, 1984), ch. 1, 1–49; ch. 3, 69–72. David Griffin, *God, Power, and Evil* (Philadelphia: Westminster Press, 1976), 268–78.
[47] Hartshorne, *Omnipotence and Other Theological Mistakes*, ch. 2, 55–63.
[48] Charles Hartshorne, *Anselm's Discovery: A Re-Examination of the Ontological Argument for God's Existence* (La Salle, Ill.: Open Court, 1965).
[49] Hartshorne, *The Divine Relativity*, ch. II, 60–94.
[50] Hartshorne, *The Divine Relativity*, ch. III, 138; Griffin, *God, Power, and Evil*, 268–78.

is instead "persuasive": Divine ideas about how the universe should develop are shared with creatures and so influence without coercing their choices towards a whole with greater complexity and higher harmony.[51]

Preserving [2] Divine personality might seem advantageous from the point of view of religious practice. If Hartshorne's and Griffin's position shares euteleology's limitation of being unable to underwrite universal salvation, their omniscient God is maximally sensitive and shares our suffering by feeling all of our feelings.[52] Moreover, their omniscient God eternally remembers and appreciates our finite careers and tries to give them greater significance by persuading the universe towards an ever greater cosmic perfection into which our past contributions will be integrated.[53] If Bishop and Perszyk were concerned to deny [1] in order to affirm that perfectly loving relationality is fully realized in history, their desideratum might be equivalently satisfied by process theology's panentheistic claim that all of human history exists in God as a focus of God's sympathetic appreciation.

Probably two factors hold Bishop and Perszyk back from claiming this advantage. First, there is their decided preference for religious naturalism over a universe of Divine and mini-minds.[54] Second, even in process theology [2] carries the downside of Divine responsibility for horrors. To be sure, the God of process theology is not omnipotent. But the personal God of process theology is responsible for exercising Divine persuasive power to persuade creatures to evolve a universe complex enough to produce and experience horrors. Perhaps Bishop and Perszyk think that God's eternal sympathetic appreciation would not be enough to make up for Divine complicity in horror-participation and hence insufficient to secure perfectly loving relationality between God and creatures.

Transcendent Suffering Love? In *The World's Redemption*,[55] C. E. Rolt advances a modified Platonism which endorses [1] and [2], but carries neither of these perceived disadvantages with process theology. A universe of Divine and mini-minds is not in view, and—as with euteleology—God is Love, not the productive but the final cause of all else. Rolt does not expound his position with analytical precision. To get a grip on his idea, it is best to approach it by stages.

[Stage 1] Begin with Plato's picture in the *Republic* and the *Timaeus*, leaving the Demiurge out of it. The Form of the Good is beyond Being and that from which the rest of the Forms derive their being. The Forms are eternally and immutably as they are. The receptacle is a mirror in which a moving likeness of eternity (= the realm of becoming) is reflected. For the reflection to occur in the receptacle, it is not necessary

[51] Hartshorne, *Omnipotence and Other Theological Mistakes*, ch. 3, 65–95; Griffin, *God, Power, and Evil*, 292–309.

[52] Hartshorne, *The Divine Relativity*, ch. I, 41–53; ch. III, 155; *Omnipotence and Other Theological Mistakes*, ch. 3, 80–3.

[53] Hartshorne, *Omnipotence and Other Theological Mistakes*, 33–7.

[54] Bishop and Perszyk, "Concepts of God and Problems of Evil," ss. 3, 116–17, s. 4, 124–5.

[55] C. E. Rolt, *The World's Redemption* (London: Longmans, Green, & Co., 1913).

for the Forms to *do* anything other than to *be* eternally as they *are* in themselves. Indeed, their doing *consists in* their being. Given the eternal Forms, the receptacle is such as to "catch" the (albeit moving) likeness.

[Stage 2] Alter Plato's picture by letting God (= Goodness Itself) take the place of the Forms, and modify the receptacle in the direction of evolutionary theory. What Plato regarded as primal chaos is now seen as material stuff with built-in causal tendencies to act and be acted upon in different ways depending on the circumstances. At first, Rolt imagines, every bit of stuff acts according to the necessity of its nature to produce a chaotic whirl. But chance and necessity together evolve patterns of fit among bits of matter, and such configurations make the sea of material stuff more mirror-like (i.e., activate its causal tendencies towards greater harmony). The evolutionary process results in a world full of many and various evils, from which we rightly recoil, although it also contains emerging elements of harmony and beauty in imitation of God.

On this scheme, God does not have power to coerce primal chaos into organization, but God's being what God is and the causal tendencies inherent in the primal stuff, result in the primal stuff's evolving towards an ever greater collective imitation of God. Thus, Rolt sometimes says, Divine power consists in being what God is and in ever patient waiting.[56] Transmogrified only thus far, Rolt's position makes God look aloof from the rough and tumble of becoming, where the pain and suffering and horrors occur, and so gives us a model that is more Platonic than Christian.

[Stage 3] Rolt goes further to Christianize the model by identifying Divine Goodness with Perfect Love, Whose power is a power to endure suffering, and Whose perfection not only involves the capacity but requires the actual endurance of suffering. Correspondingly, Rolt identifies the tendencies on which primal stuff initially acts as tendencies to self-assertion (recall how Aristotelian natures—barring obstacles—act to the limit of their powers), while the tendencies on which it later acts as tendencies towards cooperation and so with self-sacrifice for the sake of the greater Godlikeness of the universe.[57]

Continuing to speak metaphorically, Rolt explains that there are two models of conquest. On the coercive model, the victor compels the opponent to surrender and/or coercively prevents any further exercise of the opponent's power. On the absorption model, there is so much to the victor that without striking out or hitting back, she or he can absorb all of the opponent's blows without losing integrity. Rolt claims that in Christ, Divine Love defeats evil the second way: by absorbing all of its blows, while yet retaining its integrity. Moreover, Rolt thinks there is an explanation of how this is possible. Divine Love just is the power to endure suffering. Actually enduring suffering perfects it. Absorbing all of evil's blows by suffering brings Divine Love to full perfection. Therefore, so far from destroying or disintegrating Divine Love, evils occasion the perfection of Divine Love.[58]

---

[56] Rolt, *The World's Redemption*, 87, 93–4. [57] Rolt, *The World's Redemption*, 85–6, 88–9.
[58] Rolt, *The World's Redemption*, 186–8, 227–8, 245, 247, 251–2.

From this analysis of the nature of Divine Love, Rolt draws a number of corollaries. First, it is a mistake to regard Christ's "Passion as a temporary defeat which was reversed only by the Resurrection. The Passion was itself the final victory won by the Son of God."[59] Moreover, Rolt insists, Christ's perfect love meant that He was more sensitive to evil and suffering and so endured infinite agony of body and mind, "all that has ever been endured."[60] Rolt thinks this required Christ temporarily to forgo a sense of His Father's presence that was with Him through His ministry. Otherwise, His suffering would have "lost its sharpest terror."[61] Rolt thinks Christ would have been self-centered to accept life in this world without being willing to suffer. Rolt's thought is that to accept life in this world is to shoulder a collective responsibility for suffering through it, while sympathetic suffering helps us to recognize our kinship with the human race.[62] Because Divine Love suffers this way in Christ, God is not aloof. Divine suffering with us makes all created suffering holy.[63]

Second, Christ's suffering love furnishes human beings with an empowering example. When we refuse to respond to evil's blows with coercive force, but instead absorb them, we become more Godlike. Rolt adds, Christians sometimes consciously experience the presence of Divine Love suffering with them, and this gives them an inner core of joy and strength, a "true happiness" that is "the transfiguration of sorrow rather than its abolition."[64] Rolt suggests that one's own experience of evil will be defeated when one is conscious of being in the presence "of an almighty and unconquerable Being Whose power consists in the burning intensity of eternal and infinite love."[65] Divine suffering with us absorbs some of the energy of the aggression so that we won't be exposed to its full force. At the same time, experience of Divine Love makes human beings more sensitive to suffering or wrongdoing yet able to experience them without the accompanying bitterness.

Rolt's resultant picture, then, is of [2] a personal God Who is [1] transcendent Love, where Love is power to absorb aggression without losing integrity. Rolt's alternative-God is eternal in the heavens, so that Love Divine is a permanent feature of the universe no matter what happens among us humans here below. Rolt's alternative-God is the final cause of the universe the way a paradigm is the aim of its copy, because ever-greater imitation of Divine Love is where the universe is necessarily tending. Where efficient causality is concerned, however, it is important to distinguish active from passive efficient causal power. God does not have *active* efficient causal power and so is not—as Bishop and Perszyk fear—the productive cause of the universe or its horror-producing causal tendencies. But God does have *passive* efficient causal power—power to be acted upon by the rest of what there is without being destroyed thereby. Primal material stuff acts out its causal tendencies by natural necessity, but it cannot

---

[59] Rolt, *The World's Redemption*, 35.
[60] Rolt, *The World's Redemption*, 35.
[61] Rolt, *The World's Redemption*, 248.
[62] Rolt, *The World's Redemption*, 229–30.
[63] Rolt, *The World's Redemption*, 230.
[64] Rolt, *The World's Redemption*, 58–9, 242–3.
[65] Rolt, *The World's Redemption*, 61.

help but do so in the presence of the ultimate absorber, who over time absorbs enough of its energy to draw it into ever greater harmony and to enable human beings to imitate Divine love by absorbing hostile force without being thereby destroyed.

My suggestion is that Rolt's position would give Bishop and Perszyk much of what they hoped to get by embracing their own euteleology. Rolt's alternative-God would not be guilty of setting the human race up for horrors. Rolt is able to recognize loving relationality here below as participation in the point of the universe. By locating *passive* efficient causal power in alternative-God, Rolt is able to do better than Bishop and Perszyk by explaining how—in such a rough and tumble world—anything approaching perfectly loving relationality could be possible for human beings: namely, that the ultimate absorber is draining off the lion's share of the aggressive energy, so that the humans can absorb some without being destroyed. The eternal persistence of the ultimate absorber helps explain why we might expect loving relationality to recur and even become ever more frequent (an optimism to which Bishop and Perszyk are not entitled). Rolt joins Bishop and Perszyk in locating a paradigm instance of such human loving in Christ. By assigning passive efficient causal power to his alternative-God, Rolt gives alternative-God more of an explanatory role in the universe's moving towards its end, and thus gives more substance to the idea that alternative-God is Savior. As Rolt says, [alternative-]God suffers for the world's redemption!

To say that Rolt's alternative-God might do better than the alternative-God of Bishop and Perszyk's euteleology is not to say that Rolt's position is free from difficulties. Rolt is not a panpsychist. For all of his metaphors, Rolt seems prepared to take the material world in whatever way science describes it. We can see at the macro-level that the universe is endowed with human-evolving, horror-producing powers. Rolt is no more able to offer universal happy endings than Bishop and Perszyk are. But Rolt's idea—that Divine suffering with us makes all suffering holy—does win him some advantage by allowing him to assign all human horror-participation positive meaning, even if those meanings cannot be recognized by the horror-participants themselves.

The laws of thermodynamics, with their eschatology of entropy, are bad news for both theories. Bishop and Perszyk's alternative-God has no power to survive, much less to stop it, as it unravels the only beings complex enough to be capable of loving relationality. Entropy contradicts Rolt's prediction of where the world is headed and so Rolt's estimate of the material world's causal propensities. Unlike personal omni-God, neither alternative-God has active efficient causal power to halt the universal march to equilibrium. Neither alternative-God is Love stronger than entropy, which might be their cue to restore the monarchy and bring personal omni-God back again.[66]

[66] John Polkinghorne identifies entropy as the cosmic face of the problem of evil in *The God of Hope and the End of the World* (New Haven and London: Yale University Press, 2002), ch. 1, 1–10.

Bibliography

Adams, Marilyn McCord (1998). "Ockham on Final Causality: Muddying the Waters," *Franciscan Studies* 56: 1–46.

Adams, Marilyn McCord (1999). "Ockham on Will, Nature, and Morality," in Paul Vincent Spade (ed.), *Cambridge Companion to Ockham* (ch. 11, pp. 245–72). Cambridge: Cambridge University Press.

Adams, Marilyn McCord (2000). "Final Causality and Explanation in Scotus' *De Primo Principio*," in Chumaru Koyama (ed.), *Nature in Medieval European Thought: Some Approaches East and West* (pp. 153–83). Leiden: Brill.

Adams, Marilyn McCord (2006). *Christ and Horrors: The Coherence of Christology.* Cambridge: Cambridge University Press.

Adams, Marilyn McCord (2013). "Ignorance, Instrumentality, Compensation, and the Problem of Evil," *Sophia* 52/1: 7–26.

Adams, Marilyn McCord and Wolter, Allan B. (1982). "Duns Scotus's Parisian Proof for the Existence of God," *Franciscan Studies* 42: 248–321.

Anselm (1968). *Opera Omnia.* Ed. Franciscus Salesius Schmitt. 6 vols. Stuttgart-Bad Cannstatt: Friedrich Frommann Verlag [Günther Holzboog].

Aquinas. *Opera Omnia. Corpus Thomisticum.* <corpusthomisticum.org/iopera.html>.

Aristotle (1984). *The Complete Works of Aristotle: The Revised Oxford Edition.* Ed. Jonathan Barnes. Bollingen Series LXXI. Princeton: Princeton University Press.

Bishop, John (2007). "How a Modest Fideism may Constrain Theistic Commitments: Exploring an Alternative to Classical Theism," *Philosophia* 35: 387–402.

Bishop, John (2009). "Towards a Religiously Adequate Alternative to OmniGod Theism," *Sophia* 48: 419–33.

Bishop, John and Perszyk, Ken (2011). "The Normatively Relativised Logical Argument from Evil," *International Journal of the Philosophy of Religion* 70: 109–26.

Bishop, John and Perszyk, Ken. "Concepts of God and Problems of Evil," Chapter 6 in the present volume.

Griffin, David (1976). *God, Power, and Evil.* Philadelphia: Westminster Press.

Hartshorne, Charles (1948). *The Divine Relativity: A Social Conception of God.* New Haven: Yale University Press.

Hartshorne, Charles (1965). *Anselm's Discovery: A Re-Examination of the Ontological Argument for God's Existence.* La Salle, IL: Open Court.

Hartshorne, Charles (1984). *Omnipotence and Other Theological Mistakes.* Albany, NY: State University of New York Press.

Ockham, William (1967–84). *Opera Theologica et Philosophica.* Ed. Gedeon Gal et al. 16 vols. St Bonaventure, NY: Franciscan Institute Publications.

Polkinghorne, John (2002). *The God of Hope and the End of the World.* New Haven and London: Yale University Press.

Rolt, C. E. (1913). *The World's Redemption.* London: Longmans, Green, & Co.

Scotus, John Duns (1950–2008). *Opera Omnia.* Ed. Carl Balic et al. Civitas Vaticana: Typis Polyglottis Vaticanis.

Scotus, John Duns (1968–9). *Opera Omnia.* Ed. Lucas Wadding. 12 vols. Lyons, 1639; repr. Hildesheim.

PART III

Further Alternatives

8

Taking the Mind of God Seriously

Why and How to Become a Theistic Idealist

Charles Taliaferro

Before providing a guide to embracing theistic idealism, I offer a backstory on a shift in the intellectual climate that makes theistic idealism far more inviting than it was at mid-century. Not long ago, theistic idealism was presumed dead, whereas there seems to have been a resurrection of sorts.

During its long history, Oxford University has often been the site for the birth, continuation, and critique of the major schools or movements in anglophone philosophy. In the mid-twentieth century, although the University of Oxford could not boast that it included Wittgenstein as a member, it had its share of linguistically oriented philosophers who maintained essentially the same diagnosis of philosophy defended in Wittgenstein's later work: *many or most traditional and current philosophical puzzles are the result of conceptual or linguistic confusion.* Championing this thesis, Gilbert Ryle (1900–76), along with J. L Austin (1911–60) and others, had a massive influence on English-speaking philosophy through celebrated books such as Ryle's *The Concept of Mind* (1949) and the role of Ryle et al. in some of the most prestigious positions in the field of philosophy (for example, Ryle was the editor of the journal *Mind* 1947–71). Ryle argued that the belief that persons are essentially minds distinct from their material bodies was the result of a category mistake. By his lights, such a mistake is akin to concluding that because some people have a good mind for philosophy, therefore people have a thing called a "mind," whereas the right thing to conclude from the phrase "some people have a mind for philosophy" is only that some people seem naturally gifted in the practice of philosophy. One of Ryle's missions was to supplant mysterious references to the mind or subjective experience with references to actual behaviour (including linguistic behaviour) and our disposition to behave in different ways.

Such an intellectual climate led to the atrophy of many of the towering philosophical positions and projects of the past, such as different sorts of idealism, mind/body dualism, theism, pantheism, and so on. The domination of Ryle in Oxford was evident in 1965 when the American philosopher Daniel Dennett came to study with Ryle. Dennett describes the scene:

Oxford was enjoying total domination of Anglophone philosophy. It was a swarming Mecca for dozens—maybe hundreds—of pilgrims from the colonies who wanted to take the cloth and learn the moves....In many regards [Ryle] ruled Oxford philosophy at the time, as editor of Mind an informal clearing-house for jobs throughout the Anglophone world. (2008, 24)

Given that, not long ago, travel to Ryle's Oxford was the equivalent of making a pilgrimage to a holy city where one was informed that idealism was not on the agenda of live philosophical options, I was surprised that when I came to Oxford in 1991, there was very little evidence of the once dominant linguistic philosophy of Ryle and Austin. To be sure, there were at least two philosophers who remained faithful to the Wittgenstein–Ryle linguistic or (as it is often called) ordinary language philosophy (P. M. S. Hacker and John Hyman), and there was a handsome, framed photograph of Ryle in a philosophy seminar room. But the seminars were anything but what Ryle would have tolerated. In one, Galen Strawson maintained with boldness and clarity that the behaviouristic mindset held by Ryle and Dennett that still has a hold on some contemporary philosophers was preposterous. Strawson actually took seriously the reality of *consciousness, experience,* and *mind*! I was then only mildly shocked to meet a philosopher who defended a form of idealism very much along the lines of George Berkeley. John Foster, a Fellow of Brasenose College, Oxford, was a brilliant, elegant thinker, a fair-minded critic, and a person of immense generosity.

How in the world was there an intellectual climate change at Oxford so that the once monolithic ordinary language philosophy might give way to allow for its polar opposite? Berkeley's idealism, with its theism and the stress on the primacy of subjective experience and the self as an immaterial subject, could not be further from the secular, confident, common sense of Ryle and his followers, such as Dennett. In this chapter, I put to one side any explanation about what transpired at Oxford, and focus instead on why we should see the kind of theistic idealism advanced by Foster as a serious challenge to contemporary naturalism and as offering an understanding of God that is an alternative to traditional theism. Sadly, John Foster died in 2009. I defend his position here both because I think Foster's philosophy of God is cogent and to honour a friend from whom I learned a great deal.

There are three sections that follow. In the first, I take note of how Ryle and many philosophers of mind today maintain that we have a far clearer idea of what is physical than what they call non-physical. They take the physical world that is evident to us in virtually all our thought and action, and as studied by physics, chemistry, and biology, to be foundational in terms of both what we may be certain about and what makes the most sense in terms of explaining events. The idea that there might be something non-physical or incorporeal seems to them obscure and confused, and the idea that a non-physical thing (a soul or God) might causally affect something physical has been deemed preposterous. I propose that there are compelling reasons for rejecting this position. Instead of the primacy of what Ryle and others think of as physical, I argue for the primacy what Ryle, Dennett, and others think of as the experiential and the mental and offer reasons for thinking the mental is distinct from what Ryle and others maintain is physical. (This leaves open the possibility that there is some other, broader account of what is physical that allows the conceptual possibility of the identity of the mental and physical.) This section will offer reasons for thinking that our concept of the mental and mental causation is more lucid and prior to our understanding of what is physical. By "mental causation" I mean causal relations in which mental states or activities play an indispensable role in explaining other mental states or activities. An at least apparent case of mental causation arises in accounting for why I am typing the sentences I am currently typing (or why my hands are moving as they are). A complete explanation will presumably involve an account of the role of brain circuitry, nerves, neurotransmitters, and various physiological mechanisms. Nevertheless, it can be said that there is mental causation when my beliefs, desires, and values play a role *as beliefs, desires, and values* in accounting for why one belief leads to another and why my hands are moving the way they are. If I am asked, "What is the smallest perfect number?" mental causation occurs when the reason or explanation of why I utter in reply "six" is because I reason that six is the smallest number equal to the sum of its divisors, including one, but not including itself $(6 = 1 + 2 + 3)$. I fill this proposal out later, but as an advance warning I shall be arguing that we have a clearer grasp of mental causation than we do of what Ryle and others think of as physical causation. The positions I advance in this section are all in line with John Foster's case for idealism, which he begins with an argument against what he called the *physical realism* of philosophers like Ryle and Dennett.

In a second section, Foster's main claims about God, experience, and creation are explored. One of the reasons why some philosophers are sceptical about theism is that they contend that the very idea of an incorporeal being is conceptually absurd. In this section, reasons are advanced for thinking it makes sense to think of God in theistic terms, as there are reasons for thinking of us as individual subjects who are embodied but who are not, strictly speaking, identical with our bodies. I propose that the cases for and against divine and human teleological (purposive) agency are interrelated. If this section is right, then there are reasons for thinking that accounting for the cosmos or events in the cosmos in terms of the mind of God is not a category mistake. I also propose some modifications in Foster's view of meaning.

A third section considers further how one might be led to adopt Foster's theistic idealism. There is often more than one plausible route to reach certain philosophical conclusions, and my aim is to end this chapter with a bit of cartography (one of Ryle's favourite metaphors for describing the task of philosophy) on how one might reach the shores of theistic idealism. The first and second sections are the most important as they make room for theistic idealism.

1. Primacy of the "Physical" or "Mental"

This subject heading is (to use the phrase of a once Oxford don) *surrounded in quotation marks* because in this chapter I am using the two terms in the way some philosophers do (Ryle, Paul Churchland, Dennett, Jaegwon Kim, Eliot Sober), and not endorsing their use at large. According to some philosophers such as John Searle, the mental exists and is a part of the physical world. From Searle's perspective, if you argued successfully for the conceptual primacy of what Searle and you mean by "mental" (consciousness, for example), you would only establish that the *physical condition of consciousness* is more readily and clearly grasped than other *physical conditions such as some movement of sub-atomic particles that is not identical with consciousness.* But here I ask you to start by considering the assumption (shared among the philosophers cited) that we have a clear grasp of the reality and causal interactions between material bodies and chemistry, physics, and biology, and yet we are not at all sure about how "mental causation" works. Whether in the context of explanations or descriptions, let us take the term "mental" to refer to states, activities, events, subjects who are or involve consciousness, subjective experience, desires, sensations, intentions, emotions, and so on.

This section includes a fair amount of citations, but I need to secure familiarity with their terms in mounting a reply. This is also the longest section, because it addresses the biggest obstacle to theistic idealism. Much of Foster's own work went into considering and replying to the ambitious claims of a materialism that either denigrates or threatens to eliminate (he used the term "annihilate") the mental.

As noted earlier, Ryle and many of the ordinary language philosophers and contemporary advocates of physicalism assert or assume that we possess a clear-headed concept of the physical world and material bodies. In the passage that follows, Ryle contrasts the commonsense understanding of the physical as a spatial, public world of causal interaction with the mysterious supposition that there may be something else, a mind that is immaterial. I cite Ryle at length.

Material objects are situated in a common field, known as "space", and what happens to one body in one part of space is mechanically connected with what happens to other bodies in other parts of space. But mental happenings occur in insulated fields, known as 'minds', and there is, apart maybe from telepathy no direct causal connection between what happens in one mind and what happens in another. Only through the medium of the public physical world can the mind of one person make a difference to the mind of another. The mind is its own place and in his inner life each of us lives the life of a ghostly Robinson Crusoe. People can see, hear, and jolt one another's bodies, but they are irremediably blind and deaf to the workings of one another's mind and inoperative upon them ...

As thus represented, minds are not merely ghosts harnessed to machines, they are themselves just spectral machines. Though the human body is an engine, it is not quite an ordinary engine, since some of its working are governed by another engine inside it—this interior governor—engine being one of a very special sort. It is invisible, inaudible and it has no size or weight. It cannot be taken to bits and the laws it obeys are not those known to ordinary engineers. Nothing is known of how it governs the bodily engine. (Ryle 2009, 3)

The above is very much vintage Ryle. If dualism is true, the mind is invisible and power to control the body is utterly enigmatic. This weightless, inaudible mind is, like Robinson Crusoe, an isolated castaway whose communication with other people is akin to telepathy.

In *Matter and Consciousness*, a book frequently used as an introduction to philosophy of mind in the English-speaking world, Paul Churchland asks us to imagine a neuroscientist at work. She is able to account for behaviour in chemical terms, but then she wonders about whether anything more might be involved. There seems no role for what she might suppose to be non-physical.

Put yourself in the shoes of a neuroscientist who is concerned to trace the origins of behavior back up the motor nerves to the active cells in the motor cortex of the cerebrum, and to trace in turn their activity into inputs from other parts of the brain, and from the various sensory nerves. She finds a thoroughly physical system of awesome structure and delicacy, and much intricate activity, all of it unambiguously chemical or electrical in nature, and she finds no hint at all of any nonphysical inputs...What is she to think? From the standpoint of her researches, human behavior is exhaustively a function of the activity of the physical brain. (Churchland 2013, 17–18)

As Churchland sets up the philosophical puzzle, the neuroscientist seems in a quandary because she appears to have a complete explanation of human behaviour only in chemistry and without appealing to more.

Consider three more examples in which philosophers set up a similar framework. Jaegwon Kim suggests:

It simply does not seem credible that an immaterial substance with no material characteristics and totally outside physical space, could causally influence and be influenced by, the motions of material bodies that are strictly governed by physical law. Just try to imagine how something that isn't anywhere in physical space could alter in the slightest degree the trajectory of even a single material particle in motion. (Kim 1996, 4)

Here is a similar claim by Eliot Sober:

If the mind is immaterial, then it does not take up space. But if it lacks spatial location, how can it be causally connected to the body? When two events are causally connected, we normally expect there to be a physical signal that passes from one to the other. How can a physical signal emerge from or lead to the mind if the mind is no place at all? (Sober 2000, 24)

Daniel Dennett's statement that follows more or less captures what many, but not all, self-described naturalists assume in the philosophy of mind.

There is only one sort of stuff, namely matter—the physical stuff of physics, chemistry and physiology—and the mind is somehow nothing but a physical phenomenon. In short, the mind is the brain...we can (in principle!) account for every mental phenomenon using the same physical principles, laws, and raw materials that suffice to explain radioactivity, continental drift, photosynthesis, reproduction, nutrition, and growth. (Dennett 1991, 33)

Dennett maintains that he does not rule out the role of subjectivity and the first-person perspective in which it may appear to a subject that she reaches certain conclusions based on her reasons and subjective experience. But in "Who's On First," Dennett claims that the only proper way of understanding what is going on subjectively in persons is by making inferences based on what we externally observe others reporting from what Dennett calls the third-person point of view. This outlook presupposes that I can be more certain of what others say than I can be about my own thinking, hearing, reasoning, feeling, interpreting, and so on. Here is an extensive passage in which Dennett advances his position as obvious and uncontroversial, but I suggest below it is anything but.

This third-person methodology, dubbed heterophenomenology (phenomenology of another not oneself) is, I have claimed, the sound way to take the first-person point of view as seriously as it can be taken...Most of the method is so obvious and uncontroversial that some scientists are baffled that I would even call it a method: basically, you have to take the vocal sounds emanating from the subjects' mouths (and your own mouth) and interpret them! Well of course. What else could you do? Those sounds aren't just belches and moans; they're speech acts, reporting, questioning, correcting, requesting, and so forth. Using such standard speech acts, other events such as button-presses can be set up to be interpreted as speech acts as well, with highly specific meanings and fine temporal resolution. What this interpersonal communication enables you, the investigator, to do is to compose a catalogue of what the subject believes to be true about his or her conscious experience. (Dennett 2003, 1–2)

I believe that all of the above claims rest on an unwarranted assumption about our awareness of the world.

Let us begin by re-visiting Ryle's starting point. It is amusing that Ryle refers to the world of bodies as if he is pointing out something that has been overlooked: "Material objects are situated in a common field, known as 'space'" (2009, 23). But what is actually overlooked or not seen as important is that his statement only makes sense and has clarity if we have a clear, intelligible *concept* of material objects, the *concept* of space, and the *concept* of what makes some thing (a field) common. It is plausible to believe that our concepts or ideas of space and objects are derived from our experience of space and objects, but without our having the relevant concepts or ideas, Ryle's statement would not make sense to us. Moreover, our grasp of the nature of spatial objects can only be as clear and confident as the reliability of *our concepts and awareness of spatial objects*. And on this point, we might pause as Ryle's statement, however brief, does raise a brief puzzle.

Looking more closely at Ryle's statement, it appears that he holds (or implies) that material objects are distinct from space; space seems to be the sort of place where one should place or find a material object. As far as I know, Ryle never (at least in print) advocated the existence of absolute space. If he did, though, this would make for an interesting test of his critique of the idea of there being a self that is non-physical on the grounds that such a self is invisible, weightless, and inaudible, because absolute space is also invisible, weightless, and inaudible (in addition to being odourless, tasteless, without temperature, lacking in any causal power, and so on). Whether or not one accepts the theory of absolute space (the position of substantivalists) or a relational theory, and we grant that being spatial may be a *necessary* condition for being a material object, an argument would be needed to establish that this is a *sufficient* condition. Historically, Henry More thought of the self as non-physical and yet spatial, as in the twentieth century H. H. Price and G. E. Moore thought of senses (sensations) as spatial and even (with Price) three-dimensional and yet not physical. Some materialists have gone to great lengths to deny that there can be three-dimensional sensory objects (that are not identical with material objects and processes), probably the most extreme being Norman Malcolm's project in his 1959 book *Dreaming*. Malcolm argued that subjects who report dreaming in which it certainly seems as though they are being (for example) chased by bears or trying to run out of a classroom after some embarrassing moment did not actually have the experiences they claimed to have had. I will not assume that three-dimensional sensory objects in dreams exist or do not exist, but it strikes me as illegitimate to rule them out as impossible, as Malcolm sought to do, on a controversial claim about how we use terms taken from the work of Wittgenstein. (Without going into details, I propose that Malcolm's argument would, at best, only secure the conclusion that we may not be in a position to know whether or not there are sensory objects in dreams. And, given the wide reports of vivid dreams, in which persons report dreams as they are having them, I can see little hope for positions like Malcolm's.) Minimally, I think it is fair to claim that the burden of proof is on a philosopher who argues that it is impossible for there to be sensory, spatial objects in dreams.

Let us move on to Ryle's further thesis about our grasping causal relations among material bodies. Ryle notes, with a (forgive me) wry sense of humour, that we are aware that "what happens to one body in one part of space is mechanically connected with what happens to other bodies in other parts of space." So we grasp that when, say, a baseball is thrown into a window at a certain speed, then the window is likely to shatter, and Churchland's neuroscientist seems to know about the motor cortex of the cerebrum and the role of active cells and various other inputs to bring about certain effects. Kim believes we seem to have a clear handle on explaining the motion of material bodies and physical laws, and Sober holds that we have a respectable grasp on the nature and role of physical signals. But, they hold, in contrast to this knowledge of the physical world, we have very little idea about how the mental, conceived of as something non-spatial, has any causal role to play in explaining events.

Apart from noting the earlier observation that the mental may include spatial objects, the most important point to appreciate is that *we could not know any of the above unless we can trust and rely on our thinking, believing, sensing, and conceiving of the relevant objects and relations at hand.* I can think about and observe the bodies around me with confidence only so long as I have confidence in (or am not actively doubting) my thinking and observing. And quite apart from Kim's and Sober's point about what is non-spatial, I assume no one could have a clear grasp of matter in motion, laws, and physical signals without satisfying the appropriate, antecedent, conceptual, and cognitive conditions ("antecedent" is the conceptual sense in that without having the relevant concepts, one cannot understand or articulate any awareness of causal relata). So, the first point in this reply about physical causation is that our grasping physical causation rests on our having confidence in or having a reliable use of the relevant concepts, observations, experiences, and so on. This point may be amplified by reconsidering Churchland's neuroscientist.

As noted earlier, Churchland raises the worry that if you can explain some human behaviour only with "unambiguously chemical or electrical in nature" and these seem to not include any sensations, beliefs, and the like ("the mental"), it seems that sensations, beliefs, and the like are idle or possibly irrelevant (2013, 18). Indeed, as Alvin Plantinga points out, if we examine and explain the human brain and human anatomy in general only in terms of the physical sciences, it appears not to involve any beliefs and propositional content:

A single neuron (or quark, electron, atom, or whatever) presumably isn't a belief; but how can belief, content, arise from physical interaction among such material entities as neurons? How can such physical interaction bring it about that a group of neurons has content? We can examine this neuronal event as carefully as we please; we can measure the number of neurons it contains, their connections, their rates of fire, the strength of the electrical impulses involved, and the potential across the synapses, with as much precision as you could possibly desire; we can consider its electro-chemical, NP properties in the most exquisite detail; but nowhere, here, will we find so much as a hint of content. Indeed, none of this seems even vaguely *relevant* to its having content. None of this so much as slyly suggests that this bunch of neurons firing away is the belief that Proust is more subtle than Louis L'Amour, as opposed, e.g. to the belief Louis L'Amour is the most widely published author from Jamestown, North Dakota. (2006, 14)

What are we to do if Plantinga is correct and Churchland's neuroscientist is able to explain human behaviour in only chemical and electrical terms?

In response to Churchland, I suggest that the very last thing that should be doubted is *whether the neuroscientist is thinking, seeing, observing, or feeling and that, as we debate Churchland's thesis, the reason why we reach certain conclusions rather than others is because of our beliefs and inferences.* In other words, if we have abundant reason for thinking that a neurologist has come up with a powerful chemical and electrical account of human anatomy and behaviour, we have even more abundant reason for believing that mental causation occurs. Kim has a useful analogy about causation in this context. In the passage that follows he is describing an unhappy view of mental (M-M*) causation, but the important point is his analogy of a car and its shadow:

In the case of supposed M-M* causation, the situation is rather like a series of shadows cast by a moving car: there is no causal connection between the shadow of the car at one instant and its shadow an instant later, each being an effect of the moving car. The moving car represents a genuine causal process, but the series of shadows it casts, however regular and law like it may be, does not constitute a causal process. (Kim 2000, 45)

Using Kim's analogy, if our beliefs, reasons, inferences are like the shadow cast by the car, then they play no role in explaining why we write essays, read books, go to conferences, and so on. Without mental causation, we could not offer a reasonable account of why Churchland's work has led to the massive movement of molecules taking place as I type this sentence.

At the risk of repetition, I emphasize the point at issue: our grasp of physical causal relations rests on our having an antecedent, reliable means of *conceiving* one thing causing another and this, in turn, rests on our having a reliable means of reasoning and remembering. When we think about acting and what causes what, we must rely on reasoning that, say, if I throw the baseball at that glass, it will shatter, unless I am mistaken and what I have is a softball and the glass has been hardened to a certain thickness, and so on. All such reasoning presupposes what I earlier referred to as "mental causation," a case in which some belief accounts for why we hold a different belief. Churchland asks us to put ourselves in the shoes of a neuroscientist and he asks us to consider what we would do under such and such circumstances. All this involves a feat of imagination and drawing conclusions based on various beliefs. And this, I suggest, is a sign that what we need to be confident about is that some beliefs account for why we are to accept other beliefs. Important to note here is that the idea of mental causation does not itself include any idea of whether causation requires spatial relations. If I accept the thesis (rightly or wrongly) that spatial relations are a necessary condition for any causal relations of any kind on the grounds of beliefs A and B (whatever), this is presumably not because beliefs A and B are spatially related to my conclusion.

The inescapability of mental causation is evident in Dennett's credo, cited earlier, about what exists. Referring to Dennett's account of what there is, we would not be able to claim to know about "the physical stuff" of physics, chemistry, and physiology or practice physics, chemistry, and physiology unless we are capable of thinking, conceiving of hypotheses, making predictions, making observations, and drawing conclusions. All of these activities carried out by scientists and philosophers who are reflecting on the implications of science, involve mental causation. We cannot form a clear concept of the causal relata Dennett identifies unless we have an even clearer concept of the "mental phenomena" involved in scientific accounts, namely the concepts of "radioactivity, continental drift, photosynthesis, reproduction, nutrition, and growth" and our concepts of inferential relations involving our concept of the laws of nature.

As for Dennett's treatment of first-person experience, I suggest that it is baffling to think you could be more sure of what vocal sounds emanate from a subject than you can be sure of your subjective experience of hearing, seeing, thinking, interpreting. Taken to an extreme, Dennett would be committed to thinking that the best, scientific way of my having self-awareness would be by listening to what others infer, based on their investigation, from the vocal noises emanating from my mouth. Or, as Dennett implies, I might listen to myself say "I feel tired" and then, upon investigation, interpret this noise as a speech act I probably undertook because I subjectively feel tired. Again, how might I be so sure I heard myself say anything unless I trust my first-person experience of listening, thinking, feeling, interpreting? As an aside, Dennett's initial way of describing speech as "vocal sounds emanating from the subject's mouth" seems bizarrely detached from any commonsense, ordinary way of describing or interpreting what it is to speak or be in conversation. Speaking is an activity, not a matter of noises that simply emanate or we find wheeling up within us. Fortunately Dennett recognizes that speech is different from belches and moans, but it is telling that he has to point this out to his readers. Why would one need to make this point explicitly unless his initial portrait of speech and self-awareness comes dangerously close to confusing speaking with belching? Using Dennett's terminology, a conversation between two persons could be (preposterously) described as two organisms whose mouths are a conduit of various noises at different times which an observer and the two persons themselves may interpret as something called a discussion about philosophy of mind.

I propose that a more reasonable place to begin thinking about human nature and the world than proposed by Kim, Sober, and Dennett is with what we know is incontrovertible, namely that we have subjective experiences and we are thinking and acting persons. We write books and go to conferences, we eat, sleep, run, make love, and so on, based on certain reasons, beliefs, desires, and so on. These I believe to be obvious. Dennett seems to have boundless confidence in "the physical stuff of physics, chemistry, and physiology" and treats "the mind" and "mental phenomena" as second-class citizens but, as noted above, physics, chemistry, and physiology are not possible without mental phenomena: experience, observation, concepts.

Consider the following objection: Certainly we use the mind (believing, thinking, sensing, conceiving, and so on) to understand the material world—we trust our faculties are reliable—but does it thereby follow that we have any understanding of it or them? Arguably, the points I have been making seem to be in line with Descartes's thesis that because we know the world via the mind, the mind is better known that the body. But one can drive a car without the slightest idea how it works. Does one even have to believe that it works? Perhaps not. You just use it. The key difference here is that between *what you think with* and what you think about. Granted, we need to think with the mental (mental concepts, ideas about reasons, and so on), that does not mean we understand what is mental better than what is not-mental. (I thank a reviewer of an earlier version of this chapter for raising this objection.)

Reply: Let's consider the analogy of the car. Is there a proper analogy about *how I could know a lot about the world using the mental without knowing how the mental works* and *I could know lots about driving a car without having any idea of how it works*? Note the last indexical "it" as this (presumably) refers to the car's engine and the mechanical engineering that went into the car's design and performance. Obviously, someone might know how to drive without having any serious grasp of the mechanical engineering. But my thesis is better seen in terms of making the point about how any of our activities (like explaining or driving) requires recognizing the primacy of the mental or, as it were, the mental engineering involved with driving. In terms of driving, I do not think it credible (except for maybe zombie drivers) to think one knows how to drive without some basic knowledge of how driving works (knowing how to turn on or off the car, how to adjust speed and direction, and so on). As such, one would need to know and be able to rely on what might be called mental engineering prior to any claims involving the non-mental. Take any automotive explanation of a car: all this relies on our having a grasp of what are ideas, concepts, notions of causation, purposes. Someone claims: I know what a battery is, but I have no idea of what an idea is. But in referencing the battery you are using *the idea of a battery* (as well as using ideas of "I"—a subject- and "know"—the concept of knowledge). I submit that the primacy of the mental is unavoidable and we can have no clearer idea of what is non-mental than what is mental.

A further, minor point in relation to the objection: It is true that my reasoning is, broadly speaking, Cartesian, but I have not made any claims about epistemic foundationalism in keeping with Descartes's project. In arguing for the primacy of the mental, I am indeed advancing a non-sceptical position about our awareness of our subjective states (or, more awkwardly put, our awareness of awareness), but I am not committed to holding that our knowledge-claims about particular judgements are apodictic (infallible or incorrigible).

2. Minds, Human and Divine

As noted earlier, one of the reasons why Foster's theistic idealism, and theism in general, is thought to be deficient, is because it rests on a category mistake. Even if the conclusions of the first section are correct, and we must recognize the primacy of the mental, why think it makes sense to believe there could be mental, conscious states, and causes independent of the physical? Colin McGinn's position is representative of many in the philosophy of mind today:

If the mind is separate from the body, then not only can the brain exist without the mind but the mind can exist without the brain. Disembodiment becomes a real possibility, not just a funny fantasy...How could such a mind be located anywhere without a body to anchor it? How can it have effects in the physical world? How could we manage to pick out and describe one disembodied mind rather than another? We can hardly *point* to a disembodied mind...Why do we have complex brains at all if they are so dispensable in the functioning of our minds? Why does brain damage obliterate mental faculties if minds do not owe their existence to brains? (1999, 27)

I sketch a reply to McGinn as well as reply to Ryle's caricature of a non-materialist (or dualist) account of persons, and then fill out Foster's overall position about human and divine minds.

First, note that those who believe that the mental or the mind is distinct from or not identical to the body do not hold that mind is "separate from the body." In the case of human embodiment (on a dualist account), persons are very much embodied in terms of their conscious mental life being bound up with the functioning of the body as a whole, its organs, central state nervous system, and there must be (for Foster as well as for mind–body dualists) ways in which the thinking, observing, sensing of the person is functioning as a unified whole with one's sensory organs, motor control, and so on. But what McGinn and Ryle seem to miss is that Foster and mind–body dualists offer accounts of why persons may be so damaged that they think they are disembodied. While under normal, healthy conditions, a person and her body are a functional whole, to see and hear someone giving a paper is to see and hear the functional whole of an embodied person. But imagine that the speaker suffers massive brain damage and is unable to talk or communicate in any way. Then, from the subject's point of view, when she is in a state of neurogenic motor immobility (or catatonia), she as a subject has become inaudible and incapable of making her wishes visible or apparent. Maybe she even feels like a castaway (alluding to Ryle's Robinson Crusoe), and she feels harnessed to her body, which, like a machine, is still able to function in rudimentary ways.

As for McGinn's point about minds and spatial location, consider five points in quick succession.

First, if spatial location is essential for there to be minds, then embodiment may be all that is needed, in which embodiment is thought of along the lines of mind–body dualism. All that would need to change from a dualist perspective is that minds are essentially embodied. But even that seems to need qualifying: it is one thing to claim that a mind is essentially embodied (every mind must have some embodiment) and it is another, more specific claim that each mind can have only the embodiment that it has. We seem to be able to imagine having a different body than we currently do, and while this may be a fantasy, it is actually true that your body today is substantially different in composition than it was seven years ago and even more different than another seven years ago.

Second, again on the assumption that minds must have spatial location, we can imagine spatial worlds as in the 1999 American-Australian film *The Matrix*, in which subjects act and interact with each other and yet their bodies are only virtual and not themselves the material objects of our world, outside the Matrix.

Third, it is not clear how far McGinn is willing to go in allowing that there cannot be minds if we cannot identify them, such as by pointing to them. Imagine some form of materialism is true and minds exist, but they turn out to be human animal bodies that think and feel and move about. But imagine these animals are severe sceptics and they do not know whether they are animal bodies. If such a world seems coherent—there could be mindful animals who are incapable of knowingly pointing to other minds— why could there not be non-physical minds who are embodied and capable of disembodiment even if they and we are unable to tell them apart after disembodiment?

Fourth, consider disembodiment. Even if two disembodied persons could not be individuated from a third-person point of view, individuation may be possible from a first-person point of view. David Lund develops the following account of first-person individuation:

That we do have a first-person access to what grounds subject-individuation seems clear from the first-person viewpoint. When I think about two qualitatively indistinguishable subjects,

S_1 and S_2, from an external third-person viewpoint, no difference appears that would justify the claim that I am thinking about two instead of one. But when I imaginatively suppose that I am (say) S_1, the difference seems transparently clear: I am one subject, and S_2 is someone else, who, remarkably, has a mental life as similar to my own as it can conceivably be. S_2 now appears to me to be just as clearly and absolutely *someone else* as does some third subject, who is not like me at all. The difference between me and S_2 would be like the difference between me and my possible-world twin, who is qualitatively and relationally identical to me. If my twin's world were the actual world, he would occupy the place I have in the world as things actually are. I would not exist—a fact that must be acknowledged to be a highly important fact about what ultimately distinguishes me from every other subject, whether similar to me or not, even though it is inaccessible to a third-person viewpoint. (Lund 2005, 233)

Fifth, the questions McGinn asks about why minds need brains or why brain damage can lead to catastrophic effects on minds are all great questions. And the fact that they are good questions provides more support for a non-materialist position than materialist. So far, materialists have not produced a compelling case that minds are brains or the mental is the physical, and they have not shown that it is impossible for the mind or the mental to exist without a material, functioning body, or that a material, functioning body cannot exist without a mind or the mental. The brain sciences can offer accounts of correlations of mental and physical life, but correlation is not the same as identity. I see no gains scientifically if one adopts a materialist account of identity in which the mental is treated as the self-same thing as the mental or as not metaphysically identical but functioning in unity (a unity that is vulnerable to damage which, presumably, both materialists and dualists want to recognize). So, I find the following claim by Dennett a bit over-stated:

This fundamentally antiscientific stance of dualism is, to my mind, its most disqualifying feature, and is the reason why in this book I adopt the apparently dogmatic rule that dualism is to be avoided at *all* costs, It is not that I think I can give a knock-down proof that dualism, in all its forms, is false or incoherent, but that, given the way dualism wallows in mystery, *accepting dualism is giving up.* (Dennett 1991, 29)

Not only is there nothing antiscientific about dualism in general, but by adopting the idea that what neuroscience reveals is correlation rather than identity, not a single scientific, well-confirmed finding is altered in any way.

One more point about McGinn: while it is evident that brain damage does indeed "obliterate mental faculties" there is no scientific evidence, strictly speaking, that the obliteration of a human body is identical with the obliteration of the person (1999, 27). For the one to be evidence of the other, we would have to have evidence that there is no God who can sustain the person in existence notwithstanding the loss of the body. And speaking of God, if we allow that there can be explanations involving a being of omnipotent power, why would we be so convinced that the laws of nature are such that God cannot conserve an individual in being at the point of her death?

I turn now to the topic of minds as subjects and then to Foster's idealism. I earlier argued that we can be more certain of the mental than what Ryle, Dennett, and others describe as the physical; I think we can go further than see this as an argument for the existence of the mental. I suggest that in our ordinary and disciplined experience, action, feeling, sensing, and so on, each of us experiences ourselves as a subject enduring and acting (or being acted upon) over time. I cannot monitor a series of MRI images unless I am the same person who saw the first image and then saw a second image and then a third. In a series of lectures by John Foster I attended in Oxford in the 1990s he brought this point home with force. When analysing Daniel Dennett's claim "The thing about brains is that when you look in them, you discover that there's nobody home," Foster asked: who is the *you* that is looking at the brain? (Foster 1993). Foster reasoned, if it is evident that brain qua brain does not itself contain nor is a subject, and it is clear that a subject exists, then there is reason for thinking that the subject is not the same thing as the brain. Given limitations on length, I refer readers to other work that amplifies this point, and provides additional reason for the coherence of theism and there being causal explanations involving the mind of God. This other literature fills out the following thesis: given that there can be or there are human persons, whose actions and lives are not identical with what Ryle and others identify as the physical, then some of the reasons for rejecting theism as incoherent are put to rest. So, in *God in the Age of Science?* Herman Philipse argues that theism is incoherent because there cannot be an incorporeal mind or consciousness. Thus far, I think we do not yet have anything like a sufficiently plausible account of what it is to be physical to come to that conclusion.

So, what about Foster's idealism? He contends that what we think of as the physical world needs to be recognized as partly constituted by sensory experience and as created and sustained in existence by God. He begins his last book, *A World for Us: The Case of Phenomenalistic Idealism*, with this claim:

Put at its simplest, the aim of this work is to establish that the existence of the physical world is logically sustained by the world-suggestive way in which under God's ordinance and authority, things are disposed to appear at the human empirical viewpoint. This idealist thesis . . . stands in sharp contrast to the commonly accepted realist view which takes the world to have an existence that is logically independent of the human mind and metaphysically fundamental. I argue that it is only by accepting the idealist theory that we can represent the physical world as having the empirically immanence it needs if it is to form a world for us. (Foster 2008, 244)

Let's fill this out.

Partly, Foster's thesis is that our commitment to what exists materially is logically dependent on experience and our concepts of what we experience. Our claims that there are unobserved trees in the quad or that our cosmos is over 13 billion years old are partly constituted (and made meaningful) by our experience and concept of trees, years, the cosmos, and the like. Foster contends, too, that our concepts of each other, baseballs, mountains, and so on, are all concepts of the way these objects appear or might appear to us. Foster would be partly supported by some work in quantum mechanics which ties human conscious intentions in accounts of what is physical. Henry Stapp writes:

> [M]any psychologists, neuroscientists, and philosophers who intended to stay in tune with the basic precepts of physics became locked to [sic] the ideas of nineteenth century physicists and failed to acknowledge or recognize the jettisoning by twentieth century physicists of classical materialism and the principle of the causal closure of the physical. Thus while the physicists were bringing the effects attributed to the conscious intentions of human agents into the dynamical description of the physically described world, mainline psychologists, embracing behaviorism, sought to remove such features even from psychology, and most philosophers of mind followed suit. (Stapp 2011, 41)

So far, Foster's thesis may be supported by quantum mechanics and a theory of meaning (our claims about the physical or about reality logically depend on claims about experience), but to fully secure his idealism, Foster employs theism. Theism will also allow us to recognize the meaning of claims about things that we think could not appear to human minds (e.g. quarks, strings, the interior of black holes, and so forth) but may be seen in terms of the divine mind.

In *The Divine Lawmaker*, Foster develops reasons why the existence of a cosmos with laws of nature is better explained given theism rather than naturalism. Given that it is reasonable to hold that the cosmos as a whole is sustained by the mind of God, then Foster has idealism in the sense that all that is recognized as material exists in virtue of mind, rather than there being material objects that can exist independent of mind. By Foster's lights, it is God who so made and sustains the cosmos such that it is experienced by us (to use Ryle's language along with one of Berkeley's favourite biblical lines) as the common field in which we live, move, and have our being.

I seek to further clarify Foster's theistic idealism in section 3.

3. The Path to Theistic Idealism

If the first two sections of this chapter are plausible, an important roadblock has been lifted to let theistic idealism into the race of live options in terms of metaphysics and theology. The existence of God in Foster's philosophy was not advanced as an alternative to the God of Christianity, for Foster himself was a Christian (a practising Roman Catholic). But he does offer a more experientially based concept of God's relationship to the cosmos. Traditional theists such as Thomas Aquinas recognized the reality of Jesus Christ experiencing the world as both fully human and divine, but they are reluctant to attribute experience to God or the Godhead (apart from the Incarnation) on the grounds that this would be too anthropomorphic and in conflict with God's eternality, immutability, and impassibility. Foster's idealism need not attribute experience to God, but he does see God's creativity in terms of God creating a cosmos that is made for and is partly constituted by divinely ordained experiences. This need not be anthropocentric or anthropomorphic, as "experience" should not (in my view) be thought of as limited to human experiences. I believe that Foster's stress on the world *for us* needs to explicitly stress that the world is not *only* for us, but for perhaps numberless other experiential creatures. Moreover, Foster's idealism can also allow that the bare existence of a cosmos prior to created experiencing beings is a great good, both for its own sake and for the sake of divine experience.

Foster's stress on experience and its central role in our understanding of reality provides an important challenge to political and ethical theories such as most forms of Marxism that diminish the importance of experience and mental causation. While views of the self and causation found in work by Churchland and Dennett seem to undermine both the reality and value of experience, Foster's idealism invites us to see selves and experience at the very centre of things.

Historically, Berkeley argued for theism on the basis of idealism. Foster has (in my view) good arguments for the ineliminability of experience (whether theism is true or not), but I suggest that he needs theism to secure his idealism. Absent theism, one may claim that *our concepts of events prior to the emergence of experiencing beings* involve some incipient or inchoate experiential content advanced by the one making the claim, but it is another thing to hold that the events themselves (prior to the emergence of experiencing beings) are sustained or constituted by human or any other experiencing creature. Theism would, however, help one make that last step in terms of God making and sustaining the cosmos as a place fit for experiencing beings.

Is Foster's theistic idealism plausible? Not surprisingly, this will depend on what you independently find plausible in the philosophy of mind, philosophy of space, the philosophy of meaning and reference, and your assessment of theistic arguments, especially the teleological argument (which is at the heart of Foster's book *The Divine Lawmaker*). If you find yourself convinced by Ryle, Churchland, Dennett, and others about the philosophically shabby state of non-materialistic philosophies, theistic idealism does not stand a ghost of a chance. But in the philosophical climate of today, Ryle's outlook and the severity of the materialism found in works by Dennett and others are not seen as invincible. So, if you were swept up in the heyday of Ryle's Oxford in the 1950s on up to 1965, Ryle's methods and conclusions may seem the only option. But today, things have changed. Peter Unger's comment below is perhaps a bit demeaning, but not unrepresentative of many. Unger writes about how Ryle's seminal, highly influential work *The Concept of Mind* had his devotion as a teenager, but not now in his mature rereading of the book:

When I was a teenager, I thought that *The Concept of Mind* was a remarkably fine work in philosophy, quite as full of profound philosophic truths as it was replete with nice stylistic turns. Well, that's teenagers, for you. But as I now fervently hope, not very many philosophers will continue to be so much like a certain mere teenager once was—so terribly impressed by just so much false and even fatuous philosophy. (Unger 2005, 409)

If you are among those philosophers who are similarly unimpressed with the outlook of Ryle and his progeny, and you are at least open to theism, then Foster's theistic idealism should be explored as an alternative form of theism that provides for the central role and value of selves and experience.

References

Churchland, P. M. (2013). *Matter and Consciousness*. Cambridge, Mass.: Massachusetts Institute of Technology Press.

Dennett, D. C. (1991). *Consciousness Explained*. Cambridge, Mass.: MIT Press.

Dennett, D. C. (2003). "Who's On First? Heterophenomenology Explained," *Journal of Consciousness Studies* 10/9: 19–30.

Dennett, D. C. (2008). "Daniel Dennett Autobiography Part 1," *Philosophy Now* June/July: 22–6.

Foster, J. (1993). "Dennett's Rejection of Dualism," *Inquiry* 36: 17–32.

Foster, J. (2008). *A World for Us: The Case of Phenomenalistic Idealism*. Oxford: Oxford University Press.

Kim, J. (1996). *Philosophy of Mind*. Boulder, Colo.: Westview Press.

Kim, J. (2000). *Mind in a Physical World: An Essay on the Mind–Body Problem and Mental Causation*. Cambridge, Mass.: Massachusetts Institute of Technology Press.

Lund, D. (2005). *The Conscious Self*. Amherst, NY: Humanity Books.

McGinn, C. (1999). *The Mysterious Flame: Conscious Minds in a Material World*. New York: Basic Books.

Plantinga, A. (2006). "Against Materialism," *Faith and Philosophy* 23/1: 3–32.

Ryle, G. (2009). *The Concept of Mind: 60th Anniversary Edition*. New York: Routledge.

Sober, E. (2000). *Philosophy of Biology*, 2nd edn. Boulder, Colo.: Westview Press.

Strapp, Henry (2011). *Mindful Universe: Quantum Mechanics and the Participating Observer*. New York: Springer.

Unger, P. (2005). *All the Power in the World*. New York: Oxford University Press.

9

God for All Time
From Theism to Ultimism

J. L. Schellenberg

1. Introduction

Western philosophy, in its conversations about religion, has been much exercised by the idea of a personal God: an omnipotent, omniscient, and perfectly good creator of any world there may be. Of course other religious ideas, as well as other versions of this idea, have also been discussed. But the God of traditional theism—the God-Who-is-a-Personal-Agent—has tended to dominate. In this respect the recent rebirth of philosophy of religion within analytical philosophy, which has almost entirely been focused on theistic ideas, is nothing new. It's just an old conversation starting up again. If we are talking about the omnipotent agent God in new ways, and with new analytical tools, it's still *the omnipotent agent God* we're talking about. Hume, Leibniz, Descartes, Augustine, Aristotle, Plato, Anaxagoras—none of these figures would have much difficulty discerning what's going on should he suddenly be transported into the twenty-first century and reanimated in the midst of one of our seminars. (He'd immediately join us in arguing about whether God was responsible for this event!)

Now there are complex historical reasons for the continuing interest in a personal God. The millennia-long influences of western religious traditions, and especially of Christianity, would obviously have to be cited, as would the way in which the idea of an omnipotent agent has lent itself to explanation in metaphysics. Both factors are much in evidence in western philosophy, as we've experienced it so far, and appear as well in the work of leading instigators of the contemporary 'revival' in philosophy of religion such as Richard Swinburne and Alvin Plantinga. Some of the historical reasons involved may go much further back. According to the youthful field of study known as cognitive science of religion, we are primed by evolution for agent-centered religion. Humans, so we are told, are built in such a way that religious agent concepts exert a special appeal (see Barrett 2004, Boyer 2001, Tremlin 2006). This recent work waits to be further confirmed, but its results certainly enjoy a strong initial plausibility.

So is the upshot that the agent God, the personal God, has been overemphasized or emphasized in the wrong way, philosophically, at least in the west? Certainly there are some philosophers—and maybe we can tell by extrapolation from the above why they are not in the majority—who are calling for increased attention to alternative conceptions of the Divine. Because of an ambiguity in the word 'God' that I shall be exploiting, which allows it to range more narrowly or more broadly, sometimes the phrase used is 'alternative conceptions of God.' Often what these people have in mind, or so it appears, is that we should be paying more attention to detailed pantheistic, panentheistic, perhaps process theistic views that have been knocked to one side in the rush to embrace or attack traditional theism. We need to be conversing with Spinoza, Hegel, and Whitehead as well as with Descartes, Leibniz, and Hume.

Others, influenced by the great diversity of the world's religious life, sensitive to the many *conflicting* details in religious concepts, have argued that we should focus on developing a concept of the Divine which puts it quite beyond any of our detailed representations, including that of traditional theism, and indeed altogether beyond human thought. Maybe we in the west need to be conversing with Pseudo-Dionysius, Meister Eckhart, and al-Farabi too, not to mention all the non-western philosophers and religious thinkers who have taught the idea of an ineffable or transcategorial Divine. One proposal in particular has captured the attention of contemporary analytical philosophers, and that is John Hick's work on the 'Real.' (The religious application of the term 'transcategorial' originates, I believe, with him.)

The directions of thought I have just distinguished are, in my view, important and worth pursuing. Let many flowers bloom, so say I. But I have my own proposal, and a novel science-informed rationale for endorsing it. As I see it, the first option about alternatives mentioned above, which advocates exploring pantheism, panentheism, and similar ideas in detail, while excellent as far as it goes, in an important sense doesn't go *far enough*. While it is ready to speak of alternative conceptions *of God*, thus suggesting a broader idea of a Divine reality not restricted to the theistic personal God (or any other detailed center of religious life to which the word 'God' has been applied), it leaves that broader framework idea and the reasons for emphasizing it obscure. This *general* idea of God—which, given our preoccupation with details, might itself be regarded as an *alternative* idea of God—is not clarified. As for the second, Hickian approach: while admirably motivated, in an important sense it goes *too far*. From detailed conceptions we move outward to a level of vagueness so deep that literally nothing can be said about the Divine. Though it might have been otherwise had the flight from detail been terminated earlier, and the reasons for seeking increased generality correctly identified, no framework is afforded for continuing religious investigation into the future.

I myself, of course, have the happy Goldilocks position that goes just far enough! Well, that is for arguments to decide. After sketching a general conception in connection with which we might more self-consciously use the word 'God,' I shall give *my* arguments, paying special attention to the ways in which, in the new context for discussion I hope to open up, traditional theism will, perforce, recede to the secondary status it should always have had.

2. Ultimism

With concepts come propositions or claims—claims to the effect that those concepts are exemplified. And so, as we have already noted, with the idea of a personal God comes the claim of traditional theism (or theism for short). In part because everything I'm doing here amounts to a debate with those who wish to think no more broadly than theism, I shall generally be speaking of my depiction of the alternative, more general way of thinking about God in terms of the proposition claiming *it* is realized. This proposition I have called *ultimism* (Schellenberg 2005).

𝕖 'Ultimism' is the name I offer for one way of developing the ultimate proposition, the way I shall defend as offering a framework appropriate for religious investigation far into the future, and as describing the reality most worthy of being called 'God.' On this approach, the basic claim religion in the twenty-first century should be seen as calling us to consider is that there is a reality *ultimate in three ways*: metaphysically, axiologically, and soteriologically. Immediately we leave behind the vague gesturing of much talk about ultimacy in contemporary religious studies. But what exactly does *my* talk imply?

To see, it may be useful first to step back a bit and say something about another notion: that of a *transcendent* reality. The reality at the heart of many religious lives past and present is conceived as transcending—as being something more than or deeper than or greater than—mundane reality, where by 'mundane reality' or 'the mundane realm' I mean (to quote part of an earlier discussion of mine that remains relevant) "those aspects of human life and its environment to which just any mature human always has quick and natural cognitive and experiential access, what might (in two senses) be called the *common* elements of human life, which all who eat, drink, sleep, play, think, relate, and so on, will explicitly know and regularly encounter" (Schellenberg 2005, 11). Now the transcendent reality of religion is certainly something 'more' than mundane in factual terms, but if that's all there is to be said about it, it might very well turn out to be something discoverable by science and completely at home in a secular picture of the world. As so many examples suggest, what the religious have in mind is also something 'more' in inherent *value* and in what we might term *importance*, by which I mean its value for us—for human life. The first, purely factual sort of transcendence we may call metaphysical transcendence, the second is axiological transcendence, and the third soteriological transcendence (I use the term 'soteriological' advisedly, recognizing that it is often employed in contexts narrower than mine). It is by embracing these three together rather than the first alone, so I suggest, that we might profitably see religiousness as instantiated.

Let's examine a bit further these three kinds of transcendence. To say that something is *metaphysically transcendent* is to say that its existence is a fact distinct from any mundane fact and in some way a more fundamental fact about reality than any mundane fact (more fundamental in a broadly causal and explanatorily relevant sense). To say that something is *axiologically transcendent* is to say that its inherent value—its splendor, its excellence—exceeds that of anything found in mundane reality alone. And to say that something is *soteriologically transcendent* is to say that being rightly related to it will make for more well-being, fulfillment, wholeness, and the like for creatures than can be attained at the mundane level alone (this leaves open the possibility that spiritual well-being might in some way be attainable *through* mundane things). The different realities believed by practitioners to be at the heart of Jewish, Christian, Islamic, Hindu, Buddhist, and Taoist practice certainly appear to be regarded as 'more' in all three of these ways (and the same goes for other forms of religion as different from one another as North American aboriginal and ancient Greek); they are regarded as transcendent not just metaphysically, but also axiologically and soteriologically. I call this complex property *triple transcendence*.[1]

Of course, as already suggested, the various religious traditions of the world typically don't let the matter rest here—they have much more to say about how the 'more' of transcendence is to be construed. Details are added to the basic content of triple transcendence. And so we hear of the nonpersonal world-soul Brahman, or of the Buddha-nature, or of a personal God or gods (perhaps many gods or a God that is Three-in-One). The religious traditions differ in the sort of detail and also in how much detail they offer us. But they also differ along another dimension, which I shall be emphasizing, and this is a dimension I call *strength*. A strong concept of the Divine says or implies that the Divine is not just transcendent; it is ultimate, and ultimate in all three of the ways we have distinguished: metaphysically, axiologically, and soteriologically. A strong concept, in other words, takes us from triple transcendence to *triple ultimacy*, in effect endorsing the content of ultimism.[2]

Before explaining a little further how the three kinds of ultimacy are to be conceived, let me record my impression that the word 'God' is typically used in connection with views that may be regarded as elaborating them. I venture to surmise that it is an apparent connection to ultimacy that elicits use of the word 'God' and that the perhaps inchoate tendency of, for example, traditional theists and monistic Hindus to regard

---

[1] The use of the word 'transcendence' that is relevant here is easily conflated with another found in religion, which focuses on a qualitative feature or features of certain *elevated human experiences*. Now technically the latter could satisfy my description of triple transcendence, but usually the 'reality' central to religion is regarded as being more than an experience. Of course, even when this is so, the former may be closely related to the latter. Perhaps especially in a soteriological context one might be moved to speak of experiences of transcendence as *attending* a right relationship to the transcendent Divine.

[2] Of course, it may do so—and a similar observation applies to the other ideas I have mentioned, such as the idea of transcendence—without any religious person ever employing the *word* 'ultimism' or 'ultimate.' The religious concepts with which we operate and the words we use to speak of them, if we ever do, are distinct matters.

the reality central to their religious practices as ultimate is a necessary condition of their inclination to call it God. Perhaps lesser realities, even if triply transcendent, would not be seen as deserving the label. But, if so, then it is natural indeed to say of the bare concept of triple ultimacy, *without* elaboration, that what it refers to is appropriately called God. In a sense, the label may be *most* appropriate when thus applied. Certainly this would be the case if only thus were exposed the more fundamental features to which any narrower usage must conform if it is to really be homing in on the Divine.

Let's look more closely now at the content of ultimism (and when using the word in this way I shall always mean unelaborated ultimism). What is metaphysical ultimacy? axiological ultimacy? soteriological ultimacy? Here I am torn between a desire to work, in each case, toward a clear notion through analysis and a sense of the need to leave room for various analyses; perhaps only if we recognize the latter need can ultimism be for us a proper *framework* proposition, stimulating much creative religious exploration that we may have occasion to value even millennia hence. Striving for a proper balance, let me offer a few remarks.

Metaphysical ultimacy, in line with what was said earlier about metaphysical transcendence, involves the property of fundamentally determining what exists and (insofar as this is determined by anything) that it exists as it does—a property that for those with interests in both what and why will be relevant explanatorily. Something is metaphysically ultimate in the sense embraced by ultimism just in case its existence is the ultimate or most fundamental fact about the nature of things, in relation to which any other fact about what things exist and how they exist would have to be understood in a correct and comprehensive account of things. Plato, in speaking of the form of the Good, and metaphysically naturalistic scientists in speaking of the elusive Theory of Everything, seem both to have in mind something bearing metaphysical ultimacy in this sense. Religious people whose conception of the Divine is metaphysically ultimistic have it in mind too.

What else do they have in mind, at the metaphysical level? Well, I suspect this varies, and we should allow it to vary—remaining open to exploring many possibilities. For as soon as we say more we are already *elaborating* the basic idea of metaphysical ultimacy at the heart of ultimism. It might, for example, seem appealing to follow up on some interesting suggestions about the idea of an ultimate reality made by Robert Nozick (1989, 200). Nozick distinguishes several senses of this notion; the labels are mine but the descriptions are his: compositional ("the ground-floor stuff out of which everything is composed"), explanatory ("the fundamental explanatory level which explains all current happenings"), generative ("the factor out of which everything else originated"), and teleological ("the goal toward which everything develops"). The second of these seems a weaker version of what I've set out in the previous paragraph, and entailed by it. The others—including the fourth (which can also be seen as suggesting a move beyond the metaphysical to the axiological)—could all be explored as indicating some of the *ways* in which metaphysical ultimacy in my minimal sense might be realized.

Perhaps they are even compatible; there are conceivable religious elaborations of metaphysical ultimacy that argue as much. (Perhaps an 'emanationist' model that pictured the embodiment of the Divine by the rest of reality deepened and enriched over time would allow for generative ultimacy to also be compositional and teleological.)

But ultimism, as I understand it, entails none of these things. Given such elaborations, we already have *alternative conceptions* of the metaphysical dimension of God or the Divine. And with them the possibility of conflict between such conceptions, and between them and metaphysical naturalism, already emerges. A naturalism which holds that the universe is infinite in past time, for example, will say there is no generative ultimate. And theism will say there is no compositional ultimate, since you and I and the Person Who Is God aren't composed of the same 'stuff.' The metaphysical component entailed by ultimism, as I am presenting it, transcends such conflicts; it is at once broad enough for many within religion and without to endorse it and precise enough to provide a basis for further inquiry into details—inquiry which might conceivably make moving further into the ultimistic realm appealing.

So what else do we find there? Let's consider axiological ultimacy. Here again we have an intensification—a totalizing or ultimizing—of what was said earlier about the relevant aspect of transcendence. If axiological transcendence is excellence and splendor surpassing anything in mundane reality, then axiological ultimacy is completely *unsurpassable* splendor and excellence. Here the famous Anselmian idea—which ironically is linked only to the broader sense of 'God' not exclusive to theism—might profitably be contemplated: the idea of something-than-which-a-greater cannot-be-thought. This is axiological ultimacy, as I have built it into ultimism. Something is axiologically ultimate just in case it is ultimate in inherent value—the greatest possible reality.

Some might be tempted to assume that I have in mind, when speaking of axiological ultimacy, some claim to the effect (or entailing) that the existence of the Ultimate is the foundation for ethics or value theory or some such thing. Perhaps the friends of Euthyphro should rejoice! But this is not the case. Of course, there are conceivable elaborations of ultimism that run in this direction, but nothing of the sort is entailed by it. The Divine could be unsurpassably great even if the 'foundations' for ethics and value theory, if such there be, allow for a fully secular appreciation—for example, by consisting of necessary truths concerning value. And if this is not the case, if somehow the Divine is the ground of value and explains why things have the value they do have, then in speaking of this we have ventured back into the domain of *metaphysical* ultimacy and left axiological ultimacy, as here construed, behind.

Notice that we are talking not only about something that exceeds in inherent value anything else in the *actual* world. By saying it is unsurpass*able* I mean to imply that it *cannot* be surpassed, in any possible world. This seems required in order to take account of ultimizing or totalizing attitudes as we find them in religion, such as attitudes of worship, which recognize no limit of any kind to the greatness of the Divine. Out of the corner of my mind, as it were, I am also glancing at the future and thinking of the sort of framework proposition we might profitably pass along to the generations that will follow us (more on this in section 3).

Notice, also, that by moving on from metaphysical to axiological ultimacy in the construction of ultimism, we move past anything that might *nonreligiously* be endorsed. Some naturalists may demur, thinking that Nature or the most explanatorily basic fact about nature might be unsurpassably great. But in making this observation, I suggest, they are in effect observing a way of stepping *from* naturalism (at least from any naturalism defined in relation to twenty-first-century empirical science) into a form of pantheism—which is one way in which the religious idea of ultimism might be elaborated.

Let's now add soteriological ultimacy to our picture of the Divine, and by doing so ensconce that picture all the more securely in religious territory. For the ultimist, it's not just some greater good than can be found at the mundane level per se that is attainable in relation to the Ultimate, but the very greatest good that can be embodied in creaturely living—our *deepest* good (thus we are still talking about value, but not—at least not more than indirectly—about the inherent greatness of the Divine). Earlier I characterized this as a good *for us*. This expression invites discussion of the extension of 'us'—what is included in its range? Over time we have seen some movement, in the religious traditions of the world, toward a universal concern, and today one often hears religious people speaking of the good of the whole world as something they are actively seeking. Should we build such a universal attainability of wholeness or fulfillment or salvation into our understanding of soteriological ultimacy?

Here we need to distinguish two levels of 'attainable good.' First, soteriological ultimacy might be thought to involve a good attainable *by the religious practitioner*. Religion in the personal sense of religiousness that most concerns me involves a *practice*. And part of what makes a conception of the Ultimate religious, so it seems, is a certain view as to how this reality is related to such a practice. The short answer: soteriologically. On this view, anyone who takes up religious practice is thereby put in a position to attain his or her deepest good.

Having noted this, we can also move to a second level, discussing how widely beneficial states of affairs will—at least eventually—be distributed in the world, if ultimism is true. Certainly it is natural to imagine the value of the Ultimate communicated *through* religious practitioners, and perhaps also in many other ways, to all the world. It is tempting to say that nothing less than a consummation of things in which all the world tastes the goodness of the Divine could be worthy of ultimism. But I am content to leave open various possible interpretations, by altogether avoiding in my definition a reference to *us*: a reality is soteriologically ultimate just in case in relation to it an ultimate good can be attained.

So we have before us my depiction of what might be called the general concept of God. Again, given our preoccupation with details, this represents an *alternative* way of thinking about God, though of course the word 'alternative' is used here in a sense that allows a great many more detailed pictures of the Divine to be compatible with my own, even if they are incompatible with (and thus logically alternatives to) each other. According to ultimism's spare vision there is a reality triply ultimate: metaphysically, axiologically, and soteriologically. Ultimism, as can be seen, is actually logically equivalent to a large *disjunction* of propositions—all those more detailed religious claims that entail ultimism and thus, if my proposal be accepted, are able to show themselves *worthy* of the label 'religious.' Theism would be thought to entail ultimism, and the same goes for various other detailed religious ideas, including pantheism as usually described. But ultimism entails none of these propositions. By claiming that ultimism is true, any religious believer is in one sense, perhaps the deepest, and also the broadest, claiming that *God* exists. But she is at the same time recognizing, admitting, perhaps even exulting in the many alternative conceptions of God—*this* God—that our species may hardly yet have begun to explore.

3. Temporalism

And with that tantalizing thought I move from a summary of our results so far to a suggestion of new ones to be gleaned in the present section of the chapter and in section 4. The central new idea is that there is a reason related to the scientific discovery of *deep time* that will support 'going general' in our thinking about God, at least for the purpose of establishing the proper framework for human religious reflection. Both in philosophy and in religion there is a striking tendency to forget our very early stage of evolutionary development as a species (and I have in mind both biological and cultural evolution). I have recently been seeking to remind us of this, and the position I am defending in doing so, which emphasizes our place in time and the importance of bending our thought accordingly, I call *scientific temporalism* ('temporalism' for short).

Temporalism tells us that the transition from human timescales involving months, years, or centuries to scientific timescales is still quite incomplete. Now it may be thought that we are actually becoming quite familiar with deep time: aren't evolutionary studies, for example, all the rage? But what we've been getting used to is really just one side of the story, which concerns the deep *past*. The rest of the story concerns the deep future and where we are located between those two—between deep past and deep future. We need to notice our *place* in time, wedged between perhaps 50,000 years on one side, part of the short inter-glacial period in which behaviorally modern humans have arisen, and another *billion* or so on the other—life's potential future on our planet. And we need to reflect carefully on this Great Disparity, humbly considering the changes in religiously relevant thought and feeling that earth might see in so much time, were we—or other intelligent and sensitive species that follow us—to occupy it. (Notice that nothing here depends on the notion that we *will* occupy it.)

These neglected scientific facts and cultural possibilities are relevant to how we should think about God. We tend to treat ourselves as intellectually and spiritually mature, but reflection on the deep future can give us some perspective, helping us to see how humans might here be misled by another error of *scale*, analogous to others science has been forced to correct (e.g., our mistaken picture of the size of the universe), thinking that we are nearing our destination when the journey has in fact just begun. Considering our true place in time, it should strike us that the alternative construals of a transcendent Divine reality we've dug up so far might mark only a bare beginning of religious investigation. Seeing how very early a stage of intelligent development *Homo sapiens* is in, absorbing that bigger scientific picture properly, a bit of humility should arise, leading us to admit that there may be many ways of adding detail to ultimism that we haven't even conceived, perhaps including ones we are presently quite unable to conceive. Maybe it would take a great deal longer than we self-importantly imagine for intelligence and spiritual sensitivity to mature to the point where detailed religious discoveries *could* be made. This state of affairs is epistemically possible, by which I mean that we have no way justifiedly to rule it out (for more on the general epistemological issues involved here, see Schellenberg 2007 and in preparation).

From the perspective temporalism opens up to us, it must seem immodest and premature to place a great deal of weight on any detailed religious proposition. So what sort of idea of God should we be most inclined to hold on to and treat as fundamental? A *general* one. At such an early evolutionary stage our best chance at working, in this intellectually rather ambitious territory, with ideas possessing what I will call *temporal stability*—ideas that even more deeply enlightened descendants of ours existing in the far future, if such there should ever be, would find valuable—is to go general. And this, I suggest, means taking as our point of reference the triple ultimacy central to ultimism—the biggest and arguably the most interesting idea that religion has yet delivered—rather than any detailed conception of God. (I, of course, am not responsible for producing this idea. It has been with us for thousands of years. All I am doing is drawing attention to it, pushing aside the weeds of thought that have obscured it from our eyes.)

Recall the disjunction to which ultimism is logically equivalent. We have no idea how big that disjunction is and whether it may not include religious disjuncts that far surpass in power and illumination any large-scale explanatory idea yet conceived by human beings. But what we can do is *emphasize the disjunction* and work at getting a better sense of the disjuncts it may contain, guided by ultimism, which determines their character. Our idea of God needs to be a *framework* idea, whose extant fillings we must indeed continue to explore, as one of the approaches mentioned at the beginning of this chapter would have it, but which we should regard as capable of being filled out in many new ways as well—ways that a few thousand years of looking have perhaps not been sufficient to reveal. Notice that *both* the religious framework idea and various attempts to fill it out should, in my view, be kept in view by investigators, even at an early stage of inquiry. I am not advocating that we ignore details, only that we should not elevate some detailed religious conception to a status of fundamentality it does not deserve.

This is the surprising perspective on thinking about God that, in my view, science supports. It is a perspective that, as I've begun to suggest, will not uphold the continuing dominance of theism in the philosophy of religion. But there are other troubling temporalist implications for theism to be explored, as I want now to show.

4. The Evolutionary Ontological Argument

The title of this section is, I confess, a bit of a tease. I have no evolutionary proof of Anselm's idea. But I do have something like an evolutionary argument for *favoring* that ultimistic idea over the idea of theism, with which it is so often conflated. In fact, one half of the argument has already been given, for we have seen how concerns about temporal stability—the stability of our most ambitious ideas over what may be enormously long periods of cultural and genetic evolution—warrant our keeping carefully in view something very like the general idea Anselm's ontological argument sought to establish as true, and considering many ways of filling it out other than theism. But there is another concern too, which I call a concern about *spiritual authenticity*.[3]

The central idea here is that in the light of ultimism, clearer than any cast by its elaborations, theism may appear less impressive than we would like an idea of the Ultimate to be. Add to this the temporalist insight that we could easily mistake an impostor for the genuine article at so early a stage of evolutionary development, and we may find ourselves wondering whether theism *really does* entail ultimism. Its advocates would surely suppose it to do so. The evolutionary ontological argument is completed by the considerations that undermine this supposition.

The idea of a personal God is, for any sensitive human being who sees it in the light it *can* compel, with the weeds of thought that obscure the vision of many contemporary *atheists* brushed aside, a deeply affecting one. The greatest possible person would be a great thing indeed. Beginning from our own experiences of power, knowledge, and goodness and extrapolating to ultimate versions thereof, recognizing that we could never fully embrace in thought the result of doing so, noting also that there may be facets of Godly greatness compatible with those just mentioned of which we can form no conception, we may think the theistic idea of God to *be* ultimate—ultimate among religious ideas. Imagining what it would be like to grow ever deeper into knowledge by acquaintance of such a being's nature, striving to appreciate what must be the limitless subtleties and nuances of a personal relationship with the personal God, we may be unable to imagine anything that could be better—more saving—for vulnerable finite lives like our own.

And yet... And yet it is significant that everything I have just described falls within the parameters of the concept of a *person*, with the attributes of personhood determined by what we and the rest of our species have experienced thus far in our own very

---

[3] I first gestured at these two concerns in Schellenberg 2009, ch. 1.

short career as persons. Could an ultimate reality be thus narrowly confined? "The concept of God," Peter van Inwagen writes in his recent Gifford lectures, is not just "the concept of a greatest possible person." It is "the concept of a *person* who is the greatest possible being" (2006, 158). But *could* a person, with personhood understood by reference to us, be the greatest possible being? Perhaps personhood as known by us is the thin end of a wedge that thickens indefinitely, with the reality of the thicker parts in some way embracing strands of what we know but also transcending them to such an extent as to be quite unrecognizable by us. Perhaps, alternatively, something like Spinoza's idea is correct and mind and matter—the modes of being with which we are acquainted—are but two of an infinite number of dimensions or modes of Divinity (for more on such possibilities see Schellenberg 2007). Who can say? We are of course ready to be content with the idea of a Divine Person. With the hymn writer I may imagine that "He walks with me and He talks with me, and He tells me I am His own," feeling that this is quite enough. But is it enough for triple ultimacy?

Especially given a temporalist perspective, there is reason to be in doubt—skeptical—as to whether it is. It could be that theism represents no more than an early attempt to fill out the Divine idea, one overly influenced by our attraction, cognitively, to agential modes of explanation, and one that, were we to share the full future of life on earth, over a period 20,000 times as long as our past, inquiring all the while, we would surpass many times over. Now to extrapolate from our experience as persons when developing religious ideas is of course quite natural for us—if the cognitive science of religion is right, then it is natural indeed! But it may also lead us to become obsessed with religious ideas that fall far short of what may remain to be encountered. All in all, even our best and fullest experience of personhood is a slender reed on which to hang a conception of the Ultimate.

Notice that the issue here isn't whether we should be in doubt as to whether theism is *true*. I have argued elsewhere that at least so much *is* justified (Schellenberg 2007), but that is not my concern at the moment. The issue is whether theism offers a contender for the status of ultimacy in the first place. Unless it does so, it can hardly hope to retain a central place in our investigations in philosophy of religion as we seek to take the idea of religious ultimacy from the past into the future. Of course, one could tack on at the end of the traditional theistic proposition with its omni-attributes the following addition: "and this being is metaphysically, axiologically, and soteriologically ultimate." That would quite trivially make of theism an ultimacy claim. But nothing is accomplished through such sleight of hand. For now we do find ourselves wondering whether theism is true, because we wonder whether the content coming *before* the tacked-on bit entails it! Indeed, the two sorts of doubt I have distinguished now coincide.

Notice how different things must be if instead of theism we make ultimism most fundamental in our religious inquiry. Ultimism's spiritual authenticity can hardly be challenged, since it provides the standard by which to *assess* claims as being authentic, spiritually, or not. So long as this more general idea of God was left obscure, theism could stand unchallenged. But with ultimism clarified, we are able to compare the two propositions. We are able, furthermore, to see that theism should entail ultimism, if the hopes for it cherished by many philosophers of religion are well grounded. And we can see that it's not at all clear that it does entail ultimism. Moreover, with an investigative orientation tempered by temporalism, we can see that there are good reasons, at so early a stage of evolutionary development, to beware of premature commitment to what could be misleading details and indeed to *look* for something much more general like ultimism to guide the much more thoroughgoing efforts in *detailed* religious investigation that are needed.

5. Ultimism and 'the Real'

I have argued that the general idea of ultimism should become foundational in philosophy of religion's discussions of God, and that the alternative ways of filling out that idea—and in particular the one offered by theism—should be regarded as having, at best, a secondary status. On temporalist grounds we can see that the general concept should provide our starting point, when the question is how to think about God. And, having settled that, and having *clarified* the general idea, we now have a decent framework for discussing *many* alternative conceptions of God—that is to say many different ways of attempting to fill out that general picture, including any renewed attempts made by theists—as we move into the future.

How does all this relate to the *second* way of seeking to get past an overemphasis on the personal God mentioned at the beginning of this chapter—the Hickian approach? If we can now see that the first approach does not go far enough, because it leaves the general idea of God and the reasons for emphasizing it unclear, can we by the same token see how the second approach, as I earlier suggested, goes too far?

I think we can, and in this final section of the chapter, I want to show how. John Hick's efforts to revive a transcategorial, ineffabilist picture of the Divine in the midst of twentieth-century analytical philosophy of religion are strikingly bold and bracing. Much can be learned from Hick's work. And his sensitivity to the facts of religious diversity—which, together with a Kantian strain of thought, form the basis for his approach—is exemplary. But the Hickian concept of the 'Real', a Divine reality that "in itself is not and cannot be humanly experienced" (Hick 1989, 249) and whose positive, nonformal properties we could not possibly grasp, leaves something to be desired. Though one can, as Hick points out, find examples of ineffabilist talk about the Divine in many different religious traditions, one wonders why it isn't to be regarded as being what Hick himself took incarnational language about Jesus to be in another context: "hyperbole of the heart" (Hick 1977, 183). That nothing can be said of the Divine, that it merits silence alone, and so on—these are the sorts of things religious people say when stunned by the apparent *greatness* of God in certain kinds of religious experience. And this is a *positive* quality. Sure, it may be that no detailed picture religion has yet produced can do it justice, but then why not retreat to talking of such greatness alone, as does ultimism? Even if none *could* do it justice because the depths of God's greatness are permanently ineffable, still we would have greatness! For reasons such as this, one wonders whether Hick, in picking up the ineffability idea and running with it, hasn't gone too far. Why isn't ultimism far enough?

Notice that ultimism, unlike the concept of the 'Real', is not insensitive to real-world aspirations to gain some understanding of God. Instead, it provides a framework within which we may seek to fulfill them. Now I am not saying that ultimism itself is today an appropriate object of belief or securely known. (Indeed, belief too may recede in importance when temporalist considerations are fully absorbed; it could easily be set on one side and replaced in our current discussions by an emphasis on such things as justified *positions*.) But it certainly provides a basis for wide-ranging and optimistic exploration. Most of the positive things that the various religious traditions of the world have wanted to say about the Divine can be investigated within the parameters of ultimism: the facts of religious diversity are fully—certainly *more* fully—accommodated here. Accordingly one wants to say that Hick goes further than his own sensitivity to religious diversity might have been expected to take him.

Now here the ineffabilist point, inspired by Kant, may be introduced again to discourage such investigative optimism. However the Kantian move has been powerfully criticized—for example, in Plantinga (2000). And within a temporalist perspective one may in any case wish to replace an application of the distinction between phenomenal and noumenal with an application of the distinction between what has become cognitively accessible so far and what would require much further evolution, biological and/or cultural—and perhaps new kinds of evolution or evolution in new directions—to be revealed. Or perhaps we should say that even if there is some absolute cognitive limit of a relevant sort, for all we know much further investigation of profound ideas, including the idea of God, could in the right circumstances be undertaken successfully before it was reached. Even if human efforts so far leave much to be desired, why suppose they could not be greatly bettered if much further extended, with science providing the criteria for interpreting 'much further'? Any temporalist investigative pessimism we may feel should be united with a certain *optimism*—these two come in the same package. Not having taken account of temporalist insights, Hick offers us pessimism alone. And thus he goes too far.

But will we ever find ourselves in 'the right circumstances'? Is this optimism I have mentioned going to be borne out by the facts of our human or by a trans-human future? There is really no way to tell. However, anyone who has truly absorbed the reality of deep time and engages in religious investigation requires both the humility and the audacity to imagine that it may be so, and will be ready for a scale of investigation that matches the profundity of its object. She will think about God in a manner that allows her to be part of a trans-generational process of inquiry—a long process weaving its way through deep time that we who recognize our place in time must imagine to be unfolding in order to give life and hope to our present inquiries. In this context it will, to say the least, appear short-sighted to make a detailed proposition like theism, so tied to our past and present experience, as central in philosophy of religion as it has recently been. It is in the very nature of the idea of God that we cannot rest with a God from our time or for our time alone. We need a God for *all* time. Better than any alternative, this is what ultimism provides.

References

Barrett, Justin L. (2004). *Why Would Anyone Believe in God?* Lanham, MD: AltaMira Press.

Boyer, Pascal (2001). *Religion Explained: The Evolutionary Origins of Religious Thought.* New York: Basic Books.

Hick, John (1977). "Jesus and the World Religions," in John Hick (ed.), *The Myth of God Incarnate.* Philadelphia: Westminster Press.

Hick, John (1989). *An Interpretation of Religion.* New Haven: Yale University Press.

Nozick, Robert (1989). *The Examined Life: Philosophical Meditations.* New York: Simon & Schuster.

Plantinga, Alvin (2000). *Warranted Christian Belief.* New York: Oxford University Press.

Schellenberg, J. L. (2005). *Prolegomena to a Philosophy of Religion.* Ithaca, NY: Cornell University Press.

Schellenberg, J. L. (2007). *The Wisdom to Doubt: A Justification of Religious Skepticism.* Ithaca, NY: Cornell University Press.

Schellenberg, J. L. (2009). *The Will to Imagine: A Justification of Skeptical Religion.* Ithaca, NY: Cornell University Press.

Schellenberg, J. L. (in preparation). *Reason and Time: Adapting Epistemology to the Immaturity of the Species.*

Tremlin, Todd (2006). *Minds and Gods: The Cognitive Foundations of Religion.* Oxford: Oxford University Press.

van Inwagen, Peter (2006). *The Problem of Evil.* Oxford: Clarendon Press.

10

Playing the God Game
The Perils of Religious Fictionalism

Robin Le Poidevin

1. A Tale of Two Churchgoers

Reginald and Fiona are regular churchgoers. They sing hymns, join in prayers, discuss the sermon afterwards, and often meet to read passages of the Bible together and explore the meanings and implications of those passages. They seem to the neutral onlooker to be equally engaged in these activities, equally inspired by them, and equally inclined to relate them to their everyday lives.

Behaviourally, then, there is nothing to distinguish the religious attitudes of these two individuals. However, on questioning, each gives a very different philosophical account of the basis of that behaviour:

Reginald is a *realist*. More specifically he is a realist believer. He takes God-talk—subject to an important qualification—at face-value, and as true by virtue of the way the world is independently of human belief. He takes statements about God to refer to a real, mind-independent being. The important qualification is that this face-value approach applies to the most central statements of his religion, including the doctrinal statements. He recognizes that a significant proportion of scripture is metaphorical, or couched in terms of stories and parables. He is a realist, but not a fundamentalist.

Fiona is a *fictionalist*. When engaging in religious language and practice, she takes herself to be engaging in a (rather complex) game of make-believe. This attitude goes together with a corresponding view of the semantics of theistic statements: she takes their truth-conditions to be definable by the theological fiction, and the apparently denoting terms to refer to fictional characters and situations. When she asserts 'God loves us', for example, she takes this to be true, but by virtue of the content of the relevant fiction. The general schema that she subscribes to is this: any given theological statement *p* is true if and only if it is true in the theological fiction that *p*.

Sometimes they get together with Andy the anthropological reconstructionist, who thinks that theological discourse is, despite its surface content, really about human ideals, Nora the non-cognitivist, who thinks that theological discourse is expressive rather than propositional, so utterances couched in that language (for the most part) simply lack truth-value—and Agnes the agnostic.[1] These positions provide an important contrast and comparison with the first two, but it is really with Reginald and Fiona that we are initially most concerned.

We might imagine the history of the interactions between Reginald and Fiona (and Andy, Nora, and Agnes, when they are around) as being divided into two phases: before they become aware of their radically different interpretations of the nature of theological discourse and afterwards, when each confesses to the other what they take the nature and point of the discourse to be. But how different would the two phases be? We might suppose that, perhaps after the initial surprise (at least on Reginald's part), the friends decide that there is no reason why they should not continue exactly as before, since the differences between them are not so much religious as *meta*-religious. That is, they concern issues that arise when we reflect on religious activity, as opposing to participating in it. Such meta-religious issues will concern questions about the content, justification, or role of religious language, beliefs, or practices. Recognizing that, in any case, there will be, within any religious community, divergence of views of one sort or another, the friends feel that a spirit of philosophical ecumenism is called for, and that this diversity of interpretative perspectives is likely to enhance, rather than undermine, their religiously motivated interactions with each other. Such, at any rate, is their hope.

We may wonder, however, how far this spirit of philosophical ecumenism can prevail. Can a religious community in which realist belief represents the dominant outlook accommodate fictionalists? We might expect the common ground between realists and fictionalists to be relatively limited, and the state of peaceful coexistence between them to be only on the surface, concealing deeper disagreements. After all, whereas the realists are genuinely trying to make contact with a transcendent being, the fictionalists are merely playing the God game. Are these sceptical doubts justified?

Before engaging with that question, let us explore Fiona's fictionalist outlook in more detail.

2. Fictionalism: Semantics and Attitude

Fictionalist approaches have been proposed for a variety of discourses: there is, for example, fictionalism about numbers, fictionalism about possible worlds, and fictionalism about moral values.[2] What characterizes these positions is a distinctive view of the *semantics* of the discourse in question. Take modal fictionalism as the model. The modal fictionalist notes that a possible world semantics of modal discourse has much going for it, in that it allows us to understand the otherwise opaque modal operators

---

[1] Apparently, Andy has read and been inspired by the writings of Tillich and Bultmann. Nora has similarly been inspired by the writings of Wittgenstein, and feels that her view of religious language captures his. Naturally, other Wittgenstein scholars disagree with her on this tricky exegetical issue.

[2] See, respectively, Field (1980), Rosen (1990), and Joyce (2005).

('necessarily', 'possibly', 'impossibly') in terms of quantifiers ranging over worlds ('in all worlds', 'in some worlds', 'in no worlds'). By this means we can justify the modal axioms in terms, for example, of relations between sets of worlds. The set of all worlds clearly includes some worlds, so 'necessarily p' entails 'possibly p', and so on. But this gain in explanatory power comes, it seems, at an ontological price: we are committed to the existence of these worlds, and the question then arises of what their nature is: concrete or abstract? The modal fictionalist wants the explanatory power of possible world semantics without its ontological cost, and attempts to achieve this by importing the standard possible world semantics into a fictional context. We therefore consider a fiction in which there are, let us say, an infinite number of concrete possible worlds, of which this is only one, all other worlds being both spatially and temporally isolated from us, the unifying principle of a world therefore being a spatiotemporal one: x and y belong to the same world if and only if they stand in spatiotemporal relations to each other. Call this the 'Concrete Possible World Fiction' (CPWF). The fictionalist semantics now proceeds as follows:

> Possibly (p) if and only if, according to the CPWF, p obtains in at least one world
> Necessarily (p) if and only if, according to the CPWF, p obtains in all worlds

This precisely mirrors the intuitive semantics for fictional truths:

> 'Pip goes to see Miss Haversham' is true if and only if, according to the fiction *Great Expectations,* Pip goes to see Miss Haversham

The crucial question for the modal fictionalist is whether this semantics really can deliver all the explanatory benefits of possible world realism. Fictionalism about numbers proceeds in a similar fashion, as does moral fictionalism, which makes use of the fiction that there really exist objective moral values.

The term 'fictionalism' is increasingly used in the literature to refer to a non-realist position on religion,[3] but it appears not to be used to refer to an analogue of the fictionalist positions above. It is defined, rather, in error-theoretic terms: the semantics for theological statements is supposed to be realist, but the truth-conditions simply do not obtain.[4] What makes such account appropriately describable as fictionalist is its characterization of the *attitude* that should be taken towards theological statements: rather than regarding them as true, we should treat them *as if* they were true, and let them guide us accordingly. The motivation for so doing is the instrumental benefits religion brings. And by 'instrumental' is not meant (here at least) 'cynically calculated'. It is not that the fictionalist intends simply to put on a display of piety in order to win certain distinctly secular goods, such as a place for their children at a religious school. Rather, the hope is that engaging in religious activities would, for example, bring latent moral ideals into sharper focus.

---

[3] See, e.g., Eshleman (2005). His characterization of the position can be found on pp. 190–1.
[4] See Eshleman (2005, 185–6).

It is important, then, to distinguish between a fictionalist *semantics* and a fictionalist *attitude*. But it is not clear that they are completely independent of each other. In particular, it is not clear that the attitude is rationally sustainable independently of the corresponding semantics. On the other hand, treating theological statements *as if* they were true clearly fits comfortably with the supposition that they are in fact fictional. That, arguably, is the purer position. So when I use the term 'fictionalism' in this chapter I intend to refer to a position which proposes a fictionalist semantics: the fictionalist attitude will be the natural corollary. Some of the concerns raised in the literature about 'religious fictionalism' may affect the 'pure' form of fictionalism at issue here; others may not.

On the fictionalist account, the logical properties of theological discourse will be those of fictions. So, for example, the world defined by the theological fiction will be incomplete: there are some propositions that are neither true nor false in it, just as there is no fact of the matter as to whether or not Miss Haversham had a George II dressing table in her bedroom. In the God-fiction, bivalence is not preserved. Nevertheless, there is no reason to deny that it is *fictionally complete*; that is, it is not part of the fiction itself that some propositions lack truth-value. Similarly, God-talk is not closed under deduction: if it is true in the theological fiction that p and also true in the theological fiction that Not-p, it does not immediately follow that it is true in the fiction that (p and Not-p). Some inconsistency, therefore, may be tolerated, and does not generate, by the principle of *Ex Falso Quodlibet*, every proposition.

With the fictionalist position characterized, let us turn back to the relations between our three churchgoers.

3. Fiona and Reginald: The Integration of Fictionalists into a Realist Community

On the face of it, Fiona and Reginald have a lot in common, making it relatively easy for them to maintain their policy of peaceful coexistence. Both agree that statements made in the language of God-talk are true. They agree on the decision procedures for deciding whether they are true: appeals to scripture, to canonical statements of doctrine, and to the implications of these. They may even both appeal to considerations of natural theology: the project of relating theological truth to natural phenomena. Natural theology is, of course, typically presented as a realist enterprise. But there is no reason why a fictionalist cannot incorporate the same kind of moves, for the religious fiction is not isolated from the real world. Features of the actual world—the fine-tuning of the universe, for example—can be incorporated into the religious fiction, and play a role within it. And indeed our understanding of ordinary fiction is almost always informed by knowledge of how things are in fact. A rudimentary understanding of the world's actual geography, for example, is a requisite for following the narrative of Jules Verne's *Around the World in Eighty Days*. Similarly, an understanding of actual Tudor history will enrich a reading of Hilary Mantel's *Wolf Hall* and similar historical novels. The authors of such novels will, of course, incorporate quite a bit of the relevant history, but some of this background readers might supply for ourselves, particularly if they are minded to extend the events of the novel in their own imagination. Such extension is precisely what the fictionalist about religious discourse may wish to engage in. So Fiona need not absent herself from conversations with Reginald about natural theology.

Nor need Fiona insist that Reginald is mistaken about the truth-conditions of the statements he utters. For if fictional discourse requires fictive intention, Reginald, who has no such intention, cannot be mistaken in providing a realist semantics for *his* statements. (He would, however, be mistaken if he extended that realist semantics to the statements made by Fiona.)

Both, too, can give religious discourse a central role in shaping their moral and spiritual outlook. Seeing the world through the interpretative framework of God-centred discourse allows them both to get more clearly in focus what is of most value in life: love for others, displacement of the self from the centre of one's projects, the voice of conscience, the subordination of short-term goals to long-term ones, etc. None of this, of course, is inaccessible from the atheistic perspective—it would be arrogant to suggest otherwise—but it is much more accessible (argue Reginald and Fiona) if one inhabits the theistic framework.

What happens when Fiona and Reginald's conversation turns to the problem of evil? Reginald feels some pressure to reconcile his realist belief in the goodness of God with the evident fact of suffering. Fiona is entirely willing to engage with this issue. After all, it is important to her that the fiction is not isolated from real human concerns, and also that the fiction is not (in any obvious way) internally inconsistent. Eventually, after having considered various theodicies which might make sense of suffering, Reginald proposes that, although there most certainly is a solution to the problem of evil, for there is both suffering and a loving God, that solution is probably beyond the comprehension of the human mind. Fiona can readily agree. For the existence of a solution to the problem of evil that is unknown to us is entirely compatible with the logic of fiction. As we observed above, a fiction is incomplete: some propositions will lack a truth-value within the fiction, since whatever account of truth-in-fiction we adopt, the truth-value of some propositions will be underdetermined by that account. Among those propositions lacking a truth-value in the religious fiction may be any statement of a particular theodicy (it is not to be found in any of the canonical writings, but only in interpretative commentaries which lack the authority of those writings). And if p is neither true nor false in the fiction, it cannot be a known fact. However, the fiction is still fictionally complete: that is, it is fictionally true that, for any proposition, bivalence holds. The fictionalist can, therefore, entirely consistently hold that there is a solution to the problem of evil—i.e. that it is true in the fiction that there is such a solution, even if for no p is p the solution.

We may wonder, however, if the appearance of genuine communication between Reginald and Fiona is genuine. Sentences uttered by Reginald will certainly *sound* the same as sentences uttered by Fiona, and there will be a significant number of sentences to which they are both prepared to give assent. But the truth-conditions of a sentence uttered by Reginald, and an apparently identical one as uttered by Fiona, will be quite different. The realist's talk of God, if it picks out anything, picks out a real, transcendent being, otherwise it simply fails to refer. The fictionalist's talk of God, in contrast, picks out a fictional character, and, given the framework, it cannot fail to do so. Different semantics, different content, and so (it seems) no genuine communication. On the other hand, it is quite implausible to suggest that sentences have completely different meanings depending on whether they occur in a fictional or non-fictional context. 'The cat is on the mat,' as uttered by a fictional character, conjures up the same image in the mind of the reader as that same sentence uttered in real life. We do not need a translation manual to be able to read a novel written in our own language. Statements about a cat in a fictional context really do represent a cat (just a purely intentional one). And any doubts that Reginald and Fiona are using words to mean the same things can be put to rest by checking that they both agree on the inferential patterns exhibited by God statements. Both agree, for example, that 'God spoke to Moses' entails 'God spoke to someone.' In the context of specific theories of meaning, admittedly, the meaning of 'Fire!', as uttered in a burning building, will not be the same as the meaning of 'Fire!', as uttered by an actor on stage. If we apply Grice's theory of meaning, for example,[5] we will understand the first in terms of what the utterer wants us to believe, the second in terms of what the author wants us to imagine. But there will be a very significant, and asymmetric, connection. As we might put it, the meaning in a fictional context is parasitic on the meaning in a non-fictional context. It is because a non-fictional utterance of 'Fire!' means what it does that a fictional utterance of 'Fire!' means what *it* does.

The apparent robustness of the agreement between Reginald and Fiona, then, provides some hope that fictionalists can be integrated into a realist community. Three difficulties, however, arise for a fictionalist appropriation of the language and practice of the realist's religion. They concern, respectively: the content of religious language, the experience of religious activity, and the relation between religious doctrine and behaviour. Let us look at these in turn.

4. Choosing the Right Fiction

Any form of fictionalism depends for its success on a clearly defined fiction. Modal fictionalism, for example, can exploit the fact that there already exists a well-worked-out modal semantics in the form of concrete possible world realism. Given that realism can provide, for any modal proposition, a statement of its truth-conditions, so can

---

[5] See Grice (1957).

fictionalism. All the fictionalist has to do is to precede that statement with the 'According to the concrete possible world fiction …' operator. This is not the only fictional story that could be told about the modal, but the fictionalist can decide, among the competing realist accounts, which offers the most satisfactory semantics,[6] and adopt that as the preferred fiction.[7] A similar procedure suggests itself for number fictionalism.

But with religious fictionalism, it is not so clear that one preferred fiction will emerge. There are at least as many religious fictions as there are religious traditions. This in itself is not troubling for the fictionalist, for part of the instrumental value of religion is its role in forming cohesive communities, unified by a common discourse and a common set of ideals. Adopting a religious tradition identifies one with a particular religious community. So the selection of any given religion is much more likely to be determined by cultural factors than by a judgement concerning semantics. Only one religion may in practice be a live contender. (This is not to deny what is plainly the case, that people occasionally move from one religion to another, but typically this happens for decidedly non-fictionalist reasons.) And it is important, for instrumental reasons, that one religious fiction is chosen. Imagine a fictionalist who simply moves at whim from one religion to another. At any one time, there is a consistent semantics for their utterances: it just happens to be a different semantics on different occasions. It is hard to see that this involves anything other than a very provisional, and perhaps also superficial, commitment to the religious life. In contrast, a fictionalist who stays true to a particular religious fiction is in a better position to explore it more deeply, to let it guide them more thoroughly.

Having selected a particular religion, however, further choices have to be made. For within a religious tradition—and this is abundantly true of Christianity—there will, within the realist community, be a variety of ideas concerning which parts of the discourse are to be taken literally, and which regarded as purely symbolic, or metaphorical. This is so even of so central a Christian doctrine as the Incarnation. There are realists who take the doctrine at face value, and assert that God the Son really did live a human life on earth. But there are others who, while taking a realist view of God-talk in general, adopt a 'non-Incarnational' Christology: that is, they take Jesus to be simply and purely human, but as having a unique relationship to God which is metaphorically captured in terms of divine incarnation. This is not a trivial difference, given the central role of the doctrine of the Incarnation in the Christian religion. So which view will the fictionalist adopt, and on what grounds?

It might be thought that a fictionalist will naturally side with the non-incarnational Christologist, as both will agree that, literally understood, the doctrine of the

---

[6] What does 'satisfactory' amount to here? Two things, at least: expressive power—i.e. the range of types of modal statements that are provided with a semantics; and respect for the inferential patterns we know to exist in modal discourse.

[7] For doubts concerning the modal fictionalist project, however, see Divers (1995).

Incarnation is false, so the point of continuing to use incarnational language must lie elsewhere. But it does not follow that *in the fiction*, incarnational language must be taken metaphorically, for else the same reasoning would recommend that every statement uttered within the fiction is to be construed metaphorically. On the other hand, the fictionalist is not obliged to say that, fictionally, God lived on earth as a human being. For even within fictional discourse, the distinction between the literal and the metaphorical can be maintained. That is, it may be fictionally true that it is metaphorical that God lived on earth. So there is a genuine choice for the fictionalist to make here. The fictionalist may choose to wait until the debate between the two realist factions is concluded, and then adopt whichever emerges as the preferred view. But this is unsatisfactory, first, because the issue will not be concluded, and second because reasons for preferring one interpretation of the Incarnation within an essentially realist context may not carry over to the fictionalist context.

This is just one case in which the fictionalist is faced with more than one story to choose between, and the grounds for choosing one over the other are not clear. How will Fiona respond? She may point out that the indeterminacy of any fiction invites us to explore different fictional paths. We might take a given fictional narrative as a trunk from which may sprout different fictional branches, corresponding to different ways in which the narrative might be developed. Engaging with the fiction might involve a certain amount of hopping from branch to branch—and so it is, explains Fiona, with the religious fiction. We do not need to prioritize one branch over another. (Though, bearing in mind the reasons given above against the practice of a fickle fictionalism that simply moves through different religious traditions, the hopping should not get out of hand.)

5. Public and Private Prayer

One very obvious difference one would expect between realism and fictionalism is an experiential one. It just isn't going to feel the same if one abandons the realist outlook in favour of a fictionalist one. Taking it all to be real, and engaging in pretence, are two very different states of mind. Shifting between active engagement with religion on the one hand, and cool reflection on its content and import on the other, is for the fictionalist likely to result in a certain amount of cognitive dissonance, or so one would have thought. For the active engagement to work, awareness of the fictionalist interpretation has to be suppressed (compare being with someone who, throughout a particularly emotional and absorbing film, says 'it's only a film: it's not really happening'). And this is likely to become especially acute when moving from the public to the private sphere. In an act of public worship, and perhaps particularly when a significant number of those participating are realists, the fictionalist will be caught up in the solemnity, joyfulness, and intensity of the occasion. It is comparatively easy, in those circumstances, to engage fully with the fiction (as the fictionalist sees it). The interpretative semantics is far from the forefront of one's mind. But public worship does not exhaust the realist's repertoire of religious practices: there is also the time spent in private prayer, time to which the realist would attach considerable value and importance. What will the fictionalist do?

Let's consider first the reasons Reginald might have for engaging in private prayer. First, he may use it to petition God for various things he desires, in the hope that God will grant his requests. Second, he may use it for companionship, to help him feel closer to God. Third, he may use it for something intermediate between these: to align his will with the will of God. By coming closer to God in prayer, he hopes to become aware of the divine will, and in so doing reorient, as far as possible, his own desires.

Can any of these have a counterpart in Fiona's outlook? The first, prayer as petition, seems ruled out at once. Fiona cannot but be aware that no one is there to grant her requests, and the attempt to make such a request will surely strike her as a sham. There can be no willing suspension of belief here. But this may not be the loss it appears. After all, even realists may have reason to be suspicious of petitionary prayer. Can we really ask God to intervene, if he does not already judge it appropriate to do so? Either what will happen, without intervention, is already in accordance with what he ordains, in which case intervention will make things worse, or it is not in accordance with the divine will, but intervention would not be compatible with the desire to allow humans to shape the world by their own unaided actions.[8] And in any case, the realist may take the view that petitionary prayer is something we should grow out of. Rather than asking God to fix things, as if we were children, we should see ourselves as the instruments of God's purpose. So although Fiona cannot, without a serious degree of self-deception, replicate the realist's use of petitionary prayer, this may not be such a problem, from the mature religious viewpoint.

What of the second use of prayer, the seeking after companionship? For Fiona, there is no companion, and praying as if there is, for the sake of companionship, invites comparison with the sad case of someone's picking up the telephone and (trying to ignore the dialling tone) having a pretend, and very one-sided, conversation, in the vain hope that they will feel a little less lonely. Surely, then, this second use of prayer can have no genuine counterpart in Fiona's life.

That might seem to rule out the third use of prayer, too: the aligning of one's will with the will of God. There is no (real) will of God if there is no (real) God. But might one nevertheless attempt to align one's will with what one imagines *would be* the will of God? Fictional character though he may be, God represents for Fiona a moral ideal, an expression of perfect love. There is nothing self-deceptive in Fiona's genuine attempt to order her will in accordance with this ideal. But then, it will be objected, there is no need for Fiona to do this through the medium of prayer. All she need do is to contemplate that ideal, and attempt to order her desires accordingly. There is no need for a fake attempt at communication. Nevertheless, Fiona may find that a cool contemplation of

---

[8] See e.g. Basinger (1983).

an ideal is not sufficient. She needs to enter more imaginatively into a vision of pure love. Prayer might be just the medium for that imaginative state. It is not, of course, an act of communication, and indeed it need not take precisely that form. It might, rather, be a meditation, and one in which Fiona might find it helpful to voice, in her head, her own thoughts, as if they were addressed to another person, and imagine what someone motivated only by love would say in response. And, without there being any actually hallucinatory experience, answers may come to her as if they did not have their origin in her own thoughts. Phenomenologically, this could have a great deal in common with the experience of prayer that many realists have.

There is one other aspect of prayer that might come under this third heading, which the fictionalist cannot wholly replicate, and that is the wrestling with doubt that even the staunchest realist is subject to from time to time. 'Help thou mine unbelief,' cries the realist.[9] Fiona is not subject to those doubts, since they cannot arise in the fictionalist framework. Is this a loss? Reginald might argue that this wrestling with doubt is part of the authentic religious experience, something that sharpens one's awareness of the demands of a religious life, and a constant test of the sincerity of one's faith. That this should find no counterpart in Fiona's life makes hers a less truly religious outlook. But perhaps, after all, there is a counterpart in Fiona's prayers. Earlier, I mentioned the cognitive dissonance that threatens the fictionalist's religious engagement. Awareness of the fictional nature of what is being said and appealed to may at any time break in upon Fiona's sincere attempt to immerse herself in the fiction. Dealing with that dissonance, resisting its disruptive effect, bears some comparison to the realist's attempt to cope with doubt. Further, Fiona's loyalty to her chosen fiction may be tested from time to time, when it confronts her with uncomfortable moral, psychological, or spiritual truths, and on those occasions some effort of will is required not simply to abandon it.[10]

6. Reasons and Causes

Another potential difference between realism and fictionalism is the role religious language plays in the shaping of behaviour. For Reginald, theistic statements stand in a reason-giving relation to moral attitudes. For example, 'God loves us' expresses a reason to love each other: we are objectively lovable! For Fiona, it seems, such statements cannot be reason-providing in the same way, since the *fictional* truth that God loves us does not give us a reason to love each other. No merely fictional truth, it seems, can give us a reason to do anything. So it does not help to point out that it is fictionally true that 'the fact that God loves us gives us a reason to love each other', for again what counts as a reason in the fiction has no implications for moral attitudes outside the fiction.

This is not to deny that engaging with fiction can shape and develop our moral understanding. Indeed this is part of its very considerable value. But more than one mechanism

---

[9] Mark 9: 24.
[10] I am very grateful to an anonymous reader for this suggestion.

is at work. A fiction might alert us to certain truths about human nature (the characters will not, typically, be presented as having a wholly alien mentality), or present us with hypothetical dilemmas which test our moral understanding. In fiction, then, we may indeed find reasons for what we do—but then those reasons aren't (or aren't wholly) fictional truths. At a somewhat more immediate level, we find ourselves emotionally involved with the fictional characters. Notoriously, our anxiety, joy, and sadness for them seem to sit side by side with a firm belief that they do not actually exist.[11] That emotional involvement may then go on to alter our behaviour towards real people, in positive ways. Here, the relation between fictional truth is not so much reason-giving but causal. Or since (as Davidson (1963) plausibly argued) reasons can also be causes, we should avoid the implication that reasons are acausal, and say just that fiction shapes our behaviour in ways that don't appeal to reasons. For the fictionalist, God-talk is wholly fictional. So the connection between such talk and subsequent behaviour is merely causal. God-talk cannot, for the fictionalist, *rationalize* moral behaviour. For the realist, it can.

Perhaps, however, this difference, though non-trivial, is not enough to prevent the integration of fictionalists into the realist community. The important thing is that religious language continues to be behaviour-shaping; the precise mechanism by which it does so need not interfere with the actual business of religion, but is only the kind of thing to exercise philosophers (!). In any case, the fictionalist can resist the suggestion that the fictional statements of religion cannot be reason-giving. It can be part of engaging with the fiction that certain fictional statements are responded to as if they were true. And that may mark the difference between religious fiction and other fictions. With a film or novel it may be entirely appropriate to respond to it as if it were true, but only *up to a point*. That is, certain emotional responses might be appropriate, the kind that would also be appropriate if it were not fiction but fact. It would not, however, be appropriate to respond to a crime novel, for example, by ringing up the police to ask what they are doing about this horrible murder. But with the religious fiction, a deeper emotional and imaginative involvement will lead, not to inappropriate attitudes and behaviour, but to ones whose value for the self and the religious community vindicates that involvement. And that vindication is a form of rationalization.

7. Andy, Nora, and Agnes

So far, the differences between Fiona and Reginald look as if they are not so serious as to break up the sense of common ground sufficiently to warrant Fiona's banishment from a realist community. It is time now to invite the other representatives into the discussion, to see if they fare significantly better, or significantly worse.

Andy, recall, is the anthropological reconstructionist. He takes theological discourse to be translatable into statements about human ideals, and not actually about a

---

[11] According to Kendal Walton (1978), however, these emotions are only quasi-joy, quasi-sadness, etc.

transcendent being at all. Does he face the same kinds of challenge as Fiona? He would say that the choice between different interpretations of religious doctrine is, if a genuine one, a choice between different ideals. It is not clear, for example, that the dispute between incarnational and non-incarnational Christology is one of ideals, rather than one that arises only for the realist (and fictionalist, insofar as every realist dispute has a fictionalist counterpart). Fiona's problem in making sense of private prayer, on the other hand, looks as if it will arise in exactly the same form for Andy. Prayer is not really an act of communication, so we need to have some other account. And the account that is available to Fiona is equally available to Andy. As for the issue of whether theological statements provide reasons for action, Andy will point out that, since theological statements are encoded moral ideals, they already contain within themselves recommendations for action. It seems overall, then, that Andy will find the challenges to fictionalism slightly less pressing.

On the other hand, Andy is faced with an objection not faced by Fiona: it is just implausible that every statement in God-talk can be mapped onto a corresponding statement about moral ideals. And when we make the attempt to do just that, some apparently different statements in God-talk will turn out to correspond to the same moral statement. The apparent richness and complexity of God-talk will then turn out to be something of a distraction. Fiona, in contrast, can do full justice to the richness of meaning in God-talk, as different statements will play different roles in the fiction. She can concede to Andy that there is a connection between God-talk and moral ideals, but still insist that it is not as direct as Andy suggests. We often do read moral messages into a fictional narrative, without supposing that each statement can be translated into a corresponding moral statement. Fiona might even point out to Andy that in some sense her position absorbs his. Sometimes, instead of directly engaging with a fiction, losing ourselves in it, as it were, we want to take a critical stance towards it. We might, for example, want to describe the Shakespearian characters of Prince Hal, Henry IV, and Richard II as representing three images of kingship. Then we are self-consciously talking of fictional characters and the way they are constructed by the author. Andy, as Fiona might provocatively put it, is simply Fiona in critical mode. But, unlike Fiona, who can readily explain the emotional impact of religion in terms of engagement with fiction, Andy has nothing to offer on this score.

Nora the non-cognitivist is a variant of Andy, the difference between that, whereas Andy will take God-talk to *assert* moral ideals, Nora takes God-talk to *express* those ideals (just as 'ow!' expresses pain).[12] Again, Fiona can say with some justification that her position absorbs Nora's. Insofar as the fiction makes us aware of certain moral ideals, when we engage with it appropriately, it could be said to express them. But Fiona, unlike Nora, is not obliged to hold that each statement in God-talk expresses a specific ideal.

[12] Cf. the distinction Ayer makes between subjectivism about moral utterances, and his own expressivist account: see Ayer (1936, ch. VI).

And so to our final character, Agnes the agnostic. The standard agnostic accepts the realist construal of theological statements: they are intended as being (more less) literally descriptive of reality. But the agnostic does not know whether they are in fact true or not, and may indeed hold that they are undecidable. So understood, there are degrees of agnosticism, corresponding to strengths of belief or doubt, and some realist believers may confess to a degree of agnosticism with respect to certain aspects of God-talk. When Reginald talks of his wrestling with doubt, he may appropriately express this in terms of 'agnostic moments'. So there will be little difficulty, one would have thought, in integrating agnostics into a realist community. Nevertheless, there will always be the suspicion that agnostics are just a bit half-hearted about religion. They are uncertain which particular religious account to adopt because they are uncertain whether one should adopt any religious account! They will approach prayer with a 'hedging one's bets' attitude. This is well expressed by Anthony Kenny: the agnostic may pray in the hope that there is someone there, rather like someone 'adrift in the ocean, trapped in a cave, or stranded on a mountainside, who cries for help though he may never be heard or fires a signal which may never be seen'.[13] And the agnostic (of this standard kind) will recognize theological statements as reasons for actions, but any doubts as to the truth of those statements will translate into uncertainty over the usefulness of the actions. Finally, any agnostic who recognizes a significant degree of uncertainty about theological statements will probably want to refrain from uttering the creeds, for fear of bad faith, in the Sartrean sense.[14] So, altogether, the agnostic looks to be in a weaker position, vis-à-vis full engagement with the religious life, than any of the other characters of this discussion.

But we have not yet asked Agnes about her views. Is she an agnostic of this standard kind? It turns out she is not. She concedes to the standard agnostic that, *given a realist semantics*, theological statements are undecidable. But she is undecided whether that is the appropriate semantics. Perhaps a fictionalist semantics is appropriate. It may be that a realist semantics is appropriate for part of God-talk, and a fictionalist semantics for the rest. But where should the line be drawn? She doesn't know. This might seem to be rather a lot of doubt, and the others might be inclined to dismiss Agnes as thoroughly confused. However, Agnes can argue that she has an advantage over the standard agnostic, for she can guarantee the truth of theological statements. She reasons as follows: 'Either the realist truth-conditions obtain or they do not. If they do, I intend the statements to have realist truth-conditions; if they do not obtain, then I intend the statements to have fictionalist truth-conditions. Either way, they come out true, but in virtue of what they come out true I cannot say. So I can utter the creeds in good faith. And I can attach at least the same value to the statements as can the fictionalist, and can contemplate the possibility that their value goes beyond that, in putting us in touch with a transcendent reality.'

---

[13] Kenny (1979, 129).
[14] That is, lying to oneself: see Sartre (1969, part I, ch. 2).

Agnes regrets that there is not a more elegant name for her position. 'Semantic religious agnosticism' is the best she can offer for the time being. Insofar as Fiona is able to address the various challenges to her call for philosophical ecumenism, so, it seems, can Agnes. Indeed, it seems that Agnes may have the advantage, after all.[15]

References

Ayer, A. J. (1936). *Language, Truth and Logic*. London: Victor Gollancz.

Basinger, David (1983). 'Why Petition an Omnipotent, Omniscient, Wholly Good God?', *Religious Studies* 19: 25–42.

Davidson, Donald (1963). 'Actions, Reasons and Causes', in *Essays on Actions and Events*. Oxford: Clarendon Press, 1982, pp. 3–19.

Divers, John (1995). 'Modal Fictionalism Cannot Deliver Possible Worlds Semantics', *Analysis* 55: 81–8.

Eshleman, Andrew (2005). 'Can an Atheist Believe in God?', *Religious Studies* 41/2: 183–99.

Field, Hartry (1980). *Science Without Numbers*. Princeton: Princeton University Press.

Grice, H. P. (1957). 'Meaning', *Philosophical Review* 66: 377–88.

Joyce, Richard (2005). 'Moral Fictionalism', in Mark Kalderon (ed.), *Fictionalism in Metaphysics* (pp. 287–313). Oxford: Clarendon Press.

Kenny, Anthony (1979). *The God of the Philosophers*. Oxford: Oxford University Press.

Rosen, Gideon (1990). 'Modal Fictionalism', *Mind* 99: 327–54.

Sartre, Jean-Paul (1969). *Being and Nothingness: An Essay on Phenomenological Ontology*. Trans. Hazel Barnes. London: Methuen.

Walton, Kendal (1978). 'Fearing Fictions', *Journal of Philosophy* 65: 5–27.

[15] Some of the ideas in this chapter were discussed at a seminar on religious fictionalism at Durham in December 2012. I am very grateful to those present for their suggestions, and especially to Chris Insole, Ian Kidd, and Nancy Cartwright. Thanks also to Andrei Buckareff and two anonymous readers for comments on an earlier draft.

PART IV

Causal versus Non-causal Accounts

11

The Divine as Ground of Existence and of Transcendental Values

An Exploration

Willem B. Drees

The white paper that contains a drawing; the space that contains a building; the silence that contains a sonata; the passage of time that prevents a sensation or object continuing forever; all these are 'God'.

Thus wrote John Fowles—better known for his novels *The French Lieutenant's Woman* and *The Magus*—in a book with aphorisms, *The Aristos* (1980, 27). His images of the divine are not theistic: God is not *a being*, an entity alongside other entities. God is envisaged as the setting that makes it possible for drawings, buildings, music, and other entities to exist. Would this count as God? Fowles uses scare quotes; he doesn't claim that this is God but that these are 'God'. In my opinion, one could do without the scare quotes and use such images to envisage the divine. Else, one should use scare quotes all the time, as we never speak of God but merely of our images of God.

We, humans, play with ideas and think through their coherence and consequences. Here I will explore some images of the divine. In this contribution, I will not focus on ideas that have come to us directly from the western Christian tradition or from the history of philosophy. As fewer people in the West identify with particular religious communities, it may be of interest to see what happens when one seeks to speak of the divine drawing on non-religious domains, in this case science, mathematics, and morality. Philosophically speaking, the question addressed here is whether these domains provide a science-inspired naturalist with meaningful options for using concepts that come from a religious vocabulary. Before turning to these three domains, I'll first consider some preliminary issues. In section 5 I will return to one of these preliminary issues, namely the question whether the images proposed can be taken to be a concept of the divine.

1. Preliminary Issues

This volume deals with *Alternative Concepts of God*. If one identifies theism with belief in a God, it seems logically impossible to envisage an alternative to theism, and still claim to speak of a concept of a God. Thus, a preliminary issue to address is: When do we consider some alternative concept a concept *of God*? What is required so that we still may speak of 'the divine'? In the following, I will assume the move from 'a God' to 'the divine'. 'The divine' need not refer to a particular being, but may serve as a label for certain features of reality.

Though not looking for a person-like being, I seek to take into account two classical motives in religious language referring to God. First, in theism God is understood to be the creator of all that exists, a necessary being—that is, not dependent upon anything else for God's existence. For any reasonable alternative, a prime context for thinking about the divine is the ultimate metaphysical question regarding *existence*.

Second, in theistic discourse God is seen as the ultimate judge. From this image, I take with me on our exploration the ultimate 'moral' question about the possibility of evaluating our behaviour from an impartial perspective that *transcends* all human interests and biases.

Last but not least, a key issue is whether these two dimensions—the cosmological and the axiological one—can be combined. I consider this combination of the two dimensions crucial for a vision to be religious (rather than just metaphysical or meta-ethical). This is in line with Clifford Geertz's anthropological definition of religions as systems of symbols that shape moods and motivations (the axiological side of things) by presenting us with an understanding of reality (the cosmological dimension) that is taken as true, thus supporting those moods and motivations (Geertz 1966, 3; 1973, 89). Let me give a theistic example: understanding of God as creator might integrate a metaphysical idea about the source of existence with an attitude of gratitude, of humility, and of respect for our fellow creatures (see Drees 2010, 76–82).

A second preliminary question: Why embark on a quest for alternative concepts of God? What is wrong with traditional theism? Is there anything wrong with theism?

There are various reasons to consider alternatives to theism. As a worldview, theism might be challenged by questions about the nature of God's existence and location and about divine action in a reality that seems to be described well by 'natural laws'. Theism faces moral challenges as well, as God's goodness is hard to reconcile with the extent of suffering and evil in the world. And if God were able to intervene in natural processes, why don't we see more positive turns of events? A further concern could be human autonomy, as a Patriarch 'up there' doesn't square well with the moral sensibilities of many. And socially, given the extent of secular attitudes in Western societies, or at least in Western Europe, an alternative concept might be fresh and thus be an opportunity to revive interest in important issues. Last but not least, concerns could be aesthetic in kind, as a dualism of Creator and creation seems arbitrary; a more monistic view might be appreciated as having greater coherence.

But if we are unhappy about theism, why not opt for atheism, and do without any concept of God? In my opinion, some questions to which theism might present itself as an answer might be too important to be disregarded: The question about existence, the fact that somehow our world with its regularities seems given, and the question about values and perfection, beyond the biases of human self-interests and limitations.

Here I will not engage in a critical discussion on theism and atheism, but seek to contribute to the quest for alternative ways of envisaging 'the divine'. Even if one does not share the concerns about theism, the effort still could be of interest as an intellectual exercise. It is as with interpretations of quantum physics. The multitude of possible interpretations is a concern to some, but one could also appreciate the plurality. The empiricist philosopher of science Bas Van Fraassen thus saw the plurality of interpretations as insight into reality. He once identified the following question as one he and a scientific realist, in that conversation Ernan McMullin, might collaborate in: 'how could the world *possibly* be the way physical theory says it is?' (Van Fraassen 1984, 171). I hope the reader will appreciate the exploration of possible ways of thinking about reality and the divine. One potential misunderstanding about the following considerations is to be avoided. The discussion in philosophy of religion often has been framed as a discussion about arguments for the existence of God, or even proofs. My ambition is far more modest, to explore a possible way of envisaging the divine.

A further preliminary remark: I draw on the natural sciences as a resource and constraint, as science provides our best available knowledge about the natural world. A major lesson of the sciences is that phenomena in nature are intelligible. Nature seems to have a multi-layered coherence and integrity. Within this reality, we have no signs of suspension of its regularities, no signs of any additional input of matter, energy, or information, no signs of any tricks played upon us. The world could have been different, with an unruly dictator changing the laws at will, or with higher-level phenomena not being in line with lower-level processes. Naturalism is not logically necessary, a priori. Rather, naturalism is an interpretation given to the success of science, a posteriori. With respect to our ideas about 'what there is' (*ontology*) all objects around us, including ourselves, consist of the stuff described by chemists in the periodic table of the elements. This stuff is understood by physicists to consist of elementary particles, and beyond that is assumed to consist of quantum fields, superstrings, or whatever. Our knowledge has not reached rock bottom yet. Thus, such a naturalism cannot be articulated on the basis of a fundamental science, at least not yet.

Nor need this naturalism imply that all phenomena can be described in terms of physics and chemistry. A naturalist can allow for genuinely new objects with new properties, even though these new objects have arisen out of other objects. With respect to *history*, naturalism understands living beings as the current stage in a bundle of evolutionary histories on our planet, which is itself a transient phenomenon in a universe that has been expanding for some 14 billion years. And in our social and mental life we are no exceptions to reality though we may be remarkable manifestations of reality. All these insights do not commit one to a particular view on ultimate origins or foundations; fundamental metaphysical issues are not settled by the sciences. Even for a science-inspired naturalist, there can be an irresolvable unfinished character to our understanding (Drees 1996).

If one accepts a science-inspired naturalism, as the best available human view of reality and of ourselves, what about the divine? Schematically one might distinguish between three options. The theist treats God as the Creator of reality (including its regularities), thus introducing a fundamental dualism of Creator and creation. The atheist might suggest that we have just nature; ultimate questions that require a response that goes beyond the framework provided by science are dismissed. And then, there is the muddle in the middle, where we are with this volume. (Not that the other options aren't in a muddle too, once analysed more closely.)

The aim of this chapter is to present approaches that might provide opportunities for thinking of the divine without the ontological dualism of theism, of a Creator and creation, and to consider to what extent these approaches might be integrated into a single concept of the divine. The first approach considers scientific cosmology. Whereas Big Bang cosmology has a first moment in time, more speculative approaches might allow one to envisage a non-temporal ground. We then will turn to mathematics. Within an axiomatic system in logic or mathematics, axioms provide the justification for theorems. This relation is not temporal or causal. And in the process of abstraction from ordinary human practices to pure mathematics, we seem to come to a realm of timeless truths—which need not be understood as a distinct Platonic realm, but might be taken as exemplifying the possibility of a transcendent perspective. Similarly, in the development of moral judgement, we abstract from particular contexts and interests, and thus also seek to envisage the possibility of evaluating behaviour as if from a position that transcends everything—a view *sub specie aeternitatis*. In considering these contexts, my ambition is to discuss building blocks for a view of the divine that is adequate to a science-inspired naturalism.

2. From First Cause to Ground of Existence: Reflections in the Context of Cosmology

The universe has particular characteristics. Existence is one of these, even though 'existence is not a predicate', to use a classic Kantian objection against Descartes's version of the ontological argument (Kant [1781] 1997, A592/B620–A 600/B628). Lawfulness, with particular constants of nature, seems another characteristic of the universe. Thus, the themes of the cosmological argument and the design argument present themselves in the context of scientific cosmology. They can be recapitulated in two general questions: Why is there something rather than nothing? And: Why is the Universe this particular way?

Some theistic arguments envisage God as the First Cause, temporally existing before all of created reality. Existence, lawfulness, and particular properties would thus be explained by referring to a meta-physical being, God. How might this issue be approached in the context of modern scientific cosmology?

A 'first cause' view of God may be integrated with cosmic natural history, with the 'Big Bang' as the initial event, caused by God. However, at the boundaries of physical cosmology our notions of time and causality break down. It therefore is doubtful whether a 'Big Bang' as the limiting event of standard cosmology provides a stable model for 'the first event'. In future theories two conceptual developments can be envisaged, namely (a) the introduction of earlier stages of existence, and hence an ever receding horizon, and (b) a change in conceptuality, due to which the question of a 'before' is dismissed as ill posed. Whatever the development that will become scientific consensus, one can always ask the question: 'Why is there something rather than nothing?' Especially when the conceptuality of space and time changes, possible answers need not to be thought of in temporal or causal terms. We'll consider the various stages of this line of thought in somewhat more detail.

2.1 The Big Bang Model

The Big Bang model of the Universe combines observational data, such as those on the distribution and velocities of galaxies and on the cosmic background radiation, with the best available theories on matter and General Relativity as the fundamental theory of space, time, and gravity. The Big Bang model concludes that the universe has been expanding, as shown by the movement of galaxies relative to each other. Counting backwards, this suggests that the observable universe had once been in a very dense and hot state. Going all the way back, there seems to have been a moment of infinite density and temperature, the beginning of the universe. Current evidence suggests that this moment was almost 14 thousand million years ago.

Within this model the limiting event at 't=0' looks like an absolute beginning. Would this be the moment of creation? Well before Big Bang cosmology had become the scientific consensus, a claim of this kind was made by Pope Pius XII, in a speech to the Pontifical Academy of Sciences on 22 November 1951. Georges Lemaître, the Belgian astronomer and priest who was one of the original proponents of the Big Bang model, was very unhappy about the way Pius XII used the Big Bang theory as a proof of creation (McMullin 1981, 53f.; Lambert 2015, 340–347). The astronomer Fred Hoyle, disliked the Big Bang theory precisely because it seemed to suggest such an initial moment and thereby open the door for a theistic understanding of the universe. It has also been argued that the Big Bang theory is religiously neutral. This is not the place for an analysis of the religious implications and reception of the Big Bang theory. However, though multiple interpretations can be given and have been promoted (see Drees 1990, 18–29), the Big Bang model seems one that is easily framed in a theistic (or deistic) perspective, if not as a proof at least as a way of envisaging a role for a Creator 'in the beginning'.

2.2 Limitations of the Big Bang Theory

The Big Bang theory is often perceived as a scientific theory about 'the Big Bang', the initial Singularity. However, this is a mistake. The theory is not about the Big Bang but about the subsequent evolution of the universe. As a theory about the evolution of the universe it is supported by increasingly precise measurements, which have resulted in well-supported refinements in the scientific understanding of our cosmic history. However, the singular event of infinite density and temperature lies outside the domain where the theory can be trusted, for at least two reasons.

(i) The theory uses current knowledge to extrapolate and understand the early universe. This study of our past is very successful, but somewhere within the first nanosecond, we don't know for sure how matter behaves: the particle physics for such high energies is not tested within human laboratories, and the theories about matter are speculative. As we aren't sure how matter behaves, and whether our concept of matter is still adequate, further extrapolation becomes speculative.

(ii) Closer to the Singularity comes a moment, presumably the 'Planck Time', about 10^{-43} seconds after the initial Singularity, where the combination of the central theories breaks down. To understand conditions at that time, General Relativity Theory must be replaced by a quantum theory of gravity. The uncertainty about the foundational theory implies that we aren't sure anymore how to think of 'time', and whether the concept is still meaningful. And once 'time' is no longer meaningful, it becomes unclear what can be intended by any reference to a state 'before the Planck Time'—and hence by the Singularity that is supposed to be the earliest moment of time.

If one were to continue backwards in time, the initial Singularity itself would be a third limit, where General Relativity and hence our concept of space-time breaks down. However, as this limit lies beyond the Planck horizon, in a realm where General Relativity may have to be abandoned, it is not clear whether this limit is really there. While the first and second limit we encounter when exploring earlier times are limits to our present knowledge, the initial singularity seems to be an ontological discontinuity, like an absolute beginning—but this discontinuity is hidden behind the two epistemic horizons (Drees 1990, 41–4).

2.3 The Big Bang as a Beginning in Time?

If—despite the reservations presented above—the Big Bang were taken as the initial moment of existence, philosophical questions arise about the understanding of this beginning with respect to time. If the Big Bang is seen as the beginning of the universe *in* time, there was an infinite period of time during which the show had not started yet. There was space-time, as a podium for reality, but nothing happening yet. As there was nothing happening yet, it is impossible to imagine any reason why the universe did start where and when it did finally get started, rather than at any earlier moment. And given the infinity of earlier times, why had it not started an infinitely long time before (Isham 1993, 55–8)?

A similar problem was raised by Augustine in book XI of his *Confessiones*, around 400 CE, as he contemplated the creation. What was God doing all those ages before God created the world? Augustine first says that he will not make the joke that God was making hell for those who ask such questions. His serious answer is that the question is wrongly posed; time is bound up with movement and change, and hence with the created order. When there was no creation, there was no way to measure time, and hence no time, and thus one cannot ask what God was doing before God created the world. Time came into being *with* the created order (*creatio cum tempore*, rather than *creatio in tempore*).

Creatio cum tempore expresses a potentially powerful way to re-envisage 't=0' by avoiding the idea that time is a container, from past infinity to future infinity. Perhaps we have to think of the beginning of the universe as the beginning *of* time. And, so some theoreticians hope, perhaps the correct quantum theory of gravity implies a quantum cosmology that does this job well. In that sense, the scientific quest for understanding fundamental physics is intertwined with the one for understanding the very beginning of our universe. If one accepts this idea of a beginning *with* time the contingency of an arbitrary moment of beginning is avoided.

Even if there is no arbitrary choice of a moment in time when the universe started, it may well be that some features of the universe are still contingent rather than explained by the theory—and the theory itself need not be the only possible one. Thus, forms of explanatory contingency may remain. However, if one treats the initial singularity as the beginning of time and of the universe, we seem to move away from language about a first cause preceding that beginning. This is even more pronounced in some approaches in speculative cosmologies that go beyond the Big Bang theory by integrating theories about space and time and quantum theories more closely, so-called 'quantum cosmologies'.

2.4 Quantum Cosmologies: A Variety of Options

Though all science is a human representation of reality, results such as the Periodic Table of Elements are so well corroborated and used in so many different ways that the constructed nature of such knowledge does not diminish its claim to truth, understood realistically, at least for the domain or scale of resolution where atoms are an adequate model. However, uncertainty creeps in when one considers finer scales and speaks of quarks and gluons, and, even further down, of superstrings. Such uncertainty results in a plurality of research programmes in 'speculative cosmology'. Observations and theories at later times or accessible scales are not necessarily consistent with just a single model of the underlying reality. There is underdetermination of cosmological theories (or, as they often are, outlines of theories) by the data, with a major role of philosophical preconceptions (Butterfield and Isham 2001, 37ff.). When we consider the issue of the beginning of time, there are genuine differences between various approaches (see Drees 1990, 48–62; Drees 1993; Isham 1993; Butterfield and Isham 2001). I will consider two major types of approach.

First, some cosmologists approach the beginning of the observable universe ('the Big Bang') as one would any beginning. Somewhere on the timeline my life has begun, this piece of art was made, or a particular city came into existence. It may be hard to define a precise moment for a city, or even for a human being, but the basic idea is that beginnings can be located on a pre-existent continuum. And hence, for any beginning one may ask what went on before: the persons who became my parents met, and, longer before, my future grandparents, or the artist had a certain idea, or there was a trade post, and so on. If that is how one envisages the beginning of the universe *in* time, the suggestion of a 'before' arises. A *regressum ad infinitum* may arise; contingency is relocated to earlier and earlier stages in time. Some cosmological models have tried to embed the Big Bang model in a larger picture of successive phases of the universe, or as a series of new space-time domains being formed out of earlier ones—like babies each having a definite beginning, but none of these beginnings being 'the beginning of humankind' in a more encompassing sense. Lee Smolin (1999) has suggested a cosmic 'Darwinism' in which universes (better envisaged as domains) may have daughters (and granddaughters, and so on), with the kind of universe that has the best conditions for generating such daughters being the most frequent within the whole set of universes; thus, one would expect our observable universe to be of that kind.

A rather different type of approach has been introduced by James Hartle and Stephen Hawking (1983): reality deep down might be timeless (for a more general articulation of such timelessness, see Barbour 1999). Time is just a parameter which may have a finite past. In his popular book *A Brief History of Time* (1988) Hawking used the analogy of degrees latitude—there is an end to the sequence, at 90 degrees latitude, the North Pole. It makes no sense to ask what is north of the North Pole. But the meaninglessness of this question is not something special about that point on earth as if we were to encounter a boundary. The peculiar features of the North Pole are a consequence of our coordinate system. Though more subtle with respect to his understanding of time, something similar applies to time in the Hartle–Hawking proposal: 't=0' is not something extraordinary. For a particular choice of parameters it looks like a boundary, but if the parameter were defined differently other states of affairs would be the boundary. Though the past is finite, there is no unique absolute beginning. Thus, the Hartle–Hawking approach has been dubbed the no-boundary proposal.

Beyond the observationally well-supported Big Bang model, the question may be not what might be 'beyond the Big Bang?' but rather what will future theories look like? If one were to ask what would be 'beyond the Big Bang' in the context of the cosmological argument, the answer might be 'the Creator', who lit the fire and thus started the cosmos. It probably was the popular appeal of this question that made a publisher decide that the title of a book of mine was to be *Beyond the Big Bang* (Drees 1990), even though I had offered the manuscript with the title *Beyond the Big Bang Theory*, the point being that future theories might be conceptually quite different.

2.5 The Persistence of the Mystery of Existence

If a future research programme in quantum cosmology would be successful in embedding Big Bang cosmology in a larger framework that integrates all known physics in a

THE DIVINE AS GROUND OF EXISTENCE   203

coherent and consistent whole, would this be the end of the cosmological question? It might be the end of a particular form of the cosmological argument, namely one that depends on a beginning of time. And other arguments may have their problems as arguments too, let alone as proofs. However, even when science is in its own terms successful, the *contingency of existence* is still there, as one may still pose the question 'Why is there something rather than nothing?'

When current questions would have been answered by future theories, new questions emerge in the context of those future theories. For instance, the inflationary model as a refinement of Big Bang cosmology solves many questions regarding the observed region of the universe, but does not explain why the universe is such that inflation happens; some assumptions are always made. The reach of scientific explanation is impressive, but explanatory successes do not exclude further questions. Again and again, questions emerge at the limits of scientific understanding. They may be resolved, but the deeper understanding will have other elements that are assumed rather than explained.

Questions remain even if physics and cosmology agree one day on a theory explaining all known phenomena in a unified, coherent way. Imagine, a single article, a single formula answering all our questions. But the article is on a piece of paper; the formula consists of symbols. Thus, it does not provide an answer to the question: Why does reality behave as described here? It is as with a drawing of the Belgian artist René Magritte. It is a careful drawing of a pipe, a pipe used for smoking tobacco. Underneath it, he has written 'Ceçi n'est pas une pipe'—'This is not a pipe'. And he is right. It is an image of a pipe. One cannot fill the image with tobacco and if one attempts to light the image, something different happens from when one lights a pipe. There is a difference between an image, however accurate it may be, and reality. This is also the case for a good scientific theory. However accurate the theory, a question always remains why reality behaves as described in the theory. And if the theory is assumed to be complete, the distance between the conceptual entity and the reality it describes becomes a challenge to the assumed completeness. Thus, though the persistent philosophical question need not be one about a first cause—in a temporal sequence—there is a genuine philosophical question, namely why the reality described by the theories is actual.

A theistic answer could be envisaged—but that too isn't much of an answer, as the same question might be posed with respect to God. However, in the philosophical-theological tradition, this has been resolved by considering God *causa sui*, God being God's own cause, the sole self-explanatory or necessary being. Thus, within such a theistic framework further questions would be ruled out. Upon such a theistic understanding of the universe, the divine relating to the universe might best be thought of as timeless (e.g., McMullin [1998] 2013).

If one does not already assume the theistic framework with God as the self-explanatory being, the question 'Why is there something rather than nothing' seems to be without an answer. One might just say: 'The world is.' Or, as did the physicist Charles

Misner (1977, 97), one may appreciate the open-ended character of the questions and answers:

Saying that God created the universe does not explain either God or the Universe, but it keeps our consciousness alive to mysteries of awesome majesty that we might otherwise ignore, and that deserve our respect.

We always work within the limitations of our concepts and ideas and within the limitations of our existence. We will never see the universe 'from outside', from the perspective of eternity, but always from within. That is also a problem when we speak of God; we are within the universe while we attempt to speak about something that is conceived to be more encompassing. Our language about a 'beyond' need not be meaningless, but our theology does require agnostic restraint if we are not to fall into an arrogant and unwarranted religious certainty.

The more we know, the more we may become aware of the limitations of our knowledge. *De Docta Ignorantia* ('About learned ignorance') was the title of a book of Nicolas of Cusa, a cardinal in Europe in the fifteenth century. The scientific road to knowledge has shown itself to be very successful; we have learned more than Nicolas of Cusa could have expected. But that does not need to result in the arrogant conviction that we can explain everything without any residue. On the contrary; through science we are confronted with fundamental questions concerning the nature and ground of our reality. Why is there a reality? Why is reality the way it is? Thunder is no longer a voice of the gods, nor a mystery. But that does not exclude wonder regarding the reality of which both we and thunderstorms are a part. To the contrary, in the end existence remains a mystery.

Above, I have argued that we might move away from the question about the beginning to a question about the actuality of existence. With this rephrasing of the cosmological question, the nature of a possible answer shifts away from a causal concept of the creator, as a pre-existing being. An alternative might be to think of the answer in more immanent terms—as the Ground of existence, which gives actual existence to the possibility described in the successful scientific theory. Just as a reference to God is not an explanation, a reference to the Ground of existence too is more a rephrasing of the open-ended character of human knowledge than an answer. But as a way of thinking about the divine, the role envisaged for such a Ground of being is somewhat like the role axioms have in a mathematical system: the axioms don't cause the various theorems to be valid, but they do ground those theorems and thus legitimize them. (Fundamental laws of nature would not serve as well, as these may allow for additional questions about the reality those laws are about, and perhaps about the initial conditions.) The mathematical analogy brings us to the next section.

3. Mathematics: Does Abstraction Suggest Transcendence?

Mathematics is a human practice, but in various ways it reaches far beyond the specifics of the historically situated human condition. If we were ever to communicate with extra-terrestrial mathematicians, we should expect them to have a different notation, but fundamentally the same mathematics. This was the basis for the design of a cosmic 'language' by the mathematician Hans Freudenthal, *Lincos* (1960).

In the present context of reflecting upon conceptions of the divine, mathematics has at least three features that I consider relevant. At the end of section 2 I already introduced the relation between axioms and theorems, not as one of causality, but nonetheless very intimate—the axioms ground all theorems. A second feature is that mathematics seems to point towards a realm of abstract immaterial entities; though human made, new insights are felt as discoveries, and not so much as inventions. Thirdly, if one does not accept such a Platonic realm of mathematical entities, there is something remarkably universal about mathematical insights. Thus, in the process of abstraction, mathematics reaches far beyond any human historical and cultural context, as if reaching for a transcendent perspective. I will call this non-Platonic view 'constructivist', as it emphasizes the human construction of explicit mathematical insights—though these insights themselves may well be logically necessary truths.

Mathematics is odd, if one comes at it from an empiricist mind set. Pure circles, triangles, cubes, and the like do not exist, nor do imaginary numbers, Lie groups, or Bessel functions. Nonetheless, we can make well-defined claims about their properties, and argue about the truth or falsity of various mathematical claims. We can even make mathematical existence claims such as that there is (or that there is not) an even number that is not the sum of two primes (Goldbach's conjecture). The fact that we currently don't know which option is correct doesn't undermine the conviction that either there is such a number or there isn't one—and that the truth is not dependent upon cultural conditions or political preferences.

One interpretation of this feature of mathematics has been 'Platonism' (used here without regard for historical accuracy relative to Plato), the view that mathematical realities exist 'out there' in an objective but immaterial world, independent of human consciousness. Thus, mathematical truth can be understood as a form of correspondence between our propositions and mathematical reality. Mathematicians explore a pre-existing world, and make discoveries. Roger Penrose (1989) is a modern advocate of such a view.

As an ontology this 'Platonic' reality is so distinct from material reality that it is hard to envisage 'where' it might be; it is not to be positioned in terms of space and time. And if one dismisses this as a non-problem, given the categorical difference between material space-time reality and this Platonic reality, a second problem arises: How do we, material beings, have access to those non-material lands? 'Mathematical intuition', the possibility to make 'observations' in this Platonic realm, would be a remarkable addition to the experiential, causally mediated repertoire we are supposed to have. Such an ontology of mathematics seems too remote to fit the epistemic challenge how mathematical knowledge is acquired and developed (e.g., Kitcher 1984, 102; Colyvan 2012, 10f.). A different but somewhat related problem is how it might be possible that mathematics is useful for the physical world, if it is categorically distinct, dealing with abstract entities rather than material objects and natural processes.

A quite different view of the nature of mathematics is constructivist in kind. Leopold Kronecker is supposed to have said that God made the natural numbers (1, 2, 3 ...); the rest is the work of humans—'Die ganzen Zahlen hat der liebe Gott gemacht, alles andere ist Menschenwerk', 'which was the poetic expression of his belief that the only legitimate mathematical objects (on the side of number systems, geometry was not included) were those that could be reduced to natural numbers' (Van Dalen 2013, 232f.). Mathematical objects are human creations, a conceptual world that is 'up to us'. Constructivism was developed in the early twentieth century by Herman Weyl and Luitzen E. J. Brouwer (Van Dalen 2013). But if mathematics is our construction, why don't we see much more variation? Why do mathematicians agree on mathematical constructions, across cultural, linguistic, and ideological differences? Unlike social and cultural products, where there is far more variation, mathematical constructivism has to do justice to the universality of mathematical insights. Mathematical truths seem to be necessary.

Both approaches offer a possible way of understanding transcendence. A Platonist view has a transcendent *reality* of abstract entities, ready to be explored. A constructivist lacks such an ontology, but our experience with mathematics as universal suggests a notion of transcendence *in the process of mathematical abstraction*.

Let us go back to the beginnings of human mathematics. The basics of counting and measuring are clearly to be found in the practical life of early hominids, as counting is useful when sharing food and keeping track of enemies, and in trade and agriculture. One of the simplest instances of Pythagoras' formula, namely $3^2 + 4^2 = 5^2$, may have been discovered early in human history as a way to create effectively straight corners. The general form would have come later, through abstraction and reflection. It would be this process of abstraction beyond the concrete natural situation that generates mathematical insight. A remarkable feature of our reality is that those abstract insights turn out to be applicable in many other situations as well. Apparently, natural processes have many features that are structurally the same.

Thus, though upon a constructivist view we are not endowed with a distinct type of perception or intuition (as needed upon a Platonist view), humans can come up with genuine mathematical knowledge developed by abstraction, generalization, and idealization from the natural. Transcendence would not be about an ontologically distinct realm, but rather reflect the possibility of abstraction from concrete processes to structures that in their abstraction are universal in kind. The related play of imagination allows for mathematical constructs that have no straightforward real world applicability, but nonetheless have a strong intellectual standing.

The philosophy of mathematics is a scholarly profession in itself, into which here I will not delve further (see for a recent introduction, Colyvan 2012), but mathematics shows that one need not abandon a naturalistic understanding of human behaviour as rooted in practices (counting, measuring) to consider the possibility of universal concepts that go beyond specific situations, and in that sense are not factual but transcendental. In section 4 I will argue that a similar argument might be made for values; these too have their origins in human practices but reach for a higher, transcendental status.

4. Universal Values: An Inaccessible Transcendent Perspective?

Upon an evolutionary perspective pro-social behaviour has its roots in enlightened, long-term self-interest, whether of the individual or of the 'selfish' genes. Biologists and others have come up with evolutionary explanations for support given to children, nieces and nephews, and other kin (the same genes), support given to one's partner (a shared project, though if one can mobilize the other and nonetheless do less, even the better; cheating co-evolves with sociality); support given to neighbours (direct reciprocity) and to the larger community (indirect reciprocity, group selection). It all seems ultimate enlightened self-interest, unconsciously pursued. What about universal values in this world of particular interests?

One might argue that evolution has delivered more than was ordered. Means can be used for new purposes. Fingers did not evolve to play a piano, but they can be used to play the piano. Intelligence and communication, brains and language will have been useful for the four F's that are essential for survival as individuals and as a species: feeding, fighting, fleeing, and reproducing. Once intelligence and language evolved, they may have been used in other tasks as well.

This 'more' that was delivered includes reflection and communication. This allows morality to become more genuinely moral, for our intelligence allows us to reconsider our own behaviour. For instance, we may discover that we are 'naturally' inclined to treat boys and girls differently. By becoming aware of this we can also act against that which would be 'natural' to us. Communication may also contribute. Imagine that once an offended hominid asked a fellow hominid: 'Why do you behave thus?' In the presence of others he or she thus was challenged to justify the behaviour in question with arguments that would be recognizable and acceptable to the others, and thus, to formulate relatively general principles justifying his or her behaviour. In the course of many incidents of this kind, natural behaviour guided by enlightened self-interest may have become reconsidered, intentional behaviour. The social context of our lives may have pushed towards universality and accountability, hallmarks of morality, and towards law rather than individual preference (Kitcher 2011).

We are occasionally open to reasons, to argument. Since ideas spread faster than genes, culture may develop enormously. There is no reason to assume that the biological basis would always overrule the effects of culture. Thanks to the emergence of culture as a second type of heritage, alongside the genetic one, and thanks to the capacity for reflection and to the impulse to public justification, we are not victims of our evolutionary heritage. We are biological beings, but as these particular biological beings we have a moderate amount of freedom with respect to our genetic drives. We therefore also have responsibility (Alexander 1987; Drees 1996, 205–10).

We are practical beings, who measure, count, evaluate, and judge, and in doing so, we reach beyond the practical, and speak of values and ideas that would be universal and timeless, transcendent relative to the world of facts. Thus, one can envisage philosophical discussions on constructivism in ethics (see Bagnoli 2013). Here I am interested in the religious vocabulary associated with such moral transcendence. In his *God, Jesus and Belief: The Legacy of Theism* Stewart Sutherland (1984) speaks of the view *sub specie aeternitatis*, that is, the view from the perspective that is not a particular perspective, and thus not serving a particular self-interest. (Any self-interest is, by definition, particular.) Sutherland refers to a story in which someone contemplating a modest job as a schoolteacher is told that if he does it well, 'You will know it, your pupils will know it; and God will know it' (Sutherland 1984, 83, quoting a play by Robert Bolt, *A Man for All Seasons*). It is the final part—the 'God will know it', that lifts the considered course of action to a higher plane. Sutherland argues that it is not accidental that the language of theism is used; it serves well. 'The language of theism embodies, offers and protects the possibility of a view of human affairs *sub specie aeternitatis*' (Sutherland 1984, 88). He points to two hopes involved, namely the belief that one may transcend the particulars of an individual, community, or age, and the belief that the ultimate context in which our behaviour is to be judged is against values that are even beyond 'the outlook of mankind' (88) and the particulars of our species.

These features are reminiscent of the universals of mathematics, though there the ability to build consensus among those with relevant expertise is far greater than in the moral domain, where cultural and individual differences are more common and persistent. (By the way, the analogy with mathematics is also considered by Sutherland, for instance when discussing a summation over an infinite series (91)—a sum that is never to be completed, and still the sum is a well defined entity.)

5. The Divine as the Ground Immanent in Existence and Transcendence

We have considered a few varieties of transcendence that might be acceptable to a science-inspired naturalist. Cosmology provided a context to reflect on the ground of existence; mathematics and morality provide contexts for reflecting upon the perfection of ideas and values. Here I will return to these approaches, and their possible coexistence. We'll begin with mathematics and morality, and the reach for a transcendent perspective that surpasses the natural.

Mathematics is a human practice that points towards the possibility of abstraction that reaches for universality and transcends the physical in which it is rooted. In morality one could argue for a similar move, towards the abstract ideal of a totally impartial view that considers all interests and concerns, a view *sub specie aeternitatis*. Thus, both could be construed as epistemic programmes that hint at an impartial perspective, as if from a transcendent perspective.

Let us briefly consider whether these two approaches are promising as models for a theistic understanding of transcendence as pointing to God's existence as real and different from the world of creatures. It may seem attractive that the notion of transcendence can be understood in terms of mathematics or morality, but there is a downside: the argument might be understood more appropriately as an argument for the non-existence of God. In an article on arguments for the existence of God, with special consideration of Anselm's ontological argument, J. N. Findlay pointed out that precisely because of the nature of the argument God is not placed with the contingent, empirically real entities that have genuine existence but rather with mathematical entities and other conceptual truths that have no claim to existence. As Findlay (1955, 54) wrote:

It was indeed an ill day for Anselm when he hit upon his famous proof. For on that day he not only laid bare something that is of the essence of an adequate religious object, but also something that entails its necessary non-existence.

This regards mathematical truth: even if there is no triangle, it is true that triangles have three angles. And all objects that would ordinarily be considered triangles are not genuine mathematical triangles, but merely material approximations. Precisely because one can suspend the question whether triangles exist, one may have mathematical conclusions of universal validity. Findlay's challenge also regards the moral perspective advocated by Sutherland—precisely because viewing our choices *sub specie aeternitatis* is not a perspective that could be said to exist, it might function as a major regulative notion.

The approach discussed first, in relation to cosmology, is more directly about reality as it exists. By tracing the sequence of explanatory theories, one might speak of a persistent mystery of existence that is an epistemic form of transcendence (something not answered by the theories) which hints at an ontological ground of existence that would answer this fundamental question beyond all specific explanatory questions: Why is there a reality for the theory to describe?

In this context, one might speak of the divine as the Ground of Being. This avoids a strong ontological dualism of God and creation. A major figure in the articulation of such a theological position has been Paul Tillich, but it has been defended more recently in the context of a naturalistic vision as well (e.g., Wildman 2006; much controversy arose over an earlier articulation, Robinson 1963). A somewhat more theistic version of this emphasis has been formulated in panentheistic terms: the world is understood to be in God, even though God surpasses the world (Clayton and Peacocke 2004). Perhaps one could rephrase this as the idea that the ground of existence has more potential in it than what is yet actualized, though what is actualized— the world—would not be actual without this ground.

I opened this chapter with an aphorism from *The Aristos* of John Fowles, but the quote given was only part of that aphorism (1980, 27; my italics):

The ubiquitous absence of 'God' in ordinary life is this sense of non-existing, of mystery, of incalculable potentiality; this eternal doubt that hovers between the thing in itself and our perception of it; *this dimension in and by which all other dimensions exist.* The white paper that contains a drawing; the space that contains a building; the silence that contains a sonata; the passage of time that prevents a sensation or object continuing forever; all these are 'God'.

Upon such a view, God need not be envisaged as the creator 'in the beginning', billions of years ago. God can be taken to be the 'dimension in and by which all other dimensions exist', the immanent ground of actuality. We are not in the business of proofs here; it is offered as a way of envisaging a possible articulation of the persistent mystery of existence. Triggered by the analogy with mathematics, where there may be multiple axioms, one might think of multiple dimensions. However, with respect to cosmology, the coherence we see in reality as scientifically understood, might allow one to prefer to speak of a single 'Ground', rather than multiple ones.

Last but not least, I have argued for two different approaches as alternative concepts of the divine—envisaging a Ground of existence rather than a Creator, and envisaging the inaccessible but relevant possibility of a view *sub specie aeternitatis* rather than a Supreme Judge. As mentioned in the section on preliminaries, a key feature of a religious view might be that these two dimensions—the cosmological and the axiological—are integrated into a single vision.

I think that such integration is feasible within the perspective presented here, though not necessary. Upon the approach indicated above, the language of values and mathematical objects is not taken to be about a reality that exists independently of the universe, but rather as a language that arises in the process of abstraction in reflection and communication. Thus, those ideal notions may be taken to be rooted in natural reality. The Ground of being which gives actuality to empirical reality, gives actuality to an empirical reality that has build into it the possibility of absolute values and mathematically perfect entities as limiting ideals, transcendent to all that is. Thus, an attitude of wonder and gratitude for all that has been given by the Ground of existence can be combined with a moral engagement in the longing for the realization of values that surpass our messy world.

This proposal should not be confused with a 'natural law' tradition that takes the natural to be normative, and thus defends, for instance, the male dominance over females or the exclusion of persons who don't fit the dominant pattern of heterosexual relationships and thus are claimed to fall outside of the 'order of creation' (see Fehige 2013, for a critical discussion). As I see it, the normative perspective is not read off from nature, but is rather approximated through critical reflection and conversation. Thus, it is not nature that is normative—the current outcomes of the processes made possible by the Ground of Being, but rather the normative arises as this Ground of Being has endowed reality with the possibility of critical reflection, of discourse that confronts what is with what should be.

So far for a philosophical reflection, exploring an alternative concept of the divine. Of course, this is quite different from the stories that people tell and the narratives that people perform, drawing on the particular features of their heritage. The music, narratives, and practices may all be meaningful and helpful in shaping human lives. This can be true of theistic traditions, but one may also envisage a spirituality for naturalists (Stone 2012) and articulations that combine a naturalistic orientation with a particular tradition (e.g. Peacocke 2007; Peters 2013; Johnston 2009). The exploration offered here is just an intellectual effort to think through a possible way of envisioning the divine, consistent with a science-inspired naturalism, knowing well that the richness of human cultural practices has its own value.

References

Alexander, R. D. (1987). *The Biology of Moral Systems*. New York: De Gruyter.

Augustine, Aurelius ([400] 1960). *The Confessions of Saint Augustine*. Translated, with an introduction and notes, by John K. Ryan. New York: Doubleday.

Bagnoli, Carla (ed.) (2013). *Constructivism in Ethics*. Cambridge: Cambridge University Press.

Barbour, Julian (1999). *The End of Time: The Next Revolution in our Understanding of the Universe*. London: Orion Books.

Butterfield, Jeremy and Isham, Christopher (2001). 'Spacetime and the Philosophical Challenge of Quantum Gravity', in C. Callender and N. Huggett (eds), *Physics Meets Philosophy at the Planck Scale: Contemporary Theories in Quantum Gravity* (pp. 33-89). Cambridge: Cambridge University Press.

Clayton, Philip and Peacocke, Arthur (eds) (2004). *In Whom We Live and Move and Have our Being: Panentheistic Reflections on God's Presence in a Scientific World*. Grand Rapids, Mich.: Eerdmans.

Colyvan, Mark (2012). *An Introduction to the Philosophy of Mathematics*. Cambridge: Cambridge University Press.

Drees, Willem B. (1990). *Beyond the Big Bang: Quantum Cosmologies and God*. La Salle, Ill.: Open Court.

Drees, Willem B. (1993). 'A Case against Temporal Critical Realism Consequences of Quantum Cosmology for Theology', in R. J. Russell, N. Murphy, and C. J. Isham (eds), *Quantum Cosmology and the Laws of Nature: Divine Action in Scientific Perspective* (pp. 331-65). Vatican City State: Vatican Observatory Press and Berkeley: Center for Theology and the Natural Sciences.

Drees, Willem B. (1996). *Religion, Science, and Naturalism*. Cambridge: Cambridge University Press.

Drees, Willem B. (2010). *Religion and Science in Context: A Guide to the Debates*. London: Routledge.

Fehige, Yiftach (2013). 'Sexual Diversity and Divine Creation: A Tightrope Walk between Christianity and Science', *Zygon: Journal of Religion and Science* 48: 35-59.

Findlay, J. N. (1955). 'Can God's Existence Be Disproved? A', in Antony Flew and Alasdair MacIntyre (eds), *New Essays in Philosophical Theology* (pp. 47-56). London: SCM.

Fowles, John (1980). *The Aristos*, rev. edn. Falmouth: Triad/Granada.

Freudenthal, Hans (1960). *Lincos: Design of a Language for Cosmic Intercourse*. Studies in Logic and the Foundations of Mathematics. Amsterdam: North Holland.

Geertz, Clifford (1966). 'Religion as a Cultural System', in M. Banton (ed.), *Anthropological Approaches to the Study of Religion* (pp. 1-46). London: Tavistock. Reprinted in C. Geertz, *The Interpretation of Cultures*. New York: Basic Books, 1973.

Hartle, James B. and Hawking, Stephen W. (1983). 'The Wave Function of the Universe', *Physical Review* D 28: 2960-75.

Hawking, Stephen (1988). *A Brief History of Time*. Toronto: Bantam Books.

Isham, Chris J. (1993). 'Quantum Theories of the Creation of the Universe', in Robert J. Russell, Nancey Murphy, and C. J. Isham (eds), *Quantum Cosmologies and the Laws of Nature: Scientific Perspectives on Divine Action* (pp. 49–89). Vatican City State: Vatican Observatory Publications and Berkeley: Center for Theology and the Natural Sciences.

Johnston, Mark (2009). *Saving God: Religion after Idolatry*. Princeton: Princeton University Press.

Kant, Immanuel ([1781] 1997). *Critique of Pure Reason*. Trans. Paul Guyer and Alan Wood. Cambridge: Cambridge University Press.

Kitcher, Philip (1984). *The Nature of Mathematical Knowledge*. Oxford: Oxford University Press.

Kitcher, Philip (2011). *The Ethical Project*. Cambridge, Mass.: Harvard University Press.

Lambert, Dominique (2015). *The Atom of the Universe: The Life and Work of Georges Lemaître*. Kraków, PL: Copernicus Center Press. Original: Un atom d'univers: La vie et l'ouevre de Georges Lemaître . Brussels: Éditions Lessius, 2011.

McMullin, Ernan (1981). 'How Should Cosmology Relate to Theology?', in A. R. Peacocke (ed.), *The Sciences and Theology in the Twentieth Century* (pp. 17–57). Stocksfield: Oriel Press and Notre Dame, Ind.: University of Notre Dame Press.

McMullin, Ernan ([1998] 2013). 'Cosmic Purpose and the Contingency of Human Evolution', *Zygon: Journal of Religion and Science* 48: 338–63. Originally *Theology Today* 55: 389–414.

Misner, Charles W. (1977). 'Cosmology and Theology', in W. Yourgrau and A. D. Breck (eds), *Cosmology, History, and Theology* (pp. 75–100). New York: Plenum Press,.

Peacocke, Arthur (2007). *All That Is: A Naturalistic Faith for the Twenty-First Century. A Theological Proposal with Responses from Leading Thinkers in the Religion-Science Dialogue*. Ed. Philip Clayton. Minneapolis: Fortress.

Penrose, Roger (1989). *The Emperor's New Mind: Concerning Computers, Minds, and the Laws of Physics*. Oxford: Oxford University Press.

Peters, Karl E. (2013). 'A Christian Naturalism: Developing the Thinking of Gordon Kaufman', *Zygon: Journal of Religion and Science* 48: 578–91.

Robinson, John A. T. (1963). *Honest to God*. London: SCM.

Smolin, Lee (1999). *The Life of the Cosmos*. New York: Oxford University Press.

Stone, Jerome (2012). 'Spirituality for Naturalists', *Zygon: Journal of Religion and Science* 47: 481–500.

Sutherland, Stewart R. (1984). *God, Jesus & Belief: The Legacy of Theism*. Oxford: Basil Blackwell.

Van Dalen, Dirk (2013). *L. E. J. Brouwer—Topologist, Intuitionist, Philosopher: How Mathematics is Rooted in Life*. London: Springer.

Van Fraassen, Bas C. (1984). 'The Problem of Indistinguishable Particles', in J. T. Cushing, C. F. Delaney, and G. M. Gutting (eds), *Science and Reality: Recent Work in the Philosophy of Science. Essays in Honor of Ernan McMullin* (pp. 153–72). Notre Dame, Ind.: University of Notre Dame Press.

Wildman, Wesley J. (2006). 'Ground-of-Being Theologies', in Philip Clayton and Zachary Simpson (eds), *The Oxford Handbook of Religion and Science* (pp. 612–32). Oxford: Oxford University Press.

12

Theological Realism, Divine Action, and Divine Location

Andrei A. Buckareff

1. Introduction

Traditional theists assert that God exists and that God acts in the world. God, according to traditional theists, essentially possesses the omni-properties associated with maximal perfection as articulated by Anselmian theism.[1] Importantly, for my purposes in this chapter, God is also regarded as a simple agent who resides outside of space who performs intentional actions and unilaterally intervenes in earthly affairs.

In this chapter I assume the truth of theological realism about at least some discourse regarding divine action. By "theological realism" I mean the conjunction of two theses. The first is theological cognitivism, the thesis that at least some of our positive theological statements about God's attributes and agency express what we accept or believe and that the statements are truth-apt. The second commitment is the supposition that at least some positive theological statements are, in fact, true. Traditional theists and most atheists are theological cognitivists. However, traditional theists are theological realists while atheists are theological non-realists. More specifically, most atheists are error theorists about theological discourse, taking all positive theological statements to be, strictly speaking, false.[2]

---

[1] For a contemporary statement of Anselmian theism on which God exhibits whatever properties are constitutive of being maximally perfect, including all of the traditional omni-attributes, see Morris 1987 and 1991. God on this view is "omniGod" (see Bishop 1998). For a more modest version of Anselmian theism on which God is not omniGod but "maximalGod," see Nagasawa 2008. Nagasawa argues that rather than conceiving of God as exhibiting maximum perfection with respect to each great making attribute, God should be conceived of as having the maximal consistent set of knowledge, power, goodness, etc.

[2] There are theological non-realists who endorse being committed to a religious life. For examples of analytic philosophers of religion who endorse theological non-realism while endorsing the value of a religious life, see Eshleman 2005 and Le Poidevin 1996.

A problem that has not been explicitly engaged with much by theological realists is what God can or cannot be like if any of our discourse about the divine is to be true.[3] In this chapter, I consider the metaphysics of divine action and some problems posed by the thesis that God is an agent who acts in the universe and is an immaterial substance without spatiotemporal location for those committed to theological realism. I shall argue that if God is an agent who performs discrete intentional actions, the effects of which can be indexed to locations in space-time, then God's actions are spatiotemporally located. If God's actions can be located in space-time, then God is located in space-time. And if God is located in space-time, then the universe embodies God in some way. I call the view that God's actions are spatiotemporally located and that God is spatiotemporally located "the embodied God thesis." I remain silent about the details regarding how best to conceive of God's relationship to the universe.[4] What I shall explicitly defend are the following two claims. First, traditional theism does not have the metaphysical resources necessary for us to be theological realists about divine agency. Second, because of this, theological realists should endorse some species of the embodied God thesis.[5]

I will proceed as follows in this chapter. In section 2, I consider what it is for an action-predicate to be partially univocal and suggest an account of ontological commitment that is tied to truthmaking that provides us with the freedom necessary to explore alternative accounts of the nature of God while maintaining a commitment to theological realism. In section 3, I offer an argument against the possibility of a disembodied agent's actions having any effect in the world and I provide a defense of two of the more controversial premises of the argument. In defending the controversial premises of the argument I present, I respond to what I believe are some reasonable objections to my argument that have actually been raised or could be raised by the traditional

---

[3] As always, there are exceptions. For instance, Timpe 2007 has recently discussed truthmaking and the metaphysics of theism—focusing on God's relationship to time—defending the doctrine of God as time-lessly eternal.

[4] I expect it to be a given that if the embodied God thesis is correct, then either pantheism or panentheism gets things right. A classic defense of a version of pantheism can be found in Spinoza 1677/1992. An early and careful defense of a version of panentheism can be found in Schleirmacher 1830/1928. An important twentieth-century statement of panentheism can be found in Hartshorne 1948. For recent defenses of versions of pantheism by analytic philosophers of religion, see Jantzen 1984, Levine 1994, Lodzonski 1998, Mander 2000 and 2007, Oakes 1983, and Steinhart 2004. For recent defenses of accounts of the divine that can be regarded as panentheistic by analytic philosophers, see Bishop 1998, 2007, 2009, Forrest 1996, Johnston 2009, and Sarot 1992. Peter Forrest 2007 defends an attractive version of the embodied God thesis that he calls "developmental theism." While Forrest's view comes close to being a version of panentheism, it stops short of full-blown panentheism. Rather, he defends a "Swiss-cheese" view of God. God is immanent in all things except individual centers of awareness and agency.

[5] Anthony Kenny (1979, 125–7) and Grace Jantzen (1984, 85–93) have defended similar claims from divine agency to the embodied God thesis. See Holtzer 1987 for a response to Kenny. For a response to Jantzen, see Taliaferro 1994, 262–4. For those familiar with the work of Kenny and Jantzen on divine action, it will be evident that my own argumentative strategy is quite different from theirs. In particular, my argument draws more heavily on recent work on mental causation than it does on accounts of the nature of basic actions.

theist. I conclude that the objections all fail to show that traditional theism has the metaphysical resources necessary to support theological realism.[6]

2. Divine Action-Predicates: Truthmaking, Ontological Commitment, and Divine Agency

Suppose that human and divine action predicates are at least partially univocal.[7] If this is the case, since our talk about human action is not always metaphorical, then neither is talk about divine action always metaphorical. But we must take care not to read our ontology off our language. That language about divine and human action is not always metaphorical does not imply that we can neatly derive the ontology that makes our statements about divine agency true and the ontology that makes our statements about human agency true from our statements about either divine agency or human agency in a neat one-to-one fashion from our statements to the world. However, if there is at least partial univocity with respect to some human and divine action predicates, then the truthmakers for statements about both divine action and human action will be similar in some respects. Importantly, for my purposes, what I will show in section 3 is that the truthmakers for both human and divine action predicates will be spatiotemporally located occurrences whose elements can be indexed to locations in space-time. For now I should say something more about the partial univocity of divine and human action-predicates and how to settle what our ontological and theological commitments are when we speak truthfully about divine action and human action.

Consider three scenarios. First, suppose that Moses, upon leaving Egypt, says to his brother, Aaron, "God has delivered us from Egyptian bondage." Suppose further that it is true that God delivered the Hebrews from Egypt. If it were the case, however, that the Canaanites, out of the goodness of their hearts, had delivered the Hebrews from Egypt, then Moses would have uttered a similar statement to the effect that "The Canaanites have delivered us from Egyptian bondage." Finally, if we suppose that the spouse of the Pharaoh took unilateral action to release the Hebrews from bondage, Moses would have uttered "Pharaoh's spouse has delivered us from Egyptian bondage."

Suppose that Moses' intention in none of the foregoing cases is to express something metaphorical that is code for something else. It is reasonable to assume that the action-predicate Moses uses in each case, namely, "delivered," is not being used in a straightforwardly univocal sense. Moses means something slightly different in each case. This is

---

[6] Some readers will notice that in many respects the structure of the argument that follows is similar to the sort of reasoning that one may offer to argue that God is in time. I recognize the similarities but wish to keep the two issues separate since it seems to me there are good reasons for arguing that God may be sempiternal rather than timelessly eternal but still non-corporeal. I have argued for the thesis that God must be in time if God acts in the universe in a paper of mine I presented in various venues that remains unpublished, "The Ontology of Action and Divine Agency."

[7] For a defense of the claim that action-predicates when applied to God and humans are at least partially univocal, see Alston 1988.

so if for no other reason than that the truthmakers for these claims on which the truth of Moses' statements supervenes are quite different (one involves divine agency, another involves social agency, and the last involves individual human agency).[8] But there is partial univocity in Moses' use of the action-predicate. In each case, the following is the case. (i) The outcome is the same (the Hebrews are liberated). (ii) There is something that occurs in each instance in response to the Hebrews being enslaved in Egypt that brought about their deliverance from captivity. And, finally, (iii) the cause of their deliverance could truthfully be said to be *personal* in some sense and directed at delivering them from captivity.[9] Of course, whether the source of their deliverance was God or the Canaanites or Pharaoh's spouse, if we assume that all three could individually deliver the Hebrews, they all can satisfy (i)–(iii), but in different ways. So while the action-predicate "delivered" is not wholly univocal, it is partially univocal.

It may help to flesh out precisely what justifies the assertion that the action-predicate is neither straightforwardly univocal nor metaphorical, but, rather, partially univocal. Compare individual human agency to social agency. If Pharaoh's wife had said "Enough is enough!" and, contrary to her spouse's wishes, released the Hebrews from their captivity, then we could truthfully say of her that she delivered the Hebrews. But if she had done this, our use of "delivered" when we speak of what she did and what the Canaanites might have done if they had delivered the Hebrews is not exactly the same. It is true that in both instances there was still agency involved and both cases would satisfy (i)–(iii). But when we talk about Pharaoh's spouse versus the Canaanites delivering the Hebrews, it is not in virtue of the means of deliverance being the same that it is true that the Hebrews are delivered in the separate cases. (In fact, the methods employed are quite dissimilar—a decree versus an act of war.) If we move to God, we find that the truthmakers are very different from both the truthmakers for claims about Pharaoh's spouse and the Canaanites. Whether God is corporeal or incorporeal, if God is an agent, then God is a very different kind of agent from either Pharaoh's spouse or the Canaanites. God is neither an individual human agent nor is God a social agent composed of individual human agents in the same way the Canaanites are.[10] God is unlike either of these and is as different from one as God is different from the other. That said, while God is unlike either, God must be similar enough to both Pharaoh's wife and the Canaanites in order for the sense of "delivered" that we use when we speak of God, the Canaanites, and Pharaoh's wife to be at least partially univocal.

It is at this juncture that I believe we are forced to think about the metaphysics of theism. If we wish to avoid treating talk of divine action as merely metaphorical and if we wish to avoid theological anti-realism, the question that naturally arises is "What

---

[8]   For more on truthmaking, see Armstrong 2004 and Heil 2012b.

[9]   While I assume that God is personal, contra Jantzen 1984 and Swinburne 1993, whether a religiously adequate metaphysics of theism requires that God be personal is not obvious. See Bishop 2009 for an attempt at defending a religiously adequate, non-personal conception of God.

[10]   Of course, I am keeping in mind that if social trinitarianism is true, then God is, in fact, a social agent.

must God *be like* if we are to truthfully employ action-predicates when we are making claims about divine action?" This question forces us to determine what the ontological commitments of our religious language are that allow us to speak truthfully about God acting in our universe.

How we determine the ontological commitments of our theoretical discourse is a contentious matter. If we are theological realists, then we take it to be the case that we speak truthfully at least sometimes when we make claims about God and God's activity in the world. Philosophers of religion have said very little about what the proper crite- rion/criteria of ontological commitment in philosophical theology is/are.[11] This is not the place to do the necessary spadework to fill this lacuna.

So I will simply assume the tenability of a truthmaker criterion of ontological com- mitment in what follows and note that I am aware that the approach I am taking will be very controversial to some readers. According to the truthmaker criterion, "the onto- logical commitments of a theory are just those things that must exist to make true the sentences of that theory" (Cameron 2008, 4). On this criterion, "<x exists> might be made true by something other than x, and hence that 'a exists' might be true according to some theory without *a* being an ontological commitment of that theory" (Cameron 2008, 4). This criterion of ontological commitment provides us with the room to explore alternative conceptions of God including variants of both traditional theism and the embodied God thesis.

Assuming that we can truthfully predicate actions of God in our statements about the divine, we can now begin to consider what God must be like in order for our action-sentences about God to be true. We have some idea of what must have taken place and what things must actually exist in order for it to be true that either Pharaoh's wife or the Canaanites delivered the Hebrews. But we have a less clear idea of what must have taken place in order for God to deliver the Hebrews. In this chapter, as mentioned above, my task is largely negative and only partly constructive. I aim to show that God cannot be a wholly immaterial substance if God performs actions like delivering the Hebrews or even more mundane things like intentionally sustaining the existence of an organism.[12] Rather, as noted earlier, I will argue that God must be spatiotemporally located and, hence, embodied in some way in order for God to act in the universe and, thus, for our action-sentences to be true. Ergo, if we wish to be theological realists, tak- ing our statements about divine action to be true and the action-predicates we use to be

---

[11] Examples of authors who have at least approximated taking on this task are Le Poidevin 1995 and Ralls 1964.

[12] I think it is actually easier to tell a metaphysical story about how God sustains an organism on either a pantheistic or panentheistic metaphysics of the divine versus coming up with a plausible story about the truthmakers for the sorts of events described in the scriptures that are best regarded as mythical, such as the story of the Hebrews' deliverance from slavery in Egypt. The sustaining story can be naturalistic and is no more problematic than the account of the truthmakers for saying of an agent *S* that they decided to perform action *A* or that a country declared war and took military action against another country. That said, I use this example from the Hebrew scriptures because it is a case of divine action that many tradi- tional theists take to be at least the sort of action God can perform.

at least partially univocal in the case of divine and human action, then we must reject the traditional metaphysics of theism that takes God to be wholly immaterial and not spatiotemporally located. Thus, some variant of the embodied God thesis is one of the ontological commitments of theological realism.

3. Making the Case for the Embodied God Thesis

Using "state of affairs" as a generic term to refer to processes, events, and states, it is true that a state of affairs obtains wherever you have an object possessing a property at a time (see Armstrong 1993, 1997, and 2010; see also Heil 2006). Consider the following argument for the embodied God thesis.

P1. Any spatiotemporally located state of affairs is caused by something that is spatiotemporally located. (Assumption)

P2. The causal consequences of God's actions in the universe are spatiotemporally located states of affairs. (Assumption)

C1. So God's actions are spatiotemporally located. (from (P1) and (P2))

P3. If God's actions are spatiotemporally located, then God is spatiotemporally located.

C2. So God is spatiotemporally located. (from (C1) and (P3))

It is a short step from (C2) to the conclusion that God is omnispatial and, hence, in some way embodied.

According to traditional Jewish, Christian, and Islamic theology, God is active throughout the universe at all times. Minimally, God intentionally sustains the entire universe. God's sustaining is clearly an intentional action of God's. God may sustain each point that constitutes a proper part of the universe at any moment or God may sustain the universe as a composite whole. In either case, given God's sustaining activity and (C2), we can conclude that God is omnispatial and located at every point in the universe. Ergo, God is embodied in some way as the universe.[13] The reasoning to this conclusion can be represented more clearly as follows.

P4. At any moment, God intentionally sustains the entire universe.

C3. So (C2) and (P4).

P5. If (C3), then God is omnispatial.

---

[13] A very different argument for God being omnispatial is offered in Helm 1980. Helm argues that God must be omnispatial if God is sempiternal. He then argues that the omnispatiality of God entails that: (i) God is a scattered object, (ii) God cannot be wholly located in more than one place at the same time, (iii) God has proper parts and hence is not simple, and (iv) God cannot occupy all spatial locations and so is finite (1980, 108–9). Ishtiyaque Haji (1989) has responded to each of these points, arguing that Helm is mistaken about (i), (iii), and (iv). He also argues that Helm is not mistaken about (ii), but (ii) is innocuous since God is not wholly located in any particular location in space-time but is rather wholly located in the entirety of space-time. That is, the entirety of God's location, if God is omnispatial, is all of space-time.

P6.   If God is omnispatial, then God is embodied in some way as the universe.

C4.   So God is embodied in some way as the universe.

Of course, none of the foregoing is uncontroversial. But some premises are more controversial than others and, hence, require sustained defense. Premise (P2) should not be terribly controversial. At least, if we assume some traditional version of Judaism, Christianity, or Islam, all three traditions have historically held that God's actions have effects in space and time. Also, (P4) should not be controversial—at least not for adherents to traditional theism. Moreover, I take it that (P5) and (P6) are not in need of defense. (P6) is non-committal regarding how the universe embodies God. And I think it is not too much of a stretch to assert that the universe embodies God somehow if God is omnispatial. (P5) may be more controversial to some. But if I am successful with respect to making the case for the other controversial premises in the argument, then it should not be problematic. Of course, that means that the reasonability of accepting (P5) as true depends upon the success of defending the most controversial premises in the argument.

(P1) and (P3) are both highly controversial. I think they are the premises of the argument that are in need of defense. In the bulk of the remainder of this chapter I will defend both premises and then turn to discussing the upshot for how we think about God's relationship to the universe and, finally, in the conclusion I will return to the question of what the ontological commitments of theological realism must be in order for our statements about divine action to be true.

4. Defending (P1): A Pairing Problem for Divine Action

In what follows, I will remain mostly neutral between different accounts of causation. In particular, I will not take a stand here on the debate between accounts that afford events a central role and those that afford processes a central role. Whether causings are best understood as being fundamentally relations between events (Davidson 1980, Kim 1973, and Lewis 1973) or states of affairs (Armstrong 1997) or as processes involving the exchange of some conserved quantity of energy (Dowe 2000) or as processes involving the interaction of causal powers of objects (Chakravarty 2005 and Heil 2012b) does not matter much for what follows.[14] What I *will* assume is that causation is more than just counterfactual dependence. Rather, C causes E if C somehow brings E about or produces/generates E. I will make reference to causal processes and I will often refer to the relata as events. But I leave it open whether such claims about events and processes are made true by some other features of the universe.

What is of utmost importance for what follows is the truth of the following claim. Our everyday experience of causal production involves causal relata that are spatio-

---

[14] I should note that I am not suggesting that these are the only proposals that have been defended in the literature on the metaphysics of causation.

temporally located being paired up. For instance, a rock hitting a window causes the glass to shatter. The rock hitting the glass triggers the event of the glass shattering. Of course, we can also speak of the structuring causes (e.g., the brittleness of the glass) that bring about the conditions necessary for a triggering cause to be effective,[15] but these are also such that they are located in space-time.

If spatiotemporally located events occur that result from a causal process involving one or more relata that are not spatiotemporally located, then such events would be the result of causal processes that involve constituents that cannot be located anywhere in space-time. Any occurrence, such as the outcome of a causal process, capable of being indexed to a location in space-time is located in space-time. But should we think that the causes of spatiotemporally located states of affairs must themselves be similarly located? If they could be caused by non-located causes, then they could be causally generated by causes that are not located anywhere in space and time. Such relations are odd. There is no causal nexus located anywhere in space-time where the cause is paired up with its effect. This problem has been highlighted by Jaegwon Kim (2005) in recent years and is one version of what has been christened the "Pairing Problem."[16]

Recall the example of the rock striking the window, causing the glass to shatter. The effect of the rock striking the window at $t1$ is that the window shatters at $t2$. The constituents of the causing, the rock, the window, and their relevant causal powers, all admit of being paired up with one another. That is to say, the constituents of the causing each have a spatiotemporal location and the epistemic upshot is that we can easily explain why the glass shattered by appealing to some locations in space-time and what occurred in those locations.

Contrast the case of the rock striking the window with a causal process involving a non-spatially located event and a spatiotemporally located event, namely, an immaterial mental event and a bodily action. Suppose that C and C* are two non-spatially located mental events. For *reductio*, assume that the occurrence at $t1$ of *either* C or C* (and not both) causes the occurrence at $t2$ of a (spatiotemporally located) bodily action, E.[17] (Suppose that C is the onset of a desire directed at opening a window in order to let out a fly and C* is the onset of a desire directed at opening a window in order to let in some air. E is the action of opening the window.) So, assuming that E is not causally overdetermined, either C or C* causes E. Hence, it is only the occurrence of C or C* that causally explains E. However, we do not know whether C or C* explains E and we cannot know. This is because E cannot be paired with its cause. That is to say, there is no spatiotemporal causal nexus in the universe where C or C* is paired up with E. C and C* are not located anywhere in space-time. They are literally *nowhere*, if

---

[15] See Dretske 1993.

[16] See Foster 1968, Kim 1973, and Kim 2005, 78–85. I am heavily indebted to Kim 2005 in what follows.

[17] This example and subsequent argument is a version of an example and argument offered in Kim 2005, 80–5.

"where" implies some location in space-time. If there is no location in space-time where the causal relation obtains that would explain the occurrence of E, then neither C nor C* could cause E. So *neither* C nor C* cause E. If this is correct, then we should expect that the results will generalize to other alleged instances of causation where one of the relata is not located in space-time and the other relatum is located in space-time. If I am right, then there cannot be any non-spatially located causes of spatiotemporally located events and we have good reason to accept (P1) as true.

4.1 Objection 1

Some may not be moved by the foregoing reasoning. The claim may be that the problem is *merely* epistemic.[18] It may be argued that *we* simply cannot *explain* the occurrence of E by specifying its cause due to our epistemic limitations. But E is caused, nonetheless. So if E is caused by C or C*, but we cannot know which event caused E, that does not show that E is not caused. We can give a disjunctive causal explanation of the occurrence of E—it is caused by either C or C*. And that we cannot definitively pair up E with either C or C* does nothing to change the fact that E is caused by one of them.

4.1.1 RESPONSE TO OBJECTION 1

That E cannot be paired up with its effect is not *merely* an epistemic problem. As John Gibbons notes, "explanation also has a metaphysical side" (2006, 100).

The failure to explain the occurrence of E by C or C* points to a deeper metaphysical problem posed by immaterial entities. As I noted above, immaterial events such as C and C* are such that they are not located in space-time and, hence, no causal nexus exists that allows for them to be paired with events in space-time. Any attempt at locating them somewhere is an exercise in futility. Because they are not spatially located, they have no spatial boundaries that place them in a particular location in space-time. To ascribe such boundaries to them would be to ascribe spatial location to them. The epistemic problem that results from our not being able to explain the occurrence of E is thus evidence of a metaphysical problem. Specifically, we have difficulty explaining the occurrence of E because it cannot be paired up with the event that explains its occurrence. This calls into question the causal relevance of C and C*. An adequate explanation of the occurrence of E requires that we can pair it with its cause or causes. Where there is no causal nexus that exists in space-time that allows us to pair up events, we lack a causal explanation of the effect. Our lack of a causal explanation gives us reason to be skeptical about the reality of any causation in this case. If the foregoing is right, then our epistemic inability to explain how C or C* could cause E is owing to a deeper metaphysical problem that is not easily waved away.

---

[18] Thanks to Michael Almeida for raising this objection. A very similar objection is raised by David Jehle (2006) against Kim's original argument.

4.2 Objection 2

The second objection also treats the difficulty raised by the pairing problem as merely epistemic. Focusing on cases of intentional agency, where C and C* are mental causes and E is an overt action, it may be argued that given an agent's privileged first-person epistemic access to the contents of her mind, the agent should simply know whether C or C* was the cause of E. So, in cases of intentional agency, even if other persons cannot detect whether C or C* caused E, the agent can be secure in knowing what the cause was and can tell others what caused E.[19]

4.3 Response to Objection 2

This response seems to assume that human agents are immune to introspective error. But both philosophical work on self-knowledge and action and evidence from empirical work in cognitive and social psychology indicate that we can and often do go wrong when it comes to our reports of why we behaved a certain way (e.g., Nisbett and Wilson 1977; Schwitzgebel 2008). So whether we assume that mental causes have spatiotemporal location or not, it is not the case that one's first-person perspective can guarantee that one is right about what caused one to behave a certain way.

What is the import of all of this? In a case where either C or C* is among the causes of an agent's behavior, an agent may think that C is among the causes of her behavior when it is not. C* is among the actual causes. The agent's claim that C was a cause may be the case because of post-hoc rationalization. For instance, suppose that C is an emotional state, such as disgust, of an agent and C* is a moral principle. C may cause an agent to judge that some action or its consequences are bad and react disapprovingly in response to the perpetrator of the action. When asked why the agent responded as she did, the agent invokes C* and not C as among the causes that explain and justify her judgment and expression of disapprobation (see Haidt 2001).

It may be argued that the final conclusion of my argument is not about human action but about divine action and the nature of God. It may be argued that God is a very different agent. Specifically, God is immune to the sorts of introspective errors that may occur in the case of a human agent.

I admit that things would be different with a divine being with infallible knowledge. Suppose that God brought about some event E in the physical universe for either reasons C or C* and only one of them could have been involved in the causal production of E. God reports that God brought about E for reason C and not C*. Assuming divine omniscience and moral perfection, in the sort of case described it seems one would be justified in believing that C was causally relevant while C* was not with respect to the production of E. But even if this is right, the original metaphysical worries about how a non-spatiotemporally located cause could have a spatiotemporally located effect remains. We are still left wondering how it is that C, which is nowhere, could play any

---

[19] This objection was raised by one of the referees for this volume.

role in the causal production of E, which has a spatiotemporal location. Appeals to divine mystery at this point or the limits of human knowledge are simply not satisfying. So while the traditional theist may appeal to scripture and tradition at this juncture to make their case, such an appeal is simply not very philosophically satisfying.

4.4 Objection 3

In response to the foregoing, some may echo William Hasker's response to critics of substance dualism in the philosophy of mind who assert that, "because of the great disparity between mental and physical substances, causal interaction between them is unintelligible and impossible" (1999, 150). Hasker claims that the critic of substance dualism's argument "may well hold the all-time record for overrated objections to major philosophical positions" (1999, 150). Hasker suggests that such reasoning is not decisive because "*all* causal relationships involving physical objects are at bottom conceptually opaque" (1999, 150). Moreover, the critic is guilty of begging the question "by assuming that psychophysical causation must work in the same way as physical causation" (1999, 151).

As I see it, there are two substantial claims being made by Hasker. First, psychophysical causation involving immaterial mental causes only seems odd and is difficult to represent conceptually[20] because what we find understandable is whatever is most similar to that with which we are most familiar, namely, physical causation. But all such physical relations are conceptually opaque. Second, critics beg the question by assuming that psychophysical causation must work like physical causation.

4.4.1 RESPONSE TO OBJECTION 3

Hasker's first claim ignores the fact that, conceptually at least, some causal relations are more opaque than others. That psychophysical causal relations involving immaterial mental causes involve causes that cannot be located in space-time because they lack spatial location cannot count in their favor. I am happy to admit that causation of all sorts is conceptually opaque at bottom. But the fact that certain types of causal relata resist being paired up counts uniquely against them. It is harder to represent such causings conceptually, if not impossible. And the argument I presented does not rely on a general claim about the *mysterious* nature of causation by immaterial events or about how such causation is conceptually opaque. Rather, it relies wholly on how such events (including immaterial mental events) resist being paired up with the physical events they allegedly cause. In other words, I take it that such causation is not merely mysterious and conceptually opaque. Rather such causings are metaphysically impossible since the relation between the cause and the effect literally occurs nowhere. Hence, there are no such causings.

---

[20] I here assume that concepts and conceivings are representations. Hasker seems to be assuming something similar. For a defense of a representational theory of concepts, see Margolis and Laurence 2007.

Regarding the second claim, my foregoing argument did not assume that psychophysical causation must work like physical causation. But it does assume that all causal relations should be such that the relata can be paired up. To say that we should not expect psychophysical causal relations to behave like other causal relations in this respect amounts to assuming without any justification that the relata in psychophysical causation do not have to be able to be paired up like other causal relata. We need a reason to think that they should behave differently. Appeals to the nature of the mental or the nature of the divine that assert that they are "just so" are not very satisfying in the absence of reasons to think that we should allow for the possibility of such causal relations at all.

4.5 Objection 4

There is one final worry I will address before moving on.[21] It may be argued that the foregoing line of reasoning presupposes causal closure of the physical. I am taking physicalism for granted. Hence, I am guilty of begging the question against traditional theism given its incompatibility with physicalism.

4.5.1 RESPONSE TO OBJECTION 4

Physicalist assumptions are not driving my argument in this section. I have intentionally tried to remain neutral with respect to causal closure in this chapter. In fact, I believe I can reject the causal closure of the physical and endorse the reasoning of this section. This would be the case if I were to admit the existence of levels in my ontology and the possibility of interlevel causation.

Suppose that biological properties are emergent properties. Suppose, further, that some biological property B that is a constituent of a biological event can exercise a top-down causal influence on some physical property P that is a constituent of a physical event without the physical properties of the emergence base of B exercising a causal influence on P. If this is possible (and it is certainly at least logically possible), then events involving irreducible biological properties can cause physical events. And since biological *events* are spatiotemporally located, they can be paired up with their physical effects. And if biological events can be paired up with physical events, the constituents of those events (including the properties manifested), qua constituents of those events, can be paired up with the constituents of physical events. Of course, none of this is terribly neat and tidy. What is important is that, as Jaegwon Kim notes, such downward causation "prima facie implies the failure of causal closure at the lower [physical] level" (1995, 193). And if I am right, then while such causal relations run afoul of causal closure, they do not face a serious pairing problem. Admittedly, I do believe the ontology of levels such top-down causation presupposes is untenable for reasons I will not explore here.[22] But it seems that I could endorse a levels ontology

[21] Todd Buras raised this worry.

[22] But see Heil 2003 and 2012b for reasons to reject the existence of levels in one's ontology. Also, see Buckareff 2012 and Kim 2005 for related but more specific worries about the tenability of non-reductive physicalism in the philosophy of mind.

and top-down causation and be moved by arguments from pairing difficulties to reject the claim that non-spatially located entities can cause effects that are spatiotemporally located.

5. Defending (P3): The Embodied God Thesis

Recall what (P3) states: If God's actions are spatiotemporally located, then God is spatiotemporally located. For my purposes here, given the connection between (C1), which states that God's actions are spatiotemporally located, and (P3), I need to show that there are good reasons for taking both the antecedent and the consequent of (P3) to be true. Merely showing that this conditional sentence (read as a material conditional) is (vacuously) true would not be enough to defend the soundness of the argument since (P3) can be true while (C1) is false. This would mean that the argument is still not sound, or worse, not even valid given that (C1) is the conclusion of (P1) and (P2) (assuming of course, that (P1) and (P2) are true). So it is necessary to defend both the antecedent and the consequent of (P3).

If the reasoning in the prior section is cogent, then the results should generalize to God's actions. So we can justifiably assert that God's actions are spatiotemporally located. Let me explain.

If the outcomes of God's actions are spatiotemporally located, we should expect the causes of those outcomes, the actions themselves, to be spatiotemporally located. Suppose, that at $t1$ Elijah is in Jerusalem and Elisha is also in Jerusalem. At $t2$ Elijah and Elisha both find themselves surrounded by the prophets of Baal. At $t3$ each one prays that God will incapacitate the prophets of Baal. At $t4$ God incapacitates the prophets of Baal by blinding them. Suppose that blinding the prophets of Baal is a basic action for God (God does not do it *by* doing anything else). If we assume that there is an event that is the incapacitation of the prophets of Baal surrounding Elijah and another event that is the incapacitation of the prophets of Baal surrounding Elisha, then each is an event we can locate in space and time. Each event is spatiotemporally located. Suppose, further, that each event is the intentional outcome of a separate divine action. If each separate action that caused the separate outcomes is not spatiotemporally located, while we can stipulate that two simultaneous divine actions occur that have different intentional outcomes,[23] we have no principled way of pairing up the intentional outcome of each action with the action of blinding that caused it. If this is right, then if God's actions are in fact causally responsible for the spatially located intentional outcomes of God's actions, then God's actions must be similarly spatially located. For if they are causally responsible for the outcomes, then each action should admit of being paired with each intentional outcome. A non-located event cannot be paired up with a located event (as shown in the previous section). So God's actions must have a location in space-time, just as their effects have a spatiotemporal location.

---

[23] On Jewish-Christian-Islamic theism, this should not be a problem since God is omnipresent and capable of acting in multiple locations at once.

Not only are God's actions spatiotemporally located, but God is located in space-time. Why think this? We should expect this because if all of God's actions are basic actions, then the actions or some aspect of them involve God's unmediated agency. Whatever the correct story is about the etiology of divine basic actions, assuming God's actions are in any way analogous to the actions of the agents in our experience (both human and non-human animals), then God's actions occur (at least partially) within God. Consider human action. Suppose that Mary punches Bill. Leaving issues of action-individuation to the side for now, whether the basic action is Mary's moving her arm (by which she punches Bill) or some mental action of deciding to move her arm, the basic action she performs by which she punches Bill takes place within Mary. Even if we assume that some part of the action does not take place within Mary some aspect of it connects up causally with something else that is its outcome. If I am right about basic actions, then pairing requires that God's basic actions be causally paired with their outcomes. If such a causal pairing is possible, then God must be located in space-time and the embodied God thesis is true.

If I am right, then both the antecedent and consequent of (P3) are true. If (P3) is true, then God must be spatiotemporally located in some way. So the embodied God thesis must be true if God acts. So, if I am right, then some version of the embodied God thesis is an ontological commitment of theological realism about divine agency (assuming, of course, that divine and human action predicates are at least partially univocal). The embodied God thesis provides us with the truthmakers for the statements we make about divine action assuming that at least some of our statements about divine action are true. And if the reasoning of my argument at the beginning of section 3 is sound, then not only is God located in space-time, but God is omnispatial and the universe in some way embodies God.

5.1 Objection 1

If we assume that intentional actions (unlike things that merely happen to an agent) are purposive and that they are purposive because they are directed at a particular outcome, then God's actions are directed at different outcomes. This is a reasonable assumption. In fact, I think it is fairly uncontroversial. What my interlocutor may conclude from this is more controversial.

I expect the traditional theist will argue that once again, the problem I have raised is *merely* epistemic. If all of God's action are intentional actions, then, even if we cannot locate God's actions in space-time and pair them neatly with their effects, this epistemic limitation on our part should not lead us to conclude that there is no causal relation that can obtain between a divine action and its outcome.

5.1.1 RESPONSE TO OBJECTION 1

Notice how this objection echoes the first objection in section 4. I will not repeat my response to that objection here. But, since it may be claimed that things are somehow different in cases of actions causing outcomes (especially where the actions are the actions of a divine agent), I offer the following in response.

At best, this objection suggests that the claim that God's actions are not spatiotemporally located but bring about certain outcomes at which they are directed is not wholly unintelligible. But it still fails to show that any such action can actually cause an outcome indexed to some location(s) in space-time. That is to say, it does not get us any closer to discerning how any such causing is actually possible since there is no causing to speak of apart from what the traditional theist merely asserts exists. And a mere assertion proves little.

5.2 Objection 2

A defender of traditional theism who takes God to be timelessly eternal and simple rather than sempiternal may argue that the dialectic I have presented is wide of the mark. I have assumed that God is in time and that God's actions can be indexed to multiple times. It may be argued that if God is wholly outside of time and is simple, then God does not perform multiple discrete actions that obtain at different times. Rather, there is only one act. What I have done is confused God's actions with the effects of God's one action. The defender of this view may contend that there is no pairing problem between the effects of God's actions and God's actions. There is only one action and it has multiple effects (see McCann 2012).

Alternatively, the defender of God as timelessly eternal and simple may identify God's actions with their alleged outcomes (see Grant 2007, 11–12). So, for instance, the escape of the Hebrews from Egyptian bondage is identical with the action of God delivering them. On this view, God's action is not some intermediate event that stands between God and the effect of an action. The effect just is the action.

5.2.1 RESPONSE TO OBJECTION 2

This objection assumes that by either reducing the number of actions from more than one to one or by identifying divine actions with their effects we can somehow avoid the pairing problem. Call the first solution "the one action solution" and the second solution "the consequence solution."

Consider the one action solution. There are two problems with this response. By moving from multiple actions and their effects to one action with multiple intentional outcomes we have only made matters worse. Now the defender of traditional theism must explain how the rescue of the Hebrews from Egypt, saving Elisha from the prophets of Baal, and delivering David from Saul can all be the intentional outcome of the same action. What we have is a position that describes what is, at best, an unintelligible state of affairs. It is unintelligible because we now have God who is not only outside of space, but is outside of time; and we cannot make sense of how God's single action can connect causally with its effects. Whether or not such a causal relation is logically or metaphysically possible is at least questionable. But showing that it is neither logically nor metaphysically possible would require more work. Suffice it to say for now that the unintelligibility of any such causal relation counts against it being reasonable to accept as metaphysically possible. But I do not wish to suggest that I have shown that it *is* metaphysically impossible.

I should quickly note another difficulty with this view. Intentional actions are directed at particular outcomes. If God only performs one single action, then that action is directed at a plethora of different outcomes, some of which are not obviously consistent with one another. For instance, outcomes may be ordered temporally in ways that require that one outcome occurs before another can be brought about. For instance, God must first direct Jacob to go to Egypt before God delivers Jacob's descendants from Egypt. That God's guiding the Hebrews to Egypt and delivering them from Egypt are the same action is odd at the very least because they are inconsistent or, if they are consistent, they cannot occur simultaneously. This problem is even more basic than the pairing problem. A traditional theist who takes God to be sempiternal and regards the doctrine of timelessly eternal divine agency to be incoherent can offer this sort of objection to the one action solution.

While the consequence solution does not face the problem of one intentional action directed at inconsistent outcomes. The causal problems are not much different if we adopt the consequence solution. Now we must pair up God qua cause with effects. A coarse-grained solution to action-individuation may allow us to identify God's delivering the Hebrews with their escape from Egyptian bondage.[24] That is not the problem. The problem is just the same problem with the one action solution. Now the problem is with how to pair God up with God's actions. The causal relation God stands in vis-à-vis God's actions is unintelligible. We cannot pair God up with God's actions.

That a theory of divine action is problematic in the ways variants of the traditional view appear to be should be reason enough for us to dispense with such theories if another theory can be offered that avoids this problem. The variants of the embodied God thesis avoid this problem. Of course, accepting the embodied God thesis comes at some ontological and theological cost, not the least of which being that we must accept the notion that the universe constitutes, is a proper part of, or is identical with God. But if this is unacceptable, we need to know why.

6. Coda: Idolatry and Tradition

I expect that some who read this chapter will not be convinced if for no other reason than two millennia of dominant theological tradition in Judaism, Christianity, and Islam do not favor endorsing any variant of pantheism or panentheism over traditional theism. But if tradition alone is what constrains us in thinking about the metaphysics of the divine, we must ask ourselves at what point our commitment to tradition

---

[24] For more on action-invivuation, including a survey of alternatives, see Buckareff 2011.

becomes idolatrous. John Bishop (2009), Mark Johnston (2009), and John A. T. Robinson (1963) have separately underscored the danger of idolatry in theologizing. And I would encourage my traditionalist interlocutors to ask whether—to the extent that they close off the embodied God thesis as an option—their own commitments to how we should constrain our understanding of the divine are possibly idolatrous.

Notwithstanding my worries about idolatry, I do not wish to suggest that the embodied God thesis is wholly inimical to tradition. In fact, I am inclined to think that if the central argument of this chapter is sound, then being a disembodied spirit would not be a great-making attribute. If being embodied is necessary for God to act in the universe, then being embodied is a great-making attribute. The sort of version of great-being theology that will deliver this sort of conclusion is not traditional Anselmian theism. Rather, a modified Anselmian theism that takes God to be maximalGod may lead us to the conclusion that the embodied God thesis is not only acceptable, it is necessary for divine greatness.[25] I cannot explore how an embodied God can be maximalGod in this chapter. But I want to finish by considering how the embodied God thesis may not only be consistent with some of what tradition has asserted about God, it may provide us with the resources to think more clearly about some traditional doctrines.

Consider divine simplicity. The standard contemporary interpretation of the doctrine is confused (or at least confusing).[26] God is taken to be identical with God's intrinsic properties, each of which is identical with the others. Perhaps the idea of God's being identical with God's properties that are all the same property under different descriptions is unproblematic. But the doctrine as recently formulated seems inconsistent with divine agency since the truthmakers for divine action-sentences that are indexed to moments of time are constantly changing (e.g., it is true of God at $t1$ that God is liberating the Hebrews from Egyptian bondage and not true at $t2$ that God is liberating them). This problem is especially troubling for those who treat God as sempiternal/everlasting rather than timelessly eternal.[27]

One way to think about simplicity that avoids the problems of recent formulations that is also consistent with some version of the embodied God thesis is to identify God with a simple substance. That God is a simple substance is not problematic, or at least not problematic in the way that the idea that God is somehow identical with God's properties that are identical with one another. On this view, God is not a complex object composed of simple substances. If God is a simple substance, then God has no

[25] See Nagasawa 2008. On maximalGod theism, God is taken to have the maximal consistent set of great-making attributes.
[26] Brower (2009) does an excellent job at diagnosing the problem with contemporary formulations of divine simplicity and proposes a more plausible way of understanding the doctrine. For reasons I cannot address here, I do not think that Brower's own proposal is entirely successful. Some of what follows is indebted to Brower's work along with the work of John Heil (2003 and 2012a) on substantial parts versus spatial parts.
[27] The locus classicus in analytic philosophical theology for a defense of the doctrine of divine sempiternality is Wolterstorff 1975/1982. See Helm 1989 for a seminal defense of divine eternality.

substantial parts—i.e., God has no parts that are themselves substances. God's properties (including those that serve as truthmakers for divine action-sentences) are particular ways or modes of God's being.

This approach makes room for God to be acting in time. Just because something has no substantial parts, it does not follow that it has no spatial or temporal parts (Heil 2012a). If a substance is spatiotemporally extended, then it can have spatial parts while having no substantial parts. It may have an infinite number of spatial parts. Hence, if God is omnispatial, God can be infinite in some sense (see Haji 1989). Spatial parts of a substance are regions in an extended substance that depend upon the substance for their existence. God is an extended substance if God is omnispatial and acts in time.

My interlocutor may insist that, if God is omnispatial, then God is a complex substance who is composed of simple substances. But this is not obviously true. If substance monism is correct, then God may be identical with the one substance.[28] For instance, space-time may be the one substance. On this view, space-time regions are spatiotemporal parts of the one substance, and ordinary material objects are just space-time regions at which properties are possessed (Schaffer 2009). Divine action-sentences could be made true by the interaction of the properties at different space-time regions. The details of such a story go beyond the scope of this chapter. But note that such an account allows for us to make sense of how God may be omnispatial (and, hence, omnipresent), acting in space-time, and have spatial and temporal parts but no substantial parts. In any case, this strategy may allow us to make better sense of divine simplicity.[29]

So, if I am right, then room can be made for a qualified notion of divine simplicity if at least one version of the embodied God thesis is true. Of course, it would require the truth of monistic substantivalism. And God would be identical with the one substance. But this strikes me as less costly than some of the traditional options articulated in the history of theology.

7. Conclusion

Assuming theological realism, if I am right, then, if divine and human action predicates are at least partially univocal, we have good reason to think that our discourse about divine action requires that we accept some version of the embodied God thesis. Specifically, if the truthmaking view of ontological commitment is correct, then I take it that our theorizing about divine action commits us to some version of the embodied God thesis. This is so because traditional theism does not provide the requisite truthmakers for true statements about divine action.

Of course, I do not expect traditional theists to grant the foregoing. But even if they react as I expect they will to the main argument of this chapter, so long as they react, I

---

[28] For a defense of substance monism, see Schaffer 2009.
[29] The strategy is consistent with either pantheism or panentheism since God's properties may not be limited to physical properties (thus making room for a version of panentheism).

believe that we will have made some progress in our thinking about the metaphysics of divine action. To my estimate, such a development would be a welcome change to the standard fare in analytic philosophical theology that excludes the embodied God thesis from the start and effectively circumscribes the scope of debates over the nature of God to variants of classical theism.[30]

References

Alston, W. (1988). "Divine and Human Action," in T. Morris (ed.), *Divine and Human Action: Essays on the Metaphysics of Theism* (pp. 257–80). Ithaca, NY: Cornell University Press.

Armstrong, D. (1993). "A World of States of Affairs," *Philosophical Perspectives* 7: 429–40.

Armstrong, D. (1997). *A World of States of Affairs.* New York: Cambridge University Press.

Armstrong, D. (2004). *Truth and Truthmakers.* New York: Cambridge University Press.

Armstrong, D. (2010). *Sketch for a Systematic Metaphysics.* New York: Oxford University Press.

Bishop, J. (1998). "Can there be Alternative Concepts of God?," *Noûs* 32: 174–88.

Bishop, J. (2007). "How a Modest Fideism may Constrain Theistic Commitment: Exploring an Alternative to Classical Theism," *Philosophia* 35: 387–402.

Bishop, J. (2009). "Towards a Religiously Adequate Alternative to Omnigod Theism," *Sophia* 48: 419–33.

Brower, J. (2009). "Simplicity and Aseity," in M. Rea (ed.), *The Oxford Handbook to Philosophical Theology* (pp. 105–28). New York: Oxford University Press.

Buckareff, A. (2011). "Action-Individuation and Doxastic Agency," *Theoria* 77: 312–32.

Buckareff, A. (2012). "An Action-Theoretic Problem for Intralevel Mental Causation," *Philosophical Issues* 22: 89–105.

Cameron, R. (2008). "Truthmakers and Ontological Commitment: Or How to Deal with Complex Objects and Mathematical Ontology without Getting into Trouble," *Philosophical Studies* 140: 1–18.

Chakravarty, A. (2005). "Causal Realism: Events and Processes," *Erkenntnis* 63: 7–31.

Davidson, D. (1980). *Essays on Actions and Events.* New York: Oxford University Press.

Dowe, P. (2000). *Physical Causation.* New York: Cambridge University Press.

Dretske, F. (1993). "Mental Events as Structuring Causes of Behaviour," in J. Heil and A. Mele (eds), *Mental Causation* (pp. 121–36). New York: Oxford University Press.

[30] Work on this chapter was done with the help of a project grant shared with Yujin Nagasawa (University of Birmingham) on Exploring Alternative Concepts of God provided by the John Templeton Foundation, a Summer Research Grant from Marist College, and course releases from Marist College. The views expressed in this chapter are entirely my own and do not reflect any explicit or implied commitments of the John Templeton Foundation or Marist College. A very early ancestor of this chapter was presented at the 2009 Metaphysics and Philosophy of Religion Workshop at the University of Texas in San Antonio. Subsequent versions were presented at a Symposium on Divine Action at the 2011 Pacific Division Meeting of the American Philosophical Association, a Philosophy Department Colloquium at William Paterson University, and at the John Hick Centre for Philosophy of Religion at the University of Birmingham. I am grateful to the members of the audience on each occasion for their feedback. I am especially indebted to Marilyn McCord Adams, Todd Buras, Peter Forrest, Stephanie Lewis, Yujin Nagasawa, Alexander Pruss, J. L. Schellenberg, and Ben Vilhauer. I also wish to thank Michael Almeida, John Bishop, Joseph Campisi, Kevin Gray, Klaas J. Kraay, Henry Pratt, James Snyder, Eric Steinhart, Christopher Tucker, and two anonymous referees for Oxford University Press for their helpful written comments.

Eshleman, A. (2005). "Can an Atheist Believe in God?", *Religious Studies* 41: 183–99.

Forrest, P. (1996). *God without the Supernatural: A Defense of Scientific Theism*. Ithaca, NY: Cornell University Press.

Forrest, P. (2007). *Developmental Theism: From Pure Will to Unbounded Love*. New York: Oxford University Press.

Foster, J. (1968). "Psycho-physical Causal Relations," *American Philosophical Quarterly* 5: 64–70.

Gibbons, J. (2006). "Mental Causation without Downward Causation," *Philosophical Review* 115: 79–103.

Grant, W. (2007). "Must a Cause be Really Related to its Effect? The Analogy between Divine and Libertarian Agent Causality," *Religious Studies* 43: 1–23.

Haidt, J. (2001). "The Emotional Dog and its Rational Tail: A Social Intuitionist Approach to Moral Judgment," *Psychological Review* 108: 814–34.

Haji, I. (1989). "God and Omnispatiality," *International Journal for Philosophy of Religion* 25: 99–108.

Hartshorne, C. (1948). *The Divine Relativity: A Social Conception of God*. New Haven: Yale University Press.

Hasker, W. (1999). *The Emergent Self*. Ithaca, NY: Cornell University Press.

Heil, J. (2003). *From an Ontological Point of View*. New York: Oxford University Press.

Heil, J. (2006). "The Legacy of Linguisticism," *Australasian Journal of Philosophy* 84: 233–44.

Heil, J. (2012a). "Substances Stressed," in P. Goff (ed.), *Spinoza on Monism* (pp. 167–80). New York: Palgrave-Macmillan.

Heil, J. (2012b). *The Universe as we Find it*. New York: Oxford University Press.

Helm, P. (1980). "God and Spacelessness," *Philosophy* 55: 211–21.

Helm, P. (1989). *Eternal God: A Study of God without Time*. New York: Oxford University Press.

Holtzer, S. (1987). "The Possibility of Incorporeal Agency," in W. Abraham and S. Holtzer (eds), *The Rationality of Religious Belief: Essays in Honour of Basil Mitchell* (pp. 189–209). New York: Oxford University Press.

Jantzen, G. (1984). *God's World, God's Body*. Philadelphia: Westminster.

Jehle, D. (2006). "Kim against Dualism," *Philosophical Studies* 130: 565–78.

Johnston, M. (2009). *Saving God: Religion after Idolatry*. Princeton: Princeton University Press.

Kenny, A. (1979). *The God of the Philosophers*. New York: Oxford University Press.

Kim, J. (1973). "Causation, Nomic Subsumption, and the Concept of Event," *Journal of Philosophy* 70: 217–36.

Kim, J. (1995). "Mental Causation in Searle's 'Biological Naturalism'," *Philosophy and Phenomenological Research* 55: 189–94.

Kim, J. (2005). *Physicalism, or Something Near Enough*. Princeton: Princeton University Press.

Le Poidevin, R. (1995). "Internal and External Questions about God," *Religious Studies* 31: 485–500.

Le Poidevin, R. (1996). *Arguing for Atheism*. New York: Routledge.

Levine, M. (1994). *Pantheism: A Non-Theistic Concept of Deity*. London: Routledge.

Lewis, D. (1973). "Causation," *Journal of Philosophy* 70: 556–7.

Lodzonski, D. (1998). "The Eternal Act," *Religious Studies* 34: 325–53.

McCann, H. (2012). *Creation and the Sovereignty of God*. Bloomington, Ind.: Indiana University Press.

Mander, W. (2000). "Omniscience and Pantheism," *Heythrop Journal* 41: 199–208.

Mander, W. (2007). "Theism, Pantheism, and Petitionary Prayer," *Religious Studies* 43: 317–31.

Margolis, E. and Laurence, S. (2007). "The Ontology of Concepts—Abstract Objects or Mental Representations," *Noûs* 41: 561–93.

Morris, T. (1987). *Anselmian Explorations: Essays in Philosophical Theology.* South Bend, Ind.: University of Notre Dame Press.

Morris, T. (1991). *Our Idea of God: An Introduction to Philosophical Theology.* Downers Grove, Ill.: Intervarsity Press.

Nagasawa, Y. (2008). "A New Defence of Anselmian Theism," *Philosophical Quarterly* 58: 577–96.

Nisbett, R. and Wilson, T. (1977). "Telling More than We Can Know: Verbal Reports on Mental Processes," *Psychological Review* 84: 231–59.

Oakes, R. (1983). "Does Traditional Theism Entail Pantheism?," *American Philosophical Quarterly* 20: 105–12.

Ralls, A. (1964). "Ontological Presupposition in Religion," *Sophia* 2: 3–11.

Robinson, J. (1963). *Honest to God.* Philadelphia: Westminster Press.

Sarot, M. (1992). *God, Possibility, and Corporeality.* Kampen: Kok Pharos.

Schaffer, J. (2009). "Spacetime the One Substance," *Philosophical Studies* 145: 131–48.

Schleirmacher, F. (1830/1928). *The Christian Faith.* Trans. H. Mackintosh and J. Stewart. Edinburgh: T&T Clark.

Schwitzgebel, E. (2008). "The Unreliability of Naïve Introspection," *Philosophical Review* 117: 245–73.

Spinoza, B. (1677/1992). *Ethics with the Treatise on the Emendation of the Intellect and Selected Letters.* Trans. S. Shirley. Indianapolis: Hackett.

Steinhart, E. (2004). "Pantheism and Current Ontology," *Religious Studies* 40: 63–80.

Swinburne, R. (1993). *The Coherence of Theism*, rev. edn. New York: Oxford University Press.

Taliaferro, C. (1994). *Consciousness and the Mind of God.* New York: Cambridge University Press.

Timpe, K. (2007). "Truth-Making and Divine Eternity". *Religious Studies* 43: 299–315.

Wolterstorff, N. (1975/1982). "God Everlasting," in S. Cahn and D. Shatz (eds), *Contemporary Philosophy of Religion* (pp. 77–110). New York: Oxford University Press.

13

Free Will and the Mythology of Causation

Hugh J. McCann

Libertarian views about human action are universally agreed on one point: that in order to be free our decisions and actions cannot have their existence accounted for by natural or event causation, at least of the deterministic variety.[1] But as to how our actions do come about there is little agreement. Some leave the issue alone, perhaps thinking that in the absence of event causation there simply is no final accounting for the phenomenon of action. Others, unhappy with the ontological void this seems to leave, seek to fill the gap in some way. Of these, some invoke so-called agent causation, wherein the agent himself rather than any combination of events is held to bring the decision or action to pass. Others appeal to the action of God as creator or primary cause of all that exists. I have defended a view of this last sort, and I shall have more to say in its defense here. In the main, however, I want to discuss the question of what it is we seek when we try to explain an event or action, and how well any sort of explanation, causal or otherwise, might or should satisfy us. What I hope to show is that at least when it comes to free decision and action, the appeal to God as first cause is our best bet.

1. Mere Existence

It will simplify things if we confine our attention to the act of deciding between alternative courses of action, since the structure of agency is somewhat clearer with strictly mental acts. Imagine therefore some example in which an agent deliberates among more than one alternative course of action and settles on one of them; that is, he decides or forms the intention to pursue one of the alternatives. It could be a simple case of making up one's mind where to have dinner tonight, or what film to see this weekend;

---

[1] In principle, probabilistic causation could be compatible with libertarianism. This possibility will however be set aside in the present discussion, which focuses on the actual relationship that obtains in the world when one event is said to cause another—a relation that is presumably the same for both deterministic and probabilistic causation.

or it might be a decision requiring considerable deliberation, such as where to spend one's summer vacation, or which of several houses to buy. Imagine too that the agent's act of deciding is free in the libertarian sense, with whatever kind of etiology that implies. As mentioned above, this will mean that the decision does not come about through any sort of deterministic event causation, either by mental states such as the agent's motives and beliefs or by physiological processes in his brain. What else is implied is of course to be debated, but the answer to this question can be left unsettled for the moment. Simply assume that whatever libertarian freedom requires, it is present in the example. And now make just one more assumption. Assume that the example you have imagined actually exists, that some agent—you, perhaps, or someone else—actually makes a decision of the precise kind you have imagined, and with just the right etiology. That is, assume the example is not abstract but concrete: it has, as Anselm might say, not just mental existence but real existence as well.[2]

One would hope it will be protested that this last move is otiose. To imagine an example of anything, it may fairly be said, is in the end no different from imagining an existent example of it. The question of existence might not have entered one's mind in thinking of the original example, but that makes no difference to what was conceived. Indeed, the reference to Anselm is appropriate, for this so-called further step only calls to mind Kant's remark in his discussion of the ontological argument, that since existence is not a real predicate, to move from conceiving of 100 Thalers in one's pocket to conceiving of an existing 100 Thalers in one's pocket neither improves one's financial condition nor enhances in any way the original conception.[3] Fair enough, and I have to admit that this is all old ground. Still, there is a lesson to be learned here. For suppose now that we are dealing with an existing decision that we take to exhibit libertarian freedom, but that it turns out we are able after all to account for its existence. We are able, that is, to locate some source from which the decision arises, not just as a matter of ongoing natural development or emergence, but in the sense that the source actually, as we might say, confers existence on the decision. The question would then arise whether this "sourcing" was such as to undermine the freedom we originally took to characterize the decision.

In pursuing this question there are two possibilities to consider. First, it might be that the sourcing works in such a way as to affect the intrinsic features of the decision itself. If so, then it could be that libertarian freedom, and the responsibility of the agent that goes with freedom, is destroyed, as it were, from within. That is, some feature of deciding that we take to be crucial to free will could be undone by the sourcing operation—so that as far, at least, as this particular decision is concerned, the agent has no freedom. Suppose, however, that this does not occur. Suppose the situation is as it is

---

[2] Anselm, *Proslogion* 2, in *Anselm: Basic Writings*, trans. T. Williams (Indianapolis: Hackett, 2007), 81–2.

[3] Immanuel Kant, *Critique of Pure Reason*, trans. P. Guyer and A. Wood (New York: Cambridge University Press, 1998), 567–8.

with Kant's 100 Thalers: the only difference the sourcing operation makes to the decision itself is that the decision exists. In all other intrinsic respects it has the same character it would if it had simply popped into existence from nowhere. If so, then this first way in which sourcing might be damaging to freedom drops out. There is, however, a second possibility, and it remains in play. It may be that even though in itself the decision has exactly the features it would have if there were no source whatever for its existence, the mere fact that it has a source—and perhaps in particular that it has the *kind* of source it does (the machinations, say, of some alien being)—is such as to undo the agent's freedom. So our question is this: is it possible to account for the existence of a supposedly free decision without destroying the agent's freedom?

2. Uncaused Existence

In answering this question we need to realize that merely to deny that our decisions have a cause is not to deny that they have an explanation. All of us, determinists and libertarians alike, feel that our decisions have explanations, in terms of the reasons that lead us to make them. If I decide to dine at an Asian restaurant tonight, I will do so because of the good I see as being achieved thereby. Perhaps my reason will simply be that I like Asian food; or it may be that there is a special discount at the Asian place tonight, or that I hope to encounter a friend there. But whatever my reasons are, they will be different from those I might have had for dining at an Italian restaurant instead, and whichever way I decide I would invoke the relevant reasons if asked to explain my decision. But if I believe that decisions are not caused I will not take this to be an event-causal explanation. I will take it as teleological, and understand the explanation to proceed in terms not of events but of what are in fact abstract entities. That is, it is not the mental event of my experiencing a desire for Asian food that I will understand to explain my behavior, but rather the mental *content* of that event, the good I take myself to be apprehending when I think, "Would that I have some Asian food this evening." Causes are supposed to be concrete things. The contents of our reason states are, by contrast, *abstracta*, and *abstracta* are generally considered to be causally inert.[4]

It is possible, then, to offer an explanation for a decision without invoking any cause at all, much less a deterministic one. But of course a determinist is not very likely to be satisfied by this sort of explanation. True, he might say, my reasons, even though they are abstract, have some explanatory force once my decision is on hand: they lay out the end to which it was ordered, the end whose achievement I was advancing toward in deciding as I did. But, he will insist, if we agree that *abstracta* are causally inert, then this will not account for the most important thing here, which is after all the fact that

---

[4] For more on this see my "Making Decisions," in E. Sosa, E. Villanueva, and B. Brogaard (eds), *Philosophical Perspectives* 22, *Action Theory* (Boston: Wiley-Blackwell, 2012), 248–63. The classical source is Thomas Reid, see *Essay on the Active Powers of the Human Mind* (Cambridge, MA: MIT Press, 1969), 283.

my decision *is* on hand.[5] The complaint can be put in more than one way. The determinist might point out that up until the moment of my decision things could have gone either way; we could have wound up in a world where I formed the intention to dine Asian, or one where I formed the intention to dine Italian. What then is the explanation for our now being in a world where I mean to visit the Asian restaurant and not the Italian one?[6] There seems to be no explanation. Alternatively, it might be said that if my decision had no cause then it has to count as a random accident, a mere fortuitous occurrence over which I had no control, and of which I am as much a victim as the agent.[7] Finally, it might be said that my deciding as I did was a matter of sheer luck, that it was blind fortune or destiny for me to have decided in favor of dining Asian.[8] And, it might be added, destiny is not always a trivial thing. If the existence of my decisions has utterly no accounting, then it must also be sheer luck that I decide to get money to purchase a new automobile by taking out a loan rather than by theft or fraud, or that I ignore a rude motorist rather than taking a shot at him. Now free will is often invoked as a necessary condition of moral responsibility. But, the objection runs, we are not responsible for accidents, fortuitous events, or what is owing to nothing but luck. How then are we to be held accountable for our supposedly free decisions, if the cost of calling them "free" is they must be understood to be out of our control, so that we become their victims rather than their producers or enactors?

3. About Luck

There is a good point underlying this objection, but it can hardly be appreciated for its true significance in these formulations. Consider first the claim that if libertarianism is true, then we have no explanation for our being in a world where I decide to dine at the Asian restaurant rather than at the Italian one. The problem with this formulation is that a general objection of this kind holds whether libertarianism is true or not. Even in a determined world I might have chosen differently than I did; all that would be required is different causes, extending back to the beginning of the world if it had a beginning, and infinitely if it did not. In short, we might have inhabited a determined world in which I opted for the Italian restaurant, not the Asian one. And this by the

[5] The determinist might add that the "for" can only be accounted for causally, a point famously argued by Donald Davidson. "Actions, Reasons, and Causes," in Davidson, *Essays on Actions and Events* (New York: Oxford, 2001), 3–19. I address this claim at some length in "Making Decisions." Briefly, the argument is this: we nearly always know the reasons for which we decide, but we do not know whether our decisions are caused. If this is the case, then our knowledge of the reason "for" which we decide or act cannot be gotten by tracing what we take to be causes. It has to be on other grounds.
[6] Unaccountable differences between our world and worlds in which agents will otherwise form an important part of an argument by Alfred Mele against decisions that are not causally determined. See his "Causation, Action, and Free Will," in H. Beebee, C. Hitchcock, and P. Menzies (eds), *The Oxford Handbook of Causation* (New York: Oxford University Press, 2009), 554–74, 564–6.
[7] This form of the objection was given by Hume. *A Treatise of Human Nature*, bk. II, pt. III, sec. II. It has since been repeated by many authors.
[8] Mele, "Causation, Action, and Free Will."

determinist's lights must be considered a matter of chance, for surely there is in the end no naturalistic explanation for our inhabiting one world instead of another. But then, if the mere fact that things might have gone differently is enough to excuse me from responsibility for my decision, then I ought to be excused whether my decision to dine Asian was determined or not. The same point applies when the determinist's objection is framed in terms of luck. If it is a matter of luck that we live in a world where I choose to dine Asian, then that will be so whether the world is determined or not, simply because in either case things might have gone differently. Again, therefore, it seems I ought to be excused.

Now of course it will be protested that this kind of response misses the point. It speaks of very general or long-run considerations in virtue of which the world might have been different. The determinist's objection, by contrast, has to do with the very short run. In a deterministic world we can be certain at the moment of my decision how it is going to go, because once the causes are in place chance and luck are taken out of the picture. There is no option other than for me to decide as I do, no possible world where I decide instead to visit the Italian restaurant this evening for dinner. Here however the libertarian has every right to stick to his guns. Select any point you wish in the chain of causes leading up to a supposedly determined decision. The fact is that conditions as they stand at that point count as lucky, in that they are owing to luck that went before. And of course this includes conditions at the moment of the agent's deciding. So if so-called chance or luck, alone and in itself, is what excuses, then it must excuse no matter where in the chain of events that led to my decision it appears. Luck is luck, long run or short run, and the same for alternative possibilities in the sequence of events. If, therefore, they alone are enough to excuse, then they must always excuse. If on the other hand luck and chance do not always excuse, then we need an argument for that—an argument to show that only when so-called chance or luck enters into my decision at the moment the decision is made am I not responsible for it. Any such argument is going to have to be a lot more specific; it will have to be based on a much narrower characterization of what the determinist is claiming constitutes grounds for exonerating the agent in such cases.

Such grounds, furthermore, are going to be hard to find. One might think not, because we have a fuller characterization of what the determinist takes to be occurring in a free choice in the remaining formulation of his objection: that an undetermined decision is a mere happenstance, a random accident that befalls the agent, and for which he is not responsible. Yet this form of the objection is even more misguided than the two already addressed. To see why, simply imagine a student who comes to his professor after class and says, "I'm sorry I missed the exam the other day, Professor. I accidentally decided not to come." Such an excuse can only rate an F, and even that grade would be generous if the course were about the will. Or consider the husband who says to his wife, "I'm sorry I have no birthday present for you, dear. By chance I made up my mind not to get you one." Again, suicidal. And in both cases the reason is the same: it is not just unlikely or unexpected that a person should decide by chance or accident to do something. It is self-contradictory. This is owing to two facts about the phenomenology of deciding. First, deciding is from the agent's perspective intrinsically active. It is experienced as something one *does*, not something that is done to one or befalls one. Second, deciding is intrinsically intentional: it is not possible for me to decide to have Asian food tonight without both intending to decide, and intending to decide exactly as I do.[9] Nor is this a matter of my having had prior intentions along these lines. Both points would hold even if I had decided entirely on the spur of the moment, at the very first thought of dining at the Asian restaurant, and with no prior consideration even of dining out, much less at this restaurant. When it comes to deciding intending is not a relational matter. If I decide at all, I must in that very act intend to decide, and to decide on precisely the course of action I select. In the present case I must intend to decide to have dinner at the Asian restaurant. Neither this nor the intrinsically active aspect of deciding have anything to do with what went before.

It is important to keep these points in mind in considering whether an action is made free in the libertarian sense by its intrinsic features or by relational ones. In order to count as a free action an event must first *be* an action. And what makes exercises of active willing, of which deciding is one type, actional is their intrinsic features—at least as far as the image they present to introspection is concerned. From my practical perspective as an agent, it is not possible for me to decide by accident or happenstance to visit the Asian restaurant, or to do anything else. As far as my experience of them is concerned, my decisions are intrinsically actional: things that I *do* and that cannot befall me. Of their very nature they cannot be events that occur by luck or chance. Now of course the phenomenal guise of deciding could turn out to be deceptive. In particular, it may be that although I appear to myself to be completely spontaneous in deciding to dine Asian tonight this is not in fact so. Perhaps, as determinists so often allege, my decision is caused, not by the abstract content of my state of desiring Asian food but by the state itself, along with my state of believing I can get some by going to the Asian restaurant. These are concrete realities, and may therefore legitimately be invoked in event-causal explanations. True, but again the causal claim itself needs to be proven, and for all our fears about determinism it has as yet not been proven. Until it is, the libertarian has every right to treat the phenomenal guise of his acts of deciding as reliable. Indeed, he has every reason to claim that when it comes to luck it is in fact the determinist who should consider his decisions owing to luck, in that he believes himself to inhabit a world whose nature as a whole must perforce lack the only kind of explanation he professes to accept—that is, an explanation in terms of natural causes— so that all he does must in the end be owing to whatever blind fate it was that made the world what it is.[10]

---

[9] I take for granted here that anything done intentionally is done with an intention. For a defense of this view see my *The Works of Agency* (Ithaca, NY: Cornell University Press, 1998), ch. 10.

[10] There are philosophers who hold that whether our actions are determined or not, we are not responsible for them. See especially Galen Strawson, "The Bounds of Freedom," in R. Kane (ed.), *The Oxford Handbook of Causation* (New York: Oxford University Press, 2002), 441–60.

4. The Real Issue

As things stand, then, there is no reason to accept the claim that a decision characterized by libertarian freedom must count as a lucky accident. Here too there is a lesson to be learned. What makes a decision free in the libertarian sense is first and foremost a matter of its relation to alleged causes. What makes it lucky or unlucky, by contrast, is whether it is under the agent's practical control, and that turns out to be a matter of its intrinsic features. This is reflected, moreover, in discourse about what are taken to be matters of luck in ordinary affairs. We call the throw of the dice "lucky" not because we take it to be uncaused but because we understand the causes to be complex and subtle enough that we are not able to make them subject to our decisions and volition as agents. Now it is certainly fair to say that this is exactly how we would treat a pair of dice that was by some miracle exempt from event causation, so that how they came up on a given throw was truly a random matter. But it does not follow that if human decision and volition are exempt from causation they too must count as random, or as lucky accidents. Just the opposite: the whole point of calling anything a lucky accident is precisely to say that it escapes what is intrinsic to decision and volition, namely the agent's practical control. We are helpless, usually, to control how a pair of dice will come up; we are anything but helpless to control our active willing, because to engage in active willing is intrinsically to be in control of what we are doing.

The determinist's complaint about libertarian freedom is not best understood, then, as about chance or luck and the import these have for questions of responsibility. Nor, I think, is it about something else that might be alleged, namely our ability to predict, and to control or influence, the behavior of others. The practical perspective of an onlooker trying to influence another is of course a far cry from that of the agent. Whereas the agent feels himself in complete control of his actions, parties with a third person perspective may struggle to have any effect at all on others' deeds. Parents agonize over recalcitrant children; employers struggle with poorly motivated workers; the criminal justice system is overwhelmed with recidivism. The task of eliciting desired or expected behavior from others is daunting even if we presume human decisions and actions are determined. It may well appear hopeless if take ourselves to be living in the world of the libertarian, where no course of action can finally be settled except by the agent, and third parties, even those entrusted with responsibility for others' behavior, are in the end helpless to guarantee any outcome. But this line of thinking too fails to reach the heart of the problem. In the first place, we do not as agents want our behavior subject to absolute control by others, nor do we often wish to be able to exert such control over them. What we want is for human decisions and actions to be autonomous while at the same time available to persuasion: to be free yet able to be guided by sound advice. This is precisely what libertarian freedom makes possible. Free actions are not done at random. They are done for reasons, so that agents can often be swayed by considerations that others bring forward. Moreover, since success in life requires of all of us both that we maintain reasonably steady habits and that we keep to the pursuit of a fair number of long-term goals, the actions of free agents can often be predicted with reasonable success even if they are not law governed. Thus, while dealing with free agents may at times be no picnic, neither is it a question of having to cope with chaos.

There is a further point to be made here as well. Questions of responsibility and of how free agents are to be dealt with, while strongly intertwined with the issue of freedom, are in the end practical matters. By contrast the randomness objection to libertarianism, despite its practical import, is at bottom profoundly metaphysical. The problem to which it points is this: determined events—the behavior of balls on a billiard table, to take the classic example—are at home in the world, at home with the past, in a way that undetermined events at not. Given the positions and momenta of the balls at any instant, we can predict with certainty what will happen for the next few moments. We are not going to be surprised, because nothing really new is going to take place. There will be no ontological break with the past. With my decision to go to the Asian restaurant things are different. There is some continuity with the past, in that the state of intending in which my decision terminates reflects in its content the content of the reason states out of which it was formed. My desire for Asian food and my belief that I can get some at the restaurant in question end up enshrined, as it were, in my intention to visit that restaurant for dinner. Here, however, there is no certainty of the outcome based on what went before, because these reasons have to compete with whatever reasons I may have for going elsewhere, so that even a friend who is familiar with my habits could end up being surprised at what I finally decide. This is because deciding does involve a break with the past, even when I decide as my friend expects me to. Billiard balls have positions and momenta after their collisions just as they did before, because their nature does not change. Only their positions and the directions and velocities of their movements change. By contrast, an act of deciding is quite a different sort of thing from what precedes it. States of desiring and believing have nothing like the actional qualities of deciding; indeed, if I were to learn tomorrow that the onset of my desire to have Asian food this evening was an undetermined event I would no more consider it an action than I do at present. It has none of the phenomenal quality of doing, and bears not a trace of intentional purpose. Furthermore my decisions do in a way alter my nature: they establish precedents and reinforce habits that form part of my character as a rational agent, and so help guide my subsequent behavior.

Because deciding has these distinctive features, our decisions and the actions that eventuate from them, even when they are pretty predictable, count metaphysically as a break with the past—a turning of a page in which if libertarianism is true something is settled that was not settled before. That this should be so may be thought a good, since it gives us a sense of practical autonomy in our lives. Framed in the language of causality, however, it has a deeply disturbing aspect, for two reasons. First, if our decisions and actions lack natural causes then there is a sense in which each of us has a nature that is incomplete. What we are and are to be, especially in moral terms, awaits the dictate of each moment, in which there is always a degree of arbitrariness. Second, if decision and volition are not products of natural causation then the prospect arises that they may have no cause whatever. Many if not most determinists, in fact, would draw this conclusion immediately. And then our practical lives begin to appear deeply enigmatic—the more so if, as is common among philosophers, we think of natural causation as an operation in which causes actually confer existence on their effects. It means that whatever their relation to our reasons for acting may be, and however much they may count to the agent and also to observers as exercises in practical control, our decisions and actions literally come from nowhere. Each of us in his practical life is acting out a puzzle wherein every step we take is an ontological mystery. Each event, each activity in which we suppose ourselves to be exerting control over our lives and destinies testifies by its very presence in the world that we live in a universe utterly indifferent, if not implacably hostile, to all that we say and do. If this does not provoke a sense of existential anxiety, the determinist might say, then it should. As so far stated, libertarianism may engender confidence in our freedom, but it is also able to provoke a sense of desperate contingency and unease. This is what is at the bottom of the "accidentalness" objection, and it is a legitimate problem.

5. Agent Causation

The difficulty just described is, as was said, not a practical but a metaphysical one. Faced with it, the libertarian need not relinquish his claims about responsible action, for no necessary condition of freedom or responsibility has as yet been shown to be violated. He would, however, be well served to find some other way of accounting for the existence of our decisions and actions. And if he agrees that the concept of causing something is simply interchangeable with that of providing for its existence, then this means he has to come up with some sort of causation other than the event causation ruled out by libertarian freedom. And of course there is a concept ready to hand, namely that of agent causation, according to which it is the agent himself who causes or brings about his decisions and volitional acts, not some combination of inner states or events.[11] It is helpful in discussing agent causation to call to mind a claim sometimes made about libertarian freedom: that a free agent must be the sole or original source of his decisions and actions.[12] This idea need not be taken to entail a commitment to agent causation. In one sense an agent with libertarian freedom is the sole source of his actions simply in that they represent a new beginning in the world that starts with something he does: each decision or volitional act stands at the head of a sequence of change that originates with the agent in the sense simply that the act of will in question

[11] Defenses of agent causation include Roderick M. Chishom, "Freedom and Action," in *Freedom and Determinism*, ed. K. Lehrer (New York: Random House, 1966), 11–44; and Timothy O'Connor, *Persons and Causes: The Metaphysics of Free Will* (New York: Oxford University Press, 2000).
[12] For development of this idea see Robert Kane, *The Significance of Free Will* (New York: Oxford University Press, 1996), ch. 5. Kane is not, however, a defender of agent causation.

is predicated of him, and is not the event-causal product of what went before. In this much alone there is no mention of existence, much less any source it might have. There is, however, a stronger notion of sourcehood that does entail agent causation. On that conception the agent is the sole source of his acts of positive willing in that he brings them about or confers existence on them. Their presence in the world, and all that follows from them, traces its existence not to any law-governed operation in which the agent engages, but directly to him as a substance, as a person possessed of a will.

The concept of agent causation has initial appeal in that the phenomenal guise of acts of positive willing, their felt spontaneity and intrinsic intentionality, makes it easy for us to believe that it is we who bring them to pass, we to whom they owe their very existence. Upon reflection, however, this idea soon begins to fall apart. In the first place, we really have no clear idea of what exactly the supposed operation of existence conferral would come to or consist in. In our example I decide to visit the Asian restaurant this evening. But what specific dimension of my deciding counts as my bringing that act into the world? What exactly do I do, what particular act or activity of mine, counts as my conferring existence on it? There seems to be none, nor to my knowledge has anyone ever described such a doing. Even if it could be located and described, moreover, such an activity would seem to face in turn the very problems it was intended to resolve. If there is some doing that is my bringing about my decision, must that doing also be brought about? If so we are headed for a vicious regress; if not, then what accounts for its being in the world? A related dilemma arises if we ask whether the activity of agent-causing my decision is ontologically separate from and independent of my deciding, or instead counts as a part of it. If it is a separate doing, then as before it seems to demand a further act of agent-causing on my part. If on the other hand my act of causing my deciding counts as part of the deciding itself, then until the deciding is on hand my act of agent causing it cannot do its work, whereas once the deciding is on hand it already exists, so that there is no work to be done. Again, therefore, the alleged doing seems to be of no legitimate use.

Worst of all, any instance of agent causing would be subject to the very sort of difficulty that it is intended to circumvent—namely, that we would lack any accounting for its presence in the world. We have seen that to frame the objection in terms of luck is infelicitous at best. But if this were a persuasive way to put the complaint, it would apply just as much to an uncaused operation of my agent-causing my decision to dine Asian tonight as to the deciding itself.[13] And certainly the legitimate essence of the complaint has force. My act of agent-causing my decision cannot, according to the basic assumption of libertarianism, be a product of event causation; were we to make it so the libertarian position would lapse back into determinism. But then my act of agent causing would seem to have no cause at all. Why, then, does it not constitute just as much a mystery as an uncaused act of deciding on my part? Again there seems to be no satisfactory answer, and if there is none then the enigma is still with us. The only

---

[13] Mele, "Causation, Action, and Free Will," 569–70.

possible conclusion is that the appeal to agent causation is misguided. If the existence of libertarian decisions and actions is to be provided for, the task is going to have to be accomplished some other way.

6. Event Causation

At this point in the argument the determinist may be tempted to declare victory, inasmuch as event causation now appears to be the only means we have of accounting for the existence of acts of decision and volition. It will turn out that this is wrong; there is another way. But there is an important point to be made first: if the arguments of section 5 are to be taken seriously, then we must in fairness reject an event-causal account of existence conferral as well. For the fact is that when treated as an operation of existence conferral, event causation is every bit as mysterious and implausible as agent causation. The first thing to be noticed here is that if the existence of any event is owing to the action of some other event, then its existential production has to be something that happens *in the world*: that is, there has to be some action, some doing on the part of the cause that counts as the generation of the effect. This being the case, we cannot settle for an account of natural causation that makes it out to be simply a matter of frequency. If the cue ball's striking the object ball causes the object ball to accelerate, this cannot consist in the fact that whenever other cue balls strike other object balls those object balls accelerate too. The key is not what goes on elsewhere but what goes on *here*, and that has to be more than the two events simply occurring together. Counterfactual accounts will not suffice as an account of event causation either, at least on the usual semantics of counterfactuals, and for much the same reason. That the cue ball's impact causes the object ball to accelerate cannot be accounted for by the fact that in worlds most similar to ours in which the impact does not occur there is no acceleration. This may of course be true, but existentially productive causation is not a matter of what does or does not go on in other worlds; it is a matter of what goes on in the world we inhabit.

An appeal to scientific laws to ground natural causation fails also, again for reasons that are similar. One way of trying to account for the force of scientific laws is to expound their meaning in terms of counterfactuals. If we do this, however, we simply revert to the business of discussing similarities among worlds, which we have just seen will not suffice as an account of existence conferral. But scientific laws bring other problems with them. We need to remember, in the first place, that laws are not principles of cosmic legislation to which the world is somehow subject. There is no plausibility at all in the idea that billiard balls behave as they do because independent of human thought, the world is inhabited by a set of propositions dictating that this is how physical bodies must behave. There is to my mind no good reason to believe there are such entities, but even if there are they would just one more class of powerless *abstracta*, and so be incapable of exerting any kind of governance over anything. The plausible story is the other way around. Things like billiard balls do not behave as they do because the laws of motion are what they are; rather, the laws of motion—which are simply our means for describing the world—are what they are because of the way things like billiard balls behave. So if laws are to be of use in helping us to understand causation, it will be because there is something going on in the world, something concretely real, that answers to them. And there is a further point: whatever that reality is, the fact is that scientific laws themselves give us excellent reason for thinking it is nothing that could be construed as an operation of existence conferral.

Event causation is almost always portrayed as a diachronic process, and if it is to count as a process of providing for the existence of things it has to be taken that way. Things are brought into being only by what already is, and in our world that means things whose existence is temporally prior. So if the event of the cue ball striking the object ball is to confer existence on the event of the latter's acceleration, the impact must come before the acceleration.[14] But whereas the causal transaction is, at least in this portrayal, diachronic, the laws of classical physics that describe it are not diachronic but synchronic. Newton's first law does not say that an object not acted upon by a net force at t will be at rest or in uniform rectilineal motion a moment later, but that it will be at rest or uniform rectilineal motion *at* t. This alone entails that the acceleration of the object ball must occur *while* the cue ball is striking it not afterward, for only while the two are in contact can the one act upon the other. The same is implicit in the third law, which calls for action and reaction that are simultaneous, not sequential; and the force law has acceleration occurring during the interval in which force is applied, not subsequently. Classical physics has of course long been superseded—but not, to my knowledge, in a way that changes any of this. Much the same can be said for most if not all of classical science.

This understanding has a far-reaching implication for the present discussion. If we are going to take scientific laws as descriptive of causal processes, we have to cease taking natural causation to be a process of the past conferring existence on the future. In our example, I think it is best understood as what has been called a transfer of conserved quantities.[15] What occurs when the cue ball strikes the object ball is not an operation of existential propagation, but a process in which kinetic energy is transferred from the former to the latter during impact, and the transfer simply *constitutes* the resultant acceleration of the object ball. This is not to deny that there is a legitimate temporal sequence in the case. There is, and we can use Newton's laws to predict how the sequence will go, provided we are prepared to *assume* that the mass and energy of system will continue to exist. But this is only an assumption. The laws do

---

[14] Refinements could be called for here in view of the fact that time is a continuum, so that no two events could be contiguous in time, as Hume supposed they could. But the refinements can be ignored for purposes of the present argument.

[15] For this model of event-causal interactions see David Fair, "Causation and the Flow of Energy," *Erkenntnis* 13 (1979), 219–50; also Phil Dowe, "Wesley Salmon's Process Theory of Causality and the Conserved Quantity Theory," *Philosophy of Science* 59 (1992), 195–216.

not in themselves determine a temporal sequence. For all they have to say the world could cease to be an instant from now.[16]

The upshot of this is that if we are going to treat natural causation as a matter of existence conferral, there is nothing in formal science that we can rely upon to back us up. Rather, we are going to have to look and see. We are going to have to discern by observation some nexus, some kind of link between cause and effect that is the process of the former conferring existence on the latter. And if we turn our attention to nature for the purpose of discerning this link what do we see? We see what Hume—who is at least on this point the theologian's best ally—long ago told us we would see. Exactly nothing.[17] There is no nexus to be observed, nothing that counts as the cause necessitating the effect, nothing that could possibly be construed as one event or condition, or any combination of them, conferring existence on some other. Indeed, we would not even know what to look for. No one has ever described what such an operation would consist in, or given the faintest hint as to what sort of observation or apparatus might serve to detect it. In short, our situation here is just as it is with agent causation—perhaps even worse, since when we engage in deciding and volitional willing there is at least the experiential sense of action that can give rise to the illusion of existence conferral. With event causation there is nothing at all, not the faintest hint of anything that could be construed as an operation by which the past somehow bootstraps itself into the future, which causation is so often imagined to be.[18]

None of this serves to show that event causation is not a legitimate notion if properly construed. Conceived as a matter of transfer of quantities like energy and momentum it is certainly legitimate. Nor is there reason to deny a relation between natural causation on the one hand, and laws and counterfactuals on the other, provided the latter are assigned no functional role in the actual operation of the world. But what we should not do is take causation, whether of the natural or of the agent variety, as resolving the existential riddle: the enigma of why the things that are are, and the things that are not are not. Viewed as a solution to this problem either sort of causation turns out to be little short of a myth. The empirical situation with both is today just as it was in Hume's time going on 300 years ago. In neither case has the alleged operation of existence conferral ever been discerned or described by anyone; and there is no reason to think matters will be any different 300 years from now.

---

[16] Exactly the same thing is true of conservation laws. These tell us not that the mass/energy of the universe is bound to continue, but that its quantity is neither increased nor diminished through physical interaction—exactly what is to be expected if, as I am alleging, natural laws are not about existence, but about how things that do exist change.

[17] Hume, *An Inquiry Concerning Human Understanding*, ed. C. W. Hendel (New York: Liberal Arts Press, 1955), 74–5.

[18] A similar point applies if causation is taken to be a synchronic phenomenon. This type of view does far better justice to the character of scientific laws. See for example Michael Huemer and Ben Kovitz, "Causation as Simultaneous and Continuous," *Philosophical Quarterly* 53 (2003), 556–65. But it fares no better at making plausible the idea of a causal nexus.

7. Primary Causation

Libertarians and determinists are, then, pretty much on an equal footing when it comes to being able to account for the existence of events, whether they be the decisions and actions of free agents or events of the ordinary, strictly physical kind. Neither agents nor events turn out to be much good at existence conferral. But libertarians should not take too much solace in this, for at least two reasons. First, it does no good to end the conversation with a *tu quoque*; that neither side should have a workable answer to the puzzle of existence is in the end to no one's advantage. Second, whereas the concept of agent causation is more or less a nonstarter, there are other models of event causation that are perfectly viable. This applies especially to the model of conserved quantity transfer, which has the added advantage that it enables us to see clearly why physically caused events are at home in the world in a way uncaused choice and volition are not. The task of accounting for the existence of events is accordingly more pressing for the libertarian than for the determinist. We may not know where our universe comes from, but to the extent that it is deterministic, we can tell a story about where the particular events that compose it at the present moment come from, about how it is that they arise from what went before. My decision to dine at the Asian restaurant is on the other hand still very much a stranger on the natural landscape, at least if it is freely made. The existential enigma is at its strongest with free decisions and actions; it cannot be laid to rest just by pointing out that one's opponents face an enigma of their own.

But the issue need not be left at this. There is a third sort of causation, namely the primary causation ascribed in traditional theology to God as creator. Primary causation is especially appropriate to discuss in the present context, since God's action as First Cause is supposed to extend to all things, and to include sustaining them in being as well as providing for their initial existence. This if true would resolve the existential difficulties of libertarians and determinists alike: all things, at each instant of their existence, would owe their being directly to God and to him alone. At this point in our discussion, moreover, primary causation is the only candidate left standing to account for the existence of free decisions and actions. Perhaps, then, the libertarian should leave the existence of free actions, along with everything else, in the hands of God as creator.[19] Libertarians are generally loath to take this step, however, since it seems to commit one to something called "theological determinism," which might appear to threaten free will just as much as natural causation. I have elsewhere defended at some length the view that this fear is misplaced.[20] Here I want to summarize the position I have taken, and to elaborate it just a little further.

---

[19] I recognize that nontheists may not feel themselves in a position to do this, but on the other hand it would seem that at least some of the philosophical support for theism had better stem from the explanatory power of what is sometimes called the God hypothesis—which, it is hoped, the discussion here may help to illustrate.

[20] Hugh J. McCann, *Creation and the Sovereignty of God* (Bloomington, Ind.: Indiana University Press, 2012), ch. 5.

Perhaps the most important point to understand about the relation between God's role as creator and our behavior as free agents is that God is not a temporal being. Neither in creating or sustaining it therefore does God enter into the world as a temporal or quasi-natural cause. Second, God does not as creator cause the world to exist by doing something *else* that causes it to exist, like issuing a command that acts in turn as a quasi-natural cause. Nothing like that happens. Rather, we should understand the world in all of its history to be the immediate product of a single act of creation on God's part, in much the way a melody or a line of poetry is the immediate product of the creative activity of a composer or poet. We are, as it were, the content of God's act of creating us, not a causal consequence of that act.[21] Finally, as creator God is related to all that exists—substances, accidents, events, processes, decisions, actions, everything—in precisely the same way. He does not provide more for the existence of some things than of others; nor, as a timeless being, does he provide for their being in series of creative acts or in stages; and he never employs any kind of means. He simply provides equally for the existence of all things, in a simple, timeless act that has all of time, and all that time contains, as its scope.[22]

It follows from all this that God is not a participant in the world. Instead he stands above it, governing things not by interference or interposition but by a transcendent providence through which from the world's foundation all things are ordered to the good. Is this determinism? Before we rush to call it that we need to realize that on this picture God never makes us do anything, in the sense in which worldly causes are said to make things occur. Rather, our position as agents is precisely that of Kant's 100 Thalers discussed earlier. Our decisions and actions lose none of their spontaneity or intentionality, because God's role as primary cause is to provide simply for their existence. As actions, they are as much to be predicated of us and stand as much as new beginnings in the world as they would if there were no God, and no such thing as primary causation. By our earlier argument, this means that if God's action as creator is to upset our freedom, this cannot be owing to any intrinsic feature of our acts of will being lost. It would have to be owing to some relational difference. It should be apparent, however, that as far as worldly relations are concerned there is also no difference. That my decision to dine at the Asian restaurant owes its being to God's creative act does not prevent its being prompted by my desire for Asian food, or its teleological explanation as a means of fulfilling that desire. The Kantian slant on existence applies here also. Indeed, the entire order of the universe is just as it would be if, *mirabile dictu*, it existed only in your and my imagination and not in reality.

That this is so should lay to rest any fear that by invoking God as responsible for the entire existence of the world we force ourselves into a crude form of occasionalism in

---

[21] Since God is not a temporal being, his action as creator is timeless also; time belongs only to created things, since they alone change. A consequence of this is that with primary causation the priority of cause to effect is not temporal but ontological.

[22] It is sometimes thought that to create a world in which time is real God must himself be a temporal being. This, however, is a mistake. Time is simply an aspect of change, and as such is every bit as much a product of God's creative activity as the change itself. God need no more enter into time to create temporal things than Shakespeare needed to enter the time (and space) of Elsinore to write *Hamlet*.

which only God does anything, leaving not just agents but everything in nature powerless. This is simply not so. The cue ball moving across the billiard table has the power to change the motion of any ball that gets in its way, and it exercises that power by striking the object ball and transferring kinetic energy to it. What it does not do is create a future or any part of it, even in the small space of the billiard table. With rational agents the situation is the same. I still have the power to act. I exercise that power when I decide to visit the Asian restaurant, and when I engage in the volitional activity needed to get myself there. What I do not do is confer existence on my decisions and actions. Furthermore, I am as much responsible for my decisions and actions as I would be in a world in which they had no cause whatever, for they are just as spontaneous as they would be in such a world, and just as fully founded in my reasons for acting.

Yet the libertarian's fears might not be assuaged, for there is still the relation of our acts of will to God as creator to consider. And it might be felt that even if primary causation does not interfere with the worldly etiology of a free action, the mere fact that it is there renders our actions fundamentally unfree. It does so because in creating our decisions and actions God is in fact settling something that we had thought we were settling—namely, whether the world would contain those very acts. In our example, he settles it that the world will contain a decision by me to dine Asian tonight. But if I am free wasn't I supposed to be the one who settled that? The answer to this question is that I do settle the issue if by this is meant is that I alone am presented with the question whether to dine Asian or Italian tonight, and I alone decide, spontaneously and intentionally, to dine Asian. The mistake is to suppose that if God is related to my decision as First Cause then he is deciding things for me, so that my autonomy in deciding as I do is destroyed or undercut.

What makes this mistake possible is that we are taught to think of God's act of creating the world as preceded by a deliberational phase, in which he considers various possible worlds and selects whatever one will best accomplish his purposes. But this picture is far from correct. Only an imperfect being would have to proceed in the task of creation by deliberating among alternatives, because only an imperfect being would be in danger of getting things wrong. A perfect creator gets things right the way a perfect composer—say, a consummate Mozart—would get a symphony right: on the first try, without any forethought, in an act of sheer improvisation. Indeed the entire deliberative picture belies the true nature of creation. Even in the human arena, by the time the poet or composer is down to selecting among alternatives the truly creative phase of artistic production is over. With God no such thing goes on. What happens is simply that he sees a world, an entire world, as good. And in the very act of seeing it as good he creates it—not as the best among many, although we of course in studying the world may come to think of it that way—but simply as good, as worthy of his approval.

The effect of this on the question of our freedom is profound: there are not, prior to creation, multiple versions of each of us on offer, among which God decides. There are not two scenarios before God, in one of which I choose to dine Asian and in the other Italian. Indeed there is not even one such scenario, for in the order of creation primacy belongs to the concrete. Prior to God's creating me nothing that pertains to me exists, not even in the abstract. And in his act of creation there exists only the person I am, the one who in this world is presented with two alternatives that are as genuine as they can be and who decides, spontaneously and meaning to decide exactly as I do, that I shall dine at the Asian restaurant tonight. For God to lend existence to my decision is simply for him to see that it, along with the world to which it belongs—the only world that, as creator, God ever sees—is good.[23] In the same way there are not, in the larger picture of my entire life, multiple destinies for me among which God decides. From my point of view there are of course possibilities to be settled, and I alone decide my destiny by employing my will as I do. But I am not pre-empted in this by God. That he should approve, and thereby lend existence to my decisions, in no way undercuts my autonomy in making them, nor does it diminish my responsibility for every intention I form, and every action I undertake.

From God's perspective, on the other hand, everything is settled from eternity, but only in the vision of his knowing will—that is, in the very act of his approving what I am, which is the same as his act of creating me, and prior to which he does not even imagine me. Someone might protest that even so my freedom is undone here, inasmuch as this account speaks of my entire being, including all of my decisions and actions, as owing their existence to God's creative act, which is accordingly ontologically prior to anything I do. If this is the case, it will be said, then I cannot have libertarian freedom, for there never was any possibility that I might have behaved differently in anything I do. This argument for thinking I am unfree fails also, but for a somewhat subtle reason. If prior to my creation there is not even a concept of me on hand, then there can at that point be no conception of any decision or action I might perform or not perform, and hence no possibilities regarding such an act. Moreover, since the act of creation is eternal and comprises in its scope my entire being—my entire career, as it were—there is from the eternal perspective no point in speaking of possibilities for decision and action in the wake of my creation either. Only within the temporal realm does talk of possibilities have application, and there they apply only to my own decisions and actions, not to God's. Furthermore, they apply perfectly well: after all, I *do* have to decide what I am going to do about dinner tonight. As creator, God of course knows and wills my deciding, but that takes away no possibility pertaining to it that ever existed. As an agent in the world, I have fully legitimate possibilities for decision

---

[23] This characterization may seem worrisome in that it makes God responsible for my bad decisions as well as my good ones—and also for those of a Hitler or an Idi Amin. But in fact the situation is very little different for the account of creation presented here from what it would be for any other. Any theory on which God knows as creator what world he is creating is a theory on which he provides, directly or indirectly, for the existence of the bad decisions of the agents who inhabit that world. Indeed, even if God does not know in advance what exercises of free will are to occur he is in a position as creator to prevent their execution, so that no objective harm will come from them. Yet he allows both them and the resultant harm to go forward. Presumably, then, God has good reasons for treating such decisions and actions as good—if not in themselves, then at least for the sake of the larger whole. Whatever those reasons are, they have as much force on the present theory as on any other.

and action. From God's perspective as creator of that world, there is at no point either necessity or unresolved possibility. I simply am what I am.

It turns out, then, that even though as First Cause God is responsible for the existence of all my decisions and actions, I do have free will in every respect that I can have it, every respect in which I would have had it even if there were no God. The difference is only that if there is a God, and if his role as creator and our role as agents are as I have described, then the existential enigma is resolved. We do not live in a world where a free decision or action has to be taken as an insult to reason. Nor need a world that has such things in it be considered threatening in any way. Indeed, if God has the nature usually associated with him—if, that is to say, he is good—then existential dread should be the farthest thing from our minds. And we don't have to choose between the twin mythologies of agent and event causation in order to get rid of it.

8. Conclusion

A word or two about some matters of terminology may be in order by way of closing. It may be wondered whether the freedom defended in this chapter deserves to be characterized as "libertarian," and whether the role assigned to God qualifies as "theological determinism." After some thought my answer to these questions has come to be that I don't much care. If by libertarian freedom we mean that our decisions and actions can have no cause of any kind, not even God as creator, then I would have to say that I do not think libertarian freedom exists. If we mean by it that we confer existence on our own doings then I don't think it even *can* exist. But I don't think most libertarians have had either meaning in mind. In the main, what they have had in mind is that our decisions and actions are not subject to worldly causation, and have the character of voluntariness that would make us responsible for them. And when this is all that is meant then unless determinism of the mundane, worldly sort turns out to be true, libertarian freedom is very much a reality. As for theological determinism, if by this is meant merely that all of our deeds fall directly under divine providence then it is a view to which I would subscribe. If on the other hand it means that God operates either in or outside of the world through the vehicle of event causation, or that in operating as First Cause he imposes our deeds and destinies on us, then I think it is dead wrong. The important thing, however we choose to use the words, is that we not fall into the trap of supposing that the moment the question of free will comes up, we enter into a contest of power in which either God or rational creatures must inevitably come out the loser. Were it so, we should far rather wish that we be the losers than God. But I do not think it is so. Rather, we need to come to see that legitimate freedom does not require our holding the upper hand on God when it comes to how we will decide and act. Equally important, we need to realize that to accord God his legitimate prerogatives as creator does not require that we surrender legitimate freedom.[24]

---

[24] I am grateful to the editor and referees of this volume for helpful comments on earlier versions of this chapter.

PART V

Naturalism and Alternative Concepts

14

Samuel Alexander's Space-Time God

A Naturalist Rival to Current Emergentist Theologies

Emily Thomas

1. Introduction

Emergentist theologies agree that the universe exhibits a hierarchy of emergence that may have developed through evolution, and that there is a sense in which God has emerged or will emerge from the universe. The first emergentist theology was advanced in the early twentieth century, by the 'British emergentist' Samuel Alexander. Today, emergentist theologies are usually construed as versions of panentheism, and such systems have been advanced by Arthur Peacocke, Harold Morowitz, and Philip Clayton. Emergentist theologies are attractive for several reasons: they are considered to be more naturalist than traditional theologies, in that they are compatible with—and arguably draw on—scientific theories such as evolution; they accord with the respect that environmental ethics affords the natural world; and they intimately and actively involve God with the world.[1] This chapter argues that if we accept the emer- 🐝 gentist theological framework, then Alexander's theology is a serious rival to existing current accounts.

The chapter proceeds as follows. Section 2 sets out Alexander's process theology, on which deity *will* emerge as the final quality—preceded by matter, life, and mind—in a temporal and logical hierarchy of emergence that is grounded in space and time. This section considers and rejects several existing readings of Alexander in the literature. For example, Alexander is sometimes taken to be a 'panentheist'. If panentheism is taken to 🖋 mean that the universe is 'in' God, then this characterization is straightforwardly incorrect; in fact, Alexander holds that deity is strictly contained 'in' the universe. This view is

---

[1] For more on these, and other advantages, see Clayton (2004b, 73–4) and Brierley (2006, 365).

also held by the British idealist F. H. Bradley. Further, against the existing scholarship, I argue that Alexander's system is naturalist. From this secure grounding in the history of philosophy, I move to offer a partial defence of Alexander's theology.

Section 3 briefly recounts the panentheist turn in contemporary philosophy of religion, before focusing on the important work of Clayton. Clayton provides an excellent foil for Alexander: Clayton's arguments for emergentism are substantial and detailed, and he has considered Alexander's system as a possible rival to his own. With this background in place, I argue that we should prefer Alexander's theology to Clayton's. I defend Alexander from various objections made by Clayton, including the thesis that naturalism cannot explain several features of the universe; against Clayton, I argue that Alexander's system is particularly well equipped to provide naturalist explanations of the features mentioned. I then show that Clayton's theism lies open to two substantial objections—there is a tension between his use of naturalism and supernatural theism, and his system is ontologically superfluous—in a way that compares unfavourably with Alexander's. On philosophic grounds, we should prefer Alexander's theology.

Section 4 offers some final thoughts. Alexander's account of God is radical, and for many its stubborn departures from tradition will be unpalatable. Nevertheless, it is a serious attempt to mount a coherent theism from a naturalist perspective, and it should be recognized as the worthy rival that it is to contemporary emergentist theologies.

2. Alexander on God and Naturalism

2.1 Alexander on God

Alexander was one of the proponents of British emergentism, a movement best known for its thesis that mind emerges from body; fellow emergentists include C. Lloyd Morgan and C. D. Broad. Alexander was the first thinker to apply this process of emergence to God. In order to understand Alexander's theology, it will be helpful to give a brief overview of his metaphysics.

Alexander argues that mind or consciousness is a new quality that emerges from matter, when matter becomes complex enough. The same thing can have many qualities, whilst still remaining one thing rather than many. For example, one thing can have both the qualities of matter and mind. This explains the co-location of one's mind with one's brain: the quality of mind, consciousness, is co-located with its quality of matter, neurons (Alexander 1920, ii. 5). Arguably, Alexander's account of mind–body emergence is close to contemporary versions of non-reductive physicalism.[2]

---

[2] Gillet (2006a) and O'Connor and Wong (2012) argue that Alexander's emergentism is very close to some contemporary physicalisms; in contrast, McLaughlin (1992) denies that Alexander is a physicalist of any kind.

In his two-volume magnum opus *Space, Time, and Deity*, Alexander extends emergence beyond body and mind. Alexander argues that space and time are the foundation of things: space-time, or Motion, is a unity that contains all motions, events, and changes within itself. Space-time sits at the bottom of an ontological hierarchy, and as 'motions' or patterns within space-time become complex enough, further qualities emerge within it: matter, life, mind, and deity. 'Empirical things or existents are…groupings within Space-Time, that is, they are complexes of pure events or motions in various degrees of complexity…as in the course of Time new complexity of motions comes into existence, a new quality emerges' (Alexander 1920, ii. 45). Against the prima facie implausibility of Alexander's space-time ontology—for example, Clayton (2004a, 27) comments that Alexander's 'hard to stomach' space-time metaphysics have not 'improved with age'—it is worth emphasizing that Alexander's core claim, that space-time is in some sense identical with matter, is a live option in contemporary philosophy of physics and metaphysics.[3]

With this background in place, I turn to Alexander's philosophy of religion. Alexander claims we will only ever be convinced of the existence of God by experience, by non-traditional arguments that do not desert the scientific interpretation of things. In this context, Alexander rejects the argument from design for God's existence, which he understands as positing a designer in the face of the wonderful adaptation of living forms to their surroundings. The problem is that we now know this adaptation to be the result of selection operating on variables, and that is why the world works out so as to produce a plan: 'Who does not see that sheep were not created for man, but that man survives because he is able to live on sheep?' (Alexander 1920, ii. 343–4). As we will see, Alexander utilizes Darwinian evolution throughout his work. In place of traditional arguments for the existence of God, Alexander offers us a non-traditional theology. As with other aspects of his metaphysics, Alexander does not argue for this theology; rather, he offers us a description of the world, and argues that it fits the facts (Alexander 1921b, 422–3). In the same way that mind–body emergence 'fits the facts'—such as the co-location of mind with body—I read Alexander as claiming that the existence of God explains our religious sentiments, by attaching that portion of human experience to the world of truth (Alexander 1920, ii. 353).

On Alexander's description of the world, the next quality that will emerge from space-time—following the highest quality that we know, mind or consciousness—is deity, and this emergence will happen in the future (Alexander 1920, ii. 345). Deity does not emerge from a single human mind, nor a collection of human minds, as human minds are finite and God is infinite (Alexander 1920, ii. 350–1). Instead, Alexander argues that deity emerges from the universe as a whole:

---

[3] For example, Schaffer (2009) has recently defended the thesis that space-time is identical with matter, and he appears to regard his position as a direct philosophical descendant of Alexander's. For further discussion of this thesis in philosophy of physics see Sklar (1977, 221) and Earman (1989, 115); in metaphysics, see Lewis (1986, 76) and Sider (2001, 110).

[Deity] is an empirical quality the next in the series which the very nature of Time compels us to postulate, though we cannot tell what it is like. But besides assuring us of the place of the divine quality in the world, speculation has also to ask wherein this quality resides. What is the being which possesses deity?...God is the whole world as possessing the quality of deity. Of such a being the whole world is the 'body' and deity is the 'mind'. But this possessor of deity is not actual but ideal. As an actual existent, God is the infinite world with its nisus towards deity, or, to adapt a phrase of Leibniz, as big or in travail with deity. (Alexander 1920, ii. 352–3).

In this difficult passage, I read Alexander as distinguishing between deity and God. I will explicate what he means by both concepts.

For Alexander, 'deity' is an empirical quality that *will* emerge from the world, or the space-time system, as whole. In this passage, Alexander states that 'we cannot tell' what deity is like. This statement is grounded in Alexander's thesis that a being can only contemplate (i.e. know) the qualities sitting lower on the ontological hierarchy than itself (Alexander 1920, ii. 104). To illustrate, a human mind can contemplate life and matter but it cannot contemplate itself as a mind, nor qualities higher than mind. As such, we cannot know what deity—a quality higher than mind—will be like. We know only that it will be 'new', and 'different in kind' from mind (Alexander 1920, ii. 347–50). Alexander offers a new take on the traditional doctrine that God is unknowable.

A difficult aspect of Alexander's system is his belief that, as higher qualities are always unknown to beings of lower qualities, in a sense deity is *always* the next highest quality:

For any level of existence, deity is the next higher empirical quality. It is therefore a variable quality, and as the world grows in time, deity changes with it. On each level a new quality looms ahead, awfully, which plays to it the part of deity. For us who live upon the level of mind deity is, we can but say, deity. To creatures upon the level of life, deity is still the quality in front, but to us who come later this quality has been revealed as mind. (Alexander 1920, ii. 348)

Creatures on the level of life can forecast a mysterious higher level—that is deity to them, though we know it to be mind—but they cannot *know* the higher level. Similarly, human minds can forecast a higher level, that we call deity, but we cannot know deity. Alexander leaves open the possibility that there are many higher levels above mind; for example, Alexander (1920, ii. 104–5) discusses the possibility of angelic beings that possess a quality higher than mind yet are not God. Alexander is not explicit on whether there is a 'final' emergent quality; however, as his universe is always in progress—more on this shortly—I am inclined to believe that there is not.

By referring to the world as the 'body' of God, Alexander is drawing an analogy between the emergence of deity from space-time, and the emergence of mind from body. The same process of emergence is involved, even though the whole world is not literally body, and the quality of deity is not literally mind. 'God' comprises both the quality of deity *and* the entity that will possess that quality; it is in this sense that Alexander identifies God with the whole world possessing the quality of deity. To return to the analogy with mind–body emergence, Alexander would distinguish between 'mind', which is an emergent empirical quality; and 'human being', which comprises both the quality of mind and the being that possesses that quality, a particular complex of space-time. However, a key difference between God–world emergence, and mind–body emergence, is that strictly speaking God does not yet exist.

In the passage above, Alexander claims that deity has not yet emerged from the world, and as such God—understood here as the 'possessor of deity'—is not yet actual. This is because Alexander's world is one of process, and it is continually growing. Indeed, the implication is that the world will be growing unto infinity, and this is one sense in which God is infinite. Although deity and the 'complete' possessor of deity does not yet exist, something does exist that Alexander also allows us to call God: the actual world with its 'nisus', or striving, toward deity. I read Alexander as holding the actual world to be the 'incomplete' possessor of deity; as the world grows, it becomes more completely the possessor of deity. As Alexander puts it later, God is 'in process' towards deity (Alexander 1920, ii. 394). It is this aspect of Alexander's account that renders Alexander's God immanent: there is a way in which God is the world.

Alexander's distinction between God and deity has a surprising consequence for the relationship between the divine and the world. In order to explain it, a short detour into Absolute idealism is required.

Alexander explicitly compares his account of God to that of the British idealist F. H. Bradley. For Bradley, the only absolutely real entity is the Absolute, a single, partless experience. However, the Absolute contains various 'appearances': things that are real to a degree. Towards the end of *Appearance and Reality*, Bradley (1893, 447–8) considers the question of God. He argues that God cannot be identified with the Absolute, because the Absolute is not a person, and 'that is not the God of religion'. Instead, Bradley allows for a personal God that is a 'finite factor' within reality, and concludes, 'God is but an aspect, and that must mean but an appearance, of the Absolute.' The influence of Bradley on Alexander is well known—Alexander frequently compares space-time to the Absolute—and Alexander accepts this part of Bradley's theology:

Deity is located only in a portion of the infinite whole of Space-Time, and therefore God...is only in respect of his body coextensive with the absolute whole of Space-Time, while his deity is empirical and belongs only to a part of the Absolute ...

Thus it is true, as absolute idealism contends, that God is (at least in respect of his deity) on the same footing as finites and if they are appearances so is he...But both God and finites are appearances only in the proper interpretation of that term, as parts of the thing to which they belong. (Alexander 1920, ii. 370–1)

It is this comparison between Bradley and Alexander's theologies that leads to a surprising result.

Alexander characterizes 'theism' as the thesis that God transcends the finite beings that make up the world, that he is an individual being distinct from them. In contrast, he characterizes 'pantheism' as the thesis that God is immanent in the universe of finite things, a pervading presence as in Spinoza. He adds that pantheism is not so much that

God is in everything, rather that everything is in God. Alexander argues that the label 'pantheism' cannot be applied to Absolute idealism, on the grounds that the Absolute takes the place of God, and God becomes an appearance (Alexander 1920, ii. 388–9). Similarly, while Alexander accepts that elements of his system are pantheist—namely, God is immanent in the sense that God's body is the as-yet-incomplete world as a whole—he argues that the label 'pantheism' cannot truly be applied to his system because the quality of deity does not belong to the whole world as if every part of that world were permeated with deity, 'as it must be on strict pantheism'. Instead, Alexander argues that his system is closer to theism, on the grounds that the quality of deity is distinct from the other finites within space-time, and God's deity is what is 'distinctive' of him (Alexander 1920, ii. 394). Alexander's divergence from traditional theism and pantheism is highlighted by his rejection of God as creator:

[A]s being the whole universe God is creative, but his distinctive character of deity is not creative but created. As embracing the whole of Space-Time he is creative; because Time is the moving principle that brings out the constant redistribution in the matrix which is equivalent to the birth of finite forms. Even then it is, properly speaking, Space-Time itself which is creator and not God...God then, like all things in the universe—for Space-Time itself is not in the universe, whereas God, since his deity is a part of the universe, is in it—is in the strictest sense not a creator but a creature. (Alexander 1920, ii. 397–8)

God did not create the universe; rather, the universe will create and contain God.

With this background in place, we are now in a position to understand the surprising consequence mentioned above. Contemporary philosophy of religion has seen growing interest in the thesis known as 'panentheism'. Whilst the details of how best to characterize this thesis are controversial, it is broadly characterized as the view that the world is *in* God, but God is more than the world.[4] Panentheism is contrasted with pantheism, which is frequently characterized as the view that the world *is* God. In the contemporary literature on panentheism, it is sometimes implied that Alexander and Morgan are early panentheists.[5] This attribution is correct with regards to Morgan. In a very brief comment, in a very early paper, Morgan (1898, 501) writes of the cause of metaphysical activity in the universe: '[I]t is neither the product of evolution nor its precursor in time; it is that timeless omnipresent existence in and through which evolution is rendered possible'. In Morgan's (1923, 89) full account of deity—given in his *Emergent Evolution* and carefully contrasted with Alexander's account—Morgan

[4] Brierley argues that panentheism can be defined as a thesis holding the following premises: God is not separate from the cosmos, God is affected by the cosmos, and God is more than the cosmos (Brierley, 2006, 639–40). Further agreement that panentheism involves this last premise can be found in Clayton (2004b, 83), Peacocke (2004, xix), Johnston (2009, 119), and Culp (2013).

[5] For example, when Clayton (2004a) discusses Alexander's work as a rival to his own panentheist system, he does not suggest that Alexander's system is not panentheist. Culp (2013) implies that Alexander should be listed as a panentheist. Other thinkers are undecided on how best to take Alexander's account of deity. For example, in a brief comment on Alexander's 'implausible metaphysics' of deity, Smart (2013) adds that it is difficult to categorize as theism or pantheism, although either way it is far from orthodox theism.

explains that this creative source of evolution is God. Morgan is a panentheist: God is beyond the universe, even though he directs it and will also emerge from it.

However, it should now be clear that, given his subsumption of both panentheism and pantheism under the label 'pantheism', and his rejection of that label to his system, Alexander cannot happily be characterized as a panentheist or a pantheist. In fact, Alexander is offering us a theology *for which there is as yet no label at all*. Alexander does not hold that God contains the universe and is not exhausted by it. Rather, the universe contains God and is not exhausted by God. As Alexander puts it in a late piece, 'I believe Bradley was right in finding God among the things of the world, and therefore not identical with the world, as Spinoza thought' (Alexander 1939, 329). This thesis is not pantheism, and it is precisely the opposite of panentheism; as such, it deserves recognition as a standalone theological position in its own right. This is especially important as the position is shared by Bradley.[6] That said, there is one important difference between the theologies of Bradley and Alexander. For Bradley, the aspects of the Absolute are only partially real. In contrast, for Alexander, the finite motions within space-time are real in their own right (Alexander 1920, ii. 369). For Alexander, God is contained with the universe but God is a reality, not an appearance.

2.2 Alexander on naturalism

Having laid out Alexander's account of God, I will now argue that it is in line with at least one major conception of ontological naturalism.

Alexander began to recognize the similarities between his system and that of Spinoza after the publication of his Gifford lectures, and he went on to rework his metaphysics as a 'gloss' of Spinoza.[7] Alexander particularly praises Spinoza for combining naturalism with a 'profound' sense of religion and he takes himself to be following Spinoza's example (Alexander 1927, 14). Alexander understands naturalism as follows:

I mean by naturalism not the mere habit of finding a place for man and his interests in a scheme of things which includes and starts with physical nature. That method is common to all honest philosophy. The distinctive feature of naturalism … is that the physical aspect of things is pervasive or that on one side of them they are all natural … Spinoza is a living example to show how needless is the fear that a physical world has no place for religion. (Alexander 1927, 14–15)

Whether Alexander's system is naturalist depends on how one characterizes naturalism, a notoriously difficult task.

---

[6] And possibly Bishop (1998, 187), who conceives God as a 'relational being' that emerges from loving relationships. Assuming that loving relationships are contained within the universe but the universe is not exhausted by them, and emergents are co-located with their bases, Bishop would seem to accept that God is contained within the universe. Like Alexander, Bishop also considers his account of God to be 'genuinely naturalist'.

[7] The similarities that Alexander perceived in their work were a great source of pride to him (Alexander 1921a, 79); in part, this may have been because they were both Jewish.

The characterization that Alexander gives in this passage is a kind of 'ontological naturalism'. For Alexander, naturalism means that the physical aspect of things is pervasive; as on Alexander's system all things are pervaded by space-time, it is naturalist by his own lights. Whilst I acknowledge that there are alternative conceptions of ontological naturalism that Alexander's system is not compatible with,[8] I restrict myself to discussing just Alexander's conception, on the grounds that a very similar conception is widely used in the literature. As Papineau's excellent (2009) article on naturalism explains, ontological naturalism is frequently understood as the thesis that reality is exhausted by nature. This is in line with Clayton's (2004a, 164) characterization of 'metaphysical' naturalism, the view that there are no things, qualities or causes other than those that might be qualities of, or agents within, the natural world. As Alexander accepts that reality is exhausted by nature or the natural world, his system appears to be naturalist according to these definitions of ontological naturalism too.

I say that Alexander's system 'appears' to be ontologically naturalist because it has been objected that, in fact, it is not. In order to explain this objection, I return to Alexander's notion of nisus. Alexander is convinced that deity will emerge due to a nisus in space-time, which has already 'borne its creatures forward' through matter and life and mind, and will bear them forward still (Alexander 1920, ii. 346). Exactly what Alexander means by 'nisus' is unclear. A nisus is a kind of drive or striving, and Alexander seems to believe that the nisus is driving emergence towards *higher* qualities, not merely different qualities. The nisus provides progress, not merely process. There is no indication that Alexander takes the nisus to be anything other than a natural law or principle operating within his space-time universe; as we saw above, Alexander rejects entirely the thesis that the universe was designed.

In itself, there is nothing inherently non-naturalist about the notion of a nisus; I have previously argued that the nisus is best read as an evolutionary principle operating within space-time (Thomas 2013, 563). Charles Darwin (1859, 129) eloquently describes the 'striving' and 'struggling' organic beings continually undergo for life, and I have argued that Alexander conceives his nisus as a similar kind of striving. The problem is that Alexander's nisus produces progress, not merely process. Evolutionary principles such as natural selection are not usually taken as progressive: neither Darwin nor contemporary biologists hold that natural selection is leading in any kind of direction, such as towards 'higher' forms. Consequently, as I have concluded previously, the workings of Alexander's nisus do not appear to be in line with the biological sciences in the way that Alexander would seem to prefer (Thomas 2013, 556). The nisus appears to be non-naturalist. This objection to Alexander is not new. It was raised

---

[8] For example, it might be argued that ontological naturalism entails not merely that one's metaphysics are *compatible* with science but that one's metaphysics should be restricted to theories or beings that are *acknowledged* by the sciences. Alexander's theology may be compatible with science but it is hardly acknowledged by science.

by Alexander's contemporaries, including Broad (1921, 149), Bradley,[9] and Morgan (1923, 14); and it can also be found in Clayton, who argues that Alexander's nisus appears to be purposeful, and such teleology is foreign to modern physics and biology (Clayton 2004a, 30).

On reflection, I believe that there is a reply open to Alexander that would rebuff this charge of non-naturalism. We have been assuming that the nisus *directs* the universe towards progress, but instead we can understand the nisus as directionless striving that *happens* to result in progress. On this reading, Alexander's belief that the universe is progressing is disconnected from the nisus and supported by something else entirely: the observation of progress in the past. Alexander can be read as observing progress in the universe, and making an inductive argument from the observation of past progress to a prediction of future progress. That reading is supported by passages such as the following:

Now since Time is the principle of growth and Time is infinite, the internal development of the world, which before was described in its simplest terms as the redistribution of moments of Time among points of Space, cannot be regarded as ceasing with the emergence of those finite configurations of space-time which carry the empirical quality of mind. We have to think upon the lines already traced by experience of the emergence of higher qualities, also empirical...Time itself compels us to think of a later birth of Time. (Alexander 1920, ii. 346)

By thinking along the 'lines already traced by experience'—by thinking inductively, as scientists so often do—Alexander's thesis that the universe will produce higher qualities receives empirical justification. And this is why Alexander writes that the universe *compels* us to forecast the next emergent quality: deity (Alexander 1920, ii. 353). 'God's deity is demanded by the facts of nature' (Alexander 1939, 275). There is no need to conceive the nisus non-naturally, and as such Alexander's system remains ontologically naturalist.

There is of course an implicit assumption here that the qualities already produced by the universe—matter, life, mind—exhibit progress, an ascent towards perfection. This assumption is controversial. Whilst some thinkers will immediately accept that rocks, plants, and conscious minds exemplify a hierarchy of progress, other thinkers will not. Consequently, it is worth speculating as to why Alexander accepts this assumption, and I suggest that one reason lies in his account of value. Alexander is a realist about value, and he argues that values—including the highest values of beauty, goodness, and truth—are constructed by conscious minds (Alexander 1920, ii. 309). If one accepted that human minds author the highest values, then consciousness would be conceived as a higher quality than life or matter.

I end this study of Alexander's theology with a comment on a wry set of remarks from Broad. Although the primary focus of this chapter is to defend Alexander's theology as a

---

[9] Bradley's objection can be found in a letter to Alexander dated 28 April 1922 (John Rylands Library, manuscript ALEX/A/1/1/33/17). Sadly, if Alexander replied, the reply has not survived.

rival to contemporary theologies, this section has also served to correct several misap-prehensions of Alexander in the scholarship.[10] Before moving on, I will correct one more. At the conclusion of his otherwise sympathetic and serious critique of Alexander's *Space, Time, and Deity*, Broad writes the following:

I do not quite know how seriously Prof. Alexander intends his theology to be taken. I suppose it is a point of honour with Gifford Lecturers to introduce at least the name of God somewhere into the two volumes, and we may congratulate Prof. Alexander on the ingenuity which discov-ered a place in his system for something to which this name might be not too ludicrously applied ... The vaulted roof of St. Pancras station seen at midnight has been known to evoke the religious emotion in one eminent mathematician returning to Cambridge from a dinner in town; and what the sight of St. Pancras has done for one man, the thought of the next stage in the hierarchy of qualities may do for others. (Broad 1921, 148)

Against the scepticism that Broad expresses so charmingly, I say that—as this study of his theology has shown—Alexander intends his theism to be taken very seriously indeed. Alexander's sense of religion is as profound as that which he perceives in Spinoza.

3. Alexander and Rival Emergentist Theologies

3.1 Clayton's Panentheism: A Contemporary Rival to Alexander's System

Having explored Alexander's theology, I will now show that there is good reason to prefer it to at least one of its contemporary rivals.

It has long been accepted that Alexander's philosophy of religion is related to, and may have influenced, A. N. Whitehead's theology and (through that) process theology.[11] However, some of the deep similarities between Alexander's theology and contempo-rary emergent theologies have not been widely recognized. Emergentist theologies agree that the universe exhibits a hierarchy of emergence that develops through evolu-tion, and that there is a sense in which God has or will emerge in the universe. This 'sense' of divine emergence includes the thesis that God literally emerges from the universe, and the thesis that God non-literally emerges from the universe in a way that is analogous to other cases of emergence. Today, emergentist theologies are usually conceived as a kind of panentheism. Recent arguments in favour of emergentist theologies or panentheism include Peacocke (1993; 2001), Morowitz (2002), Robert

---

[10] In addition to Broad (1921) and the other works already mentioned, further—albeit somewhat vintage—studies of Alexander's theology can be found in Titus (1933), McCarthy (1948), and Brettschneider (1964).

[11] In a letter to Alexander dated 3 September 1924, Whitehead encloses a draft of his Gifford lectures, and writes that he believes them to be 'in general agreement' with Alexander's *Space, Time, and Deity* with 'attempts at further developments' (John Rylands Library, manuscript ALEX/A/1/1/307/1). Whitehead's lectures, later published as *Process and Reality*, argue amongst other things for an immanent God that is constantly in flux with the world (Whitehead 1929, 493). For more on Alexander and Whitehead, see Lowe (1949) and Emmet (1992).

Hermann (2004), Clayton (2004a; 2004b), Niels Gregersen (2006), and Mark Johnston (2009). Of the theorists included in this list, Peacocke, Morowitz, and Clayton particularly use notions associated with the emergentist framework, including emergence, evolution, complexity, and levels. Morowitz and Clayton argue that there is a sense in which God has or will emerge as the final level in a hierarchy of emergence. Indeed, Morowitz (2002, 176) speculates that we may already be 'in the middle of' the emergence of God.

I say that, if we accept the emergentist theology framework, then Alexander's system should be preferred. There is no space here to compare Alexander's system with all of the emergentist theologies mentioned above, so I will focus on a comparison with one of the most important systems on offer today: Clayton's panentheism. As explained earlier, Clayton provides a logical choice of rival to Alexander, for Clayton's metaphysics is set out in substantial detail, and he compares his work with Alexander's at various points. The arguments given here against Clayton's theology may have force against other emergentist theologies too.

We will begin with an overview of Clayton's theology, principally expressed in his *Mind and Emergence*. Clayton argues at length for the reality of emergence, claiming that emergence provides the best way of understanding various scientific theses, including biological evolution. In arguing for emergentism against its rivals, Clayton frequently calls on naturalism. For example, whilst comparing mind–body emergentism to its rivals mind–body dualism and physicalism, Clayton writes: '[O]f the three, emergence is the naturalist position most strongly supported by a synthetic scientific perspective—that is, by the study of natural history across the various levels it has produced' (Clayton 2004a, 2). Later, Clayton faces a choice between 'strong' emergentism, which he characterizes as the thesis that emergent levels are ontologically distinct, characterized by their own laws and causal forces; and 'weak' emergentism, which he characterizes as the thesis that as new emergent patterns emerge, the fundamental causal processes remain those of physics (Clayton 2004a, 9). Once again, Clayton appeals to naturalism to make his case: 'strong emergence represents the better overall interpretation of natural history' (Clayton 2004a, 31).

With this emergentist ontology in place, Clayton asks what account we can give of it. Assuming we accept it, he offers three possibilities. The first two responses are naturalist. First, one could hold that the universe and its hierarchy of emergence is a 'brute given', a contingent reality produced naturally and accidentally. Second, one could deny that emergence is a contingent feature of the world yet still provide a purely naturalistic account of its inevitability; for example, one might argue that, in the course of biological evolution, the natural laws are constrained in such a way that life would inevitably give rise to mind. Clayton recognizes that Alexander could be read as endorsing either the first or the second option, on which the universe—by accident or some unknown law of necessity—produces various emergents including deity; this position does not imply any 'broader' metaphysical consequences, such as a creator of the universe. The third and last response is non-naturalist. One could hold that the universe with its emergent hierarchy was created by a conscious being, who put certain laws in place and intended that the universe would arrive at something like its present outcome (Clayton 2004a, 160–2). Clayton endorses this option, as do Peacocke and Morowitz. Clayton argues that it is legitimate to endorse naturalism in some domains but not in others; I will discuss this move below.

In support of his non-naturalist theology, Clayton argues there are various features of the universe that naturalism cannot explain. He offers us a smorgasbord of such features, including the perennial question, Why is there anything at all? Clayton contends that there is something unsatisfying about explaining aspects of parts of the natural order in terms of natural causes; one also wants to know what produced the natural order as a whole. Naturalism also struggles to make sense of our moral striving. Further, many human beings claim to have had supernatural experiences, and this lends some evidential weight to non-naturalism (Clayton 2004a, 172–3). However, Clayton's central argument for non-naturalism concerns the 'fit' that we presume exists between our beliefs and the external world.

As humans we investigate the universe and reason about it. Thomas Nagel has argued in several works—including his (1986) and (2001)—that the fact humans reason successfully about the universe requires an explanation. As Nagel (1986, 74) puts it, a complete conception of our place in the world would close over itself, 'describing a world that contains a being that has precisely that conception, and explaining how the being was able to reach that conception from its starting point within the world'. Clayton builds on Nagel to make a case for theism, arguing that the success of our reasoning pushes us to ascribe a rational structure to the world, and the fact that the world has this structure is either a brute given, or it has a reason. 'But the only reason that could function at this level is that the world was made to be reasonable, that is, that it was designed to be that way by an intentional agent' (Clayton 2004a, 177–8). This intentional agent, the creator of the world, is God. Clayton summarizes his argument against metaphysical naturalism using a cost–benefit analysis (Clayton 2004a, 179). On the one hand, one can endorse either the first or second option and remain a naturalist in every domain, but that leaves various features of the universe unexplained. On the other hand, one can endorse the third option and provide explanations for the features that naturalism cannot explain, but in doing so one ventures beyond the natural world. Clayton believes that the benefits of non-naturalism outweigh the cost.

Having argued for a creator God, Clayton goes on to 'radicalise' his immanence. Clayton argues that if theism is to be more than the postulation of a divine source that has since grown mute, it must entail some sort of divine involvement in the world (Clayton 2004a, 185). In another piece, Clayton sketches this involvement in panentheist terms. In an attempt to characterize the 'in' of the panentheist thesis 'The world is in God', Clayton describes what he labels the 'panentheistic analogy'. The analogy is drawn between the body in mind–body emergence, and the world in God–world emergence. 'The world is in some sense analogous to the body of God; God is analogous to the mind which indwells the body, though God is also more than the natural world taken as a whole.' Clayton argues that the power of the analogy lies in the fact that mental causation is more than physical causation yet still a part of the natural world; analogously, we are offered the possibility of conceiving divine actions in a way that does not break natural law (Clayton 2004b, 83–4).

Clayton's panentheist analogy is strongly reminiscent of Alexander's claim that the world is the body of God. A deeper similarity may be present here too: Clayton appears to argue that God will emerge from the universe. '[E]mergence provides the best available means, for those who take science seriously, to rethink... the immanence of God in the world' (Clayton 2004b, 87). Unlike Morowitz, Clayton is coy as to whether he believes that God has or will literally emerge from the universe, but some of his remarks are certainly suggestive.

How can God be source of all things and yet at the same time *a* thing or agent that arises in the course of the history of the cosmos? It is this conundrum that has forced many panentheists to accept a form of ultimate or theological dualism... God is, for us, the source and (we hope) ultimate culmination of this cosmos, the alpha and omega, the force or presence within which all is located ...

Emergentist panentheism thus represents a superior means for thinking God's relation to the world. (Clayton 2004b, 90–1)

Clayton seems to be arguing that, while God existed before the cosmos and created it, he also has, or will, emerge from the cosmos as its culmination.

3.2 Defending Alexander's Theology

Let's assume that the emergentist theological framework is correct: the universe is best understood as a hierarchy of emergence, and there is a sense in which God emerges from it. Against Clayton's argument for a non-naturalist creator God, I argue for ● Alexander-style naturalism. The universe, including minds and deity, should be conceived as a wholly *natural* phenomenon. I will defend Alexander's account from Clayton's objections, before making some objections to Clayton's account.

In addition to the charge (already considered above) that Alexander's system is not fully naturalist, Clayton accuses Alexander of 'divinising' human beings, and 'finitising' God.[12] I will discuss each of these objections in turn. Citing Alexander's (1920, ii. 358) thesis that minds are infinite because they stand in relations to all of space-time, Clayton argues that it is 'an all-too-noble place' to which Alexander's emergentism assigns humans. 'Such a deification or divinization of humankind may have been attractive to Feuerbach, to Victorian England, or to German thinkers early in the twentieth century... [but] the twentieth was, by any account, a bad century for the so-called

---

[12] Clayton also gives several arguments against weak emergence, and he reads Alexander as a weak emergentist. I will not discuss these arguments for two reasons. First, Clayton does not offer them as objections to Alexander's theology, and that is my concern here. Second, Alexander may not be a weak emergentist; Gillet (2006b, 811–12) provides an extended argument for reading Alexander as a strong emergentist.

infinite goodness of Man' (Clayton 2004a, 168–9). This objection is not well aimed. In the passage that Clayton cites, Alexander is merely arguing that a single mind is 'compresent'—is present in the same universe—with every other thing that exists. '[I]n one sense our minds and all finite things are infinite... our minds, which are extended both in space and time...are in relation to all Space-Time and to all things in it' (Alexander 1920, ii. 358). This hardly divinizes humans. Even David Lewis (1986, 71–2) is committed to the thesis that, in any given universe or possible world, any given thing is related *at least* spatiotemporally to every other thing. It is unclear why Clayton makes reference to the unhappy events of the twentieth century; perhaps he is implicitly reading Alexander as claiming that minds are in some sense infinitely good.[13] But if this is the case, Clayton does not say so, and Alexander himself makes no such claims.

Clayton's second objection against Alexander is much better aimed. Clayton objects that Alexander renders God finite. Against the view that God does not create the world, but rather the world deifies itself, Clayton quotes from Pierre Bayle's famous attack on Spinoza's panentheism, explaining that if one is a radical theist of this sort, one cannot be 'too squeamish' (Clayton 2004a, 168). Alexander is very aware that his theology is radical, and at points he seeks to reconcile it with tradition. For example, Alexander (1920, ii. 359–60) argues that there is a sense in which God is infinite: his quality of deity will occupy an infinite part of space-time, and his body is identified with the whole of space-time. On Alexander's system, there is a *sense* in which God is infinite. However, the body of Alexander's God is limited to the space-time manifold, and—as we saw above that Alexander's theology is the opposite of a panentheism—there is a also very real sense in which God is *contained* within the world, as the quality of deity will only be lodged in a part of space-time. As such, Clayton is correct to say that Alexander finitizes God, and this divergence from traditional theology arguably counts against his system.

Having discussed Clayton's particular objections to Alexander, I ask how Alexander would reply to Clayton's general objections to naturalism. Let's begin with the smorgasbord. Oddly, Clayton presents these objections to naturalism as though they have never been previously considered, and ready replies aren't available; however, these objections are well known, and ready replies are available to the naturalist. Clayton asks, 'What explains the existence of the natural world?' Clayton's answer to this old theological chestnut is: God. But this prompts the old reply, 'What explains the existence of God?' The theistic answer to this further question is that God is self-grounded, and as such does not require further explanation, whereas nothing else is self-grounded. Whilst this *arguably* provides a more satisfying explanation than the naturalist who argues that the natural world is not in need of further explanation—who 'explains' it as a brute fact—this is extremely controversial, and Clayton offers no further argument. Moving on, Clayton argues that naturalism struggles to make sense of our ethical or moral striving. In

---

[13] In a later piece, Clayton (2006, 24) implies that for Alexander the quality of deity will emerge from the collection of human minds; perhaps that is what leads him to claim here that Alexander is divinizing humans. However, as we saw above, that would also be an incorrect reading of Alexander.

response, Alexander could point to his *Beauty and Other Forms of Value* (1933a), a book-length naturalist account of value, which seeks to explain our striving towards the highest values in evolutionary terms. Lastly, Clayton cites the evidentiary weight of recorded supernatural experiences. Unless these experiences can be verified in some way as being supernatural, this weight means little; not so long ago, human beings could have claimed that all the evidentiary weight pointed to the earth being flat.

We will move on to Clayton's central argument against naturalism. As we have seen, Clayton makes use of the problem Nagel raises concerning the 'fit' between our reasoning activity and the world. In the face of this problem, Clayton believes that non-naturalist theism is the best response. However, many other responses are possible. For example, one could take (what might be described as) a Kantian line: the fit between our reasoning activity and the external world is explained by the fact our minds *impose* categories, aka a rational structure, on the universe. Whilst there is hardly room to discuss all possible responses to Nagel here, this Kantian reply provides a neat contrast to the reply that I will offer on Alexander's behalf. Alexander is deeply concerned with the 'categories', the pervasive features of the world that apply to all things, including identity, existence, universal, relation, parts, wholes, and number. Why are these categories pervasive? Alexander's answer is not that our minds impose the categories on the world, but rather that the world imposes the categories on us. The categories are pervasive because they are features of space-time, and as all things are pieces of space-time the categories apply to all things (Alexander 1920, ii. 186–9). With this in mind, here is an Alexander-inspired reply to Nagel.

Let's accept, with Nagel and Clayton, that the universe really has a rational structure that is open to investigation by our reasoning activity. Why is that the case? Alexander could reply that it is because we are *part* of the universe, and as parts of the universe our minds are subject to the same structural features—the same categories—as the stuff of the universe itself. This reply is especially plausible once we consider that on Alexander's account of emergence, there is just one thing that is at once a piece of space-time, and a body, and a living organism, and a mind. For any account of emergence sharing that thesis it would be bizarre if the reasoning activity of minds did *not* echo the rational structure of the universe. Against Clayton, it is indeed a brute fact that the universe has a rational structure. But there is nothing mysterious about the fact that our minds echo that rational structure: as emergents of the universe, our minds share whatever structure the universe happens to have.[14] Once the mystery surrounding the 'fit' between mind and world is dissipated, Clayton's argument collapses into his earlier objection that naturalism cannot explain why there is a world at all, and that objection lacks force.

---

[14] As Alexander writes, '[T]he real greatness and value of mind is more likely to be established on a firm and permanent basis by a method which allows to other existences than mind an equally real place … epistemology, is nothing but a chapter, though an important one, in the wider science of metaphysics' (Alexander 1920, i. 6–7).

With the exception of the worry that Alexander finitizes God, sound replies can be made on Alexander's behalf to all of Clayton's objections. Now we will turn the tables. Two serious objections can be made against Clayton's account, and as such it compares unfavourably with Alexander's.

The first objection concerns Clayton's use of naturalism. As we saw above, Clayton relies heavily on appeals to naturalism in defence of emergence, but he later endorses a non-naturalist theology. Clayton is aware that this might seem inconsistent, and in defence of his methodology he distinguishes between the proper domain and the proper parameters of naturalism. Clayton believes that we should take seriously the methods and results of the natural sciences but he also believes that naturalism only applies to domains to which science is applicable; in the case of at least one domain, metaphysics, science is not applicable and it is consistent with his larger position to leave naturalism behind (Clayton 2004a, 169). Clayton is not a thoroughgoing naturalist because he rejects metaphysical naturalism as he defines it: the view that there are no things, qualities, or causes other than those within the natural world. Clayton is also not a naturalist according to the characterizations of ontological naturalism given above. Whilst in principle distinguishing between the domain and parameters of naturalism is a respectable move, in Clayton's case I argue this move poses a problem for his larger system.

The problem is that one of the central set pieces in Clayton's philosophic machinery is the panentheist analogy: the idea that we can understand the relationship between God and the world using mind–body emergence. But how close can this analogy possibly be, given that mind–body emergence is a natural phenomenon within the domain of science, and God is a non-natural phenomenon lying outside of science? Clayton has already pulled away from some of the implications of the panentheist analogy. For example, he is explicit that God—unlike minds and bodies—is not intrinsically spatial and is not correlated to time (Clayton 2004b, 83; 2004c, 256). Given that Clayton is also pulling the analogy apart with regards to naturalism, it is unclear exactly what *is* supposed to be analogous between mind–body and God–world emergence. In contrast, Alexander follows through on his ontological naturalism. Just as mind–body emergence is a natural phenomenon, so is the emergence of deity. Alexander also embraces the consequences of his emergentist analogy; for example, just as minds are spatiotemporal, so is deity (Alexander 1920, ii. 347).

The second objection to be made against Clayton is that it is unclear why he posits an emergent God. Once we have posited the God of traditional theism, whose existence predates that of the universe he creates, why *also* posit that God has or will emerge from the universe? The additional posit is ontologically gratuitous, and it is unclear what motive there is for making it. If one is merely concerned that God should be a real, immanent presence in the world, it would seem far simpler to posit a literally omnipresent creator God, than to posit a creator God *and* bother with all the complicated mechanics of God–world emergence. For Alexander, the world—or at least, the world with its nisus towards deity—is sufficient, and positing a creator God is 'superfluous' (Alexander 1933b, 131). In contrast, I argue that for Clayton, a creator God is sufficient, and positing an emergent God is superfluous.

In response to this second objection, Clayton could offer the following reply. Above, I wrote that Clayton is coy as to whether he believes God literally will emerge or has emerged from the universe. Perhaps, if pushed, Clayton would deny that God literally emerges, thereby evading this charge of superfluity. The problem with this response is that it casts the role of the panentheist analogy even deeper into shadow. We have already established that the analogy is weak in a significant regard: mind–body emergence is naturalist, while God–world emergence is not. If Clayton goes on to deny that God literally emerges from the world, then the analogy is weakened to breaking point: it is unclear how the literal emergence of mind from body is supposed to elucidate the non-literal emergence of God from world. Far from being a metaphysically robust analogy that can help us to understand divine immanence, the panentheist analogy slides into the realm of murky metaphor.

In effect, the foregoing discussion presents Clayton with a dilemma. On the one hand, he could hold that God creates, and then literally emerges from, the universe. On this view, the panentheist analogy has a clear role, but it leaves open the question *why* we should posit a creator God and God–world emergence. On the other hand, Clayton could hold that God creates the universe, and that God–world emergence is non-literal or metaphorical. While this blocks the charge of superfluity, it raises new questions over the role of the panentheist analogy, which becomes so shadowy as to be unusable. I believe this dilemma to be in the spirit of Alexander:

[God] must be transcendent indeed to men but still in the world, else there remains a gulf between him and the world which no metaphors can bridge … [and] he must not be a superfluous repetition of the world itself but a being within it which involves the whole world because it is rooted in that world.

Such a conception of God appears to me the immediate suggestion of a philosophy which regards the world as essentially in process … a world in process might create a God by the same continuing impulse by which it has already produced stones and plants and men. (Alexander 1933b, 131–2)

And the answer to the dilemma, is, of course, to endorse Alexander's emergentist theology.

4. Final Thoughts

This chapter has argued that, within the emergentist theology framework, Alexander's system should be recognized as a serious contender to contemporary accounts, and it should be preferred to at least one of its major rivals. Clayton's system lies close(r) to traditional theology than Alexander's but that does not outweigh the problems surrounding his non-naturalist—and possibly non-literal—panentheist analogy. Alexander follows through on the emergentist principles underlying his system, and he does not shy away from the consequences of the analogy he draws between the emergence of mind and the emergence of God. Further, Alexander is able to offer a naturalist explanation for divine emergence, a route not open to his rivals. For

Alexander, the universe is the vast, evolving entity space-time, a continually progressing theatre of motion that contains or will come to contain all things. It is the Bradleyian element of this view that renders it the very opposite of panentheism: deity will be contained within space-time, it is not the container itself.

I am not optimistic that Alexander's system, even with its advantages, will attract many converts; few theists are willing to endorse a theology as radical as this. It may be that, as Bayle (1826, 299) said of Spinoza, it will be said of Alexander that he asserts the most infamous, 'maddest extravagances' that can be conceived. But this by itself does not devalue the philosophic, naturalist worth of Alexander's theology.[15]

References

Alexander, Samuel (1920). *Space, Time, and Deity*. 2 vols. London: Macmillan & Co Ltd.

Alexander, Samuel (1921a). *Spinoza and Time*. London: Unwin Brothers.

Alexander, Samuel (1921b). 'Some Explanations', *Mind* 30: 409–28.

Alexander, Samuel (1927). 'Lessons from Spinoza', *Chronicon Spinozanum* 5: 14–29.

Alexander, Samuel (1933a). *Beauty and Other Forms of Value*. London: Macmillan & Co.

Alexander, Samuel (1933b). 'Spinoza and Philosophy of Religion', *Septimana Spinozana* 77: 127–33.

Alexander, Samuel (1939). *Philosophical and Literary Pieces*. Ed. John Laird. London: Macmillan & Co.

Bayle, Peter (1826). *An Historical and Critical Dictionary, Selected and Abridged from the Great Work of Peter Bayle*, vol. 3. London: Hunt and Clarke.

Bishop, John (1998). 'Can There Be Alternative Concepts of God?', *Nous* 32: 174–88.

Bradley, F. H. (1893). *Appearance and Reality*. London: Swan Sonnenschein.

Brettschneider, Bertram (1964). *The Philosophy of Samuel Alexander*. New York: Humanities Press.

Brierley, Michael (2006). 'The Potential of Panentheism for Dialogue Between Science and Religion', in Clayton and Simpson (2006).

Broad, C. D. (1921). 'Professor Alexander's Gifford Lectures II'. *Mind* 30: 129–50.

Clayton, Philip (2004a). *Mind and Emergence*. Oxford: Oxford University Press.

Clayton, Philip (2004b). 'Panentheism in Metaphysical and Scientific Perspective', in Clayton and Peacocke (2004).

Clayton, Philip (2004c). 'Panentheism Today: A Constructive Systematic Evaluation', in Clayton and Peacocke (2004).

Clayton, Philip (2006). 'The Conceptual Foundations of Emergence Theory', in Philip Clayton and Paul Davies (eds), *The Re-Emergence of Emergence*. New York: Oxford University Press.

Clayton, Philip and Peacocke, Arthur (eds) (2004). *In Whom We Live and Move and Have our Being*. Grand Rapids, Mich.: William B. Eerdmans Publishing Company.

Clayton, Philip and Simpson, Zachary (eds) (2006). *The Oxford Handbook of Religion and Science*. Oxford: Oxford University Press.

[15] I owe thanks for helpful comments on earlier drafts of this article to James Connelly, Michael Rush, Anthony Fisher, both editors of this collection, and two anonymous referees.

Culp, John (2013). 'Panentheism', in Edward Zalta (ed.), *The Stanford Encyclopedia of Philosophy*. URL = <http://plato.stanford.edu/archives/spr2013/entries/panentheism/>.

Darwin, Charles (1859/1968). *The Origin of Species*. London: Penguin.

Earman, John (1989). *World Enough and Space-Time*. Cambridge, Mass.: MIT Press.

Emmet, Dorothy (1992). 'Whitehead and Alexander', *Process Studies* 21: 137–48.

Gillet, Carl (2006a). 'Samuel Alexander's Emergentism: Or, Higher Causation for Physicalists', *Synthese* 153: 261–96.

Gillet, Carl (2006b). 'Hidden Battles Over Emergence', in Clayton and Simpson (2006).

Gregersen, Niels Henrik (2006). 'Emergence and Complexity', in Clayton and Simpson (2006).

Hermann, Robert (2004). 'Emergence of Humans and the Neurobiology of Consciousness', in Clayton and Peacocke (2004).

Johnston, Mark (2009). *Saving God: Religion after Idolatry*. Princeton: Princeton University Press.

Lewis, David (1986). *On the Plurality of Worlds*. Oxford: Basil Blackwell.

Lowe, Victor (1949). 'The Influence of Bergson, James and Alexander on Whitehead', *Journal of the History of Ideas* 10: 267–96.

McCarthy, John (1948). *The Naturalism of Samuel Alexander*. New York: Macmillan & Co Ltd.

McLaughlin, B. (1992). 'The Rise and Fall of British Emergentism', in A. Beckerman, H. Flohr, and J. Kim (eds), *Emergence or Reduction?* (pp. 49–39). Berlin: Walter de Gruyter.

Morgan, C. Lloyd (1898). 'The Philosophy of Evolution', *The Monist* 8: 481–501.

Morgan, C. Lloyd (1923). *Emergent Evolution*. London: Williams and Norgate.

Morowitz, Harold (2002). *The Emergence of Everything*. New York: Oxford University Press.

Nagel, Thomas (1986). *The View from Nowhere*. New York: Oxford University Press.

Nagel, Thomas (2001). *The Last Word*. New York: Oxford University Press.

O'Connor, Timothy and Wong, Hong Yu (2012). 'Emergent Properties', in Edward Zalta (ed.), *The Stanford Encyclopedia of Philosophy*. URL = <http://plato.stanford.edu/archives/spr2012/entries/properties-emergent/>.

Papineau, David (2009). 'Naturalism', in Edward Zalta (ed.), *The Stanford Encyclopedia of Philosophy*. URL = <http://plato.stanford.edu/archives/spr2009/entries/naturalism/>.

Peacocke, Arthur (1993). *Theology for a Scientific Age*. Minneapolis: First Fortress Press.

Peacocke, Arthur (2001). *Paths from Science Toward God*. London: Oneworld Publications.

Peacocke, Arthur (2004). 'Introduction', in Clayton and Peacocke (2004).

Schaffer, Jonathan (2009). 'Spacetime as the One Substance', *Philosophical Studies* 145: 131–48.

Sider, Theodore (2001). *Four Dimensionalism*. Oxford: Oxford University Press.

Sklar, L. (1977). *Space, Time and Spacetime*. Berkeley: University of California Press.

Smart, J. J. C. (2013). 'Atheism and Agnosticism', in Edward Zalta (ed.), *The Stanford Encyclopedia of Philosophy*. URL = <http://plato.stanford.edu/archives/spr2013/entries/atheism-agnosticism/>.

Thomas, Emily (2013). 'Space, Time, and Samuel Alexander', *British Journal for the History of Philosophy* 21: 549–69.

Titus, Harold (1933). 'A Neo-realist's Idea of God', *Journal of Religion* 13: 127–38.

Whitehead, A. N. (1929). *Process and Reality*. Cambridge: Cambridge University Press.

15

On Religious Naturalism

Eric Steinhart

1. Introduction

A *religious naturalist* says (1) that all religiously significant objects are natural and (2) that some natural objects are religiously significant.[1] Recent religious naturalism tends to be defined by writers affiliated with the journal *Zygon* (e.g. Crosby, Goodenough, Peters, Raymo, Stone, etc.). But these Zygoners are not the only religious naturalists. It seems fair to characterize some of the New Atheists as religious naturalists (e.g. Comte-Sponville, Dawkins, Dennett, Harris).[2] Groups like the World Pantheist Movement, the Spiritual Naturalist Society, the Humanistic Pagans, the New Stoics, the Kopimists, and the Burners (participants in the Burning Man festivals) can plausibly be classified as religious naturalists. Several other groups, even though they are not entirely naturalistic, incorporate many of the ideas and practices developed by stricter religious naturalists. These other groups include the Wicca, the Catholic Green Sisters, and the Evolutionary Christians (e.g. Berry, Dowd, Swimme).

While all these groups are currently small, they appear to be growing. At least in the United States, surveys indicate a movement away from traditional theism. As they move away from traditional theism, many Americans increasingly combine New Age and Eastern beliefs and practices with a nominal Christianity (Pew Forum 2009). Many of those new beliefs and practices are represented in religious naturalism. And, as they leave traditional theism, many Americans also increasingly self-identify by marking "None" on surveys asking for their religious affiliation (Kosmin et al. 2009; Pew Forum 2012). Among the Nones, the Pew survey indicates that nearly 60 percent

---

[1] According to Stone, *religious naturalism* affirms "that there are religious aspects of this world that can be appreciated within a naturalistic framework" (2003, 784). Drees says religious naturalism entails that "naturalism, properly understood, allows for religiously significant language, questions, answers, ways of life, etc." (in Cavanaugh 2000, 243). Conger writes that religious naturalism is "the view that the Object of religious devotion is identical with the universe or some portion of the universe, some process or direction or trend in it, as studied in the sciences" (1940, 205).

[2] Dawkins (2004) and (2008, ch. 1) mark him as a religious naturalist. Dennett (1995, 520) suggests religious naturalism: "This world is sacred." Spiritual atheists are religious naturalists (Harris 2005, ch. 7; Comte-Sponville 2006).

often feel "a deep connection with nature and the earth" (2012, 9–10). Some people, migrating from traditional theism, say they are "spiritual but not religious". Ammerman (2013) has analyzed these "spiritualists" into four categories. People in her "Extra-Theistic" category locate spirituality "in various naturalistic forms of transcendence" (2013, 258). This category is very close to religious naturalism. Among those who self-identify as atheists, Silver (Silver et al. 2014) says that about 12 percent lie within a group he refers to as the "ritual atheists." Many embrace practices close to those in religious naturalism. All these data suggest growing interest in religious naturalism.

Some surveys indicate that a large flight from theistic institutions has already happened (Pew Forum 2010). American college students now appear to fall into three roughly equally large groups: the traditional theists, the spiritualists, and the secularists (Kosmin and Keysar 2013). The traditional theists are mainly Christians. The spiritualists are open to Eastern, New Age, and neopagan beliefs and practices. The secularists include New Atheists, Nones, and the spiritual but not religious. If these three groups mark the corners of a triangle, then religious naturalism lies mainly on the line which runs between the secular and spiritual corners. The Kosmin and Keysar data suggest that young Americans may be increasingly interested in religious naturalism. Data from Europe, while less detailed, suggest similar trends.[3] If these statistics are correct, and these trends continue, then religious naturalism may begin to significantly challenge traditional theism. Since the religious landscape is changing rapidly in the West, anyone who is interested in those changes should become familiar with religious naturalism.

Since there are many ways to define nature, and many ways to define religious significance, there are many versions of religious naturalism. Some of these are mentioned above. And yet much of the diversity is merely apparent. Underneath the apparent diversity, there exists a deeper shared framework. This shared framework, which is developed here, is a generic version of religious naturalism. It includes *most but not all* of the ideas and practices of *most but not all* of the religious naturalists mentioned above. The sole purpose of this chapter is to present this deeper shared framework, and to thereby provide a *systematic introduction* to the currently emerging forms of religious naturalism. Although this systematic introduction is sympathetic, that sympathy should not be mistaken for uncritical acceptance or endorsement. Religious naturalism needs to be critically scrutinized, and it is hoped that the introductory work done here will suggest strategies for future critical engagement. Nevertheless, the critical assessment of religious naturalism is a distinct project, which must be saved for later work.

Most (but not all) of the religious naturalists mentioned above discuss five natural contexts.[4] The *concrete* context is associated with nature in the largest and deepest

---

[3] For supporting data on Europe, see Jackson et al. (2014), the European Values Study <http://www.europeanvaluesstudy.eu>, and Lambert (2006).

[4] Some Zygoners (e.g. Goodenough 1998) and Evolutionary Christians (Swimme and Berry 1992; Dowd 2009) use the *Epic of Evolution* to describe the religiously significant aspects of nature. The Epic of

sense; the *physical* context is associated with our universe; the *chemical* context with our solar system; the *biological* context with our earth; the *personal* context with individual human animals. Within each context, most religious naturalists argue for the existence of some natural creative power; most of them talk about the eruption of that power from some initial object or event; most of them regard that eruption as a gift which establishes a gift economy; and most regard that power as divine or otherwise religiously significant. Within each context, most religious naturalists focus on the cyclical patterns (the wheels) in the evolution of natural creative power; most argue that the evolution of that power builds complexity; most argue that evolved complexity is intrinsically valuable; and most argue that things involving high degrees of evolved complexity are sacred. Finally, most religious naturalists build their practices around these ideas.

2. The Concrete Context

It has long been traditional for people to turn to religions for answers to ultimate questions. These include *metaphysical questions* like: Why are there some concrete things rather than none? Why is nature lawful? Why are the laws of nature the way they are? Specifically, why do those laws seem to be so congenial to the evolution of complexity, including intelligent life? Zygoners discuss these questions (e.g. Goodenough 1998, 11, 167; Raymo 2008, 27). Dawkins takes these questions seriously (2008, 184–6). And, to these questions, one might add another: "What is it that breathes fire into the equations and makes a universe for them to describe?" (Hawking 1988, 174).

One way to answer these questions is to provide an account of *nature* that is metaphysically ultimate. Of necessity, any such account is speculative and controversial; yet it is also unavoidable—it is irrational to ground reality in mystery (contra Goodenough 1998, 11–13, 167). One plausible way to provide a metaphysically ultimate account of nature is to run the *cosmological argument* starting with our entire universe: Our universe is obviously a complex contingent thing. But what is complexity? Modern theories of complexity are *informational*.[5] They say that all complex things arise along "graded ramps of slowly increasing complexity" (Dawkins 2008, 139).[6] Hence our universe lies on some graded ramp of slowly increasing complexity. The cause of our universe lies in some simpler prior thing. Perhaps this simpler prior thing

---

Evolution traces the history of our universe from the big bang to the present. As it moves from past to present, the Epic of Evolution moves from larger to smaller contexts (universe, galaxy, solar system, earth, humanity). The Epic of Evolution is used here. However, here the Epic starts with the multiverse.

[5] The best informational measures of complexity involve *depth*. These include *computational depth* (Antunes et al. 2006) and *logical depth* (Bennett 1988). Dawkins appears to measure complexity in terms of depth (1987, 6–9).

[6] Bennett (1988, sec. 3) and Antunes et al. (2006, sec. 5) prove *slow-growth theorems*, which mathematically confirm the Dawkinsian thesis that all complex things arise on "graded ramps of slowly increasing complexity."

is some earlier universe. But the cause of that simpler prior thing lies in some even simpler prior prior thing. And this chain or strand of decreasingly complex things runs back until it bottoms out in some simplest original thing, the first cause of all physicality: "[t]he first cause that we seek must have been the simple basis for a self-bootstrapping crane" (Dawkins 2008, 185).

The first cause is the ultimate uncaused simple object. It is the ground of all complex concreteness. It is necessary in the sense that it is the invariant root of every possible way of working out the content of concreteness. Since this original object is the ground of all complex concrete things, it can be called the *urgrund*. Will it be objected that the urgrund is supernatural? The objection is defeated like this: nature is causally closed; since nature is causally closed, the cause of any natural thing is itself a natural thing; but the urgrund is the ultimate cause of all natural things; hence the urgrund is a natural thing. The urgrund resembles various ultimate causes.[7] On the basis of that resemblance, it seems appropriate to classify the urgrund as *divine*. But the urgrund is not any kind of god, and the religious naturalism developed here includes no gods.[8] The urgrund is the naturally divine alpha, the ultimate source of all natural power or energy. It contains the power of self-surpassing, which is the capacity to produce greater versions of itself. Poetically speaking, this power is the fire of actuality which the urgrund breathes into its greater potentialities.

As the ultimate origin of all things, the urgrund is creative. Since the urgrund is simple, and all other things are complex, its creativity increases complexity. The simplest way to define that creativity looks like this: for every way the urgrund can make some more complex version of itself, it does make that version of itself.[9] Every more complex version of the urgrund is one of its offspring, and the urgrund gives its power of self-surpassing to its offspring. This power, which grows during its transference, is a self-amplifying *gift* which the urgrund bestows on its offspring.[10] Every descendant of

---

[7] There are some ways in which the urgrund is similar to the Platonic Form of the Good or to the Plotinian Unity. There are ways it resembles the ground of being (Tillich 1951, 21, 235–9). And it resembles the Wiccan ultimate deity (Farrar and Farrar 1981, 12, 117; Buckland 1986, 19; Cunningham 2004: 9; Silver Elder 2011, 9, 18). But the urgrund is not beyond being; it does not transcend nature; and it is not a god or deity of any kind.

[8] The urgrund is not personal in any sense. It is neither the God of Abraham nor the God of Christianity. Any attributions of personal qualities to the urgrund are idolatrous (Raymo 2008, 19–20, 28, 103). The urgrund is not any kind of god at all (Dawkins 2008, 184–5). Of course, some religious naturalists use the term "God" in non-standard ways (Stone 2008, ch. 2; Peters 2002). Yet Crosby agues that "God" is so "hopelessly anthropomorphic" that it must be rejected (2002, 9). For the sake of neutrality, the generic religious naturalism developed here does not include any gods. However, specific religious naturalisms are free to define naturalistic gods as they see fit.

[9] This account of nature resembles the *evolutionary cosmology* of Peirce. Peirce argues that the self-organization of an original chaos produces a branching tree of universes. See Peirce 1965, 1.175, 1.409–16, 6.13, 6.33. 6.189–220, 6.490, 7.513–15, 8.317–18. For Peirce, evolution moves towards an omega point; however, the evolutionary cosmology developed here is open-ended. The Second Law of Thermodynamics is merely a local law, operative in our universe. It does not constrain this evolutionary cosmology.

[10] The concepts associated with *giving* are central to much religious naturalism (e.g. giving, gifts, gratitude and gratefulness, thanksgiving, gift economies). Givers need not be persons (Goodenough 1998, 169; Harrison 1999, 88; Crosby 2002, 153). Bishop (2010, 533) motivates the thesis that givers are creative

the urgrund therefore inherits its essence and energy. So, for every way every descendant of the urgrund can make a more complex version of itself, that descendant does make a more complex version of itself. The result is a series of generations of increasingly complex concrete things, in which each next generation is populated with every more complex version of every object in its previous generation. Thus the urgrund is the root of an endlessly ramified *tree* of ever more complex objects (objects which are the nodes of the tree, connected by its branches). Since this tree grows through the endless distribution of gifts, the economy of concreteness rooted in the urgrund is a *gift economy*. Eventually, the nodes of this tree become so complex that they contain spatiotemporal-causal structure, and can therefore be called *universes*. Less complex universes perpetually give birth to more complex universes—they give birth to universes ever more *finely tuned* for the evolution of internal complexity. Eventually, our universe appears.

The endlessly ramified tree of ever more complex objects (including its root, the urgrund) is the whole of nature. This account of nature agrees in many ways with the account offered by one of the Zygoners, namely Donald Crosby. Crosby says that nature is an all-inclusive and metaphysically ultimate system of things (2002, 21). It is "self-originating, self-renewing, self-transforming" (2008, 55).[11] It is one great spatiotemporal-causal process which *infinitely* exceeds our universe (2008, 94). For Crosby, nature can be thought of both as *natura naturata* and *natura naturans* (2002, 34; 2008, 6–7).[12] *Natura naturans* is an "unceasing creative energy" (2002, 114). On the version of religious naturalism developed here, the urgrund is the ultimate source of this energy. This creative energy works in a *cyclical* way, bringing one universe after another into being, creating the next out of the ashes of the previous (2002, 35–44). For as long as it lasts, each universe is an instance of *natura naturata*. It is a cosmic epoch whose lawful form is merely temporary and contingent (2002, 154). But while each universe is contingent, "that which exists necessarily...is the creative power (*natura naturans*) underlying and producing all of the systems of nature that ever have been or ever will be" (2002, 154).

On the left hand, Crosby says that "the *whole* of nature is inviolably holy or sacred" (2008, 44). On the right hand, Crosby acknowledges that many religious naturalists regard as holy or sacred *only* those aspects of nature that are "creative and constructive, and that express or produce unequivocal goodness" (2008, 62). There are at least two

optimizers which cause their creations to gain value. The urgrund and all its descendants are such optimizers. But religious naturalists have much work to do on the logic of giving.

[11] Crosby also says our universe is one member of a series of universes that is endless both into the future and past (2002, 39–44; 2003, 252–3, 2008, 55, 491). The troubles with two-way endlessness are both scientific (Mithani and Vilenkin 2012) and philosophical (Leibniz 1697; Geach 1967, 64–5). Two-way endlessness is rejected.

[12] The concepts of *natura naturans* and *natura naturata* originate with Spinoza (*Ethics*, book 1, proposition 29, Scholium). For Spinoza, these concepts are associated with God; however, for religious naturalists, they are non-theistic.

objections to the left hand. The first is that the sacred has always been defined as a highly exclusive category, containing only highly intrinsically valuable or *precious* things.[13] Thus the sacred is contrasted with the profane (Eliade 1959). Likewise the idea of the holy does not include everything (Otto 1958). The second is that if the sacred is not defined in an exclusively positive way, then religious naturalism cannot have any distinctively positive focus for its ritual activity. It would be wrong for a religious naturalist to celebrate destructive processes as sacred (e.g. to celebrate violence, crime, war, famine, plague, and disaster). On the basis of these objections, which appear fatal, the advantage goes to the right hand: an aspect of nature is *sacred* if and only if (iff) it is creative or constructive.

Against this analysis of the sacred, it may be objected that every aspect of nature is creative in some sense. The only way to defeat this objection is to qualify the creativity: an aspect of nature is sacred iff it is *appropriately* creative or constructive. Of course, this qualification now demands its own analysis. For the religious naturalist, sacredness must be some type of intrinsic value. On the basis of the informational concepts used to develop the gift economy of concreteness, it seems appropriate to identify intrinsic value with complexity (see Dennett 1995, 511–13). If this is right, then more complex things are more valuable; hence they are more sacred. Degrees of sacredness are degrees of complexity. The profane is the least yet still positive degree of sacredness. Since the urgrund is simplest thing, it is also the least sacred thing; as the root of all complexity, it is the only profane thing. The profanity of the urgrund does not negate its divinity.[14] On the contrary, that profanity is entirely appropriate in an evolutionary theory of the sacred: just as life emerges from non-life, so the sacred emerges from the profane.

Since any religiously significant change either decreases or increases sacredness, there are two kinds of religiously significant changes: those that decrease sacredness are negative while those that increase it are positive. But any change involves some energy. Hence the energy involved in complexity-destruction is *negative energy* while the energy involved in any complexity-creation is *positive energy*. Positivity and negativity are merely religiously significant yet entirely naturalistic qualities of entirely natural energy. Since complexity and energy are both defined scientifically, positive and negative energies are also both defined scientifically. The religious naturalism developed here explicitly excludes all unnatural meanings of concepts like energy, complexity, positivity, and negativity.[15]

---

[13] The pantheist Harrison says that to be sacred is to be "imbued with profound value" (1999, 63). Many New Atheists affirm that the sacred is highly valuable (Blackburn 2004; Dawkins 2004; Comte-Sponville 2006, 18; Dennett 2006, 23).

[14] For traditional theists (especially Anselmians), the profanity of the urgrund contradicts its divinity; but religious naturalists are not traditional theists. They have their own ways of defining the divine, the sacred, and the holy.

[15] Some groups associated with religious naturalism, especially pagans, tend to use the term "energy" in occult or New Age ways (e.g. crystals store occult energies). All unscientific meanings of energy are entirely and emphatically rejected here.

For many Zygoners, this natural positive energy is *divine*.[16] Following those Zygoners, the religious naturalism developed here affirms that positive energy is *divine energy*. Of course, to refer to positive energy as divine is merely to give it a religiously significant meaning. For religious naturalists, to refer to something divine does *not* mean that it is supernatural; on the contrary, for them all divinity is natural. And this religious meaning is not merely subjective: since complexity is objectively definable, divinity is also objectively definable. The eruption of divine energy into any new form is *hierophantic*. The eruption of divine energy from the urgrund is the *original hierophany*.[17]

According to the evolutionary account of concreteness given here, the activity of divine energy has a *cyclical* form: the creative process repeats itself in all its products. On each cycle, the previous generation of created objects produces the next generation. The abstract shape of this cyclicality resembles the spinning of a *wheel*. The cyclical form of concrete creativity is the wheel of concreteness. Since this wheel generates all dependent concrete things, it is the deepest wheel of all—it is the self-rolling *wheel of nature*. All other natural cycles supervene on this wheel. It is worth noting here that cyclicality plays a central role in paganism. York writes that "Paganism…reflects or develops from the rhythms and cycles of the natural world. It does not seek to escape or obliterate the great round of nature but to work within it and to celebrate it" (2003, 167).

As the form of divine creativity, the wheel of nature is divine—it is the divine *logos*. As the wheel of nature rolls ever further uphill in the abstract landscape of complexity, as it rolls up Mount Improbable, divine energy pours itself into ever more concentrated forms. The objects that realize these forms burn ever more hotly and brightly. With every turn, this wheel builds the next generation of nodes in the great *world-tree* of ever more complex objects. Poetically speaking, divine energy rises like a current of fire through the branches of this tree, concentrating itself ever more intensely in ever more complex nodes. As the total product of divine energy, the world-tree is divine.[18] Of course, the world-tree is a familiar motif from many types of paganism (e.g. Druidism).

---

[16] Stone lists many twentieth-century American religious naturalists who used the term "God" to refer to some sort of creative power (2008, ch. 2). Gordon Kaufman defines God as creativity (2007). Peters says God is "the universal creative process, continuously at work to give rise to new forms of existence" (2002, 4). Stuart Kauffman says that "God is our name for the creativity in nature" (2008, 284). Aquinas reports that the positive side of *natura naturans* is sometimes said to be God (*Summa Theologica*, I.II, q. 85, art. 6). To refer to this creative power as God means only that it is divine.

[17] Zygoners like Crosby refer to this ultimate energy as *natura naturans* (2002, 114, 154; 2008, 7, 51). Goodenough refers to this ultimate energy, especially as it appears in the aroused body, as "Immanence." She says that during mystical experiences, we are "invaded by Immanence" (1998, 101) and that we become "a recipient of Immanence and grace" (1998, 164). Wiccans affirm that this ultimate energy is sacred. Cunningham writes that "All natural objects … are manifestations of sacred energy" (2004, 92).

[18] Hartshorne says God is "the self-surpassing surpasser of all" (1948, 20). Since the world-tree is the self-surpassing surpasser of all, the world-tree resembles Hartshorne's God; thus it seems appropriate to say that the world-tree is divine.

For religious naturalists, the religious distinction between positivity and negativity grounds both axiology and morality.[19] More precisely, the sources of moral obligation are grounded in the nature of divine energy. Religious naturalists therefore tend to be ethical naturalists (Hogue 2010, ch. 4). Since divine energy is active in every natural system, and since that energy is the power of self-surpassing, it provides every natural system with the goal of surpassing itself. Granted that obligations can be grounded in goals (Black 1964), it follows that if you *can* help any natural system to surpass itself, then you *ought* to help it to surpass itself. To the extent that you can help your body, family, society, species, and the entire earthly ecosystem to surpass themselves, you ought to help them in their self-surpassing. Since a natural system surpasses itself by increasing its complexity (or by creating something more complex than itself), you ought to work as far as you can to increase complexity.[20] Since health tracks the maintenance of complexity, religious naturalists advocate the maximization of personal, social, and ecological health. They also advocate the maximization of social and ecological diversity.

On this analysis of the morality of religious naturalism, the *good* and the *right* correspond to complexity-creation while the *evil* and the *wrong* correspond to complexity-destruction. If this analysis is correct, then you ought to do what the wheel of nature does: you ought to continue the gift economy. When you do what the wheel does, you are engaged in *religious mimesis*—in the ritual imitation of the act of unreciprocated giving. So, when you work to maximize the health of your body, and the healths and diversities of your society and your ecosystem, you are engaged in religious mimesis. Hyde argues that science is a gift economy (1979, 77–83). If that is right, then scientific research is religious mimesis—it is sacred work, in service to the wheel. The view that reality is ultimately a gift economy in which energy concentrates itself into ever more complex forms has been taken up by the naturalistic religion of *Kopimism* (George 2012).[21] For Kopimists, information is sacred and copying and copymixing are sacred acts. And surely there are other ways to ritually imitate the self-accelerating wheel of nature.

---

[19] Some religious naturalists have discussed ethical issues (see Harrison 1999, ch. 6; Peters 2002; and Crosby 2008). And there are many books on Wiccan ethics. However, religious naturalists have made few efforts to link their ethical discussions to well-known ethical theories (e.g. virtue ethics, deontology, utilitarianism). And their ethical ideas sometimes conflict with their metaphysical ideas. The conflict appears in Crosby (2008, ch. 5, pp. 85–6). It also appears in efforts to ground Wiccan ethics in Wiccan metaphysics. Religious naturalists need to do much more work in this area.

[20] Although you ought to increase complexity (and you ought not to decrease it), that imperative is extremely abstract. Hence it is likely to conflict with itself (by increasing complexity in one way, you decrease it in some other way). Religious naturalists need to develop a system of ethical rules to resolve such conflicts.

[21] For more on Kopimism, see the website of The First Church of Kopimism for the USA, at <http://www.kopimistsamfundet.org/>. Accessed 22 June 2012. Sadly, Kopimism has been tainted by its association with illegal file-sharing; but religious naturalists may develop Kopimist rituals without such improprieties.

On the account of concreteness offered here, the wheel of nature has actualized your form and thereby given you the gift of concrete existence. On the one hand, you are obligated to continue this gift economy. Given this gift, you are obligated to pay it forward. On the other hand, if you are given any gift, then you ought to be grateful for it, and you ought to express your gratitude by giving something back to the giver in return. You therefore have these obligations to the natural sources of your existence. Remarkably, many New Atheists experience this gratitude and its associated obligations (Young 2005; Solomon 2006; Aronson 2010, ch. 2; Bishop 2010; Walters 2010, 169–71). Some Zygoners think that prayers of thanksgiving are an appropriate way to reciprocate the gift of existence (Goodenough 1998, 47; Crosby 2002, 153). However, in any gift economy, paying it forward already entails paying it back (see Franklin 1784; Emerson 1841, 147). Through ritual mimesis, you discharge both your obligation to pay it forward and your obligation to pay it back. By continuing the gift economy, you express your gratitude to the wheel for your concrete existence; you thank the wheel of nature for your being.

3. The Physical Context

According to our best physics, our universe begins with an initial creative event, namely, the *big bang*. The big bang is an immense eruption of creative (and therefore divine) energy into the form of our universe—into our system of physical laws. It is the divine alpha of our universe, the endocosmic or physical *hierophany*. The hierophany is an immense squandering with no reciprocation—it is not possible to give anything back to the big bang. The physical economy whose first event is the big bang is a pure gift economy.

At the moment of the big bang, our universe does not contain any complex things. At that moment, *every* change produces some increase in complexity. Every change is creative: the initial emergence of radiant energy is creative; the initial condensation of that radiation into particles and atoms is likewise creative. Since these first steps towards complexity are creative, they are divine. However, after complex things have been created, they are there to be destroyed. After the first atoms emerge, energetic interactions divide into those that are creative and those that are destructive. Changes in the cores of stars that fuse simpler nuclei into more complex nuclei are creative, positive, and divine. But changes that break more complex atoms into simpler atoms are destructive and negative. Changes that bind atoms into more complex molecules are creative, positive, and divine. But changes that break complex molecules into their simpler parts are destructive and negative.

Over time, events become linked together into strands. A strand is positive iff its end is more complex than its beginning. Of course, the overall tendency of a strand may be positive even though it contains many internal booms and busts. So long as any internal negativities are surpassed by greater positivities, the strand as a whole remains positive. Over time, a small percentage of nuclear events link up into positive atomic strands; a small percentage of atomic strands become woven into positive molecular strands; and a small percentage of molecular strands become woven into even more positive molecular strands. Over time, through rare events, some of the energy released by the big bang self-organizes. The complexities of the most complex things become greater as time goes by. Of course, this does not imply that every thing in our universe becomes more complex. On the contrary, the levels of complexity form a growing *pyramid* in which all higher levels are always smaller. Since the self-organization of this energy takes place in our universe, it is *endocosmic evolution*. Endocosmic evolution begins with simple particles and builds more complex structures. It builds atoms; molecules; cells; bodies; societies.

Over time, divine energy concentrates itself into ever more complex forms. The nature of this divine self-concentration is clarified by Chaisson. He defines the complexity of a thing as the number of ergs of energy that pass through one gram of its matter in one second (2001, 134). He shows that the history of our universe reveals an *exponentially increasing* curve of complexity (2001, 2006). Chaisson (2006) defines of eight epochs of ever greater complexity. These epochs are centered on the emergence of particles, galaxies, stars, planets, chemicals, organisms, cultures, and technologies. Chaisson argues that the evolution of complexity in our universe is ultimately driven by the expansion of space itself (2006, 45). If that is right, then the evolution of complexity in our universe is built into the natural laws of our universe—it is encoded in the form of our universe.

Kurzweil (2005) presents a similar series of epochs. The progress from each epoch to the next adds objects at ever higher levels of complexity. For Kurzweil, endocosmic evolution has a cyclical pattern. He says that "Evolution works through indirection: each stage or epoch uses the information-processing methods of the previous epoch to create the next" (2005, 14). Thus endocosmic evolution is a positive feedback loop (2005, 40). This evolution of complexity is self-sustaining and self-accelerating. The cyclical pattern which generates ever increasing levels of physical complexity is the *wheel of physics*. The wheel of physics is a *logos* that supervenes on the deeper wheel of nature. Looking at the curves drawn by Chaisson and Kurzweil, it is a *wheel that rolls uphill*. It is a divine wheel driven by divine energy to ever higher heights in a landscape of sacredness.

More locally, the focus of religious naturalism zooms in on our galaxy. Our galaxy begins with its own divine alpha: the collapse of the star that made the black hole at its center. This alpha is the eruption of divine energy into the form of our galaxy; it is the *galactic hierophany*. Our galaxy exhibits many cyclical patterns—these patterns are the divine *wheels of the galaxy*. Our galaxy slowly orbits great centers of mass (celestial barycenters). And our galaxy rotates around its central black hole. As the result of that rotation, our solar system orbits that black hole. It takes about 225–50 million years to make one cycle—this is the *galactic year*. Your body traces a very small part of this cycle.

On the account of our universe offered here, the wheel of physics has given you the gift of physical existence. You are obligated to respond to that gift. Through ritual mimesis, you can discharge both your obligation to pay this gift forward and to pay it back. At the physical level, ritual mimesis includes the *Cosmic Walk* (Taylor 2007, 249–52). The Cosmic Walk imitates the evolution of divine energy in our universe. It uses a large spiral, laid out on the ground, to illustrate endocosmic evolution. Its central point refers to the big bang. As the spiral uncoils, time flows into the future. Points on the spiral are marked with the divine events in the *Epic of Evolution* (Sagan 1977, ch. 1; Swimme and Berry 1992; Modis 2002). The end of the spiral is the present. Large unlit candles are placed at the marked points on the spiral. Two people perform the Cosmic Walk: a reader and a walker. As the reader narrates the history of the universe, the walker moves along the spiral. As the walker passes a candle, a gong is struck, and the walker lights the candle. There are plenty of variations on this general script, and the entire ceremony may be watched by an audience, who may also one by one walk the spiral after the candles are lit.

4. The Chemical Context

Our solar system begins with its own alpha—the ignition of fusion in the sun. As the eruption of divine energy into a novel form, this solar alpha is hierophantic—it is a divine event. The emission of power from the sun reveals that the solar economy is a gift economy: the sun is squandering itself. As it squanders itself, the sun provides our earth with energy. But the earth is also a source of energy. It is filled with internal heat, generated by nuclear decay as well as by its original gravitational formation. This energy manifests itself through thermal vents at the bottoms of the oceans, which may have seeded life. This earth-energy is divine. Yet there is nothing mysterious about it—it is fully open to rational study and is accurately described by science. The generation of power in the center of the earth reveals that the earthly economy is also a gift economy.

The sun rotates on its axis, and imparts its rotation to the entire solar system. Our earth thus rotates in many ways: it spins daily on its axis (making the day–night cycle); and it precesses on its axis (making the seasonal cycle). Likewise, as the moon orbits the earth, it waxes and wanes. The orbit of the moon causes the periodic tides. And the entire earth–moon system orbits the sun. This orbit involves many subtle cyclical patterns (e.g. the Milankovitch cycles). These cycles of moon, earth, and sun are the *wheels of the solar system*. Each of these celestial wheels is a divine *logos* which supervenes on the deeper wheels of nature. And these wheels produce oscillating polarities that drive chemical reactions on all solar satellites (planets, moons, asteroids). These oscillating polarities support the evolution of complexity in the solar system. They are divine.

Your body participates in all these solar cycles. Although you do not feel it, as the earth rotates your body traces a circular path relative to the axis of the earth. As the earth orbits the sun, your body traces an even larger circular path relative to the axis of the sun. Since your life is powered by energetic gifts from the sun and earth and moon, you may feel gratitude towards those sources of energy. To express this gratitude, some pagans offer prayers to those celestial bodies. However, most naturalists are likely to think that offering prayers to unintelligent objects makes little sense. And some naturalists may therefore urge that it makes equally little sense to give thanks to unintelligent objects. After all, they cannot appreciate our gratitude. But the expression of gratitude may have for its aim, not the perpetuation of an imaginary symbolic economy, but the perpetuation of our positive involvement in the cycles of nature (Goodenough 1998, 171). We are parts of nature, and, by giving thanks, we orient ourselves towards the continuation of natural creativity (Bishop 2010, 532). We orient ourselves through ritual mimesis.

By participating in rituals focused on the seasonal cycles, you can give thanks to the wheels of the solar system of chemical existence. For many pagans (e.g. Wiccans and Druids), the seasonal cycle of earthly life is revered by means of *sabbat* celebrations on the eight solar holidays on the *Wheel of the Year* (Sabin 2011; Silver Elder 2011). The solar holidays on the Wheel of the Year are the solstices, the equinoxes, plus the four "cross-quarter" days that lie half-way between solstices and equinoxes. Other activities associated with the sabbat celebrations on the solar holidays include rituals like *silent suppers* to honor the dead (on Halloween). The eight solar holidays are also celebrated by many Green Sisters, who refer to them as "Earth Holy Days" (Taylor 2007, 252–8). Pantheists celebrate at least the solstices and equinoxes. The purpose of these pantheistic celebrations is to "strengthen our vision of human life as a part of the great natural cycles" (Harrison 1999, 84). Pagans revere the moon through *esbat* celebrations. Religious naturalists can easily celebrate the solar and lunar holidays without affirming any superstitions.

Although the energy of the sun powers the evolution of complexity, that energy can also be destructive. Religious naturalists talk about the destructive side of nature (e.g. Goodenough 1998; Peters 2002; Crosby 2008). Fortunately, destructive energies can be harnessed to serve creative ends. The power of fire to consume things is often thought to symbolize the power of goodness to overcome negativities. Hence practices that aim at ethical purification often involve fire. On this view, solar fire (involving thermonuclear fusion) is the power to burn away all negativities. And the power of ordinary chemical fire (involving only oxidization) can symbolize the cleansing power of solar fire.

Several fire purification ceremonies involve the symbolic destruction of personal negativities by burning. These include the *Vinotok* festival (Peterson 2008, 99–100; Grout 2010, 145–6) and the *Zozobra* festival (Gilmore 2010, 24). Participants write down their personal negativities on pieces of paper, which are placed into the chest of a wooden man, known as the Grump or Old Man Gloom. At the climax of the ceremony, the Grump is burned, symbolically destroying the negativities of the participants. Burning the Grump resembles the Wiccan fire purification ritual described by Buckland (1986, 99–101). Green Sisters have also performed fire purification rituals, by placing inscriptions of personal negativities onto a raft which is burned on the Winter Solstice (Taylor 2007, 255).

The *Burning Man* festival is an especially interesting fire festival. It is celebrated in the Black Rock Desert, in north-western Nevada, around Labor Day. Much has been written about its ritual aspects (e.g. Doherty 2004; Gilmore 2010). Burning Man is explicitly based on a gift economy. An enormous amount of free creative (and thus religiously positive) energy goes into the construction of Black Rock City and the great wooden Man. Each year, the Man is set on fire. During many years, the fire that will ignite the Man is derived from the light of the sun via parabolic mirrors. And so the Man burns. The creative energy is squandered in radical self-expression.

The yearly Temples at Burning Man illustrate the association of fire with the destructive side of nature (Gilmore 2010, 87–94). These Temples are elaborate constructions, involving considerable collective work. Since 2001, they have served as sacred places for the consolidation and release of the memories of the dead; they are sites for ritual grieving and catharsis. Mourners write inscriptions honoring their dead on parts of the Temple or on flammable items which they then place inside the Temple. The Temples are themselves flammable. At the climax of the Temple ritual, the Temple is burned. This is purification by fire. It is surely not implausible to interpret this ritual burning as a way of giving thanks to the solar wheels for the lives of those who have died.

5. The Biological Context

The earthly bio-process begins with the first self-replicators. The formations of the first self-replicators are the ultimate original events for earthly life, they are the divine alphas for biological being, the openings into which divine energy bursts into the form of earthly life. The eruption of divine energy into this form is the biological hierophany.

These self-replicators replicate, replicate again—and so it goes. Goodenough writes that "cell cycles have an inherent life of their own . . . once the first cycle was traversed, the engine has never stopped" (1998, 56). The reproductive cycle ensures the perpetuation of life: "The continuation of life reaches around and, grabs its own tail, and forms a sacred circle" (Goodenough 1998, 171). This sacred circle is the *wheel of life*, and through its revolutions, it produces generation after generation of organisms. Dawkins (1996, 72, 326) describes biological evolution as an enormous distributed computation. And Dennett (1995) argues that biological evolution is algorithmic. The wheel of life is a divine *logos* which supervenes on all the deeper cyclical algorithms of nature.

Over time, organic life evolves. It has been argued that the history of life is the history of gradually increasing complexity: the complexity of the most complex organisms grows greater over time (Bedau 1998). Evolution constructs an ascending complexity hierarchy. The wheel of life rolls uphill. And the revolutions of the wheel of life weave the strands in the earthly tree of life. This tree is the sum of all the careers of all earthly organisms. Every such career is a spatially and temporally extended fiber in the tree. Species are strands woven of these fibers. Every ascending fiber in the tree of life is divine. As a generally ascending structure, the tree itself is divine (see Dennett 1995, 520).

Since the celestial cycles produce oscillations in energy flows across the entire earth, those cycles drive many biological cycles. As the seasons oscillate between their polarities, plant life waxes and wanes; and with those plants, animal life also waxes and wanes. The cycles of life (at least on the surface of the earth) closely follow the Wheel of the Year. Since so much life rolls with that Wheel, the Wheel of the Year is an appropriate symbol for all biological wheels. Many aspects of the pagan sabbats are focused on the cycles of plant and animal life. By celebrating the solar and lunar holidays on the Wheel of the Year, you can give thanks to the wheels of life for the gift of your biological existence.

On the account of biology offered here, the wheel of life has given you the gift of biological existence. You are obligated to respond to that gift. Through ritual mimesis, you can discharge your obligation both to pay this gift forward and to pay it back. The *earth body prayer* celebrates, through ritual mimesis, the interaction of the sun and earth in the daily solar cycle, as well as the chemical elements. It is practiced by the Green Sisters (Taylor 2007, 231–6). It begins at sunrise, with the celebrant facing the rising sun. The basis of the ritual involves turning to face each of the four cardinal directions in a sunwise (deosil) direction: east, south, west, north, then finally back east to close the circle. At each cardinal direction, the celebrant performs a scripted sequence of bodily movements. Each cardinal direction symbolizes one of the four classical groups of elements (earth, air, fire, and water) and the four seasons (winter, spring, summer, and fall).

On the assumption that you are obligated to participate in complexity-creation, it follows that you are obligated to continue the biological gift economy. You ought to keep the wheels of life rolling (Goodenough 1998, 171). She says that the only purpose of life is that "the continuation continue until the sun collapses or the final meteor collides. I confess a credo of continuation" (1998, 171). After arguing that intrinsic value is complexity, Dennett infers that you ought to work to ensure the evolution of as much earthly life as possible for as long as possible (1995, 511–13). All groups affiliated with religious naturalism endorse eco-positive action. Eco-positive action, which aims to continue the biological gift economy, is sacred work—it is service to the wheel.

Of course, one of the strands in the tree of life is the human species. And, obviously enough, the human species is regenerated through sex. By participating in rituals focused on sex, you can give thanks to the wheels of life for the gift of human existence. Done for its religious significance, sex is ritual mimesis. Pantheists affirm the religious value of sex (Harrison 1999, 79–81). Wiccans also affirm the religious value of sex (Farrar and Farrar 1981, ch. XV; Cunningham 2004, 13; Sabin 2011, 32). Many Wiccan rituals involve considerable sexual symbolism (and, in the "Great Rite", may involve actual sex). Many groups affiliated with religious naturalism have developed naturalistic ceremonies marking the stages of human life (such as birth, puberty, marriage, and death).

If it is true that you are obligated to participate in complexity-creation, then you ought to continue the gift economy that has brought humanity into being. You ought to keep the wheels of humanity rolling by ensuring the perpetuation of the human species (Goodenough 1998, 171). This *does not* imply that you ought to have children (indeed, ecological concerns with over-population may entail that you should *not* have children). To say that you ought to keep the wheel of humanity rolling does entail that you ought to work to ensure the sustainability of humanity. You ought to work to preserve and enhance the positive aspects of human cultural diversity (Dennett 1995, 512–17).

On the basis of their focus on natural cycles, many Wiccans endorse some type of reincarnation (Farrar and Farrar 1981, 113–16; Buckland 1986, 26–7; Cunningham 2004, ch. 9; Silver Elder 2011, 56–7; Sabin 2011, 31–2). Of course, these Wiccan theories, like most other traditional reincarnation theories, contradict our best science; consequently, religious naturalists reject them. And most traditional theories of resurrection or disembodied life also contradict our best science. Generalizing, many Zygoners declare that *all possible* soteriologies are false: our earthly lives are our only lives (Goodenough 1998, ch. 11; Peters 2002, ch. 15; Crosby 2002, 129; 2008, 4–5, 58–9, 99–100). Of course, that is an invalid generalization, and those Zygoners who object to life after death offer no arguments against every possible soteriology.

Although science may close the doors on older soteriologies, it also opens doors to newer soteriologies. Stone writes that "since patterns of information can outlast their original physical substratum, just as music can outlive its composer, immortality is not definitively foreclosed in a naturalistic framework" (2008, 228).[22] Our entire earthly ecosystem, from start to finish, is a single informational pattern. It is the form of earthly life, the form of a great computation. It is surely *consistent* with our best science to say that all the information encoded in our entire earthly ecosystem can be naturally reinstantiated in some new natural structure, perhaps in some other universe. A program, once run, can be debugged and upgraded. Thus enhanced, it can be run again.

6. The Personal Context

Although you are surely already alive when you take your first breath, it seems plausible to say that your first breath is your first act as a *distinct* human body. For pagans, the body is sacred (Davy 2007, 24). For pantheists, "The body is a sacred part of nature" (Harrison 1999, 80). For Zygoners, like Goodenough, the body is also sacred (1998, 59). As she talks about her birth, she says that "I sanctify myself with my own grace" (1998, 60). If your body is sacred, and if your first breath is your first self-directed act, then indeed you sanctify yourself with your first breath. It is the divine alpha of your

---

[22] The pattern associated with the life of any organism is the form of its body. Aristotle says that the form of the body is the *soul* (*De Anima*, 412a5–414a33). This concept of the soul is entirely naturalistic. Barrow and Tipler define the soul as a computer program (1986, 659). Tipler writes that "the human 'soul' is nothing but a specific program being run on a computing machine called the brain" (1995, 1–2).

body. Your first breath is an eruption of divine energy into a new form; it is a *hierophany*.

Your body-process is animated by your divine energy, which is just the natural physical energy generated by the metabolic processes in your cells. The divine energy running through your body organizes itself into cyclical patterns. These patterns include the cycles of breathing, the cycle of the heartbeat, the wake–sleep cycle; the cyclical motions of the limbs in walking; the menstrual cycles of women; and so on. They also include the deeper metabolic cycles inside our cells (e.g. the Krebs cycle). Since all these *wheels of the body* are driven by divine energy, they are divine. Each visceral wheel is a divine *logos* which supervenes on all the deeper cyclical algorithms of nature. For Wiccans, the wheels of the body symbolize the deeper cycles of nature (Silver Elder 2011, 8, 19, 43).

On the assumption that you ought to give thanks for the gifts you receive, you ought to give thanks to the wheels of the body for the gift of your personal existence. You can give thanks to those wheels by participating in rhythmic physiological activities. Drumming, chanting, and dancing are important for Wiccans and other pagans (Davy 2007, 66; Sabin 2011, 72). Since one essential way of giving thanks to the wheels of your body is to keep them rolling, this means that you ought to keep them rolling. You ought to perform all the self-regulatory actions that keep those wheels finely tuned and healthy.

An essential way to give thanks to any wheel is by rolling it forward, by rolling it higher uphill, by continuing the gift economy. You can do this by performing exercises (*askesis*) that minimize your expression of negative energy and maximize your expression of divine energy. All dualism is rejected: these exercises are entirely *both* physiological *and* spiritual. They are exercises for arousal regulation. Wiccans advocate the use of breathing exercises for arousal regulation (Farrar and Farrar 1981, 230–1; Cunningham 2004, 86–7; Sabin 2011, 55, 70–1). And some Wiccans also advocate the use of meditative or mindfulness exercises (Cunningham 2004, 87; Sabin 2011, 75–7). Harrison writes that breathing exercises and meditation are central practices for pantheists (1999, 91–4). Zygoners also advocate arousal regulation exercises (Goodenough 1998, 101–2; Peters 2002, ch. 13; Crosby 2007, 496). Some New Atheists advocate arousal regulation exercises (Harris 2005, ch. 7; Comte-Sponville 2006; Walters 2010, ch. 8). And the New Stoics advocate a wide variety of personal psychological exercises (Irvine 2009, part 2).

On the basis of the cyclicality of nature, Nietzsche argued that our lives would be exactly repeated in future replications of our universe. For Nietzsche, this eternal return of the same is satisfactory. However, it is not satisfactory for Benjamin Franklin (1771, 1). After his death, Franklin hopes for the existence of a better version of his life (he refers to it as a "second edition"), in which some of the defects and misfortunes are corrected. On the basis of the evolutionary view of nature developed here, it is more likely that Franklin's desires will be satisfied. After all, the wheels of nature do not merely repeat the same old patterns without modification. On the contrary, they generate simple patterns and then cause their more sacred potentials to be actualized; they build endlessly ramified trees in which every pattern is surpassed by more sacred versions of itself.

A pattern is *amplified* by a natural wheel iff it produces some more sacred version of that pattern. Thus a pattern is amplified by a wheel if that wheel causes some more complex version of that pattern to be instantiated on some future cycle. On the view of nature offered here, *every* pattern is amplified; its amplifications are further amplified; and so it goes.[23] Of course, since the wheels of nature roll uphill, this amplification is selective. Those parts of patterns that tend to negativity are not selected for further amplification, while those parts of patterns that tend to positivity are selected. Consequently, your actions have an influence on your future lives (see Leslie 2001, 132–3): the more you contribute to the evolution of the sacred, the more of your life is worthy of its own further evolution; the less you contribute to that evolution, the less of your life is worthy of its own further evolution. This can be put into a slogan: the more you give to the wheels, the more you get from the wheels.

Theravedic Buddhism offered highly naturalistic ways of thinking about life after death (Rahula 1974, 34). These accounts are consistent with the amplification of your life from universe to universe (Steinhart 2008). Granted that nature is rational, Godel argues that the positive potentials of our lives will be realized in future versions thereof (1961, 429–31). He argues for amplification. If science depends on the rationality of nature, then his argument is a reasonable inference from the very possibility of science. Of course, the amplification of your life on some future cycle of the wheels of nature does not entail that you *survive* death. It merely entails that you have future counterparts who will actualize all your positive personal potentials. For every way your life can be improved, you have some future counterparts in some future cycles whose lives will be improved in that way.

7. Conclusion

A unifying framework for religious naturalism has been developed here, one to which many groups have contributed their ideas and practices. This framework suggests ways that religious naturalism may continue to evolve. It therefore seems appropriate to end with a speculative note concerning the future of religious naturalism. Surveys mentioned in the Introduction suggest that, at least in the United States, social trends have produced a religious landscape with three distinctive yet overlapping identities.

---

[23] Amplification is just an application of Dennett's Principle of Accumulation of Design. His Principle says "since each new designed thing that appears must have a large design investment in its etiology some-where, the cheapest hypothesis will always be that the design is largely copied from earlier designs, which are copied from earlier designs, and so forth" (1995, 72). Amplification occurs at every level of nature: the patterns of universes, galaxies, solar systems, ecosystems, and organisms are all amplified. Since the patterns of all things are amplified, it follows that the patterns of all organisms are amplified.

These identities, whose cores mark the corners of a triangle, have been referred to as the traditional theists, the spiritualists, and the secularists (Kosmin and Keysar 2013).

Religious naturalism lies mainly on the line between the secular and the spiritual. Many new religious movements, discussed here, are already emerging on this line. They tend to take their beliefs from the secularists and their practices from the spiritualists. Perhaps some of them will mature into stable religions. Peters believes that religious naturalism "could lead to a new significant form of organized religion with a structured community, ritual practices, and ways of moral living" (2010, 435).

But a less organized future is also possible. It may be that religious naturalism will become a widespread folk spirituality with few institutions. On this hypothesis, its core beliefs and practices will be those most commonly found in the groups discussed in this chapter. Those who identify with this folk spirituality will dismiss all personal gods and goddesses; they will find spiritual satisfaction in the grandeur of nature; they will meditate; they will gather to celebrate the solar holidays. Of course, these remarks, while grounded in data, remain highly speculative. The future of religious naturalism is far from clear. Nevertheless, perhaps the most interesting thing about religious naturalism is that it shows that nontheistic religions are possible in the West.

References

Ammerman, N. (2013). "Spiritual but not Religious? Beyond Binary Choices in the Study of Religion," *Journal for the Scientific Study of Religion* 52/2: 258–78.

Antunes, L., Fortnow, L., Melkebeek, D., and Vinodch, N. (2006). "Computational Depth: Concept and Applications," *Theoretical Computer Science* 354/3: 391–404.

Aronson, R. (2010). *Living without God*. Berkeley: Counterpoint Press.

Barrow, J. and Tipler, F. (1986). *The Anthropic Cosmological Principle*. New York: Oxford University Press.

Bedau, M. (1998). "Philosophical Content and Method of Artificial Life," in T. Bynum and J. Moor (eds), *The Digital Phoenix: How Computers are Changing Philosophy* (pp. 135–52). Malden, Mass.: Basil Blackwell.

Bennett, C. (1988). "Logical Depth and Physical Complexity," in R. Herken, *The Universal Turing Machine: A Half-Century Survey* (pp. 227–57). New York: Oxford University Press.

Bishop, J. (2010). "Secular Spirituality and the Logic of Giving Thanks," *Sophia* 49: 523–34.

Black, M. (1964). "The Gap between 'Is' and 'Should'," *Philosophical Review* 73: 165–81.

Blackburn, S. (2004) "Salvaging the Sacred," in B. Rogers (ed.), *Is Nothing Sacred?* (pp. 128–34). New York: Routledge.

Buckland, R. (1986). *Complete Book of Witch Craft*, 2nd edn revised and expanded. St Paul, Mich.: Llewellyn Publications.

Cavanaugh, M. (2000). "Exploring the Resources of Naturalism: What is Religious Naturalism? Report of an ongoing conversation," *Zygon* 35/2: 241–52.

Chaisson, E. (2001). *Cosmic Evolution: The Rise of Complexity in Nature*. Cambridge, Mass.: Harvard University Press.

Chaisson, E. (2006). *The Epic of Evolution: The Seven Ages of our Cosmos*. New York: Columbia University Press.

Comte-Sponville, A. (2006). *The Little Book of Atheist Spirituality.* Trans. N. Huston. New York: Viking.

Conger, G. (1940/1969). *The Ideologies of Religion.* Freeport, NY: Books for Libraries Press.

Crosby, D. (2002). *A Religion of Nature.* Albany, NY: SUNY Press.

Crosby, D. (2003). "Transcendence and Immanence in a Religion of Nature," *American Journal of Theology and Philosophy* 24/3: 245–59.

Crosby, D. (2007). "A Case for Religion of Nature," *Journal for the Study of Religion, Nature and Culture* 1/4: 489–502.

Crosby, D. (2008). *Living with Ambiguity: Religious Naturalism and the Menace of Evil.* Albany, NY: SUNY Press.

Cunningham, S. (2004). *Wicca: A Guide for the Solitary Practitioner.* St Paul, Mich.: Llewellyn Publications.

Davy, B. (2007). *Introduction to Pagan Studies.* New York: Altamira Press.

Dawkins, R. (1987). *The Blind Watchmaker.* New York: W. W. Norton.

Dawkins, R. (1996). *Climbing Mount Improbable.* New York: W. W. Norton.

Dawkins, R. (2004). "The Sacred and the Scientist," in B. Rogers (ed.), *Is Nothing Sacred?* (pp. 135–7). New York: Routledge.

Dawkins, R. (2008). *The God Delusion.* New York: Houghton-Mifflin.

Dennett, D. (1995). *Darwin's Dangerous Idea: Evolution and the Meanings of Life.* New York: Simon & Schuster.

Dennett, D. (2006). *Breaking the Spell.* New York: Viking Penguin.

Doherty, B. (2004). *This is Burning Man.* New York: Little Brown.

Dowd, M. (2009). *Thank God for Evolution.* New York: Penguin.

Eliade, M. (1959). *The Sacred and the Profane: The Nature of Religion.* Trans. W. Trask. New York: Harper & Row.

Emerson, R. W. (1841). "Compensation," in P. Norbert (ed.), *Essays and Poems by Ralph Waldo Emerson* (pp. 136–53). New York: Barnes & Noble, 2004.

Farrar, J. and Farrar, S. (1981). *A Witches' Bible.* Blaine, Wash.: Phoenix Publishing.

Franklin, B. (1771). 'The Autobiography', in A. Houston (ed.), *The Autobiography and Other Writings on Politics, Economics, and Virtue* (pp. 1–142). New York: Cambridge University Press, 2004.

Franklin, B. (1784). Item 1498: Letter to Benjamin Webb (22 April 1784), in A. Smyth (ed.), *The Writings of Benjamin Franklin,* vol. 9 (p. 197). New York: MacMillan Company, 1907.

Geach, P. (1967). 'Commentary on Aquinas', in D. Burrill (ed.), *The Cosmological Arguments* (pp. 57–82). Garden City, NY: Anchor Books.

George, A. (2012). 'Kopimism: The World's Newest Religion Explained', *New Scientist* 213/2847 (14 January): 25.

Gilmore, L. (2010). *Theatre in a Crowded Fire: Ritual and Spirituality at Burning Man.* Berkeley: University of California Press.

Godel, K. (1961). Letter to Marianne Godel, 23 July 1961, in S. Feferman et al. (eds), *Kurt Godel: Collected Works,* vol. 4 (pp. 429–31). New York: Oxford University Press, 2003.

Goodenough, U. (1998). *The Sacred Depths of Nature.* New York: Oxford University Press.

Grout, P. (2010). *Colorado Curiosities.* Guilford, Conn.: Globe Pequot Press.

Harris, S. (2005). *The End of Faith.* New York: W. W. Norton.

Harrison, P. (1999). *Pantheism: Understanding the Divinity in Nature and the Universe.* Boston: Element Books.

Hartshorne, C. (1948). *Divine Relativity: A Social Conception of God*. New Haven: Yale University Press.

Hawking, S. (1988). *A Brief History of Time*. Toronto: Bantam Books.

Hogue, M. (2010). *The Promise of Religious Naturalism*. Lanham, Md: Rowman & Littlefield.

Hyde, L. (1979). *The Gift: Imagination and the Erotic Life of Property*. New York: Vintage Books.

Irvine, W. (2009). *A Guide to the Good Life: The Ancient Art of Stoic Joy*. New York: Oxford University Press.

Jackson, D., Memory, J., and Appleton, J. (2014). "Spirituality and Religion in Europe," *Vista: Quarterly Bulletion of Research-Based Information on Mission in Europe*.

Kaufman, G. (2007). "A Religious Interpretation of Emergence: Creativity as God," *Zygon* 42/4: 915–28.

Kauffman, S. (2008). *Reinventing the Sacred*. New York: Basic Books.

Kosmin, B., et al. (2009). *American Nones: The Profile of the No Religion Population*. A report based on the American Religious Identification Survey 2008. Hartford, Conn.: Trinity College.

Kosmin, B. and Keysar, A. (2013). *Religious, Spiritual, and Secular: The Emergence of Three Distinct Worldviews among American College Students*. A report based on the ARIS 2013 National College Student Survey. Hartford, Conn.: Trinity College.

Kurzweil, R. (2005). *The Singularity is Near: When Humans Transcend Biology*. New York: Viking.

Lambert, Y. (2006). "Trends in Religious Feeling in Europe and Russia," trans. A. Jacobs. *Revue française de sociologie* 47: 99–129.

Leibniz, G. W. (1697/1988). "On the Ultimate Origination of the Universe," in P. Schrecker and A. Schrecker, *Leibniz: Monadology and Other Essays* (pp. 84–94). New York: Macmillan Publishing, 1988.

Leslie, J. (2001). *Infinite Minds: A Philosophical Cosmology*. New York: Oxford.

Mithani, A. and Vilenkin, A. (2012). 'Did the Universe have a Beginning?' Online at <arXiv: 1204.4658v1>.

Modis, T. (2002). "Forecasting the Growth of Complexity and Change," *Technological Forecasting and Social Change* 69: 377–404.

Otto, R. (1958). *The Idea of the Holy*. Trans. J. W. Harvey. New York: Oxford University Press.

Peirce, C. S. (1965). *Collected Papers of Charles Sanders Peirce*. Ed. C. Hartshorne and P. Weiss. Cambridge, Mass.: Harvard University Press.

Peters, K. (2002). *Dancing with the Sacred: Evolution, Ecology, and God*. Harrisburg, Pa: Trinity Press International.

Peters, K. (2010). "*Zygon* and the Future of Religion-and-Science," *Zygon* 45/2: 430–6.

Peterson, E. (2008). *Ramble Colorado*. Golden, Colo.: Speck Press.

Pew Forum (2009). *Many Americans Mix Multiple Faiths: Eastern, New Age Beliefs Widespread*. Washington, DC: The Pew Forum on Religion & Public Life.

Pew Forum (2010). *Religion among the Millenials*. Washington, DC: The Pew Forum on Religion & Public Life.

Pew Forum (2012). "*Nones*" on the Rise: One-in-Five Adults Have no Religious Affiliation*. Washington, DC: The Pew Forum on Religion & Public Life.

Rahula, W. (1974). *What the Buddha Taught*. New York: Grove/Atlantic.

Raymo, C. (2008). *When God is Gone Everything is Holy*. Notre Dame, Ind.: Sorin Books.

Sabin, T. (2011). *Wicca for Beginners: Fundamentals of Philosophy and Practice*. Woodbury, Mich.: Llewellyn Publications.

Sagan, C. (1977). *The Dragons of Eden*. New York: Random House.

Silver, C., et al. (2014). "The Six Types of Nonbelief: A Qualitative and Quantitative Study of Type and Narrative," *Mental Health, Religion & Culture*. Online DOI: 10.1080/ 13674676.2014.987743. Accessed 7 January 2015.

Silver Elder (2011). *Wiccan Celebrations: Inspiration for Living by Nature's Cycle*. Winchester: Moon Books.

Solomon, R. (2006). *Spirituality for the Skeptic*. New York: Oxford University Press.

Steinhart, E. (2008). "The Revision Theory of Resurrection," *Religious Studies* 44/1: 1–19.

Stone, J. (2003). "Is Nature Enough? Yes!," *Zygon* 38/4: 783–800.

Stone, J. (2008). *Religious Naturalism Today*. Albany, NY: SUNY Press.

Swimme, B. and Berry, T. (1992). *The Universe Story*. New York: Harper Collins.

Taylor, S. M. (2007). *Green Sisters: A Spiritual Ecology*. Cambridge, Mass.: Harvard University Press.

Tillich, P. (1951). *Systematic Theology*, vol. 1. Chicago: University of Chicago Press.

Tipler, F. (1995). *The Physics of Immortality: Modern Cosmology, God and the Resurrection of the Dead*. New York: Anchor Books.

Walters, K. (2010). *Atheism: A Guide for the Perplexed*. New York: Continuum Publishing.

York, M. (2003). *Pagan Theology*. New York: New York University Press.

Young, D. (2005). "Being Grateful for Being: Being, Reverence, and Finitude," *Sophia* 44/2: 31–53.

Index